Essen

explc

FLORENCE & TUSCANY

Tim Jepson

AA Publishing

Essential

Written by Tim Jepson
Original photography by Clive Sawyer
Edited, designed and produced by AA Publishing
Maps © The Automobile Association 1995

Distributed in the United Kingdom by AA Publishing, Norfolk House, Priestley Road, Basingstoke, Hampshire, RG24 4NY.

Colour separation by LC Repro
Printed by LEGO SpA, Italy

Cover picture: Detail of Baptistry doors, Florence
Page 4 (top): Pitigliano, Tuscany
Page 5 (top): Ponte Vecchio detail, Florence
Page 5 (bottom): The 19th-century mosaics of the Duomo, Siena
Pages 6–7 (top): Olive grove near San Gimignano
Page 6 (bottom): Il Porcellino, Mercato Nuovo, Florence
Page 7 (bottom): Palazzo Vecchio detail, Florence
Page 9: Duomo detail, Florence
Page 27: *Four Seasons*, Santa Trinita Bridge, Florence
Pages 48–9: The city of Florence
Pages 188–9: Tuscan countryside near Volterra
Page 251: San Gimignano rooftops
Page 273: Delicatessen, Lucca

Tim Jepson has written or contributed to many books on Italy, including *Wild Italy* (Aurum Press), *Italy by Train* (Hodder & Stoughton), *The Fodor Guide to Italy* and *The Rough Guide to Tuscany and Umbria*, as well as *Rome*, *Italy* and *Venice* in the AA Explorer series. For several years he lived in Italy, during which time he was Rome Correspondent for the *Sunday Telegraph*.

Vineyards near Pienza

How to use this book

This book is divided into five main sections:

❏ Section 1: *Florence Is*
discusses aspects of life and living today, from tourism and restoration to café life

❏ Section 2: *Florence Was*
places the city in its historical context and explores those past events whose influences are felt to this day

❏ Section 3: *A to Z Section*
is broken down into two chapters, covering Florence and Tuscany, and covers places to visit, including walks and drives. Within this section fall the Focus-on articles, which consider a variety of topics in greater detail

❏ Section 4: *Travel Facts*
contains the strictly practical information vital for a successful trip

❏ Section 5:
Hotels and Restaurants
lists recommended establishments in Florence and Tuscany, giving a brief résumé of what they offer

How to use the star rating
Most places described in this book have been given a separate rating:

▶▶▶ **Do not miss**

▶▶ **Highly recommended**

▶ **Worth seeing**

Not essential viewing

Map references
To make the location of a particular place easier to find, every main entry in this book is given a map reference, such as 176B3. The first number (176) indicates the page on which the map can be found, the letter (B) and the second number (3) pinpoint the square in which the main entry is located. The maps on the inside front cover and inside back cover are referred to as IFC and IBC respectively.

Contents

Quick reference 6–7

My Florence and Tuscany 8
by Valeria Nardi
by Franco Bianchini

Florence Is 9–26

Florence Was 27–47

A to Z
Florence 48–187
Tuscany 188–249

Itineraries 250

Travel Facts 251–72

Hotels and Restaurants 273–81

Index 282–7

Picture credits and
contributors 288

Quick reference

6

This quick-reference guide high-lights the features of the book you will use most often: the maps; the introductory features; the Focus-on articles; the walks and the drives.

Maps and plans

Florence and 3-star sights	IFC
The city of Florence in 1830	43
Th e heart of the city walk	54
Dante's Florence walk	72
The Duomo	79
Fiesolè walk	83
The north of the city walk	94
San Lorenzo	133
Santa Croce	140
Frescos in Cappella Brancacci	146
Santa Maria Novella	149
Walk to San Miniato al Monte	156
Arezzo	193
San Francesco frescos	195
The heart of Chianti drive	199
Cortona	201
Lucca	205
Pisa	219
Pistoia	225
San Gimignano	229
Siena	235
Siena to Montepulciano drive	243
Volterra	249
Tuscany and 3-star sights	IBC

Florence Is

An artistic shrine	10–11
Florentines	12–13
Fashion and style	14–15
Music and festivals	16–17
Art and craft	18–19
Food	20–1
Café life	22–3
Tourism and restoration	24–6

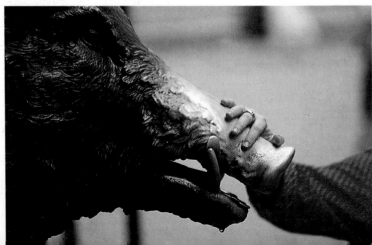

Florence Was

Myth and legend	28–9
Romans and emperors	30–1
Textiles and banking	32–3
Guilds	34–5
Guelphs and Ghibellines	36–7
The Medici	38–9
Savonarola	40–1
Dynastic decline	42–3
Medici family tree	44
Austrian and French rule	45
Modern times	46–7

Focus on

Michelangelo	66–7
Dante	70–1
The Pazzi Conspiracy	74–5
The dome	80–1
The art of fresco	98–9
Galileo	106–7
Markets	114–15
Machiavelli	124–5
The flood of 1966	130–1
The Cappella Brancacci	146–7
The Pre-Renaissance	158–9
The Renaissance	166–9
Peace and quiet	196–7
Tuscan food	210–11
Tuscan wines	212–13
A 'Paradise of Exiles'	222–3
Monasteries	232–3
The Palio	240–1
The Etruscans	246–7

Walks

The heart of the city	54
Dante's Florence	72
Fiesole	83
The north of the city	94
To San Miniato al Monte	156

Drives

The heart of Chianti	198–9
Siena to Montepulciano	242–3

Travel Facts

Arriving	252–3
Essential facts	254–5
Getting around	256–9
Communications	260–1
Emergencies	262–3
Other information	264–7
Opening times	268–9
Glossary	270–1
Language	272

7

Valeria Nardi
Valeria Nardi was born in the Tuscan port of Livorno. After completing Liceo Classico she took a degree in art history at the University of Pisa, going on to write a doctoral thesis on Florentine and Sienese miniatures of the 14th century, which was published in the magazine *Ricerca di Storia dell' Arte*. She is now a tour guide and Italian language teacher in Florence.

8

My Florence

by Valeria Nardi

Florence is slow to reveal her true self to visitors. It is all too easy to be bewitched; to be preoccupied by Florence – *la bella* – shamelessly parading her beauty before her many admiring visitors. But this is to limit one's understanding of the city to her façade. To discover the heart of Florence demands a different approach.

There is no escaping her beauty. It strikes you as soon as you arrive, confirmed by the throngs of tourists – frenetic and tired, yet eager to seize everything that the city offers them with such generosity. But beware: with the tourist's eye you will only ever see one Florence. The other – the real Florence – is seen only by those who, instead of running, stop; instead of looking, feel; instead of talking, listen.

To begin to grasp the true Florence you must depart from the usual itinerary of 'sights'. As soon as you arrive, head across the Arno, ignore the museums, monuments and souvenir shops, and lose yourself in the alleys of San Frediano or the evocative scents of Santo Spirito. Only now are you ready to forget that you are a tourist and head back to the other Florence – the one of beauty and artifice; the one most visitors see. But now you will perceive her differently, understanding the often forgotten truth that Florence's architecture and art are not here simply as attractions for *us*, but that we have come to render homage to *them*. Only now will this most special of cities truly bestow herself upon you.

My Tuscany

by Franco Bianchini

Most visitors come to Arezzo on a day-trip to see Piero della Francesco's frescos in San Francesco or Vasari's elegant loggia in Piazza Grande, but few decide to stay. So what are they missing?

Arezzo stands on a hill between the valleys of three rivers. The Tiber springs from the harsh mountains east of Arezzo, while the sluggish Chiana flows from the south through undulating fields of sunflowers and maize. High on the hills on the eastern side of the Valdichiana stand the towers of the perfect 11th-century castle of Montecchio and the beautiful medieval town of Cortona.

Enjoy the views from the town's many belvederes. They stretch as far as Lago Trasimeno, with its three mysterious islands, encircled by hills of pearly olive trees. Also visible are the verdant cone of Mount Amiata and the Val d'Orcia, where you can find 'lunar' landscapes, the utopian model town of Pienza and the hot springs at Bagno Vignoni.

Or go north through the mountainous Casentino valley, with its quiet history: the castle of Poppi, where Dante wrote the *Divine Comedy*; the great rocks of La Verna, where St Francis received the stigmata; the remote monastery of Camaldoli surrounded by thick forests.

These are some of the (relatively) untrodden places of my Tuscany. One thing they have in common is that near each of them there are enough *trattorie*, *pizzerie* and *gelaterie* tucked away to make a satisfying end to any adventure.

Franco Bianchini
Franco Bianchini was born and brought up in Arezzo where he organised outdoor theatre and opera festivals before moving to England and becoming an academic. He currently runs an MA course in European Arts and Cultural Policy at De Montfort University in Leicester.

He once attempted to walk from Siena to the Tyrrhenian Sea, and in the process learnt a lot about public transport in rural areas in his region...

■ **Florence is a city-sized shrine to the Renaissance. Its churches, museums and galleries catalogue an epoch that shaped history and produced some of the greatest works of art of all time. But if you come here only for art and architecture you will have missed the heart of a living city.....■**

Museum city You go to Rome to look at Rome, to Venice to look at Venice, but to Florence to look at paintings – or so it might sometimes seem. As a city to see for its own sake, Tuscany's capital has always ranked below its big Italian rivals. It has no ruins (unlike Rome) and no fairy-tale setting (unlike Venice). Florence, one is told, lacks romance, lacks an atmosphere to call its own. This city has no lost lagoons, no crumbling layers of history. It is neither timeless like Venice, nor eternal like Rome. This is the received wisdom, and being wisdom

A detail of Pietro Tacca's fountain in Piazza Santissima Annunziata

it contains a truth of sorts. If approached in the wrong way Florence *can* seem an indoor city: its sights, for the most part, are concealed within churches and museums. Its streets can, at times, seem gloomy. Its architecture *is* often stolid and forbidding. Seen from a different angle, however, the picture looks very different.

Another side Florence's appeal goes way beyond the world of sculptures and gallery Madonnas. It has a river to give it heart, markets to give it life. Its citizens are proud and stylish (unlike those of Rome), its streets part of a living city (unlike those of Venice). Old-world artisans flourish, and designers – Gucci and Ferragamo the most famous – dress it in a fashion to match Milan. Its cuisine – rustic but refined – is superb, its cafés stylish and sedate. Cultural life abounds: the Maggio Musicale is one of Italy's finest arts festivals. The Giardino di Boboli is Italy's most visited garden (giving the lie to the idea of Florence as an indoor city). And this is without the art, without one of Europe's greatest galleries (the Uffizi), without Michelangelo's *David* or the world's finest Renaissance sculptures (in the Bargello).

Romance Florence is also a city with its share of romance – the Ponte Vecchio, for example, glimpsed across the Arno on a summer's evening; a late-night drink sipped in Piazza della Signoria; the flower-hung streets of the Oltrarno explored on a warm afternoon; or the majestic cityscapes to be enjoyed from San Miniato or Giotto's lofty Campanile. It is also a city to fire the historical

10

imagination. Picture, for example, Dante, Machiavelli, Boccaccio and Galileo wandering its streets. Or Lorenzo the Magnificent in the Duomo fleeing his would-be assassins; or Michelangelo striding the city's defences in preparation for the siege of the city by the combined armies of the emperor and the pope; or Savonarola's huge Bonfire of Vanities crackling in Piazza della Signoria.

Seeing it all At first glance, Florence might seem an easy sightseeing touch. It is small, and all the sights are close together. Don't be fooled. Every gallery, however modest, is essential; every church a treasure-house of art. A week's stay here is only going to scratch the surface. And that is without the big draws – the Uffizi and the Bargello – or the churches of Santa Croce and Santa Maria Novella, each worth a whole morning on its own.

At the same time you should avoid trying to see more than is pleasurable. Nothing is worse than the misery of museum fatigue. Accept your limitations and pick out the highlights. Plan ahead, don't tackle too much, and avoid the streets in the heat of the afternoon. Head-on confrontation with the city, however energetically you join battle, will always leave you the dispirited loser. Allow time for lounging in gardens, an hour in a sun-drenched café, a quiet meal under a starry sky, or an ice-cream from Italy's best *gelateria* (Vivoli). And then, of course, when you have exhausted the city, the rest of Tuscany – Italy's most beautiful region – is waiting on its doorstep.

Make time to relax in Florence's beautiful Boboli gardens

■ **Florentines, like any group of Italians, are a breed apart, riddled with their own particular faults and foibles, vices and virtues. Stereotypes are invidious things, but no-one meeting a Roman or a Neapolitan, for example, could confuse them with a Florentine.....■**

12

Foreigners in their own country

Italians are never simply Italians. Centuries of divisive history have left them fiercely provincial, bound by that force known neatly as *campanilismo* – the idea that all that matters is what takes place within the sound of your own church bells, and that everything else belongs to a foreign country. Tuscans are never Italians, therefore – except perhaps when the national football team is playing. Nor, however, are they simply Tuscans.

Art, architecture – and daily life

Someone from Siena is Sienese, and proud of the fact; someone from Pisa is Pisan, and woe betide anyone who calls them otherwise.

> ❏ 'Beyond all others, a treacherous and mercenary race.'
> Walter Savage Landor
> (1775–1864) ❏

Florentines on Florentines

Michelangelo, who grew up in Florence, said 'I never had to do with a more ungrateful and arrogant people than the Florentines.' Dante, a native of the city, described his fellow citizens as '*gente avara, invidiosa e superba*' (mean, envious and proud people). A Renaissance proverb described them as perpetual moaners – possessed of 'sharp eyes and bad tongues'. Leaving aside personal agendas – Michelangelo was habitually bad-tempered and Dante was exiled by his fellow Florentines – the assessments, if deliberately overpitched for rhetorical purposes, mention qualities still seen today as distinctively Florentine: pride and arrogance.

> ❏ 'Prodigal of cry and gesture when the world goes right.'
> Elizabeth Barrett Browning
> (1806–61) ❏

Florentine pride

The proverbial Florentine pride is an affront to many Italians, who wonder what it is, exactly, of which Florentines are so proud. The Renaissance, it seems, is one answer, a golden age that merely reflects qualities – hard work,

genius, flair, ambition, verve, civic pride – that are still possessed by the average Florentine. Certainly there is much of which Florence can be proud – poets, painters and sculptors, scientists and political theorists; Dante and Boccaccio; Botticelli and Michelangelo; Galileo and Machiavelli; Europe's first public library; the western world's first chair of Greek; the creation of a literary language; the rediscovery of perspective; the foundation of capitalism; the invention of opera, eyeglasses, the piano – the list is long.

Somehow the past still reflects well on modern Florentines. And yet their pride is no retrospective reaching after past glories. Nor does constant confrontation with their past produce an incipient inferiority complex. Rather the past provides people with a powerful sense of their own identity, a sense of self-confidence borne of the knowledge that Florence – through good times and bad – has prospered for over 2,000 years. And the reason it has prospered, of course, as any Florentine will tell you, is the Florentines themselves.

Culture and civilisation Italians, albeit grudgingly, concede almost

Enjoying the bright lights of Via dei Calzaiuoli

without exception that the Florentines are some of the most cultured and civilised people in Italy. Florentines are also hard-working – not something Italians would say of the Romans or the Neapolitans, for example. They are also active and enterprising – witness the city's army of artisans – and, unlike the people of much of modern Italy, they still have a healthy respect for those who work the land (Tuscan peasants have long been considered the most intelligent of Italy's farmers). Yet for all their supposed pride, Florentines are also decorous and dignified people. And though individual in the extreme, they never cultivate the cult of the individual. Urbane, busy, cultured and quietly self-satisfied – these are the Florentine watchwords.

❏ 'The Florentines ... invented the Renaissance, which is the same as saying they invented the modern world – not, of course, an unmitigated good.' Mary McCarthy (1912–89) ❏

■ **Florence's wealth was founded on textiles and its artistic reputation on the sublimities of its Renaissance painters. No wonder, then, that cloth and the cult of the beautiful, together with the work of designers and craftspeople, continue to make Florence one of Italy's capitals of fashion and style.....■**

14

Good taste and high quality You have to look a long way in Italy to find a scruffy Italian. You have to look even further in Florence, where old and young alike parade the city streets dressed as if preening on some vast outdoor catwalk. Nowhere, with the exception of Milan, is the art of the *bella figura*, of creating a good impression, more keenly practised. Cool and intellectual, the Florentines look to subtle and sober-minded clothes, mixing tweedy English classicism with dashes of Renaissance opulence. On the business side, the city's textile barons plump for quality. Artisans and up-market couturiers cohabit quite happily, weaving their magic from the most luxurious cloth, or conjuring up the jewellery and leatherware, for which the city is famous, from the most exclusive of materials.

Goodbye Gucci? Three big names roll off the tongue when talk in Florence turns to fashion. Biggest of all, though perhaps not the most fashionable, is Gucci, still based at Via de' Tornabuoni 73r where the firm was founded three generations ago. The company has been going through some difficult times, though the problems of widely available fakes and the over-large product range that threatened to sink the firm have been fought off. In the wake of those difficulties came some bitter infighting and a run-in with the

US and Italian tax authorities. Where it counts, however, in the shop window, the company's leather goods – made from fine-quality, honey-cured hide – continue to appeal to those who covet the quiet panache of the famous 'double G'.

Emilio Pucci With his aristocratic bearing and ambassadorial aplomb, Il Marchese Emilio Pucci is the *doyen* of Florentine fashion, a popular society figure who often entertains visiting royalty and heads of state. He launched his fashion career in the 1950s with dramatically dyed silks – still fashionable today, when his company's design credentials extend to cars, perfume and *objets d'art*. Pucci even dresses Florence's local

Emilio Pucci: high priest of Florentine fashion

15

Stepping out in style: hat, handbag and all the trimmings

❏ Machiavelli complained that the main preoccupations of Florentines were 'to appear splendid in apparel and obtain a crafty shrewdness in discourse'. ❏

traffic police (the *vigili urbani*). In 1957 he launched his famous lingerie range – made from scraps of discarded silk. Unashamedly romantic, Pucci can also be refreshingly down to earth, once describing his fashion empire as a 'modest endeavour in the rag trade'.

Salvatore Ferragamo Born in Naples, Ferragamo emigrated to America when he was 15. He made his fortune in Hollywood, crafting shoes for the likes of Greta Garbo,

Vivien Leigh, Gloria Swanson and the gladiators in Cecil B de Mille costume epics. His spiritual home was really Florence, however, where his family still administer a fashion empire that now produces accessories and clothes to accompany the trademark shoes.

❏ The average Florentine spends something approaching a million lire annually on clothes. Some 10 per cent of Florence's income is generated by its fashion industry, whose main showcase is the famous trade fair, Pitti Moda, held in the Fortezza da Basso. ❏

■ **Sober and hard-working they may be, but Tuscans happily let the mask slip when it comes to celebration. Florence and Siena have the big set-piece festivals – Calcio in Costume, Maggio Musicale and the Palio – but not even the smallest village lets the year go by without at least one excuse for riotous celebration......■**

16

Music and the arts Tuscans, and Florentines in particular, pride themselves on their culture. Colourful medieval memories may be evoked in their most famous pageants, but it is past glories of a cultural kind that they seek to celebrate in their more highbrow arts festivals.
Performances of music, dance and drama are held throughout the

Poster for a Saracen joust

region, often in magnificent medieval settings or, as in the case of Fiesole, in outdoor theatres of Roman vintage. Concert cycles fill Florentine churches, or tuck themselves away in green secluded corners (as in Barga's famous opera festival). Some festivals, such as San Gimignano's, are provincial affairs confined to the town square. Others, such as Florence's Maggio Musicale (see

❑ Art and music festivals in Tuscany include the following:
Arezzo Choral music (late August)
Barga Opera and theatre (late July)
Fiesole Estate Fiesolana – music, film, ballet and drama (June–August)
Florence Maggio Musicale – orchestral concerts, ballet, film and fringe events (April–June)
Lucca Sacred music (April–June)
Montepulciano Cantiere Internazionale – music and arts (end July/beginning August)
Siena Settimana Musicale – concerts by pupils and staff of the Accademia Musicale Chigiana (August)
Torre del Lago Puccini operas performed outdoors (August) ❑

page 183), are among Italy's most popular and prestigious arts events. Visit any Tuscan tourist office for details of current festivals.

Food and wine It need not be much – an obscure saint, the humble potato – anything will do as long as it provides an excuse for a party. Small *feste* or *sagre* erupt across Tuscany throughout the year. Most take place in the summer, when long balmy evenings provide the perfect background for a night of festivities. Autumn, however, will do just as well, for then the grapes are brought in, and what better reason for celebration than a good harvest? Most village festivals begin with a special Mass, followed by much dancing, over-indulgence (of food rather than drink) and a rousing fireworks finale. Brass bands provide a musical accompaniment (often of excruciating quality but quite remarkable enthusiasm). You should stumble across many such festivals by accident. If not, they are widely advertised on street posters and in local newspapers.

Medieval echoes Italians love nothing more than spectacle and sensuality. Siena's famous Palio (see pages 240–1), therefore, like many similar pageants, may seem to be little more than an excuse to dress up and indulge in days of rampant (but motiveless) merry-making. To the cynical, such festivities can also appear like attempts to woo the wealthy tourist. Nothing, however, could be further from the truth. Many such events recall ancient but still passionately felt enmities (Siena's Palio, with its inter-district rivalries, is a perfect example). Most are means of expressing fiercely felt civic pride. Some, like Florence's Scoppio del Carro (see page 75), wear a spurious religious mantle – often no more than a mask for an event whose origins have pagan roots. The majority revel in competition, usually between neighbouring districts. Encounters can range from the ferocious – as in Siena's horse-race – to the faintly ridiculous, as in Montepulciano's comical barrel-rolling contest, the

❑ Among the more entertaining traditional festivals are:
Arezzo Giostro del Saracino (September)
Florence Scoppio del Carro (Easter Sunday); Festa di San Giovanni (June); Calcio in Costume (June); Festa del Grillo (15 August); Festa del Rificolone (7 September)
Lucca San Paolino (July); Luminara (13 September); Santa Croce (14 September)
Montepulciano Bravio delle Botti (August)
Pisa Luminara & Regatta di San Ranieri (June); Gioco del Ponte (June)
Pistoia Giostro dell'Orso (July).
Prato Festa degli Omaggi (September)
Siena Palio (2 July and 16 August) ❑

17

Bravio delle Botti (see page 215). Ludicrous or not, the stakes are always high, the battles furiously contested. For example, Florence's Calcio in Costume – a mass game of football in medieval dress – involves bruising passages of play and a medley of viciously underhand tactics.

The Campo in Siena during the Palio, Italy's most famous pageant

■ **Old traditions of craft and artistic endeavour die hard. Florence's modern artisans, worthy successors to their Renaissance forebears, are still part of the city's mythology, whether carving furniture in dusty workshops or crafting jewellery in the venerable environs of the Ponte Vecchio.....■**

Craft on every corner Few modern cities would find a place in their hard-pressed hearts for a breed straight out of the Middle Ages. In Florence, however, artisans (*artigiani*) are very much a part of life. Although rising rents have driven craftsmen out of some parts of the city centre, other areas buzz with skilled activity. On Via della Porcellana, for example, near Ognissanti, every doorway is a tumult of chair-legs and dismembered tables, every interior a vignette of wood shavings and leather-aproned carpenters. A similar scene greets you around Santa Croce, where the smell of wood-glue fills your nostrils and the clank of wrought iron rends the air. The picture is repeated (though in a different guise) on the Ponte Vecchio, where you can look over the shoulders of latter-day portrait painters as they flatter their eager clients. Around them, as likely as not, will be the wares of less subtle deceivers – the fake Chanel bags and Gucci watches of less reputable artisans, tucked away in more discreet workshops. Shops on the bridge itself are packed with glittering jewellery, the work of skilled successors to Renaissance goldsmiths such as Ghiberti and Benvenuto Cellini. Nowhere is the lack of distinction between artist and artisan more apparent than in Florence.

Continue beyond the bridge into the Oltrarno and you enter another artisans' heartland. Whilst fine antique shops front the thoroughfares, small ateliers jam the back streets, home to leather workshops (that of Santo Spirito the most famous) and some of the city's longest-established cabinet-makers. If their wares prove too expensive, visit the market around

Artisans are still an integral and important feature of the city

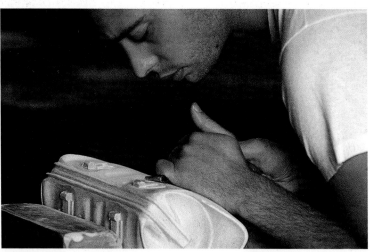

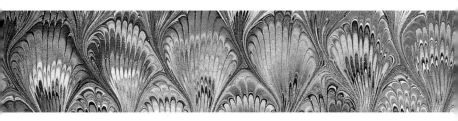

San Lorenzo for a huge choice of leather and clothing. If not, broaden your scope by visiting the stores on Via de' Tornabuoni, a shop window for the city's finest craftsmanship (see Shopping, pages 178–81, for details).

Tradition Artisans provide a living reminder of the past in a city whose history otherwise seems confined to museums and galleries. Not only in their workshops (whose appearance has probably changed little in five centuries) but also in the crafts they carry out, these workers continue to provide a glimpse of a lost world. They may not produce paintings of Renaissance calibre, but in virtually all other areas their skills are as sharply honed as ever. The variety of craftspeople, too, is as broad as ever: from frame-makers, ceramicists, stone-cutters and jewellers, to furniture-makers, silversmiths, weavers and textile-designers.

Pressed into service At no time was the strength of the city's craft tradition more dramatically revealed, nor more desperately needed, than in the aftermath of the 1966 flood. Dozens of skills old and new had to be found to deal with the deluge of damaged artefacts. Many ancient crafts had to be revived (notably the art of illuminating manuscripts): others were virtually unknown (such as the restoration of paper). For the most part, however, the city was able to draw on talent still latent in its thriving artistic subculture.

The Opificio delle Pietre Dure provides an excellent example of tradition merging with modern techniques in the service of art. Founded

In the shadow of the Uffizi gallery, local artists look for work

in 1588, the institute started life making mosaics from *pietre dure* (literally 'hard stone') – usually semi-precious stones like agate and amethyst. The epitome of its work is found in the Medici Chapels' Cappella dei Principi (see pages 64–5). These days its teaching departments and modern laboratories are world leaders in restoration of all kinds, trawling among the craftspeople of Florence not only for *pietre dure* specialists, but also for experts in furniture, painting, stone, marble, bronze and textiles.

■ **Good food is as much a part of the pleasure of a holiday in Florence and Tuscany as visiting the region's museums and art galleries. Eating out in a wayside trattoria or a city-centre restaurant should provide a medley of memories every bit as satisfying as a Donatello nude or a Masaccio fresco.....■**

Florence and French cuisine

Florentines never tire of telling visitors how they invented French cuisine. In 1533, so the story goes, Caterina de' Medici, aged just 14, married Henri de Valois, later to become Henri II of France. Loath (like any good Italian) to leave the joys of home cooking, and appalled by the prospect of foreign food and French table manners, the young Caterina ensured that a train of chefs and an encyclopaedia of recipes followed her to Paris. Hence, supposedly, the range of classic Gallic dishes with

Mushrooms are a speciality of the region in the autumn

more than a hint of Tuscan seasoning: *dolce forte* (from *lepre dolce e forte*); *canard à l'orange* (Tuscany's *papero alla melarancia*); and *vol au vents* (sold in Florentine *pasticcerie* as *turbanate di sfoglia*). Caterina is also supposed to have introduced the French to that most vital piece of table equipment, the fork.

Rich repasts Whatever the truth of the story, medieval Tuscan meals, at least on big occasions, were far richer than the simple dishes that make up today's regional cuisine. The banquets of Pope Leo X, the Medici pope, for example, featured delicacies such as peacocks' tongues, and spectacles such as nightingales flying out of pies and children springing naked from puddings. At the other extreme, poor Florentines might sup off little more than dried figs and oak-bark bread. The average family, by contrast, would settle down to something resembling a modern meal – wine, pasta, ravioli, sausage and grilled meat, and fruit or cheese to finish. Medieval flavourings, however, would raise eyebrows in a modern kitchen. Soups, for example, might have been seasoned with cloves, cinnamon and ginger, and garnished with sugar, cheese and almonds. Pies overflowed with oil, orange and lemon juice, cloves, nutmeg, parsley, saffron, dates, raisins, bay leaves and marjoram. One sauce, *savore sanguino*, boasted cinnamon, raisins, sandal and sumac, the last now used only for tanning leather.

Today's temptations You would be hard pressed to find anything as exotic in today's restaurants. Quite

the contrary: Florentines – wrongly – are now known for their culinary parsimony, and are labelled by other Italians as mere *mangiafagioli* (bean-eaters). Beans, in many forms, certainly feature in many Florentine dishes, but they are symbols rather than staples of the city's healthily robust cuisine. There is much else to appeal, from warming Tuscan vegetable soups like *ribollita* and *acqua-cotta*, to that mother of all steaks, the hearty *bistecca alla fiorentina*. Fruit and vegetables, locally grown and market-bought, are superb, and in season there are such delights as truffles and *porcini* mushrooms to tempt the tastebuds.

As in Rome, which loves its brains and offal dishes, Florence can also taunt the palate with specialities which some might consider a little beyond the culinary pale. Tripe and pigs' intestines (*lampredotto*) are two

❏ City-centre restaurants run the gamut, from expensive post-modern to tatty *trattorie*. The areas around Santo Spirito (in Oltrarno) and Santa Croce are rewarding, with many small, interesting restaurants. Cheap pizzerias and lively *osterie* cluster around the station and Santa Maria Novella. ❏

classic dishes, as are the combs, livers, hearts and testicles of freshly killed roosters. You may wish to pass over such delicacies, but do try to move beyond staples like spaghetti and tomato sauce to sample some of Florence's more interesting specialities (see also pages 210–11).

A tempting sight – take your pick of the city's trattorie

Trattoria

■ **No-one pretends that Florentines revel in the *dolce vita* to the extent of their Roman counterparts. With a café on every corner, however, and a summer sun overhead, opportunities for the *dolce far niente* – the sweet doing of nothing – are as rich in Florence as almost anywhere in Italy.....■**

Time out The simple pleasures of a quiet *cappuccino*, or a calming *aperitivo*, are as much a part of enjoying Italy as trudging round museums and galleries (and this is as true for a native as it is for a foreigner). No self-respecting Italian city, therefore, can do without its bars and cafés. And while Florence's streets and piazzas may seem less welcoming than some, they still provide a colourful and more than adequate stage for lazy self-indulgence. They also provide the wherewithal for that other passive pastime – people-watching.

Cafés are there to be used – and not merely as bolt-holes for a gulp of coffee before another round of Giotto and Michelangelo. After hours of paintings and sculpture, of churches dutifully seen, treat yourself to an hour or two of more

❏ Florence's best-known cafés are the 'Big Four' on Piazza della Repubblica: **Donnini** (excellent coffee and cakes), **Paszkowski** (literary associations, music on the terrace summer evenings), **Giubbe Rosse** (peruse the daily papers with your coffee) and (best of the lot, one-time haunt of the intelligentsia) the *belle-époque* **Gilli**. ❏

wholehearted self-indulgence. Such simple delights may be denied you on your return to daily routines.

A choice of styles There is a bar on almost every Florentine street corner – functional, stand-up places designed for a kick-start *espresso*, a breakfast *cornetto* (a horn-shaped, custard-filled croissant) or a hurried lunchtime snack. All human life is here, together with all it needs to keep body and soul together. Bars are shops, pubs, phone-booths and social meeting places rolled into one. Cafés are a little different. You can still stand and fight for service, but more often than not they provide oases of leisurely and sun-drenched contemplation. Relaxation, not to mention waiter service, comes at a price (you pay extra to sit down), but even the most humble purchase buys the right to read, day-dream or take in the streetlife for as long as the mood takes you.

Service with a smile

A slightly different experience awaits in the city's wine cellars, old-fashioned institutions that parade under a variety of names – *vinaio, fiaschetteria, mescita*. Some, like the *Cantinetta Antinori* (in Piazza Antinori) are smart, rather up-market affairs. Others, like the hole-in-the-wall *Vini del Chianti* (Via dei Cimatori) are rough-and-ready neighbourhood joints. Most offer places to meet for a chat and a bite to eat (with, of course, a glass or two of wine).

People-watching There comes a time – when the postcards are written and you are dead on your feet – when the world has to come to you. Then is the moment to forget the galleries, ignore the churches, and sit back, drink in hand, to watch the Italians and your fellow travellers at play. People-watching in Italy is a rare delight. No time is better to indulge in it than during the social ritual known as the *passeggiata*, a stylised evening parade when the object is to

Taking time, with a cup of coffee, to catch up on the news

dress up and then to see and be seen (in Florence its ebb and flow centres on Piazza della Signoria and the streets around Via dei Calzaiuoli). Traffic and narrow streets preclude ranks of Parisian-style boulevard cafés (premium spots for the amateur voyeur): in Florence, the most famous cafés crowd Piazza della Signoria or the more dour margins of Piazza della Repubblica. Many equally picturesque spots await discovery in the quieter corners of the Oltrarno. None lack for passing interest.

❑ The expensive but essential **Rivoire** on Piazza della Signoria is one of Florence's most famous cafés, perfect for admiring the clothes-conscious Italians carrying out their evening *passeggiata*. ❑

■ **Tourism in any great city is invariably a double-edged blessing. On the one hand it offers revenue and employment, on the other it encourages the less scrupulous and adds to the wear and tear on the very monuments visitors come to see. Restoration, as a result, is a constant Florentine preoccupation. Today more than ever, the city is struggling to maintain a balance between protecting the legacy of its illustrious past and carving for itself a realistic and economically sound future.....■**

Weight of numbers Estimates vary as to how many people visit Florence every year. The evidence of one's own eyes, however, suggests it is too many. It is as well, therefore, to come expecting to share the city's attractions with a great many other people: prepared for the crowds forever clustered around the Uffizi's Botticellis, and for the numbers of young visitors of many countries sprawled around the Duomo and the Ponte Vecchio.

Overcrowding is a problem that touches the Florentine at least as much as the harassed tourist. Those who live in Florence are the ones, day in, day out, who bear the intolerable strain visitors place on the city's infrastructure – though they are also, of course, the ones who reap tourism's financial benefits. Visitors, however, can only be partly blamed for the city's traffic, a daily threat to life and limb (quite apart from the effects of vehicle-induced pollution on the health of statues and stonework). Here locals are their own worst enemies: there are, on average, 2.7 cars for every Florentine family. And cars – with food, family and football – are the things closest to an Italian's heart. Getting rid of them, therefore, has been an uphill battle: city-centre restrictions were introduced only in 1988, and then only after considerable argument.

Florence fossilised? Florentines are currently faced with a difficult choice: whether to go for broke (perhaps literally as well as metaphorically) and

retain Florence as a living city, or whether to turn it over entirely to the demands of tourism. If they tend towards the latter, Florence may be in danger of becoming a historical fossil, a moribund city dressed up as a Renaissance theme park. Death by tourism can be brought on by a variety of causes. They include slow strangulation by traffic, paralysis by depopulation, food shops replaced by souvenir stands, workshops replaced by boutiques, neighbourhood *trattorie* sacrificed to the gods of fast food.

The problem echoes that of Venice, whose population has dropped to 70,000 today from 180,000 in 1945. Florentine figures show a similar trend, down from 400,000 before the 1966 flood to an estimated 150,000 today. But for Florence, such discouraging statistics are generally tempered by glimmers of optimism.

Firenze Nuova One much-heralded way forward for Florence is the new town on the city's northwestern outskirts, around the airport. Firenze Nuova, so the theory goes, will encourage urban decentralisation and create the focus for a broad-based industrial and municipal metropolis, its economy increasingly intertwined with that of its booming neighbour, Prato. Florence itself, the planners hope, will increasingly be freed to develop as a culture- and service-orientated city. Critics (of which, as ever in Italy, there are many) complain that the scheme could have the opposite effect, creating a

24

desiccated city centre on the one hand, and a steel and glass wasteland on the other. So far, the critics appear to have been confounded: many of the traditional businesses, such as banking, publishing, architecture and legal services, seem likely to remain in central Florence. Many Florentine professionals perhaps prefer the more stimulating environment of the city centre, with its Renaissance palaces and statues, and have no intention of surrendering Florence to tourism.

Crime Whatever the impression given by the city's urbane citizens and benign-looking streets, all is not well below the surface. Florentines talk of *Firenze snaturata* (Florence corrupted), a phrase used to describe both the threat of the city's surrender to tourists and its growing catalogue of crime. Prostitution and drug-dealing are mainstays of the Florentine underworld, just as in many cities in the 1990s. It can be hard not to notice the drug deals on Via de' Neri, or the late-night low-life cluttered around the station and the Cascine park, proving that there is more to the city than statues and sweet-

The volume of visitors (top, Uffizi and below, Piazza SS Annunziata) increases wear on the monuments

Making friends with the Porcellino near the Mercato Nuovo

faced gallery Madonnas. However, this is not to say that Florence is particularly dangerous, nor is it plagued with the petty crime of, say, Rome or Naples. Pickpockets aside, the city's criminal element is unlikely to affect most reasonably vigilant visitors.

Pollution and restoration Still on the down side, but again in common with cities the world over, air pollution is an increasing worry in Florence. It is true that the city has some way to go before it faces the pollution problems of Rome or Milan. Nonetheless, the danger signs are already there, and are of special concern in a city that has more than its share of outdoor art treasures. The begrimed Battistero is a prominent victim, its bronze doors now removed from their proximity to belching exhausts and replaced by copies. Gone, too, are most of

Orsanmichele's exterior statues, removed – like the Campanile's corroded reliefs and Michelangelo's *David* – to the pollution-free sanctuary of museums and galleries.

The unending task of restoring works of art damaged by time and pollution is one thing; repairing the damage done in a mere few hours by the 1966 flood is quite another. The deluge created one of the greatest artistic (and human) disasters in Italy's recent history (see pages 130–1). Some of the thousands of damaged artworks were lost for ever and many are still waiting to see the light of day. Most, however, were restored, almost miraculously in many cases, testament to the dedication and technical skills of Florence's restorers.

The sheer size of Italy's artistic heritage means that funds for restoration are constantly at a premium. After the 1966 flood, however, huge additional sums of money were donated to Florence. Much of the money is still being put to good use in a massive restoration project that looks set to last another 20 years.

Not all the city's restoration projects have been without incident. Piazza della Signoria provided the worst recent upheaval: excavations turned the square into a building site, then the original medieval paving stones were mysteriously 'lost'. The pedestrianisation scheme (the *Zona Blu*) has also been a mixed success. It is, however, typical of the projects increasingly needed by a city struggling to reconcile two disparate sets of demands – the requirements of visitors seeking its Renaissance past and the needs of citizens looking to its 21st-century future.

❏ Almost 30 years after the 1966 flood, some 80 full-time staff are still employed restoring books and manuscripts in the National Library, where more than a million volumes were ruined. About 2,000 of the 3,000 paintings and sculptures dredged from the mud have so far been returned to public view. ❏

FLORENCE WAS

Myth and legend

■ Although Florence was a late arrival on the historical stage – only six decades before the birth of Christ – its beginnings have become entangled in a heady mix of myth and counter-myth. Even the origins of its name are obscured by an opaque combination of fact and fantasy.....■

The Etruscans Florence was probably first inhabited by Italic tribes from latter-day Emilia-Romagna around the end of the 10th century BC. The main attraction of the site was simple: it provided a crossing point over the Arno, one of the region's more formidable natural barriers (the ford was close to the site of the present-day Ponte Vecchio). When the Etruscans drifted into the area five centuries later, however (see pages 246–7), they ignored the river in favour of a more easily defended position in the hills to the north. In time their craggy fortress

became Fiesole (see pages 82–3), a colony that developed into a leading member of the Etruscans' 12-city federation. At the same time, the Etruscans probably kept a small market on the Arno, and a breakaway group from Fiesole may also have established a community near the river in the 4th century BC.

The end of Fiesole By this time, Rome was rapidly encroaching on the Etruscan dominions. Fiesole was first defeated in 283BC, but it continued, like many Etruscan cities, to enjoy a relationship of benevolent neutrality with the ever more powerful city of Rome. Fiesole's end, according to legend, came around 60BC, when Rome sent an expedition to hunt down Catiline, a fugitive from Roman justice. Catiline, it seems, had fled to Fiesole and assumed control of the city (to the delight of its inhabitants). Fiorino, commander of the Roman forces, realising Fiesole was powerfully defended, decided to build a camp on the Arno and take the city by siege. Killed in a surprise raid, however, his plans came to nothing, but his successor, Julius Caesar, consolidated the riverside camp and eventually defeated Fiesole. As for Catiline, he escaped, only to be hunted down and killed near Pistoia.

Fact and fiction Most of this colourful account is pure fiction – and with it the notion that Florence took its name (and owed its existence) to the slain commander, Fiorino. Catiline

Etruscan art: (top) black figure vase and (left) funerary urn from Chiusi

was a historical figure, *was* in Fiesole, and *was* defeated at Pistoia in 62BC. Fiorino, however, seems to be an entirely literary invention. Julius Caesar probably never fought in Tuscany; nor did he found Roman Florentia (though he is often described as doing so). His role in the city's birth was passive. It was his agrarian law of 59BC that – by making provision for land to be granted to retired army veterans – actually created the conditions for Florence's establishment and early growth.

The name of Florence How Florence came by its romantic name is a mystery. Many would still like to believe it was named after Fiorino and his fictitious camp (and, though history is silent on the subject, there may well have been such a general in Caesar's army). Others think it derives from *fluentia*, after the fact that the Arno 'flows' through the city (though plenty of rivers flow through

Wandering among the ruins of Fiesole, Florence's Etruscan predecessor in the hills above the Arno

cities). Another theory, along similar lines, suggests that *fluentia* refers to the 'confluence' of the Arno and Mugnone (the river that joins the Arno 2km west of the city).

Popular tradition, however, favours more poetic semantic possibilities – centring on Florence as a 'city of flowers' (*fiori*). Roman Florentia, for example, might have taken its name from the wild flowers that strew the city's hills and plains. Or it may have derived from the Ludi Floreales, a programme of spring games held to honour the goddess Flora. The city's cathedral is still known as Santa Maria del Fiore, after the *giaggiolo*, or *Iris florentia*, the violet-scented iris of the Florentine hills. The purple flower (shaped like a fleur-de-lis) is also the city's emblem and the symbol of the Virgin Mary.

■ **Under Roman domination, Florence enjoyed a period of quiet prosperity. After Rome's fall the city took the barbarian invasions more or less in its stride. Lombard and Carolingian rule then laid the foundations of an independent city, and with it the prospect of Florence's medieval power and prosperity.....■**

A Roman city Florence's Roman stalwarts established a walled *castrum*, a camp whose grid-iron outline is still clearly imprinted on the city's present-day streets. Its northern and southern limits, for example, are marked by Via de' Cerretani and Via Porta Rossa, its eastern and western boundaries by Via del Proconsolo and Via de' Tornabuoni. Piazza della Repubblica was the old Forum, Via degli Strozzi its main street (the *Decumanus Maximus*). The old theatre lay behind the Palazzo Vecchio, the amphitheatre within the curve of Via Torta and Piazza dei Peruzzi (near Santa Croce).

Today, only a few columns remain as direct memorials of the colony of Florentia. Some are in the church of San Miniato al Monte, others form part of the Battistero, site of the Roman *praetorium* or guardhouse (and possibly the Roman governor's residence). Otherwise monuments amount to no more than historical echoes, vague memories recalled by street names such as Via delle Terme (Street of the Baths) or Via del Campidoglio (Street of the Capitol).

Decline and fall Florence's main role under the Romans was strategic. Florentia not only provided a route over the Arno, but also controlled the passes across the Apennines into Emilia-Romagna. Although the settlement's first walls took no account of the Arno, it was the river – navigable to this point – that provided a conduit for trade and generated the colony's early prosperity. Consular roads, too, made the camp their focus, notably the Via Cassia, a link between Rome and its big colonies at Bononia (Bologna) and Mediolanum (Milan). The Via Aurelia, the Via Clodia and

Top: the façade on the Roman villa at Poggio a Chiano. Below: the great Roman theatre at Fiesole

the Via Flaminia – built before Florentia's rise – also criss-crossed the region, further emphasising the new colony's strategic importance. Although Florentia was never a major player in the Roman world, by around the 3rd century (after expansion during the Augustan period) the city's population had probably reached about 10,000.

The Barbarians After Rome's fall Florence suffered repeated attacks from Goth and Byzantine invaders. Ultimately, however, it was the Lombards, a Germanic people from the north, who dominated the city during the Dark Ages. After taking Tuscany in AD570, they brought two centuries of relative peace to the troubled region, which they administered from Pavia and Lucca. Their reign was cut short by the Franks (another northern race), first under Pepin the Short, and then under his more famous son, Charlemagne, who probably visited the city on a couple of occasions. Tuscany became part of the Franks' Carolingian Empire (later the Holy Roman Empire), ruled on behalf of its northern emperors by a series of Lucca-based princes known as the Margraves.

The rule of the Margraves The Carolingian empire's hold over the Margraves grew progressively weaker. As it waned, the Margraves were becoming increasingly fond of Florence. Willa, widow of the Margrave Uberto, for example, founded the Badia Fiorentina, the city's first abbey (see page 55), in 978. By 1001 Willa's son, the Margrave Ugo, transferred the

Rome continued to influence the art of Tuscany long after the fall of the empire

region's capital from Lucca to Florence. Thereafter, Margrave allegiance to northern-based emperors slackened still further. By 1077 the pious Margrave Matilda (1046–1115), founder of many churches and one of the era's most successful rulers, had transferred her loyalties to the pope (by now already involved in virulent disputes with the emperor – see pages 36–7). At her death she bequeathed her titles to Pope Gregory VII – all, that is, except Lucca, Florence and Siena, all three of which found themselves on the verge of independence and self-determination.

Textiles and banking

■ **The medieval prosperity of Florence was based on Europe's greatest woollen and textiles industry. This enterprise in turn nurtured a banking system whose success laid the foundations of modern capitalism and made Florentines bankers to much of the known world.....**■

Early success At its peak, the textiles industry in Florence employed an estimated 30,000 people – about one-third of the city's population. During the 12th century, barely 100 years after the trade began, some 300 textile workshops were scattered across the city. Even by the end of the 13th century, when production had dropped by almost 90 per cent, Florence still provided the Western world with at least one-tenth of its textiles.

There were several reasons for Florence's success. One was water, fundamental to the woollen industry (both sorted wool and finished cloth, for example, had to be washed and rinsed). In the Arno, therefore, the city had a primary resource. Another was the availability of expertise and cheap labour. The expertise was provided by the Umiliati, a group of monks introduced to the city from Lombardy. Their riverside workshops made Ognissanti (see page 109) one of the industry's main centres. They helped train the city's teeming ranks of carders, combers, weavers, shearers, spinners and other specialised artisans. Money, too, was of prime

importance, and here Florence's bankers came into their own, providing the industry with capital investment and extended lines of credit.

Florence was also renowned for the quality of its cloth. Its reputation for dyeing, in particular, was second to none. Exotic dyestuffs came from every corner of the Orient and the Mediterranean basin, Florentine reds becoming particularly prized (many of the dyers' secrets, incidentally, are now lost – one of history's more tantalising mysteries). All Florence lacked was wool. This problem was solved by the city's enterprising merchants who – 'in the name of God and profit' – travelled to England, Portugal, Spain, Flanders and the Barbary Coast to buy raw materials to feed their flourishing businesses.

Europe's bankers Florentine bankers championed the use of bills of exchange, and invented cheques, credit, life insurance, double-entry book-keeping and Europe's first single currency, the gold florin. On their own these might seem dry achievements. In the context of what a banker might do with his profits, however, they provided the financial wherewithal for

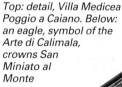

Top: detail, Villa Medicea Poggio a Caiano. Below: an eagle, symbol of the Arte di Calimala, crowns San Miniato al Monte

many of the greatest buildings and works of art of the Renaissance.

The best-known of the bankers, of course, were the Medici, whose bank, in its day, was Europe's single wealthiest business. A 15th-century phenomenon, the family were late-comers to an industry that by 1250 already dominated the world of European commerce. The Bardi and the Peruzzi, for example, were chief bankers to the kings of England and France; the Acciaiuoli dealt with the Angevin monarchs of Naples and Sicily; whilst the Pazzi, the Alberti (and the Medici) handled the highly lucrative papal account. Lesser financiers from among Florence's 24 banking dynasties – involved with Holy Roman Emperors, German potentates and Burgundian princes – are remembered today in the city's palaces and street-names – Alberti, Albizzi, Antinori, Capponi, Cerchi, Davanzati, Guardi, Mozzi, Portinari, Ricci, Strozzi and Tornabuoni.

The florin One of the bankers' key achievements was the *fiorino d'oro* (gold florin), a coin which was adopted across Europe after its introduction in 1252, and which remained in use until the middle of the 15th cen-

Top and above: details, the Palazzo dell'Arte della Lana

tury. Florentines had previously used the *mark*, minted in Pisa, whilst the only internationally accepted coin had been the Byzantine *hyperper*. (The English florin, whose name survived in British coinage until recently, took its name from the *fiorino*.) Purity was vital to the coin's stability, and standards at the Zecca (Mint), alongside the Palazzo Vecchio, were rigorously applied. By 1422 two million *fiorini* were in circulation. One side bore a likeness of John the Baptist, Florence's patron saint: the other was inscribed with the city's Latin name, Florentia, and its floral emblem.

❏ In the 1430s, a family could live comfortably on 150 florins a year; a *palazzo* could be bought for 1,000, a Botticelli painting for 100, a slave for 50 and a servant for 10. The Medici accounts for the years 1433–71 showed 663,755 florins spent over 38 years on 'buildings, charities and taxes'. ❏

■ The city's great mercantile endeavours were organised into *Arti* (Guilds). Their leading lights were invariably to be found either running the city as office-holders in the official machinery of government, or manipulating affairs more subtly through their position at the head of its supposedly independent institutions.....■

A society of merchants As early as the 11th century, Florentine merchants organised themselves into a *societas mercatorum*. Ranged against them was the *societas militium*, a grouping of nobles and leading Florentine families. The former provided the backbone of the *comune*, the independent city-state, run by a 100-strong assembly and established in Florence after Margrave Matilda's death in 1115. In time the *societas* was replaced by the first of the guilds, the Arte di Calimala, an umbrella organisation devoted to most mercantile vocations. By the end of the 12th century, however, splinter groups had broken away to form seven major guilds, the Arti Maggiori.

The Arti Maggiori The most prestigious of the guilds, though not the wealthiest, was the lawyers' Arte dei Giudici e Notai. Next came the wool, silk and cloth merchants – the Arte della Lana, the Arte di Por Santa Maria and the refashioned Arte di Calimala. Lower down came the Arte del Cambio, or bankers' guild (bankers preferred the term 'money-changers', usury being a sin in the eyes of the Church). The Arte dei Vaccai e Pellicciai looked after the furriers. The Arte dei Medici, Speziali e Merciai embraced a hotch-potch of doctors, apothecaries and spice- and dye-merchants (as well as the occasional poet, painter and craftsman).

The Arti Minori While the Arti Maggiori embraced wealthy merchants, the 14 minor guilds (founded in 1289) catered more to middle-ranking tradesmen. These included anyone from butchers, bakers and armourers to carpenters, masons and inn-keepers (not to mention vintners, tanners, cooks, locksmiths and leather-workers). Ordinary workers, however, the so-called *Popolo Minuto,* had no representation at all – despite making up 75 per cent of the population. Those employed in the wool, silk and cloth industries, moreover, were prevented by law from forming guilds.

The power of the merchant class Merchants, known as the *Popolo Grasso* (literally the 'fat people'), controlled Florence during much of the 13th and 14th centuries. Sometimes the control was covert, at other times plain to see, as in the so-called Primo Popolo (1248), a quasi-democratic regime dominated by mercantile elements (whose 10-year rule, according to Dante, was the only period of civic peace in Florence's history). During the Secondo Popolo (1284), the Arti Maggiori introduced the *Ordinamenti della Giustizia* (1293), a written constitution that, while theoretically the blueprint for republican rule, in fact entrenched mercantile power still further.

Government by guilds Florence's much-vaunted republicanism worked well in theory. The names of selected guild members (and only guild members) were placed in eight leather bags (*borse*) kept in Santa Croce. Names were then drawn at random in public. Those selected were known as *Priori*, the government they formed the *Signoria*. There were usually nine *Priori*, six chosen from the Arti Maggiori, two from the Arti Minori, and one standard-bearer, the

Gonfaloniere. The *Priori* served a maximum term of office of two months – a deliberately short period, in order to reduce the chances of corruption or favouritism. In times of crisis a *Parlemento*, or assembly, was summoned, consisting of all male citizens over the age of 14. When a two-thirds quorum was reached, the *Parlemento* was asked to approve a *balia*, a committee delegated to deal with the crisis as it saw fit.

Florence's republican system looked good on paper. In practice it was far from democratic. The lowliest workers, the *Popolo Minuto*, were totally excluded, as were the *grandi*, or nobles. Despite the random selection process, merchant cliques easily ensured that only the names of likely supporters found their way into the *borse*. If things did not go their way, it was easy enough to summon a *Parlemento* and form a *balia* whose first act would be to replace the offending *Priori* with more pliable candidates. It was thus, through the long decades of Medici rule, that the family retained the reins of power while only rarely holding formal office.

Top: sails, symbol of the Rucellai family, S Maria Novella. Below: patron saints of the major guilds decorate Orsanmichele's exterior

■ **Florence was torn by internal disputes throughout the medieval period. Matters came to a head during the 13th century with the so-called Guelph–Ghibelline conflicts. Ostensibly encounters between papal and imperial supporters, these divisions were often no more than labels for any number of different feuds and factions.....■**

36

Endless enmity There has hardly been a time in Florence's 2,000-year history when the city was not divided into two or more rival camps. Dante compared its constant political struggles to a sick man forever tossing and turning in bed. So unending was the discord that contemporaries believed two different races had settled Florence: the nobles, descended from Roman soldiers, and the commoners, descendants of Fiesole's ancient Etruscans. Trying to follow

Emperor Barbarossa – 'Red Beard' – and (top) his court at Mayence

the city's litany of feuds is pointless – and makes monotonous reading. All one can do is trace the main divisions, and remember that, for all the apparent conflict, Florence went from strength to strength.

Pope versus emperor The Guelphs and the Ghibellines took their names from 'Welf' – the family name of Otto IV and the dukes of Bavaria – and 'Waiblingen' – the name of a castle belonging to their rivals, the Imperial family of Hohenstaufen. The Guelphs, broadly speaking, were supporters of the pope, the Ghibellines supporters of the Holy Roman Emperor. Disputes between emperor and pope dated back to the investiture of Charlemagne, who had given lands conquered in Italy to the papacy (the beginnings of the Papal States). In return he had been anointed and crowned Holy Roman Emperor. This was the root of irreconcilable differences: the popes claimed the right to crown emperors; the emperors claimed the right to sanction popes. Even more importantly, both parties claimed the right to rule the lands that made up the ancient Roman empire: the pope argued that Constantine the Great had bequeathed the empire to the Church, while the emperor cited lineal descent from the Roman and Byzantine emperors.

The dispute first came to a head in 1079 when Emperor Henry IV rejected Pope Gregory VII's proposals for radical reform (aimed at securing exclusive papal powers to control the selection and investiture of bishops). Gregory responded by excommunicating the emperor, in theory thereby freeing his subjects from imperial

The Bargello's courtyard, scene of countless executions during the Guelph and Ghibelline conflicts

allegiance. While diplomacy eventually settled this dispute (in the Concordat of Worms), subsequent disagreements were to involve violent confrontations on Italian soil, the most notorious of which was Emperor Barbarossa's 12th-century rampage to restore imperial authority.

Flags of convenience Conflicts within Italy's city states, including Florence, rarely divided along simple Guelph–Ghibelline lines. By the time the words entered the language (in the 12th century) they were little more than convenient labels for a variety of feuding factions. Cities used alliances with pope or emperor, for example, as means to their own ends, the terms 'Guelph' and 'Ghibelline' serving as mere window-dressing for squabbles between cities, or feuds between families within cities. If your sympathies were broadly Guelph (like those of Florence), the chances are your neighbour (and enemy) would be nominally Ghibelline (like Siena).

Florence divided The main division among the citizens of Florence was between the old nobility, who had Ghibelline sympathies, and the new class of entrepreneurs, who were Guelphs. By 1193 the in-fighting was so disruptive that the *Comune* introduced political refinements such as the post of *Podestà* (a chief magistrate) to help defuse the situation

(see pages 56–7). In 1216, in one famous incident, street battles were triggered by the murder of one Buondelmonti, stabbed for reneging on a promise to marry a member of the Amidei family. (This was the supposed spark of Florence's Guelph–Ghibelline conflicts.) Although Ghibelline regimes reigned briefly (in both 1237 and 1260), Florence was predominantly a Guelph (mercantile) city – though, in keeping with the divisive spirit of the times, the Guelphs themselves managed to quarrel and split into two factions – the Whites and the Blacks (see page 71).

Civil chaos in most cities of the period invariably had the same outcome – the emergence of a single man or family with the wealth and power to cut through the tangle of feuding and factionalism. It was only a matter of time before just such a family emerged in Florence.

> ❏ 'Nearly every form of government was tried … in Florence', but Florentines were 'too articulate, politically, for government to be possible at all'. Mary McCarthy (1912–89) ❏

■ Few families' names are more associated with a city than that of the Medici with Florence. The phenomenal wealth of their banking business sustained them as the city's effective rulers for 350 years. During this period, Medici patronage produced some of the greatest buildings and works of art ever seen.....■

38

Casting into the future, Giovanni di Bicci de' Medici (1360–1429), founder of the Medici banking business, could scarcely have dreamed that his descendants would rule Florence until 1737, that they would include popes and cardinals, and that they would marry into the noble families of Spain and Austria, providing spouses for such illustrious names as Charles I of England, Philip II of Spain, Philip IV of Spain, Henri II of France, Henri IV of France, Emperor Ferdinand II, the Elector Palatine, and Mary Queen of Scots.

The Medici family crest – object of much historical speculation

The family symbol You come across the Medici emblem time and again in Florence – a cluster of red balls on a gold background. Yet its origins are a complete mystery. Legend claims the family were descended from Averardo, a Carolingian knight who, passing through the Mugello (south of Florence), had fought and killed a giant in battle. During the encounter his shield received six massive blows from the giant's mace. Charlemagne, as a reward for his bravery, allowed Averardo to represent the dents as red balls on his coat of arms. Others say the balls (*palle*) had less exalted origins: that they were pawnbrokers' coins, or medicinal pills (or cupping glasses) that recalled the family's origins as doctors (*medici*) or apothecaries. Others say they are *bezants*, Byzantine coins, inspired by the arms of the Arte del Cambio (the bankers' guild, to which the Medici belonged).

❏ Whatever the origin of the Medici family emblem, it is interesting to note that the number of *palle* (balls) depicted in it varied. Originally there were 12; in Cosimo de' Medici's time it was seven; the ceiling of San Lorenzo's Sagrestia Vecchia has eight; Cosimo I's tomb in the Cappelle Medicee has five; and Ferdinand's coat of arms in the Forte di Belvedere six. ❏

Cosimo de' Medici (1389–1464)
From humble origins (two wool workshops), Giovanni di Bicci had engineered a business that put the Medici in the first rank of Florentine

society. His son, Cosimo, was to prove the greatest of the Medici. A patron of the arts, he increased his fortune tenfold and established the family's political credentials.

Cosimo (later to be known as 'Il Vecchio' – 'the old man', enabling posterity to distinguish him from later Medici also called Cosimo) took on and defeated the ruling Albizzi family after briefly leading the opposition party and being exiled for his pains in 1434. By 1458 Pope Pius II could describe him as 'master of the country ... Political questions are settled at his house. The man he chooses holds office ... He it is who decides peace and war and controls the laws ... He is King in everything but name.'

Lorenzo the Magnificent (1449–92)

Cosimo's son Piero (1416–69) was cursed by ill-health, outliving his father by only five years. Lorenzo, Cosimo's grandson, carried on where his grandfather had left off. His 23-year reign, a period of relative peace in the city (and in Italy), was to be looked back on as a golden age. A scholar and accomplished poet, Lorenzo was perfectly at one with his times, which coincided with the height of the Renaissance. He enjoyed country villas, and sponsored a host of humanist thinkers and writers (though he commissioned surprisingly few paintings and buildings). He was a skilled diplomat, despite occasional disagreements with the papacy (and the trauma of the Pazzi Conspiracy – see pages 74–5). Only in business, where it mattered, did he lack the family touch (both Medici fortunes and the Florentine economy were in decline during his period of ascendancy). His death marked the close of an era. 'The peace of Italy is at an end,' remarked Pope Innocent VIII on hearing of his demise.

❏ 'Do not appear to give advice,' Giovanni di Bicci de' Medici told his son Cosimo, 'but put your views forward discreetly in conversation ... never display any pride should you receive a lot of votes ... Avoid litigation and political controversy, and always keep out of the public eye.' ❏

Top: medieval Florence: Below: Botticelli's Adoration of the Magi *contains portraits of Cosimo, Piero, Giovanni and Lorenzo de' Medici*

■ **Few periods in Florence's history can have been as bizarre as the four-year reign of Savonarola, a charismatic but fanatical Dominican monk whose dazzling sermons fired the city to moral and literal revolt before papal ire and mob rule brought his downfall and eventual execution.....■**

Early life On his deathbed, Lorenzo the Magnificent had sent for two clerics – Fra Mariano and a 40-year-old firebrand named Girolamo Savonarola. Few who had known the young Girolamo would have prophesied such an honour. Born in 1452, the son of a Paduan physician, he was a man unpromising in looks – hook-nosed and thick-lipped – and of uncompromising personal habits. He slept on straw or on wooden boards, ate little, drank no liquor and rarely addressed women (except when

Fra Bartolomeo's portrait of the fiery Girolamo Savonarola

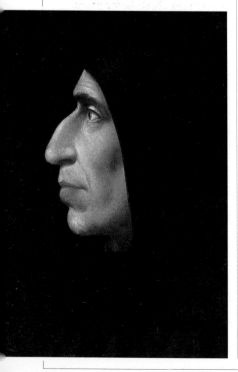

preaching). His youth passed in the study of scripture, or in the composition of religious poetry. Only his eyes suggested passion – green orbs that sometimes (according to one source) gave forth red flashes. At 23 he ran away to a Dominican monastery in Bologna, later moving to Florence's San Marco convent. The pope appointed him Vicar General of the Order in 1493.

A stirring preacher In his first sermons, to quote a chronicler, Savonarola scarcely knew 'how to move a hen'. By 1491, despite his continuing awkwardness, the content and apocalyptic passion of his preaching were drawing large audiences: 10,000 people came to the Duomo to hear his Lenten sermon that year. In old age Michelangelo claimed he could still hear the friar's speeches ringing in his ears. Savonarola's sermons, however, were not mere harangues. He believed them to be divinely inspired: 'It is not I who preach,' he said, 'but God who speaks through me.' Florence, he thundered, had condemned itself to perdition by its idolatries. Its painters made the Virgin 'look like a harlot'; its prostitutes were 'pieces of meat with eyes'; its sodomites were to be burnt alive. 'Repent, O Florence, while there is still time', he warned, conjuring visions of plague, war and foreign invaders 'armed with gigantic razors', should Florence reject the 'white garments of purification'.

Savonarola in power When Charles VIII of France entered Italy in 1494 (pressing a claim to the Neapolitan throne) Savonarola saw him as a vehicle of divine retribution: 'Behold!

the sword has descended; the scourge has fallen; the prophecies are being fulfilled'. Lorenzo's son and successor, the ineffectual Piero, fled Charles's military advance. Savonarola, who held the terrified populace in his palm, filled the power vacuum to become the city's effective ruler. Decrees and invocations flowed from San Marco: there was to be continual fasting; treasures were to be removed from churches; 'blessed bands' of children were to spy on their parents. Most famous of all, a vast 'Bonfire of Vanities' was built in Piazza della Signoria, stacked with books and board games, clothing, wigs and false beards, paintings, mirrors and pots of rouge.

Downfall and death Charles, meanwhile, had won Naples and retreated to France. Every two of his soldiers, it is said, were accompanied by a mule burdened with treasure pilfered from the peninsula. Savonarola, for his part, declined to involve Florence in the Holy League convened against the French king (an alliance of the papacy, Milan, Venice, Ferdinand of Aragon and the Emperor Maximilian).

The execution of Savonarola in Piazza della Signoria: the scene depicts three separate episodes

Furthermore, he denounced Alexander VI (the corrupt Borgia pope) as an agent of Satan. Alexander summoned him to Rome to explain his conduct. Savonarola refused. Alexander pleaded, even offering him a cardinal's hat. Eventually, in July 1497, Savonarola suffered the inevitable fate: he was excommunicated.

By now the tide of Savonarola's popularity had turned. He had always had enemies, the so-called *arrabbiati* ('the angry ones'), mobsters who derided his followers as *piagnoni* (snivellers). Poor harvests, plague and war with Pisa now strengthened their hand (while excommunication chastened the Florentines). In 1498, when Savonarola ducked a trial by fire (a Franciscan idea), the mob, robbed of its spectacle, dragged the friar from San Marco. Tortured half to death, he was found guilty of heresy and burned in Piazza della Signoria. The place of execution is still marked by a commemorative plaque.

■ **The Medici heyday lasted a little over 100 years, from the birth of Cosimo in 1389 to the death of Lorenzo in 1492. The rule of their hapless descendants, however, kept Florence in thrall for much longer – from the rise of Cosimo I in 1537 to the dynasty's extinction in 1737......**■

Troubled times Republican rule returned briefly to Florence after Savonarola's execution. However, a decade of peace under Piero Soderini, assisted by Machiavelli, proved to be the calm before the storm. In 1512 Florence found itself France's only Italian ally against the combined papal and Spanish armies. Defeat was swift, and was followed by the return of Giuliano de' Medici (Lorenzo's vicious son) and the syphilitic Lorenzo, Duke of Urbino (a grandson of Lorenzo the Magnificent). Real control of the city, however, now lay with Lorenzo the Magnificent's second son, Giovanni, better known as Pope Leo X.

Medici popes The papal account had long been the mainstay of Medici fortunes. What better way to secure it, therefore, than by creating a Medici pope? Plans for just such an eventuality had preoccupied the Medici for years. In the 1470s, for example, bribery and diplomacy had seen the eight-year-old Giovanni ordained. Similar tactics five years later had bought him a cardinal's hat (at 13 he was the youngest cardinal in history). Given his route to success, it was heartening to find that Giovanni, for all his jollity and love of pleasure, was not entirely without papal merit. On assuming office in 1513, following the death of Julius II, he launched his pontificate with the cry 'God has given us the papacy. Let us enjoy it!'

He proved as good as his word. He patronised the arts, threw lavish feasts and generally ran papal (and Medici) finances into the ground. He 'could no more save a thousand ducats', wrote a friend of Machiavelli, 'than a stone could fly through the air.' While free-spending, he was also shrewd. Into a Curia packed with Medici supporters (31 new cardinals were created) he launched Giulio de' Medici (previously Archbishop of Florence), the illegitimate son of Lorenzo the Magnificent's brother, Giuliano (murdered in the Pazzi Conspiracy – see pages 74–5). In 1523, after the brief rule of Adrian VI (1522–3), Giulio duly became Pope Clement VII, reigning until his death in 1534.

Top: grotto in the gardens of Cosimo I's Palazzo Pitti. Right: Pope Leo X

Like Leo before him, Clement VII ruled Florence from Rome. Two thoroughly unattractive Medici bastards were used as stooges – Ippolito and Alessandro (the latter probably Clement's son). The Sack of Rome by Charles V's Imperial army in 1527, however, destroyed Medici papal ambitions at a stroke. With Clement powerless and humiliated, Florence rid itself of the Medici – only for them to return when Charles and Clement made peace in 1529. Alessandro, created the first Duke of Florence, was married to Charles's bastard daughter, Margaret of Parma. The marriage, an obviously political affair, proved a pointer to Florence's subsequent role as a minor supporting actor to the main players, Austria and Spain.

Cosimo I After Alessandro was murdered by a distant cousin in 1537, the city elders and their imperial puppeteers fished around for a suitably pliable replacement. No directly descended Medici figurehead being available, they chose Cosimo, descended from Cosimo de' Medici's brother via an obscure branch of the family tree. In the event Cosimo I, as he was known, turned out to be more than they bargained for, proving determined to remain his own man. More than 30 years of autocratic and conceited rule under the thumbs of foreign powers saw him take the title of Grand Duke of Tuscany in 1570.

The beginning of the end Cosimo I was succeeded by two sons, Francesco I and Ferdinando I, both more or less capable and honourable rulers. They were also, in the family tradition, inveterate collectors and patrons. Under them, universities were founded and the port of Livorno was created; they sponsored the work of Galileo and promoted the exploratory voyages of Amerigo Vespucci into the New World. Sadly, their successors began the dynasty's steady decline: the sickly Cosimo II and the cultured but ineffectual Ferdinando II presided over a period of failing trade and dwindling prestige. The eccentric and foolish Cosimo III was succeeded in 1723 by Gian Gastone – the decadent and debauched last male member of a once-great dynasty. He died without an heir in 1737. Fortunately for the future of Florence, his sister Anna Maria Luisa bequeathed the entire Medici estate to the city in perpetuity.

The city of Florence as it appeared on a map of 1830

43

1	Porta S. Gallo
2	P.ta Pinti
3	P.ta alla Croce
4	P.ta S. Niccolò
5	Forte di Belvedere
6	P.ta Romana
7	P.ta S. Frediano
8	Porticciola
9	P.ta al Prato
10	Fortezza da Basso
11	Piazza S. Marco
12	P.za S. Maria Novella
13	P.za del Duomo
14	P.za S. Croce
15	P.za del Gran Duca
16	Ponte alla Carraja
17	P.te a S. Trinita
18	P.te Vecchio
19	P.te alle Grazie
20	Piazza dei Pitti
21	Arno Fiume

FIRENZE

1	Porta Nuova
2	P.ta Lucchese
3	P.ta alle Piagge
4	P.ta Fiorentina
5	P.ta Mare
6	Piazza del Duomo
7	P.za de' Cavalieri
8	P.za S. Caterina
9	Il Bagno
10	Ponte a Mare
11	P.te di Mezzo
12	P.ta alla Fortezza
13	Piazza S. Silvestro
14	P.ta S. Martino
15	Fortezza
16	Arno Fiume

Medici family tree

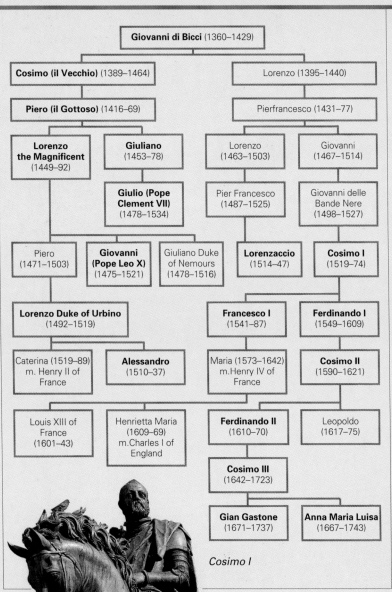

Giovanni di Bicci (1360–1429)

Cosimo (il Vecchio) (1389–1464)

Lorenzo (1395–1440)

Piero (il Gottoso) (1416–69)

Pierfrancesco (1431–77)

Lorenzo the Magnificent (1449–92)

Giuliano (1453–78)

Lorenzo (1463–1503)

Giovanni (1467–1514)

Giulio (Pope Clement VII) (1478–1534)

Pier Francesco (1487–1525)

Giovanni delle Bande Nere (1498–1527)

Piero (1471–1503)

Giovanni (Pope Leo X) (1475–1521)

Giuliano Duke of Nemours (1478–1516)

Lorenzaccio (1514–47)

Cosimo I (1519–74)

Lorenzo Duke of Urbino (1492–1519)

Francesco I (1541–87)

Ferdinando I (1549–1609)

Caterina (1519–89) m. Henry II of France

Alessandro (1510–37)

Maria (1573–1642) m. Henry IV of France

Cosimo II (1590–1621)

Louis XIII of France (1601–43)

Henrietta Maria (1609–69) m. Charles I of England

Ferdinando II (1610–70)

Leopoldo (1617–75)

Cosimo III (1642–1723)

Gian Gastone (1671–1737)

Anna Maria Luisa (1667–1743)

Cosimo I

■ **After almost 350 years of direct and indirect Medici rule, Florence passed first to Austria (by treaty) and then to France (under Napoleon). Its days of glory past, the city became a favoured haunt of foreign writers, artists and poets.....■**

Austria In the end, Florence's independence, so often at issue, was extinguished with barely a whimper. Two years before Gian Gastone's death, when it was clear no Medici heir was to be forthcoming, Gastone's sister, Anna Maria Luisa, signed a treaty handing the Tuscan Grand Duchy to Francis Stephen, the Duke of Lorraine (later to marry the Empress Maria Theresa and become Emperor Francis I of Austria). The new incumbent positively shone by comparison with his predecessors. Under his enlightened rule, and that of his successor, Pietro Leopoldo (1765–90), Tuscany enjoyed the brisk benefits of Teutonic reform. Its administration was modernised, its religious houses were reorganised, and improvements were made to its agriculture (notably the draining of areas in the Maremma and Valdichiana).

France and Austria Austria's defeat by France in 1799 brought Napoleon into Italy. His troops occupied Tuscany – though to little lasting effect – for some 15 years. Renamed the Kingdom of Etruria (1801–2), the region was placed under the control of the Infante Louis of Bourbon. In 1809 it was conferred on Napoleon's sister, Elisa Bonaparte Baciocchi. Napoleon's fall in 1814 saw the return of the exiled House of Lorraine. The 1815 Congress of Vienna ceded Elba, Piombino and the Argentario to Tuscany. (Lucca, then still a separate duchy, was absorbed in 1847.)

Ferdinand II and then Leopold II (1824–59) continued their predecessors' reforms. The march towards Italian independence, however, was by now well under way, and the nationalist uprisings of 1848 saw

Leopold briefly exiled. In 1859, as the Risorgimento reached its climax, he stepped aside for good. A year later Tuscany voted in favour of annexation to a united Italy.

Napoleon ruled Tuscany for 15 years until 1814

■ **Florence's centuries-long struggle for self-determination finally came to an end in 1861 with the birth of the Italian state. Florence became its temporary capital. The city was then destined to share Italy's fate in two world wars, its artistic heritage emerging safely from the second only to be devastated by the tumultuous flood of 1966.....■**

Moment of glory Proclaiming the Italian state was one thing. Creating it was another, for Rome, its natural capital, was still in the hands of the papacy (defended by a garrison of French troops). In 1865, therefore, Florence became the country's provisional capital. King Vittorio Emanuele moved into the Palazzo Pitti, and the Italian Parliament was installed in the Palazzo Vecchio (together with the country's Foreign Ministry). The honour, however, was to be short-lived. When France was defeated in the Franco-Prussian war of 1870, its Rome-based troops were withdrawn from papal sentry duty. Italian troops made a ceremonial entry into Rome and within a few months the city had taken over from Florence as capital.

Two world wars World War I had a devastating effect on Italy. War memorials are poignant features of even the smallest Tuscan villages. After the war, when economic and political turmoil ushered in Mussolini and Fascism, Florence appeared to rediscover the enmities of old. Florentine Fascists, it seems, were some of the country's most vociferous. Yet, at the same time,

The Ponte Vecchio – a landmark that has survived floods, wars and seven centuries of political turmoil

Florence proved an intellectual centre of anti-Fascism, and when the chance came to fight, Tuscany's hill-towns provided some of the country's strongest partisan bands.

As World War II unravelled, the battle for Italy became one of grinding attrition, of step-by-step advance in the face of a determined and well-organised German retreat. In its wake the country's artistic heritage came under severe threat. The great abbey of Monte Cassino had already been destroyed. Rome, however, had been saved, thanks to its status as an 'open' or demilitarised city. Hopes that the same could be achieved in Florence proved to be in vain. The Arno in general, and Florence in particular, were simply too important as strategic redoubts to be surrendered without a fight.

The American 5th Army took Rome in June 1944. As it marched on Florence, the Nazis made plans to remove as many works of art as possible to Germany (they failed only because of a shortage of trucks). Ludwig Heydenreich, director of the Kunsthistorisches Institut (the body overseeing the city's treasures), still had to fight bravely to prevent works falling into the hands of Goering and Himmler's SS. Parachutists under Adolf Fuchs were charged to slow the Allied advance by mining the Arno's bridges and their main approaches. All were dynamited on

Some of the thousands of catalogues and manuscripts damaged by the 1966 flood

4 August except the Ponte Vecchio – spared, it appears, on Hitler's direct orders (the medieval quarters on both banks were not so lucky).

To the present day The flood of 1966 (see pages 130–1) inflicted more damage in a day than had been suffered during four years of war. Florentines, backed by a massive international effort, rallied magnificently in a valiant attempt to set the city and its works of art back to rights. It was perhaps the first time this century that Florence had been obliged to take stock of its future. Recently, though, Florence has been forced to look to its laurels with increasing frequency. Measures to combat pollution and congestion, for example, were introduced in 1988 (though not without considerable prevarication). Still more heart-searching now seems certain in the light of the city's over-dependence on tourism (see pages 24–5). Florentines must also be casting a wry eye over the turmoil currently convulsing Italy's body politic. The death of a political system, after all, is something the Florentines have lived through – and survived – time and again during their city's troubled but ultimately triumphant history.

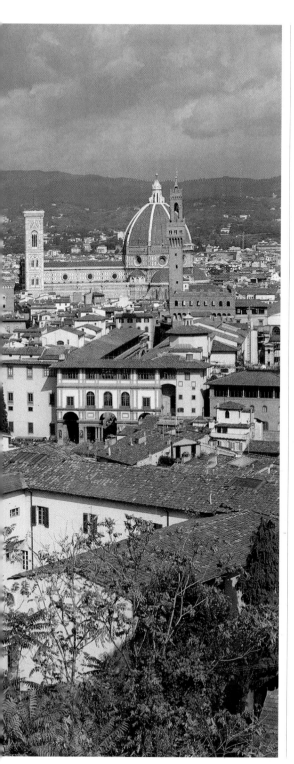

Florence orientation

Opening times
Of all Florence's potential problems, juggling opening times will cause you the most headaches. To avoid disappointment, double-check all the opening times before starting a day's sightseeing. Visit the tourist office at Via Cavour 1r (a minute from the Duomo) to collect a copy of the *Orario di Apertura dei Principali Musei e Monumenti*, a list of current hours and prices. Most museums close on Sunday afternoon and all day Monday. To confuse matters, however, some close on Tuesday or Wednesday instead.

Its compact size and dense concentration of 'sights' means there is no obviously useful way to compartmentalise Florence into manageable chunks for the visitor. The city has few 'old quarters' such as might be found in Rome or Venice. Even in the Middle Ages Florence was only divided into four ill-defined districts (known as *rioni*). It is the Arno that really defines the city, a watery divide that separates the **centro storico** (historic centre) on the north bank from the hillier **Oltrarno** ('Over the Arno') district to the south. This makes the job of sightseeing somewhat arbitrary. What you see, and when, is often determined by opening times (see panel), and by which sights happen to be in the same area. Other itineraries are possible of course – Brunelleschi's churches, say, or the Florence of Dante and Michelangelo – but they require considerable planning and much legwork.

Old boundaries Although the city has few Roman remains, Florence's tight-knit city centre still conforms to the grid-iron plan of the first Roman colony (see page 30). The successive walls built by the Byzantines, the Carolingians and by the Countess Matilda mostly followed those of the Romans (except where they paralleled the Arno along Borgo Santi Apostoli). The city's first major expansion came in 1173, when a new set of walls more than doubled Florence's metropolitan area. In the west they ran up Via del Moro and Via del Giglio, enclosed San Lorenzo (then the city's northernmost point) and continued east and south along Via dei Pucci, Via Giuseppe Verdi and Via de' Benci. Succeeding centuries saw the building of new walls as the city grew, but today only fragments of these survive, since they were demolished in the 19th century to create the broad *viali* (boulevards) that divide the city centre from the suburbs.

The tower of the Palazzo Vecchio

Tackling the 'sights' Since there are no convenient city-centre divisions to guide your sightseeing, the best way to approach Florence is to break the city's sights into clusters within manageable areas – although the areas may have little geographical distinction and the sights within them may have little or nothing to tie them together. Before you begin, however, do walk around the centre to get the feel of the city. Diving into the Duomo on your first morning is too intimidating a start to any holiday. See page 250 of this book for some suggested itineraries to help you plan your sightseeing.

Piazza del Duomo Once you are acclimatised, Piazza del Duomo makes the most obvious place to start a visit. The **Battistero** (Baptistery), the **Campanile di Giotto** (Giotto's Campanile) and the **Duomo** (Cathedral) form Florence's finest religious ensemble. Near by lies the **Museo dell' Opera del Duomo** (Cathedral Works Museum), home to works of art removed from these three world-famous religious buildings over the centuries. The city's second-ranking sculpture gallery, the Museo dell'Opera del Duomo could well be combined with the **Bargello**, housing Italy's greatest collection of Renaissance sculpture (and more besides). A monastery church, the **Badia Fiorentina**, is easily seen at the same time.

Piazza della Signoria After Florence's religious heart, it makes sense to see the piazza that is the city's civic set-piece. Enjoy its people-watching possibilities (perhaps from the famous **Rivoire** café), then take in its statues, particularly the masterpieces of Cellini and Giambologna in the **Loggia dei Lanzi**. Then visit the **Palazzo Vecchio**, home to sculptures by Michelangelo and Donatello, as well as frescos by Ghirlandaio and several Mannerist masters. More paintings await next door in the **Uffizi**, Italy's greatest art gallery.

Also within easy reach of Piazza della Signoria are the distinctive church of **Orsanmichele** and the **Museo della Casa Fiorentina Antica** (Museum of the Old Florentine House), a lovely Renaissance house complete with period furniture and fittings. Spare time, too, for the little-visited **Museo di Storia della Scienza** (Museum of the History of Science).

East, west and north Florence's greatest church, **Santa Croce**, is the starting point for visits in the eastern part of the city – to the **Casa Buonarroti** (Michelangelo's House), the **Sant'Ambrogio market**, the **Museo della Fondazione Horne** and, just across the Arno, the **Museo Bardini** (Horne and Bardini museums).

Another fine church, **Santa Maria Novella**, is the focus of more dispersed sights in the west, namely the **Palazzo Strozzi** and nearby **Palazzo Rucellai**, and the churches of **Ognissanti** and **Santa Trinita**.

In the north, wander through the **San Lorenzo market** to the **Mercato Centrale**, the city's covered food market, then see the church of **San Lorenzo** and the **Cappelle Medicee** (Medici Chapels) with their Michelangelo sculptures. Moving on, try and drop into the **Palazzo Medici–Riccardi** (for frescos by Benozzo Gozzoli) and **Sant'Apollonia** (for Andrea del Castagno's *Last Supper* fresco). You can then enjoy the **Museo di San Marco** (frescos by Fra Angelico), the church of **Santissima Annunziata** and its attractive piazza, and Michelangelo's *David* in the **Accademia**.

Oltrarno The shop-lined **Ponte Vecchio** leads to the Oltrarno, a quieter part of the city and one of the nicest areas to explore for its own sake. Two days at least are needed here, with at least a morning devoted to the **Palazzo Pitti**'s several museums (notably the paintings of the Galleria Palatina). Close by, the macabre medical wax-works of the **Museo Zoologico – La Specola** (Zoological Museum) make essential, if eccentric, viewing. Among the churches, **Santa Maria del Carmine** stands out for the famous fresco cycle in the adjacent **Cappella Brancacci** (Brancacci Chapel), whilst **San Miniato al Monte**, away on its hilltop, is among Tuscany's most beautiful Romanesque buildings.

Views
Florence is a beautiful city, particularly when seen from above. Enjoy the best views of the city centre from the top of the Duomo or the Campanile. For more complete panoramas climb to the Forte del Belvedere, Piazzale Michelangelo or San Miniato al Monte.

Essential sights
General: Duomo; Battistero; Campanile di Giotto; Ponte Vecchio.
Frescos: Cappella Brancacci (Santa Maria del Carmine); Cappella Bardi (Santa Croce); Cappella Filippo Strozzi, the chancel and Masaccio's *Trinità* (Santa Maria Novella); Museo di San Marco; Chiostrino dei Voti (Santissima Annunziata).
Churches: Santa Croce; Santa Maria Novella; San Miniato al Monte; San Lorenzo; Orsanmichele.
Museums: San Marco; Casa Fiorentina Antica; Storia della Scienza.
Paintings: Uffizi; Palazzo Pitti.
Sculpture: Bargello; Museo dell'Opera del Duomo; Cappelle Medicee; Accademia; Loggia dei Lanzi.

51

ACCADEMIA

Giambologna's Rape of the Sabines

Four Slaves

Michelangelo's unfinished *Slaves* (or *Prisoners*) – the Accademia's other highlight – illustrate the sculptor's maxim that sculpture was the liberation of a form already within the stone. Originally intended for the tomb of Pope Julius II and sculpted between about 1521 and 1523, they were presented to the Medici in 1564 and installed in the Boboli gardens. The figures may have been intended to represent the liberal arts, left 'enslaved' by Julius's death. The Accademia also houses Michelangelo's *St Matthew* (1504–8), intended as one of 12 figures commissioned for the Duomo, but the only one that the sculptor actually started.

The paintings of the Accademia

Eleven of the Accademia's rooms are filled with paintings, but many are by minor or unknown artists. The exceptions are Botticelli's *Madonna and Child* and *Madonna of the Sea*, and works by Perugino and Filippino Lippi (downstairs); the canvases of Pontormo (*Venus and Cupid*) and Bronzino (in the tribune); and the first floor's 14th-century and early 15th-century paintings, notably Lorenzo Monaco's *Christ in Pietà*.

▶▶▶ **Accademia, Galleria dell'**   *IFCE5*

Via Ricasoli 60

Europe's first artistic academy (founded in 1563) is today visited by most people almost solely for Michelangelo's *David*. Viewing the world's most famous sculpture, however, can be anything but an unmitigated pleasure. Long queues build up outside the gallery, tripping over sheets spread with fake Chanel and Louis Vuitton accessories, laid out for sale by hopeful street vendors. Then visitors are herded through battered railings into a cramped atrium desperately in need of a coat of paint. Here, finally, one of the city's highest admission charges admits you into the company of *David*, five other Michelangelo sculptures, and a collection of only intermittently interesting Gothic and Renaissance paintings.

David is not the first thing in the gallery, but it is the beacon to which most people gravitate. The image's familiarity does little to dull the statue's impact: in the chill, marble flesh its sheer size still comes as some surprise. Commissioned by the Opera del Duomo in 1501 (when Michelangelo was just 26), the work's theme (David defeating the tyrant Goliath) was deliberately designed to symbolise the virtues of Republican Florence and its free-dom from foreign and papal domination (and perhaps also its recent liberation from Savonarola and the Medici). More recently, it has come to represent the ultimate symbol of the artistic and intellectual ambitions of the Renaissance.

The 5m-high block of marble that Michelangelo used, known as *Il Gigante* (the Giant), had been quarried in Carrara 40 years earlier. Not only was it thin and riddled with cracks – adding a technical challenge which Michelangelo relished; it had also been partly spoiled by earlier sculptors (including Agostino di Duccio) and offered to other artists such as Andrea Sansovino and Leonardo da Vinci. Once in Michelangelo's hands, however, the crude stone was transformed, in just three years, into a work which, with the Rome *Pietà* of six years earlier, was to establish Michelangelo's reputation as the foremost sculptor of his day.

Its masterpiece completed, Florence was left with the problem of displaying it. Thirty leading artists were asked to select a site, among them Leonardo, Botticelli, Filippino Lippi, Perugino, Sansovino and Andrea della Robbia. Leonardo and Botticelli favoured the Loggia dei Lanzi (see page 86); others suggested a plinth in front of the Duomo. In the end the statue was placed in Piazza della Signoria (see panel). Here it remained until 1873, when it was removed to the specially built tribune in the Accademia where it is now displayed. Before its initial installation, the statue remained under wraps while a skirt of copper leaves was prepared, to spare citizens' blushes. This is now long gone, along with the gilding of the hair and of the band across the chest, worn away by sun and rain during the centuries the work spent out of doors.

David was always intended as a piece of outdoor public sculpture rather than for indoor display. This perhaps helps explain some of its extraordinary physical distortions such as the over-large head and hands, probably designed to emphasise its monumental effect. By discouraging the admiration of beauty for its own sake, the deformities may also have been designed to focus more attention on David's character – on the 'heroic conception of human will'. The statue's lack of identifying props may have served the same purpose – compare the obvious sling and severed head of Donatello's equally idealised *David* in the **Bargello** (see page 58).
Open: daily 9–7 (winter and Sunday 9–2).
Closed Monday. Admission charge (expensive).

53

The 'heroic conception of the human will': Michelangelo's David

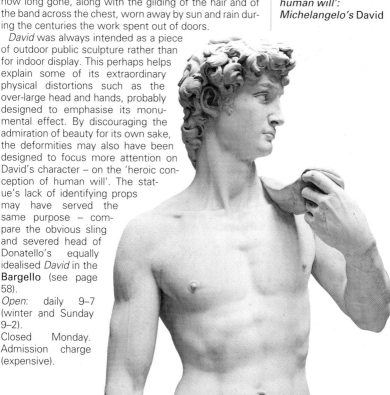

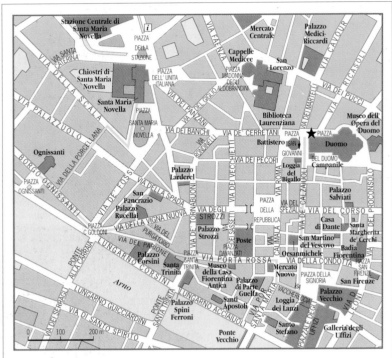

Walk **The heart of the city**

A good introduction to the city's main streets and piazzas, taking in several of the smaller churches and palaces, quiet lanes of artisans' workshops and the great church of Santa Maria Novella (2km; allow 1 hour).

Start at Piazza del Duomo, one of Florence's three main piazzas and the city's religious heart. The **Duomo**▶▶▶ (pages 76–81) and the **Battistero**▶▶▶ (pages 60–2) are among Italy's most familiar landmarks.

Walk south on the pedestrianised Via dei Calzaiuoli, passing the distinctive church of **Orsanmichele**▶▶ (pages 110–11) to reach **Piazza della Signoria**▶▶▶ (pages 126–7), the second of the big piazzas and the city's civic forum since medieval times. Leave the square on Via Vacchereccia and turn right then left into Via Porta Rossa. From here you can glimpse Piazza della Repubblica, third of the piazzas, a dour 19th-century creation

carved out over the heart of the old Roman city.

In Via Porta Rossa stands the Palazzo Davanzati, now home to the **Museo della Casa Fiorentina Antica**▶▶▶ (pages 90–1), an excellent introduction to medieval Florence. A short distance beyond it is the church of **Santa Trinita**▶▶ (page 154). Take Via del Parione, to the right of Santa Trinita, then the first or second alley on the right to emerge on Via del Purgatorio, turning left into Via della Vigna Nuova. The elegant façade of the **Palazzo Rucellai**▶ (pages 120–1) faces you at the end of Via del Purgatorio.

Cross Piazza Goldoni, beside the Arno, and walk up Borgo Ognissanti to see the church after which the street is named, **Ognissanti**▶ (page 109). Walk up Via della Porcellana, a street of artisans' workshops, and turn right at the end to emerge in the huge piazza fronting the Gothic **Santa Maria Novella**▶▶▶ (pages 148–53).

54

▶ **Badia Fiorentina** *IFCE3*

Via del Proconsolo – Piazza San Firenze

Restorations in the Badia, Florence's oldest monastery, mean you may have to make do with a view of its façade and beautiful campanile, one of the city skyline's most distinctive landmarks. The Benedictine abbey was founded in 978 by Willa, the widow of Umberto, Margrave of Tuscany, in memory of her husband, and later re-endowed by their son, Ugo (see panel). The city's focal point for centuries, its bell tolled the divisions of the Florentine day and its cells housed one of Florence's earliest hospitals, established in 1031. In 1285 it was rebuilt along Cistercian Gothic lines, probably under the eye of Arnolfo di Cambio, architect of the Duomo and the Palazzo Vecchio. The hexagonal campanile was completed between 1310 and 1330, its base Romanesque, its delicate upper registers more decidedly Gothic.

Inside, the church is something of a disappointment, the result of a baroque remodelling inflicted during the 17th century. Two outstanding works of art survive, however – Filippino Lippi's *The Madonna Appearing to St Bernard* (1485), left of the entrance (on Via del Proconsolo), and the tomb of Count Ugo (1481) by Mino da Fiesole, close to Lippi's *Madonna* on the transept's left wall. The figure of Ugo, who died in 1001, lies above his tomb, hands calmly folded, the edge of his cloak hanging casually over the edge of his marble plinth.

Also well worth seeing is the **Chiostro degli Aranci**, a double-storeyed cloister entered by way of a staircase through a door off the right-hand side of the choir. It contains a lovely series of frescos on the life of St Benedict painted by an unknown hand around 1440.

Open: Under long-term restoration – check times locally.

The Badia and Dante
The Badia is one of only three Florentine churches mentioned by Dante. He alludes to the Badia's bell and remembers gazing on Beatrice here. Boccaccio also used the church to deliver celebrated lectures on the *Divine Comedy*.

Visionary warning
Ugo's generosity to the Badia was not entirely philanthropic. The story goes that he experienced a vision of 'black and deformed men ... tormenting others with fire and hammer ... damned souls all'. He was told that his own soul was condemned to similar pains 'by reason of his worldly life, unless he should repent'. Ugo took the hint, sold his family lands in Germany, and endowed the Badia and six other Tuscan monasteries.

55

The Badia (to the left) and the Bargello

A tough job
The post of *Podestà* was created in 1193 to bring an unbiased governing magistrate to arbitrate in the violent internal feuds then threatening to tear Florence apart. Elected for just one year, the incumbent was always a 'foreigner', supposedly above local political machinations. He had to hail from a town at least 80km from the city.

▶▶▶ Bargello, Museo Nazionale del   IFCE3

Via del Proconsolo 4

Behind its fortress-like walls, the Bargello shields Italy's greatest collection of Renaissance sculpture. This museum is second only to the Uffizi in its importance – an essential morning's viewing on any Florentine itinerary. Sculpture aside, it also devotes a surprising amount of space to the decorative arts, its collection ranging from enamels, majolica and ivories to carpets, tapestries, silverware, glassware and paintings.

The museum building – all bristling towers and battlements – was Florence's earliest public palace (1255–1350), and the first seat of the city's government. Its tower and airy courtyard were a model for the **Palazzo Vecchio** (see pages 122–3). Initially home to the *Capitano del Popolo*, a post created just before the palace was built (see panel), the building was given over to the *Podestà*, (chief magistrate) in 1261, when it also became the city's main law court. When the Medici abolished the post of *Podestà* (in 1574), the palace passed to the chief of police, and served as a prison, torture chamber and place of execution. It continued as a prison until 1859 (though torture and execution were abolished in 1786). The Bargello became a museum in 1865.

The ground floor The Bargello spreads over three floors, its ground plan rather confusing at first glance. In fact the key sculptures reside in just two rooms (on the ground and first floors), and in a delightful courtyard – a fine spot to escape the crowds clustered around the ground-floor masterpieces. To join the fray, turn right from the ticket hall into the main hall, a room whose open-plan scheme and generously spaced exhibits make a pleasant change from some of the city's dustier and more claustrophobic museums. The modern setting dates from the 1966 flood, when the whole floor wallowed in 4m of water.

Room 1 concentrates on the late-Renaissance works of Michelangelo, Giambologna and Benvenuto Cellini and their followers. The works are arranged almost at random, encouraging pleasantly casual inspection. Most people head for Michelangelo's sculptures – three dramatically contrasting works whose variety vividly illustrates the sculptor's versatility. Most delicate is the *Madonna and Child* tondo (1503–5), half-finished except for a slight polish to the Virgin's cheeks and forehead. It represents a fine example of *sciacciato*, or low relief, a technique in which subtlety of line is more important than the depth of a sculpture. Notice the more rounded but less effective treatment of the same subject by Rustici, whose tondo is placed behind Michelangelo's to provide a telling contrast. The drunken *Bacchus* (c.1497), loutish and soft-bellied, was Michelangelo's first large free-

A stained-glass stemma *(coat of arms) from the Bargello*

The Bargello's airy courtyard has been a showcase for numerous statues since it became a national museum in 1865

Slaughter outside the Bargello
The Bargello has seen many dark deeds. Augustus Hare, a biographer and travel writer (1792–1834), described the events of 1 August 1343. 'The Duke of Athens had taken refuge in the fortress, and the members of the noble Florentine families ... who had suffered from his tyranny were besieging him. They demanded, as the price of his life, that the Conservatore Guglielmo d'Assisi and his son, a boy of eighteen, who had been the instruments of his cruelty, should be given up to them. Forced by hunger, he caused them to be pushed out of the half-closed door to the populace, who tore them limb from limb, hacking the boy to pieces first before his father's eyes, and then parading the bloody fragments on their lances through the streets.' *Florence* (1834)

standing statue, a character piece carved in Rome. The tipsy tilt of the head and the lurching shoulders are as convincing a portrayal of drunkenness as you could find. Still more impressive is the powerful *Brutus* (1539–40), a much later work and Michelangelo's only known portrait bust. Perhaps intended as a celebration of republicanism, it was carved after the assassination of the tyrannical Alessandro de' Medici.

Other highlights of the room include Giambologna's famous *Mercury* (1564), a study in speed, from pointed finger to discreetly winged feet. Lithe, slim and full of athletic grace, the figure has been copied for centuries as the definitive interpretation of the subject. The same sculptor's *Victory of Florence over Pisa* (1570), by contrast, is lumpen in the extreme. Cellini's many works include several small statuettes; a model for the infamous *Perseus* (see page 86); and a bust of Cosimo I, his first work in bronze (on the entrance wall). Also eye-catching, if only for their scale, are Bandinelli's statues of Adam and Eve, deemed unsuitable for the Duomo, for which they were designed; two statues by Ammannati – one standing, one reclining – designed for the Nari tomb in Santissima Annunziata (but never installed because of Bandinelli's jealous opposition); and Ammannati's erotic *Leda and the Swan*, inspired by a picture of the subject that was painted by Michelangelo but later destroyed.

From the exit, enter the sunny courtyard, once site of the Bargello's gallows but now crammed with sculptural fragments and the coats of arms (*stemmi*) of its successive *Podestà*. Cross over to the small **Room 2**, whose cruder collection of exterior 14th-century sculpture contrasts with the more delicate exhibits of Room 1.

The people's choice
The *Capitano del Popolo* – a post created in 1250 – performed a similar role to the *Podestà*. Also elected for a year from a distant city, he had the dual task of safeguarding middle-class interests against the aristocracy, and of commanding the local militia, an often unruly body raised predominantly from the city's working population. He was helped by two councils, one of 90 men, the other of 300.

BARGELLO

Palazzo Pazzi-Quaratesi
Based on designs by Brunelleschi, this palace is north of the Bargello at Via del Proconsolo 10. It was built in 1462–72 for Jacopo Pazzi, who was executed after its completion for his part in the Pazzi Conspiracy (see pages 74–5). Note the dolphins on the capitals of the inner courtyard's columns, taken from the Pazzi coat of arms, and the vases, symbols of the Pazzi's right to take a flame from the high altar on Easter Sunday. The privilege was awarded to Pazzino de' Pazzi, who in 1101, during the First Crusade, was the first to scale Jerusalem's walls and plant a Christian flag in the Holy City.

The most impressive works are Paolo di Giovanni's vast *Madonna and Child* (on the end wall) and the figures of St Peter and St Paul, removed from the city's Porta Romana. **Room 3** is used for temporary exhibitions.

The first floor Climb the courtyard's grand staircase to the *verone*, a lovely arched loggia which provides the setting for some charming and eccentric bronze novelties by Giambologna. Created for the **Villa di Castello** (see page 170), they include a menagerie of cockerel, peacock, and vividly detailed turkey.

Now turn right to enter the immense Salone del Consiglio Generale, a glorious vaulted hall (the former courtroom) now filled with masterpieces of early-Renaissance sculpture. Here, too, the room's arrangement encourages random wandering, though the works of Donatello, star of the room, invite attention almost immediately. Pride of place goes to his *St George* (centre of the far wall), carved for the Armaiuoli (armourers' guild) in 1416 and brought here from Orsanmichele. The figure epitomises fresh-faced Christian chivalry and 'the beauty of youth, courage and valour of arms' (in Vasari's words). In front and to its left stands Donatello's debonair *David* (c.1430–40), the first free-standing nude since antiquity. Famously androgynous, the figure sports only a dipped, dandified hat and long boots, one of which rests on Goliath's bloodied head. Mary McCarthy described the statue as 'a transvestite's and fetishist's dream of alluring ambiguity' (*The Stones of Florence*, 1959).

Other works by Donatello include a smaller marble *David* (1408); the *Atys-Amorino* (1440), a bronze putto of unknown mythological significance (perhaps Cupid); the shallow bas-relief *St George Slaying the Dragon* (*c*.1430–40, alongside the Orsanmichele *St George*); and the stone *Marzocco*, Florence's heraldic lion symbol (1420; see the panel on page 127). Two easily missed panels, reliefs of the sacrifice of Isaac, by Ghiberti and Brunelleschi, sit on the right wall. Both were entries in the 1401 competition to choose an artist to design the second set of doors for the **Battistero** (see page 61). Numerous other sculptures (all well labelled) decorate the walls, dominated by the blue-and-white glazed terracottas of Luca della Robbia.

The gallery's remaining 10 rooms (on the first and second floors) are explored clockwise from the rear of the Salone. Starting with **Room 7** – dimly lit and full of rugs, carpets and tapestries – all the rooms are beautifully appointed and packed with artefacts running the gamut of the decorative arts. It would be easy to spend at least as much time here as in the four rooms of sculpture. Worthy of special attention are **Room 9**, the **Cappella di Santa Maria Maddalena** (see panel), the **Sala delle Maioliche** (**Room 12**) and (on the second floor) the **Salone del Camino** (**Room 16**), the most important collection of small bronzes in Italy. It includes works by Giambologna, Bandinelli and Benvenuto Cellini.

Open: daily 9–2 (Sunday 9–1). Closed Monday. Admission charge (moderate).

Santa Maria Maddalena
This chapel's frescos, once attributed to Giotto, were discovered in 1841 during its conversion from a prison cell. Among the scenes of Heaven and Hell on the end wall is a portrait of Dante (in maroon in the right-hand group, fifth from the right). The fine wooden pulpit, lectern and stalls (1498) all came from the church of San Miniato al Monte (see pages 136–7). The striking triptych is by Giovanni di Francesco and dates from the mid-15th century. Entry to the chapel is by steps leading from the blue-and-gold vaulted Room 8.

59

Sculptors of less renown
Desiderio da Settignano (1428–64) specialised in portrait busts and low reliefs, using techniques pioneered by Donatello. Several of his busts are in the Bargello. Other works in Florence include a fine tomb in Santa Croce and a tabernacle in San Lorenzo.
Benedetto da Maiano (1442–97) also concentrated on portrait busts, examples of which can be seen in the Bargello. He worked as well on bas-reliefs, the best of which adorn Santa Croce's pulpit.

A resplendent setting for one of Italy's most important collections of sculpture

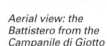

*Aerial view: the
Battistero from the
Campanile di Giotto*

▶▶▶ Battistero (Baptistery)   *IFCD4*
Piazza San Giovanni

Mystery surrounds the origins of Florence's Baptistery,
one of the oldest and most appealing of the city's buildings. During the Renaissance it was thought to be a
Roman temple to Mars, built to celebrate the defeat of
Fiesole and the founding of Florence. Pavement fragments confirm the existence of a Roman building – probably part of a 1st-century palace – but most scholars now
date the core of the building to the 6th or 7th century (the
4th at the earliest). It is first mentioned in documents in
897, when it is recorded as the city's cathedral.

The exterior The octagon's largely Romanesque appearance dates from a period of remodelling (1059–1128) initiated by the Arte di Calimala, the most powerful of the
city's guilds and the body responsible for most of the
building's subsequent embellishments. Clad in white and
green marble, the classically inspired exterior decoration
– friezes, cornices, triangular window heads and grooved
pilasters – was stunningly innovative in its day. The geo-
metrical design in coloured marble was, however, to
inspire generations of Florentine architects and provide
the model for countless Tuscan churches.

The interior The rather disappointing first impression of
being bare and sparsely decorated evaporates in the light
of the breathtaking ceiling mosaics. In early Christian
basilicas, mosaics were arranged along the naves, or in
the straightforward domes of churches such as San
Marco in Venice. Here, however, where they are forced
into an awkward octagonal space, their narrative scheme
is difficult to decipher. It was precisely these early churches, nonetheless, that the Calimala wished to emulate
(particularly those of Rome and Venice, then in the process of being restored). Venetian craftsmen, at the time

Baptisms
In the early Middle Ages,
all the children born in
Florence in each year were
brought to the Battistero
for a communal baptism on
21 March, which was New
Year's Day in the old
Florentine calendar. When
a child was born, a bean
was dropped into an urn in
the Battistero, a black
bean for a boy, a white one
for a girl. By this means,
the average annual birth
rate during the 14th century was estimated at 6,000,
out of a total population of
90,000.

Europe's most accomplished mosaicists, were drafted in to start the panels, instructing local artists in their Byzantine intricacies.

The earliest mosaics (c.1225), above the square apse (*scarsella*), depict the Virgin and John the Baptist, to whom the Battistero is dedicated. (The Baptist is also the patron saint of Florence.) Above them stands a complicated wheel of prophets circling the Lamb of God. Immediately over the *scarsella*, in the main vaults, is the unmistakable figure of Christ, flanked by three bands depicting the Last Supper. Detail and narrative in the rest of the ceiling's four bands are almost impossible to follow. From the inner ring outwards they depict the story of Genesis, the life of Joseph, the life of Christ and the life of John the Baptist. Parts of the last band are believed to be the work of Cimabue.

The mosaic's splendour is mirrored in the pavement, a tessellated patchwork of multi-coloured marble. The site of the original font is still obvious, clearly marked in the pavement's centre by a large octagonal inlay.

Floor and ceiling aside, the interior seems to boast few artistic afterthoughts. Closer inspection, though, reveals a lower ring of granite columns (probably removed from the city's Roman Capitol); a fine mosaic frieze; a beautiful upper gallery; and – to the right of the *scarsella* – the distinctive tomb of the antipope, John XXIII (see panel).

The south doors (1328–36) Just as the Calimala had looked elsewhere for its mosaics, so they cast an envious eye to Pisa when it came to decorating the Baptistery's exterior. Not only was Pisa's cathedral famous for its 12th-century bronze doors, but Pisan craftsmen had recently cast similar doors for the cathedral of Monreale in Sicily. It was decided that Andrea Pisano was the man to do the same for Florence. Commissioned in 1328, the Pisan artist completed working wax models of the proposed doors within three months. Over the next eight years these were cast by Venetian bell-makers, then Europe's most accomplished bronzesmiths. The result, 28 simple and uncluttered reliefs, describe the life of John the Baptist and the theological and cardinal virtues.

The north doors (1403–24) Sixty years of plague and political upheaval ensued before another set of doors could be comfortably considered. A famous competition was arranged to award the commission in 1401, a date widely considered as the 'start' of the Florentine Renaissance. The doors were to be a votive offering to spare the city a repeat of the 1348 plague. Lorenzo Ghiberti was left to do the work alone after the haughty Brunelleschi, with whom he had jointly won the competition, refused to share the task. Ghiberti proceeded to emulate Pisano's 28-panel plan – though not its speedy execution. Another 20 years passed before the reliefs were finished, a period during which Ghiberti's style inevitably matured. Something of this maturing process reveals itself in the doors, from the simple narrative of their early reliefs to the crowded, perspective-filled schemes of later panels. The scenes described are the life of Christ (upper five registers) and the Evangelists and Doctors of the Church (lower two registers).

Papal favour
The controversial antipope John XXIII (deposed in 1415) was lucky to be given a memorial of any sort, let alone the only one in Florence's Holy of Holies. However, the tomb of John XXIII, carved by Donatello and Michelozzo in 1427, is one of the city's earliest Renaissance tombs – a reward for services rendered. It was through his patronage that Giovanni di Bicci de' Medici, who commissioned the tomb, became chief banker to the Papal Curia and thus laid the foundations of the Medici fortunes (half of the Medici income came from just two branches in Rome).

Florence's own miracle
A column north of the Battistero commemorates a miracle that occurred as the body of St Zenobius, Florence's first bishop, was being moved from San Lorenzo to Santa Reparata. One writer tells the story as follows: '... take notice of a little round pillar ... with the figure of a tree in iron nayled to it, and old words engraven upon it importing, that in this very place stood anciently an Elmtree, which being touched by the hearse of St Zenobious ... budded forth with green leaves of sweet odour though in the month of January.' Richard Lassels, *The Voyage of Italy* (1603)

BATTISTERO

A Pisan gift
Two pitted maroon columns flank the east doors of the Battistero. In 1117 the Pisans set off to conquer Mallorca. Fearful of attack from Lucca in their absence, they begged Florence to watch over Pisa. In gratitude, on their return, they offered Florence two porphyry columns plundered from Mallorca – reputedly magic columns whose polished surface foretold acts of treason against the state. Before making the gift, however, the Pisans are said to have ruined the pillars by baking them in embers. In any event they proved too weak to be used structurally inside the Battistero and have remained outside ever since.

The east doors (1425–52) Such was the success of Ghiberti's doors that he was immediately commissioned to produce another set. This second labour – when he strove 'to imitate nature to the utmost' – was to occupy him 'with the greatest diligence and greatest love' for almost 27 years. The result was the finest of the Battistero's three pairs of doors, sometimes known as 'The Gates of Paradise'. All the panels, however, have now been replaced with copies and the originals are being restored. Four of the renovated originals are already on show in the **Museo dell'Opera del Duomo** (see pages 96–7). Even the copies, however, suggest Ghiberti's virtuosity. More like paintings than sculpture, the ten rectangular panels depict their Old Testament episodes with extraordinary clarity, often weaving several narrative episodes into a single frame (see below).
Open: daily 1:30–6 (Sunday 9–1).

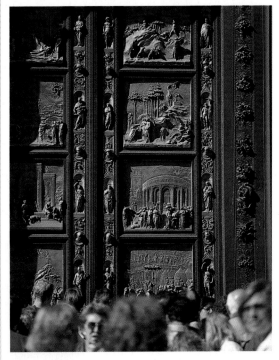

Although the original panels have been replaced by copies, Ghiberti's 'Gates of Paradise' still attract the crowds

The east door panels
Moving from the top left (and then across and down) the panels depict:
1 Creation, original sin, the expulsion from Paradise
2 Cain and Abel, Cain slays Abel, the wrath of God
3 Noah's Ark, Noah plants the vine, Noah's drunkenness
4 Three angels visit Abraham, Sarah at the tent
5 Esau sells his birthright, Rebecca talks with God and advises Jacob
6 Joseph pulled from the pit and sold to merchants, Joseph explains the Pharoah's dreams
7 Moses receives the Tablets
8 Crossing the Jordan, Joshua at the Battle of Jericho
9 David beheads Goliath, Battle with the Philistines
10 The Queen of Sheba visits King Solomon.

▶▶▶ Campanile di Giotto   IFCE4

Piazza del Duomo

Next to the **Duomo** (see pages 76–81) stands the 85m-high, multi-coloured Campanile – 'the Duomo's fit ally', in the words of poet Robert Browning. One of the most beautiful bell-towers in Italy, Longfellow described it as 'the Lily of Florence blossoming in stone'. Ruskin thought it 'the model and mirror of perfect architecture', adding that an hour's study of its decorative reliefs would 'give you strength for all your life'. Views from its summit (see panel) are a highlight of any trip to Florence.

The tower was begun by Giotto in 1334 during his reign as city architect and *capomaestro* (head of works) of the Duomo. Only the base, however – the first of its five present levels – had been completed at his death in 1337. Andrea Pisano, fresh from work on the south doors of the **Battistero** (see page 61), took over the second storey (1337–42). When he moved on, Francesco Talenti rounded things off (1348–59). Before Giotto died, he had apparently drawn up detailed plans for the tower's decoration, but he seems to have given rather less thought to its 12m base, whose walls Pisano and Talenti were forced to double in thickness to prevent their collapse.

Two sets of reliefs decorate the first storey, the lower tier set in hexagonal frames, the upper tier in diamonds. Both cycles are copies; the originals are now in the **Museo dell'Opera del Duomo** (see pages 96–7). The hexagonal panels, some designed by Giotto but all executed by Pisano and his pupils, depict Creation, the Seven Planets, the Seven Sacraments and the Seven Virtues: the Five Liberal Arts on the north face are by Luca della Robbia (Grammar, Philosophy, Music, Arithmetic and Astrology). The upper reliefs are also by Pisano. The niches of the second storey contain copies of the *Prophets* and the *Sibyls* by Donatello and others (the originals are in the Museo dell'Opera del Duomo).

Decorative detail

Climbing the Campanile
Though it may not offer the structural insights to be enjoyed in the cathedral dome, the Campanile offers an outstanding view of the city. Notice, on the way up, the pulleys and central stays used to keep the bell ropes in place. Be warned, though, that it is a stiff 414-step climb: not for nothing is there a first-aid post at the top.
Open: daily 8:30–6:50 (winter 9–4:30). Admission charge (moderate).

An astonished author
'Giotto's tower, with its delicate pinkish marble, its delicate windows with twisted columns, and its tall lightness … is a thing not easily to be forgotten … This evening we have been mounting to the top – a very sublime getting-upstairs indeed – and our muscles are much astonished at the unusual exercise.' George Eliot, *Letter* (1861)

Dynastic decay
Forty-nine Medici coffins were opened in 1857: 'some had been broken into and robbed, some were the hiding place of rats and every kind of vermin. In many nothing remained but bones and a handful of dust … some were in a dreadful state of putrefaction. Ghastly and grinning skulls were there, adorned with crowns of gold. Dark and parchment-dried faces were seen, with thin golden hair, rich as ever, and twisted with gems and pearls and golden nets. The cardinals still wore their mitres and red cloaks … the dried bones of Vittoria della Rovere were draped in black silk trimmed with lace, with a golden medal on her breast, and the portrait of her as she was in life lying on one side … while all that remained of herself was few bones … Anna Luisa, almost a skeleton, robed in rich violet velvet, with the electoral crown surmounting a black, ghastly face of parchment … Francesco, her uncle, lay beside her, a mass of putrid robes and rags.' William Wetmore Story (an American sculptor, writing in 1857)

Michelangelo's Lorenzo
No other work 'that ever came from a sculptor's hand' was like Michelangelo's *Lorenzo*, said the poet Longfellow. 'No such grandeur and majesty have elsewhere been put into human shape. It is all a miracle: the deep repose, and deep life within.' *Outre-mer: A Pilgrimage Beyond the Sea* (1833–4)

▶▶▶ **Cappelle Medicee (Medici Chapels)**   *IFCD4*
Piazza Madonna degli Aldobrandini

The Medici Chapels consist of three distinct areas: the Crypt, a mausoleum for minor members of the Medici family; the Cappella dei Principi, a gaudily opulent chapel for six of the Medici Grand Dukes; and (what most people come to see) the Sagrestia Nuova, last resting place of four family members, two of whom are commemorated with tombs sculpted by Michelangelo. Although the chapels are part of **San Lorenzo** (see pages 132–5), their entrance is located separately in the piazza to the rear of the church.

The Crypt This dimly lit, low-vaulted space is dotted with the brass-railed tombs of many lesser Medici. Today everything in the crypt seems suitably decorous, a far cry from 1791, when Ferdinand III piled the family corpses 'together pell-mell in the subterranean vaults … caring scarcely to distinguish one from another.' This rather unseemly arrangement lasted until 1857, when, after much prevarication, the bodies were exhumed for a more dignified burial. The operation was enjoyed and recorded in fine detail by an American eyewitness (see panel).

The Cappella dei Principi Steps at the rear of the crypt lead up to the Cappella dei Principi, an enormous space whose extraordinarily opulent decoration has aroused much comment over the years – most of it derogatory. Lord Byron called it 'fine frippery in great slabs of various expensive stones, to commemorate fifty rotten and forgotten carcases.' Others have talked of its 'insane, trashy opulence', the epitome of a 'mentality that thinks magnificence is directly proportional to expenditure'. Conceived by Cosimo I as a family mausoleum and begun in 1604, this was to be the most expensive project ever commissioned by the Medici. It was still draining dynastic coffers when the family died out in 1743, and finishing touches were still being added as recently as 1927.

Plans for the chapel suggest the extent of the Medici family's conceit. Its octagonal blueprint, for example, was based on the Battistero, whilst its interior was designed to accommodate the Holy Sepulchre, which was to be stolen from Jerusalem. This plan was abandoned only when the expedition to the Holy Land failed to accomplish the burglary. Instead, colossal slabs of porphyry and fine Roman marbles were carted to Florence, captured Turkish slaves being ordered to hack the pilfered stone into pieces of manageable size. Everything in the chapel except the frescoed ceiling is smothered in these marbles, or with swathes of magnificently worked semi-precious stones (*pietre dure*): *verde antica*, jasper, oriental agate, alabaster, mother-of-pearl, red coral, chalcedony and many more. The Medici's six-ball symbol is omnipresent.

The chapel's best feature is the 16 coats of arms, a series of white-backed mosaics ranged at head height around the walls. Each represents a different Tuscan town. Otherwise, all there remains to marvel at before leaving is the vulgarity of it all: the gloomy, mismatched colours and the bombastic, almost Fascistic, lines of the Grand Dukes' huge tombs. Looking around this monument to a dynasty's decadent decline, it is hard to remember that earlier members of the same family were responsible for commissioning some of Europe's most sublime art.

The Sagrestia Nuova A corridor leads left off the chapel to Michelangelo's New Sacristy, whose medley of calm whites and airy greys was designed as a riposte to Brunelleschi's Sagrestia Vecchia (Old Sacristy) in San Lorenzo (see page 134). The space contains three groups of sculpture (1520–34), two wholly and one partly by Michelangelo. On the left, as you stand with your back to the entrance, is the tomb of Lorenzo, Duke of Urbino (grandson of Lorenzo the Magnificent). Lorenzo, head in hand, is intended as a symbol of the contemplative life (see panel opposite). The figures at his feet are *Dawn* and *Dusk*. On the chapel's right-hand side stands the tomb of Giuliano, Duke of Nemours (third son of Lorenzo the Magnificent), intended to symbolise the man of action, with the figures *Day* and *Night* below. Both dukes were minor to the point of insignificance, making it ironic that the tombs of the chapel's real stars were never completed – those of Lorenzo the Magnificent and his brother Giuliano (murdered in the Pazzi Conspiracy, see pages 74–5). Only the unfinished *Madonna and Child* of the third sculptural group was ever started. The illustrious pair are now buried in a simple tomb close to the *Madonna*.
Open: daily 9–2. Closed Monday. Admission charge (expensive).

Michelangelo's graffiti
Some of the faint drawings on the Sagrestia Nuova's altar walls and in a side room are by Michelangelo. He reputedly made them while hiding from the Medici in 1530 under the protection of San Lorenzo's prior.

Possessed
' ... I am become the slave of a demon. I sit gazing, day after day, on that terrible phanthom, the Duke of Urbino ... the visage ... under that scowling and helmet-like bonnet is scarcely visible. You can just discern the likeness of human features; but whether alive or dead, whether a face or a skull, that of a mortal man or a Spirit from heaven or hell, you cannot say. 'Samuel Rogers, *Italy* (1836)

65

The Sagrestia Nuova

■　　Poet, painter, sculptor and architect, Michelangelo was a consummate genius. His prodigious energy and virtuoso technique overcame the political and artistic vicissitudes of almost a century to produce some of the greatest sculpture of his – or indeed any – age......■

Definitions
'By sculpture,' said Michelangelo, 'I understand an art that takes away superfluous material; by painting, one that attains its result by laying on.'

Ingested genius
Michelangelo claimed that his sculptural prowess came from marble dust in the milk of his wet-nurse, a woman from Carrara in the quarry- and marble-streaked mountains of Tuscany's Alpi Apuane.

Beauty or bust
'Michelangelo detested to imitate the living person unless it were one of the most incomparable beauty.' Vasari, *Lives of the Artists* (1550)

Architecture
'There is no question,' wrote Michelangelo, 'that architectural members reflect the members of Man and that those who do not know the human body cannot be good architects.' His own architectural career began in Florence, with San Lorenzo's Sagrestia Nuova and Biblioteca Laurenziana. Here, and in his later projects in Rome – Piazza del Campidoglio and the dome of St Peter's – he laid the foundations of Mannerist architecture, deliberately subverting classical ideals in favour of dynamism, expressiveness and originality.

Michelangelo (1475–1564) was born in the small and remote village of Caprese, in the mountains about 100km east of Florence. His father, of impoverished noble stock, was an administrator in the village. The family returned to Florence soon after their son's birth and settled there permanently.

Artistic beginnings Michelangelo's father, it seems, may have objected to an artistic career (then something of a social come-down) for his son. This was perhaps the reason for Michelangelo's late apprenticeship, taken up when he was around 13. 'Why, this boy knows more than I do,' remarked his teacher, Ghirlandaio, then one of the city's leading painters. Michelangelo left his studies within a year, partly because he had nothing to learn, and partly because he was showing a marked preference for sculpture (a bias that remained with him all his life).

Michelangelo quickly found himself in a charmed circle, working with a group of artists sponsored by Lorenzo the Magnificent. It was his first brush with patronage, a system whose constant demands – those of the popes in Rome, those of the Medici in Florence – were to prove a source of lifelong frustration. Many of his works remained unfinished because of it.

A flawed genius At the same time, Michelangelo could be his own worst enemy. His personal habits were 'repulsive': he never washed (on his father's advice), and when working he would only eat crusts of bread. He was consumed by worry, and desperate to accumulate property. He was also jealous of other artists: 'they want to ruin me', he once wrote, and (referring to Raphael) 'all he had in art he had of me.' Over-ambition also proved to be a fatal flaw. 'No particular work could satisfy the magnitude of his ambition,' wrote Mary McCarthy in *The Stones of Florence* (1959).

Florence and Rome Fate, however, was no kinder, political turmoil frequently intervening to disrupt his work. One such upheaval, the Medici's exile in 1494, saw him leave Florence for Bologna. A little later he was in Rome, where he produced the Bargello *Bacchus* (see pages 56–7), his earliest surviving large-scale sculpture (c.1497). A year later, still in Rome, came the work which secured his reputation: the *Pietà* (1498), now in Rome's St Peter's.

The Accademia's *David*, sculpted on his return to Florence in 1501, consolidated his position. This Florentine interlude also produced the Uffizi's Doni Tondo, one of his rare excursions into easel painting. In

1504 he started work on murals in the Palazzo Vecchio (of which only copies survive) and also began a set of 12 Apostles for the Duomo (of which only the Accademia's *St Matthew* was ever started). Both projects were abandoned in favour of the tomb of Pope Julius II in Rome – a proposed 40-figure sculpture that distracted him intermittently for almost 50 years. Soon after he began that project came his most famous commission, the painting of the Sistine Chapel (1508–12).

By 1516 he was back in Florence, dispatched by Leo X (a Medici pope) to work under the pope's cousin, Cardinal de' Medici (later Pope Clement VII). During this period, though turning increasingly to architecture (see panel opposite), he embarked on San Lorenzo's Medici tombs (1523–33), yet another unfinished work. Chastened by the Republic's overthrow, he also helped to design the city defences before the siege of Charles V.

Poetry and architecture Michelangelo finally left Florence in 1534, spending the rest of his days in Rome. During this period he wrote the best of his 300-odd poems. He also painted the Sistine Chapel's *Last Judgement* (1534-41), its tone more sombre than that of his earlier work in the vaults. Architecture again dominated as old age encroached: Piazza del Campidoglio and the dome of St Peter's were the two great works of his later years. Two tortured sculptures also materialised, one of which – the *Pietà* in the Museo dell'Opera del Duomo – was intended for his tomb.

He died at the age of 88 and was buried in Florence's Santa Croce.

Opposite: one of four unfinished Slaves, commissioned by Pope Julius II for his tomb

Michelangelo in Florence
Sculpture: Madonna della Scala, Battle of the Centaurs, Torso (Casa Buonarroti); *Bacchus, Madonna and Child* tondo, *Brutus* (Bargello); *David, St Matthew, Four Slaves* (Accademia); *Lorenzo, Dawn* and *Dusk, Giuliano, Day* and *Night, Madonna and Child* (Cappelle Medicee); *Pietà* (Museo dell'Opera del Duomo). *Architecture*: Sagrestia Nuova (Cappelle Medicee); Biblioteca Laurenziana (San Lorenzo). *Paintings and drawings*: Doni Tondo (Uffizi); six drawings (Casa Buonarroti); graffiti and wall drawings (attributed to Michelangelo; Sagrestia Nuova, Cappelle Medicee).

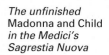

The unfinished Madonna and Child *in the Medici's Sagrestia Nuova*

CASA BUONARROTI

*Man of action:
Michelangelo's
Giuliano de' Medici*

More Michelangelo
Among the Casa
Buonarroti's decorated
salons, the cases of
bozzetti (models) in Room
IX contain smaller works
attributed to Michelangelo:
a torso of a hermaphrodite;
a fragment of a female figure (perhaps intended as
part of Giuliano's tomb in
the Cappelle Medicee); a
tiny wooden crucifix (possibly the model for a work
the sculptor intended to
execute in his old age);
and a terracotta study for
statues of Hercules and
Cacus which, if they had
been realised, would have
partnered the famous
David outside the Palazzo
Vecchio.

►   **Casa Buonarroti**   *IFCF3*

Via Ghibellina 70
Michelangelo's house is something of a fraud for,
although he bought the property in 1508, he never lived
here. The present house, its decoration and its collection
of Michelangelo memorabilia were arranged by his
nephew Leonardo (his sole descendant), and subsequently by Leonardo's son, Michelangelo the Younger.
The admission charge is exorbitant, given that the collection contains only four minor works and a handful of drawings by the master. And whilst the small maze of
decorated rooms is pleasant enough – full of furniture,
objets d'art and frescoed ceilings – the house is impersonal, and does not impart the *frisson* it might have
induced had Michelangelo ever lived here.

This said, the museum is beautifully presented, its
smart appearance the result of restoration precipitated by
the 1966 flood. Climb the stairs and turn left (at the case
of swords) for the sculptural highlights. The first, the
Madonna della Scala (*c.*1491), is a delicate, shallow relief
showing the influence of Donatello. Carved when
Michelangelo was 15 or 16, it is the sculptor's earliest surviving work. The second, the *Battle of the Centaurs*
(*c.*1492), was executed during his period at the court of
Lorenzo the Magnificent. A more complex and tangled
carving, it already suggests the sense of the heroic and
sfinito (unfinished) effects characteristic of his subsequent work.

In the adjoining room (left) is a wooden model of
Michelangelo's plan for the façade of San Lorenzo (never
implemented). Alongside sprawls an age-darkened wood-
and-wax model of a torso, part of a huge river god, perhaps intended for the **Cappelle Medicee** (see pages
64–5). It is the only such model by the sculptor in existence. Return to the swords at the top of the stairs: the
room straight ahead contains a selection of Michelangelo
drawings. To the right is a room with a slender, poplar-
wood *Crucifix*. Found in 1963, this long-documented
work was previously believed lost.
Open: daily 9:30–1:30. Closed Tuesday. Admission
charge (expensive).

► **Casa di Dante** *IFCE4*

Via Dante Alighieri–Via Santa Margherita 1r

Dante's supposed birthplace certainly looks the part. Its old stonework, wooden eaves and wrought ironwork conspire to produce one of the city's most convincing-looking medieval houses. Sadly the whole thing is a 19th-century pastiche: not only that, but Dante probably never set foot in the place (though he was almost certainly born near by, doubtless on the street that now bears his name). Before turning into the house, now a modest museum, look at the small plaque on the wall opposite, etched with buildings pertinent to episodes in Dante's life (see page 72).

The museum entrance is not under the prominent porch, but a little way down Via Santa Margherita on the left. Little of the material inside is original, and nothing relates directly to the poet's life. Nonetheless the modest offerings are worth a few minutes, particularly the collection of antique editions of the *Divine Comedy*. The best of these are a poster produced by a demented Milanese printer, presenting the entire work in miniature, and copies of Botticelli's line illustrations for the epic.

Open: daily 9–1. Closed Tuesday. Admission by donation.

Outside the museum, just down Via Santa Margherita, stands the small church of **Santa Margherita de' Cerchi** (*open*: daily 9–12 and 3–6:30; Sunday 9–12). Dante's Beatrice attended Mass here with her father, Folco Portinari, and some claim the church witnessed Dante's marriage to Gemma Donati (see page 70). In fact the nuptials probably took place in the parish church of the Donati and Alighieri families, **San Martino del Vescovo** (see panel), positioned immediately across from the Casa di Dante on Piazza San Martino (*open*: daily 10–12 and 3–5; closed Sunday).

Dante's spyhole
At the northern end of Via Santa Margherita, at Via del Corso 6, stands the Palazzo Salviati, located on the site of the house owned by Beatrice's father, Folco Portinari. Its courtyard harbours the so-called Nicchia di Dante (Dante's Niche), from which Dante is supposed to have watched his beloved.

Dante's church
San Martino del Vescovo was founded in 986 but the church as Dante knew it was rebuilt in 1479, when it became the headquarters of a charitable body, the Compagnia dei Buonomini. They commissioned the church's frescos – *The Life of San Martino* and *Works of Charity* (by the school of Ghirlandaio), delightful vignettes of daily life in 15th-century Florence. The church also has two renowned paintings of the Madonna, one attributed to Perugino.

Medieval pretensions: the largely 19th-century 'Casa di Dante'

■ **Dante (1265–1321) signed himself 'Dante Alighieri, a Florentine by birth but not by character'** – an ironic allusion to the city he served as a politician but which later cast him into exile and which was to inspire some of the most bitter passages in his great epic poem, the *Divine Comedy*.....■

First love

Dante (aged nine) records his feelings on first seeing Beatrice (aged eight). 'Love ruled my soul ... and began to hold such sway over me ... that it was necessary for me to do completely all his pleasure. He commanded me often that I should endeavour to see this so youthful angel, and I saw in her such noble and praiseworthy deportment that truly of her might be said these words of the poet Homer – *She appeared to be born not of mortal man but of God.*' La Vita Nuova (1293)

Top: Dante mural in the Duomo: Right: a belated honour: Dante in Piazza Santa Croce

Dante was born in 1265, a member of a minor and genteelly impoverished noble family. He was educated at Bologna, one of Europe's leading universities at the time, and later at Padua, where he studied philosophy and astronomy.

Dante and Beatrice Learning was one thing; love was to be another. Dante first glimpsed Beatrice, the daughter of Florentine nobleman Folco Portinari, when he was nine years old. She was to be his lifelong muse, and the inspiration for one of Europe's greatest works of literature (the dramatic *coup de foudre* of their first meeting was described by both Boccaccio and Dante himself – see panel). Sadly for Dante, however, Beatrice was never to be his lover: when she was eight, her family had arranged for her to marry Simone de' Bardi. Such marriages, designed to cement alliances between families, were nothing new. Beatrice's began in 1283 (when Dante was 18), only to end seven years later with Beatrice's death.

Marriage and politics Dante, for his part, had also been coaxed into a pragmatic marriage, to Gemma Donati, arranged when he was 12. The ceremony – tellingly, perhaps – did not take place until he was almost 30. Married, and muse aroused sufficiently to write *La Vita Nuova*, his first major work, Dante moved into a political career. He signed up to the Apothecaries' Guild as a 'poet', and operated on a variety of minor city councils. In 1300 he was sent from Florence to San Gimignano, charged with winning the town over to an alliance against Pope Boniface VIII. Boniface, who had designs on Tuscany, was among the most violent and vice-ridden of popes. (One of his tricks was to have the tongues of heretics nailed to doors.) Dante was later to pay a heavy price for provoking such a powerful enemy.

In 1300 the poet joined the Priorate (see page 35). As one of the city's *Priori* he continued his campaign

against Boniface, attempting at the same time to heal the rifts between the Black (anti-Imperial) and White (more conciliatory) factions of Florence's ruling Guelph party. The division had its origins in money. Members of the White faction included prominent bankers to the imperial powers such as the Cerchi, Mozzi, Davanzati and Frescobaldi. The Blacks, by contrast, included a roll-call of the most powerful papal bankers, notably the Pazzi, Bardi and Donati. Boniface, as was to be expected, sided with the Blacks, who eventually emerged triumphant.

Poetry and exile Dante's White sympathies and anti-papal stance were his undoing. In 1302, following spurious charges of corruption, he was sentenced – with other important Whites – to two years' exile. Most of the exiles were later able to return, but Dante rejected his city of 'self-made men and fast-got gain', wandering far and wide for several years before settling in Ravenna, where he probably wrote most of the *Divine Comedy*, completed just before his death.

Dante's epic of history, philosophy, science and theology, in which he seeks to bring about his own and humanity's redemption, begins on Maundy Thursday in 1300. The poet finds himself in a dark wood, a symbol of his moral and love-lorn darkness since the death of Beatrice. Grace, however, in the person of the poet Virgil, appears to point the way to salvation, guiding him through *Inferno* and *Purgatorio* (thronged with a cast of historical and contemporary characters) before delivering him to *Paradiso*.

Dante's exile perhaps makes it fitting that his body was never returned to Florence (though Santa Croce has a commemorative monument). Every year, however, on 14 September, the anniversary of his death, the city sends a gift of Florentine oil to Ravenna to light the votive lamps on Dante's tomb.

In a fanciful 19th-century interpretation, a wedding party emerges from the Church of Santa Margherita de' Cerchi, where Dante is supposed to have been married – but not to Beatrice

Fateful encounter
Boccaccio describes the meeting of Dante and Beatrice at a party thrown by the girl's father: 'Beatrice [had] habits and language more serious and modest than her age warranted; and besides this with features so delicate and so beautifully formed, and full, beside mere beauty, of so much candid loveliness that many thought her almost an angel … Dante … though still a child, received her image into his heart with so much affection that from that day forth, as long as he lived, it never again departed from him.' *Life of Dante* (1321)

[Map of Dante's district of Florence, showing the area from the Battistero and Duomo in the north to Santa Croce and the Arno in the south. Key locations labelled include: Battistero, Piazza San Giovanni, Duomo, Campanile, Loggia del Bigallo, Palazzo Salviati, Casa di Dante, Santa Margherita de' Cerchi, San Martino del Vescovo, Badia Fiorentina, Museo Nazionale del Bargello, Orsanmichele, Mercato Nuovo, Palazzo di Parte Guelfa, Loggia dei Lanzi, Palazzo Vecchio, Galleria degli Uffizi, Santo Stefano, Ponte Vecchio, Museo di Storia della Scienza, Museo della Fondazione Horne, Santa Croce, Biblioteca Nazionale Centrale, Casa Buonarroti, Museo di Firenze com'era, and various streets. Scale bar: 0 – 100 – 200 m.]

Walk **Dante's Florence**

A short walk through Dante's district and the eastern part of the city to the church of Santa Croce (1km; allow 30 minutes).

Start at the **Battistero▶▶▶** (pages 60–2), Dante's *bel San Giovanni*, one of only three churches in the city mentioned by the poet. Dante was baptised here but in his day the building still lacked most of its marble veneer. The Campanile did not yet exist and work on the Duomo had only just started. To the south of the Duomo, hunt out the so-called **Sasso di Dante** (Dante's Stone), set into the wall between Via dello Studio and Via del Proconsolo. Dante is supposed to have sat here and watched the building of the cathedral.

Walk down Via dello Studio to the junction with Via del Corso where, at No 6, the site of Beatrice's home, the Palazzo Salviati's courtyard still boasts the **Nicchia di Dante** (see the panel on page 69). Go down Via Santa Margherita to reach the **Casa di**

Dante▶ (see page 69) and the churches of **Santa Margherita de' Cerchi** and **San Martino del Vescovo** (see page 69).

Near by, on Via del Proconsolo, pass the **Badia Fiorentina▶** (page 55), where Dante often saw Beatrice. During the poet's lifetime the **Bargello▶▶▶**, opposite, was still being built (pages 56–9). Streets dotted with artisans' workshops lead to **Santa Croce▶▶▶** (pages 138–43) where you can see a monument raised in Dante's honour in 1829 – more than 500 years after his death.

Florence's only large public park, and once a fashionable meeting place for the city's élite, the Cascine is nowadays especially popular for its Tuesday market

Cascine, Le   *IFCA5*

Ponte della Vittoria – Piazza Vittorio Veneto
Bus: 17c from the Duomo or the railway station
Florence is not blessed with generous expanses of green space, making it unfortunate that the Cascine, its one big public park, is tatty round the edges and a long way from the city centre (30 minutes' walk). It also has a well-deserved reputation as somewhere to avoid after dark. If you want readily available peace and quiet, therefore, make for the more bucolic pleasures of the **Giardino di Boboli** (see page 84).

This said, the park is not all bad. Mothers bring their children here, and on a summer's afternoon there are worse places to escape the traffic and enjoy a break from sightseeing. If you decide to come here, try a Tuesday morning, when thousands of people flood in for the city's largest general **market** (see page 114).

The park is barely 100m wide in places, but stretches along the Arno for almost 3km, petering out at the river's confluence with the Mugnone. Originally a tract of wilderness known as the *isola* (island), the area that is now the park later became a Medici-owned dairy-farm (*cascina*), later serving as one of the family's favourite hunting estates. Napoleon's sister, Elisa Baciocchi Bonaparte, laid it out as a public park in 1811.

Over the next 100 years the Cascine emerged as the most fashionable meeting place for Florence's social élite. Charles Lever, a visitor in 1856, observed the great jam of carriages 'side by side like great liners', noting that 'the Cascine is to the world of society what the Bourse is to the world of trade.' He also added, 'Scandal holds here its festival', a sentiment echoed by several commentators on the more salacious undercurrents of the Cascine's social intercourse (see panel).

73

Shelley and the Cascine
'Yellow and black and pale and hectic red, pestilence-stricken multitudes' – Shelley's description of the Cascine's autumn leaves. The park occupies a small place in the annals of literary history, for it was here, 'on a day when the tempestuous wind ... was collecting the vapours that pour down the autumnal rains', that the poet wrote his famous 'Ode to the West Wind'.

Outdoor overtures
Elizabeth Barrett Browning, who came to live in Florence in 1847, hints at the Cascine's potential for sexual dalliance, talking of 'carriages alive with Florentine beauties,/ Who lean and melt to music as the band plays,/ To smile and chat with some one ... afoot ... in observance of male duties.' Alexandre Dumas also analysed these 'male duties': 'everyone makes or receives visitors. It goes without saying the visitors are men. The women remain in their carriages, the men go from one to another and, some on foot, some on horseback and some, more familiar, standing on the pavement, converse at the carriage doors ... glances are exchanged ... meetings fixed.' *Une Année à Florence* (1851)

The Pazzi Conspiracy

■ In its execution and aftermath, the attempted assassination of Lorenzo and Giuliano de' Medici in 1478 – the Pazzi Conspiracy – was perhaps the most blood-thirsty and compelling of all Florence's murkier acts of treachery. Had it succeeded, Florentine history might have been very different......■

Jacopo de' Pazzi

Jacopo escaped Florence after the conspiracy but was recaptured, tortured, stripped naked and hanged from the Palazzo Vecchio. After his burial in Santa Croce his corpse was dug up by the mob (who blamed his evil spirit for heavy rains), tossed in a ditch and then dragged through the streets. It was then propped up outside the Palazzo Pazzi, where the decomposing head was used as a door knock-er. Eventually the rotting body was thrown in the Arno, then fished out, flogged and hanged again by a gang of children, before finally being tossed back into the river.

Giuliano's death

'Baroncelli, crying out "Take that, traitor" ... brought down his dagger in a ferocious blow that almost split [Giuliano's] skull in two. Francesco de' Pazzi thereupon stabbed him with such frenzy, plunging the blade time and again into the unresisting body, that he even drove the point of the dagger through his own thigh. Giuliano fell to his knees while his assailant continued to rain savage blows upon him, slashing and stabbing until the corpse was rent by nine-teen wounds.'Quoted in Christopher Hibbert, *Rise and Fall of the House of Medici* (1974)

Pope versus Medici When Sixtus IV was elected pope in 1471 he began to distribute money and favours with a largesse remarkable even by medieval papal standards. One nephew in particular, Girolamo Riario (widely believed to be the pope's son), came in for special atten-tion. Having decided to buy Imola, a town near Bologna, as a present for the youth, Sixtus petitioned his banker Lorenzo the Magnificent for the necessary loan. Lorenzo refused, despite the importance of the papal account, viewing Imola as too important to be handed over to papal control. Angered by the snub, Sixtus looked to the Pazzi, the Medici's leading rivals as Florentine bankers in Rome.

Further friction arose when Lorenzo refused to recog-nise Francesco Salviati as Archbishop of Pisa. Sixtus had ignored an agreement by which such appointments in the Republic – of which Pisa was a part – could only be made by mutual agreement. Thus, by 1477, three men (as well as the pope) were ready to challenge Lorenzo: Riario, who was now in possession of Imola but desperate for greater spoils; Salviati, outraged at Lorenzo's veto and keen to become Archbishop of Florence; and Francesco de' Pazzi, head of the Pazzi's Rome operation, and eager to usurp Medici power in Florence.

The plot Any conspiracy worthy of the name required mil-itary muscle. The man chosen to provide it – a bluff mer-cenary known as Montesecco – proved wary of the whole business: 'beware of what you do,' he counselled, 'Florence is a big affair.' Eventually he was won over by the promise of papal backing for the project. When the plotters met with Sixtus, approval was quickly forthcom-ing. 'Go, and do what you wish,' he told them, adding the disingenuous caveat 'provided there be no killing'.

It then remained to win over Jacopo de' Pazzi, the head of the family, a grizzled godfather who proved 'colder than ice' when appraised of the proposed coup. He was on rel-atively good terms with the Medici, despite the bulwark they formed against his family's ambitions. His nephew, moreover, was married to one of Lorenzo's sisters. Like Montesecco, however, he was quickly won round by the pope's mealy-mouthed support.

Murder in the cathedral Lorenzo and his brother Giuliano were to be murdered while they attended Mass in the Duomo. The day of destiny was to be Sunday, 26 April 1478. The reluctant Montesecco, however, now refused to add sacrilege to murder in a place where 'God would see him'. Lorenzo's murder, therefore, was

Pope Sixtus IV (opposite page) and the assassins' targets: Giuliano (left) and (below) Lorenzo de' Medici

A papal hypocrite
Pope Sixtus – though desiring Lorenzo's death – made sure to distance himself from the Pazzi conspirators: 'I do not wish the death of anyone,' he lied, 'since it does not accord with our office to consent to such a thing. Though Lorenzo is a villain, and behaves ill towards us, yet we do not on any account desire his death, but only a change of government.'
Quoted in Christopher Hibbert, *Rise and Fall of the House of Medici* (1974)

Scoppio del Carro
Reviled by posterity for their conspiracy against the Medici, the Pazzi ironically inspired one of the city's most popular festivals. During the Crusades, Pazzino de' Pazzi brought back three flints from Jerusalem's Holy Sepulchre. At Easter these flints are used, in celebration of Christ's Resurrection, to relight lamps that were extinguished on Good Friday. On Easter Sunday they are used to ignite a dove-shaped rocket suspended on a wire above the Duomo's high altar. This is then sent whizzing down the wire to the piazza outside, where it sets off a cart (*carro*) full of fireworks. The size and splendour of the resulting bang and conflagration is taken as an omen, predicting the likely outcome of the year's harvest.

handed over to two twisted priests, Maffei and Bagnone. Giuliano was to be dispatched by Francesco de' Pazzi and Bernardo Baroncelli, the latter a violent Pazzi acolyte deeply in debt to the family. Salviati, meanwhile, accompanied by a band of armed men, would seize the members of the Priorate.

It all went wrong. Giuliano was killed, but the bungling priests were only able to wound Lorenzo, who took refuge in the Duomo's Sagrestia Nuova. Across the city, Salviati, separated from his troop, was arrested by the Gonfaloniere, Cesare Petrucci. An angry mob – most of them Medici supporters – was then summoned to Piazza della Signoria by the Palazzo Vecchio's famous bell. On discovering the plot, they dispensed summary justice to several of the conspirators, and then, despite entreaties from Lorenzo, indulged in a five-day rampage through the city in which 80 people were killed.

The day of reckoning After the plot's failure, Salviati's armed troop were massacred in the Palazzo Vecchio. Francesco de' Pazzi was dragged from hiding, stripped naked, and hanged alongside Salviati. The humanist, Poliziano, recorded that 'as the Archbishop rolled and struggled at the end of his rope, his eyes goggling in his head, he fixed his teeth into Francesco de' Pazzi's naked body.' Maffei and Bagnone were castrated and hanged. Montesecco was tortured, but given a soldier's execution in the Bargello. Baroncelli escaped to Constantinople, but was extradited and executed.

The crypt

The Duomo was rebuilt on top of the remains of Santa Reparata, its predecessor on the site, which was demolished but not completely destroyed. Remains of the old church can be seen in the crypt (see the plan on page 79). The ruins, however, are confusing, and it is not worth paying to see more than can be glimpsed from the bottom of the crypt's steps. The most interesting feature, moreover, can be seen for free: the tomb of Brunelleschi, located to the left of the steps. Such a burial place was a singular honour for the architect of the cathedral dome.

▶▶▶ **Duomo (Santa Maria del Fiore)** *IFCE4*

Piazza del Duomo

Rising above close-packed streets and houses, the Duomo's colourful exterior and orange-tiled dome form not only Florence's heart, but also a landmark that has become the city's virtual emblem. Europe's fourth largest church, it is surpassed only by St Peter's in Rome and the cathedrals of Milan and London; big enough, in Leon Battista Alberti's estimation, 'to cover with its shadow all the Tuscan people' (*De re aedificatoria*, 1452). Something tawdry, however, hangs around its square, the result of too many people, too much traffic and too little space. The mood is hardly lightened by the begrimed Battistero, nor by the tacky souvenir stands.

Santa Reparata The first church here was founded in the 7th century (possibly earlier) and dedicated to Santa Reparata, a somewhat obscure Syrian or Palestinian martyr. Remains of this church were rediscovered in 1965 (see panel). By the 13th century, when Florence had become a burgeoning commercial capital, the Priorate deemed the old building too 'crudely built and too small for such a city'. In its place was needed something to rival the cathedrals of Pisa and Siena, something, as an edict

of 1294 put it, of 'the most exalted and most prodigal magnificence, in order that the industry and power of men may never create or undertake anything whatsoever more vast and more beautiful'. The building was to be 'so magnificent in its height and beauty that it shall surpass anything … produced in the times of their greatest power by the Greeks and Romans.'

Building the Duomo The job of creating this architectural *nonpareil* was given to Arnolfo di Cambio, architect of the Palazzo Vecchio, who in 1296 proposed a vaulted basilica, polygonal apse and magnificently domed octagon. Quite how the dome – the largest since ancient times – was to be built, he neglected to say. Some 10 per cent of the building's cost was raised by a property tax levied on all citizens. As late as 1800 a tax of two *soldi* was still being deducted from every Florentine will and diverted to the Duomo. All fines for drunk and disorderly behaviour were also turned over to the building.

After a hiatus caused by Arnolfo's death in 1302, work restarted on the project in 1331 under the auspices of the Arte della Lana (Wool Merchants' Guild). Giotto was appointed master of the works in 1334, but spent most of his time preoccupied with the **Campanile** (see page 63). Francesco Talenti (1357–64) and a string of lesser architects then nursed the nave to completion (1380). The tribunes (apses) and drum of the dome were finished by 1418, but the problem of how to build the dome remained unresolved (see pages 80–1).

The exterior Some may find it hard to fault the Duomo's decorative impact – originally intended to mirror that of the Battistero – but its rainbow of coloured marbles (green from Prato, white from Carrara and red from the Maremma) has raised many an aesthetic eyebrow. 'A huge architectural zebra … a gigantic harlequin', said James Johnson in 1831, who abhorred the whole 'gothic and tasteless idea'. 'Like Victorian wallpaper', and 'a cathedral wearing pyjamas' have been two more recent comments.

Most of the fault lies with the façade, added as recently as 1887. Arnolfo di Cambio's projected frontage, only a quarter finished by 1420, was demolished in 1587 on the orders of Ferdinand I. (A few statues saved are now in the **Museo dell'Opera del Duomo**; see pages 96–7.) A competition then drew five new façade designs (the architects' models are in the same museum), but none was deemed worthy. Nothing happened for three centuries and then, between 1861 and 1868, a total of 92 plans were considered, that of Emilio de Fabris emerging triumphant. Its adoption has been generally regretted ever since.

The interior The simple austerity of the interior comes as a shock after the exterior's decorative exuberance. Its size, though, is overwhelming, the crowds that mill about in the vast open space dwarfed by doughty pillars and

Detail from the Duomo doors

Carping criticism
Not every visitor has found the Duomo or its piazza to their liking. 'A temple to damp the spirit, dead or alive, by the immense impression of stony bareness, of drab vacuity,' wrote the American novelist W D Howells in 1891. 'A vast pile that has been sapping the purses of her citizens for five hundred years,' commented Mark Twain in 1869. A 'hackney coach stand and omnibus station,' complained John Ruskin, full of the 'smell of variously mixed horse manure … cigars, spitting, and harlot-planned fineries …'

The Misericordia
Established in the 13th century, this hospital charity, in the manner of the Red Cross, has its headquarters to the south of the Duomo, in a building usually surrounded by ambulances. Today the organisation has 6,000 volunteers, each of whom devotes an hour's service a week for life. During services, the members traditionally wear black hoods, their identities kept secret out of humility.

Marking time

Paolo Uccello's remarkable clock of 1443 uses the so-called *hora italica*, whereby the 24th hour of the day ended at sunset. This system of telling the time remained common in Italy until the 18th century.

The Sagrestia Nuova

Lined with exquisite intarsia work of the mid-15th century, this (also known as the North Sacristy) is one of the Duomo's most fascinating corners. It was here in 1478 that Lorenzo the Magnificent took refuge during the Pazzi Conspiracy after the murder of his brother Giuliano (see pages 74–5). Above the entrance to the Sagrestia Nuova is another lunette by Luca della Robbia, the *Resurrection* (1442), his first important work in the enamelled terracotta for which he was to become famous. The sacristy doors (1446–67), easily overlooked, are also by Luca della Robbia (his only work in bronze) assisted by Michelozzo. Above them stood della Robbia's exquisite choir loft, now on display in the Museo dell'Opera del Duomo (see page 97).

Dante and the Duomo

Domenico di Michelino's painting, *Dante with the Divine Comedy*, was commissioned to celebrate the bicentenary of the poet's birth. Notice the drum of the cathedral dome, painted before it received its marble cladding. Dante stands outside the city walls, a symbol of his exile.

lofty arches. Unlike the piazza outside, where people seem to clutter the surroundings, the constant throng inside the Duomo only emphasises the building's epic scale. Capable of accommodating up to 10,000 people, its most dramatic moments came during the Pazzi Conspiracy, when men were hacked down in the apse (see pages 74–5), and when huge congregations crammed the nave to hear the sermons of Savonarola (see pages 40–1).

These days there appears little to see at first glance, as if the exterior had taken the lion's share of the decoration. On closer inspection, however, there are several fine works of art, as well as two interesting smaller excursions, into the crypt and up into the dome. The principal features of interest are identified on the plan on page 79. *Open*: daily 9:30–6. Crypt open daily 10–5, closed Sunday.

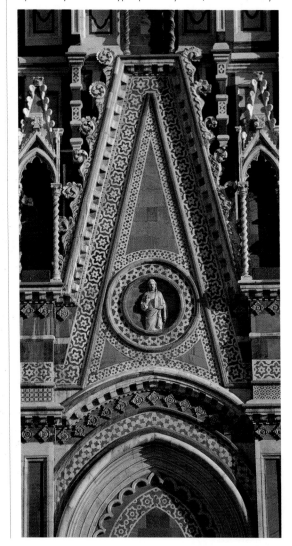

A rainbow of Tuscan marbles on the cathedral's exterior

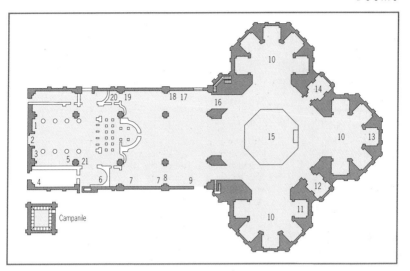

1. Tomb of Antonio d'Orso, Bishop of Florence, by Tino da Camaino (1323).

2. Mosaic *The Coronation of the Virgin* (c.1300), attributed to Gaddo Gaddi (c.1260–1332).

3. Clock, decorated by Paolo Uccello (see panel opposite).

4. Bust of Brunelleschi (in a tondo) by his pupil and adopted son, Andrea Cavalcanti (1447).

5. Gothic water stoup (c.1380). The angel and basin are copies.

6. *St Blaise* by Jacopo Franchi (1408).

7. Two frescoed cenotaphs, to Cardinal Pietro Corsini and Fra Luigi Marsili, by Bicci di Lorenzo (1422–39).

8. Stained-glass windows depicting six saints, designed by Agnolo Gaddi (1394–5).

9. Bust of Marsilio Ficino, philosopher friend of Cosimo de' Medici, holding a copy of Plato's works.

10. The three apses. Each is divided into five chapels, of which each one has two levels of stained glass. Most of these 30 windows were designed by Lorenzo Ghiberti.

11. Fresco fragment, the *Madonna del Popolo*, attributed to Giotto. Heavily restored frescos lie below he stained-glass windows in all the chapels.

12. Sagrestia Vecchia (Old, or South, Sacristy). A large terracotta lunette of the Ascension by Luca della Robbia (1446–51) is situated above the entrance. Above this originally stood Donatello's great choir loft, now reassembled in the Museo dell'Opera del Duomo.

13. Two kneeling angels holding candles, by Luca della Robbia, and a superb bronze reliquary (1432–42) by Lorenzo Ghiberti. This contains the relics of St Zenobius, Florence's first bishop (see the panel on page 61). Note: this third chapel of the central apse is often roped off for prayer and confessions.

14. Sagrestia Nuova (New, or North, Sacristy – see panel opposite).

15. Vasari's dome frescos (1572–9), long covered for restoration, depict the Last Judgement. Over the years many have felt them to be unworthy of the dome, and debate rages over whether they should be removed elsewhere.

16. Entrance to the dome (see panel on page 81).

17. *Dante with the Divine Comedy* (1465), a painting by Domenico di Michelino. (See panel opposite.)

18. *St Cosmos and St Damian*, the Medici's patron saints, by Bicci di Lorenzo (1429). (See panel on page 134.)

19. Large frescoed equestrian cenotaph by Paolo Uccello (1436) of Sir John Hawkwood, an English mercenary who headed the Florentine army between 1377 and his death in 1394.

20. Frescoed equestrian cenotaph of Niccolò da Tolentino, another mercenary hero, by Andrea del Castagno (1456).

21. Entrance to the crypt. (See panel on page 76.)

■ **The largest and highest dome of its day, the crowning glory of Florence's cathedral not only is a miracle of Renaissance engineering, but also symbolises the unbounded aspirations and achievements of its era......■**

Strange solutions

The problem of building a dome drew several eccentric proposals. One was to build it entirely from pumice-stone. Another was to support it, during its construction, on a vast mound of earth, liberally seeded with small coins (*quattrini*). Once the dome was finished, the people of Florence were to be invited to dig away the earth, spurred on by the prospect of carrying away a small fortune.

Michelangelo's praise

Richard Lassels, in *The Voyage of Italy* (1670), comments that Michelangelo, coming now and then to Florence while he was planning the cupola of St Peter's in Rome, reputedly viewed Florence's cupola attentively and said of it: 'Come te non voglio, meglio di te non posso' (Similar to you I will not; better than you I cannot).

A miracle of medieval engineering: Brunelleschi's dome

By 1418, the cathedral – its shell complete – possessed a yawning gap (45.5m wide) patiently awaiting its long-projected dome. Domes were nothing new. The cathedrals of Pisa and Siena already had them, and Rome's Pantheon had stood unbowed for over 1,000 years. None, though, approached the scale of Florence's endeavour, destined to be grander than anything attempted since antiquity. The problem of how to build it had preoccupied the committee of the Opera del Duomo for years. The members bickered constantly over the final design (signs of collapse in the Battistero further focused their minds on the project's potential pitfalls). In August 1418, in desperation, they threw the scheme open to competition.

Brunelleschi and Ghiberti Brunelleschi had been appointed engineering consultant to the Opera del Duomo in 1404, two years after being chosen as joint winner, with Lorenzo Ghiberti, in the competition to design the doors of the Battistero. The fiery Brunelleschi, who thought he should have won outright, refused to work with Ghiberti, leaving the plodding former goldsmith to create the doors alone. Revenge of sorts came Brunelleschi's way in 1418, when he defeated Ghiberti in the competition to build the dome. Ghiberti, however, proved an equally poor loser and, as a part-time consultant, joined the chorus of doom-mongers who poured scorn on Brunelleschi's plans. Brunelleschi, in an attempt to counter his critics, built a scale model on the banks of the Arno. The interfering Ghiberti, however, continued to dog his steps. In the end, as an excuse for abandoning the dome, Brunelleschi feigned illness. His ploy had almost immediate success: Ghiberti, left to his own architectural devices, soon found the project beyond his abilities. By 1423 Brunelleschi had been formally recognised as the dome's sole 'inventor and chief director'.

The problem and Brunelleschi's solution Domes were conventionally built using a wooden scaffold, the stone shell being supported on a temporary wooden dome until the last brick was in place and the mortar had hardened fully. In Florence, however, the cost of such an undertaking was deemed to be

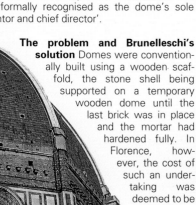

prohibitive. It was also unclear where the sheer quantity of wood required for such a frame would be found. Worse still, the cathedral's masons were unable to calculate the dimensions and the stresses generated by such a structure. The *impasse* generated many suggestions, many of them remarkably far-fetched (see panel opposite).

Brunelleschi's solution consisted of two shells; a light outer covering around 1m thick, and a concentric inner shell about 4m thick. Leon Battista, a contemporary, described the engineering as being of a kind that 'not even the ancients knew or understood'. Indeed, many of its finer points are still not understood today. At its most basic, the plan copied the octagonal vaults of the Battistero, the dome being arranged around eight principal and 16 lesser ribs, all bound together with horizontal brick rings designed to absorb some 25,000 tonnes of lateral thrust. No additional buttressing was required. Key to the scheme's success, however, was the herringbone patterning of the inner shell's brickwork (arranged in cantilevered rings, a technique that allowed the dome to support itself as it rose). Innovative tools, lightweight materials and quick-drying mortar were also devised, some now on show in the **Museo dell'Opera del Duomo** (see pages 96–7).

Finishing touches The dome took 16 years to complete, a period during which Brunelleschi was also busy on San Lorenzo and the Ospedale degli Innocenti. Despite these distractions, however, no detail was too small for the architect, whether it was providing the labourers with meal-kitchens in the dome (to save time), or creating a labyrinth of corridors – still in use today – to speed up movement around the shells. He even thought to provide scaffolding hooks for future cleaning and repairs.

Despite such diligence, and notwithstanding the dome's successful completion, Brunelleschi had to endure another competition to convince the authorities that he was the right person to complete the dome's lantern. His design prevailed, but was realised only in 1461, 15 years after his death. The external gallery around the dome's base – not Brunelleschi's design – was abandoned half-built in 1515, leaving raw brickwork on seven sides (reputedly because the design was ridiculed by Michelangelo).

Take the climb to the top for a look at the dome's construction, as well as fine views

The way to the top
The reasonably able-bodied (except those who suffer from claustrophobia or vertigo) should be sure to climb the 463 steps that lead up the dome. The entrance is at the eastern end of the nave's north aisle. On the way up, enjoy the views and the engineering insights offered by the corridors between the dome's two shells. Mid-way, an internal balcony provides close-up views of Vasari's dome frescos and of the seven stained-glass windows designed by Uccello, Donatello, Castagno and Ghiberti. *Open*: daily 10–5. Closed Sunday. Admission charge (moderate).

Egghead
At a meeting of the Opera del Duomo, called to quiz him on his plans, Brunelleschi produced an egg, saying that he alone knew how to make it stand on end. When other committee members admitted defeat he cracked its end and left it – broken, but standing. 'But we could all have done that,' they argued. 'Yes,' Brunelleschi replied, 'and you would say the same thing if I told you how I intend to build the dome.'

A detail of the exquisitely decorative inlaid marble façade of the Badia Fiesolana. The 9th-century church was Fiesole's cathedral until 1028

▶▶ **Fiesole**   *IBCD5*

The hill town of Fiesole, to the Florentines' chagrin, is centuries older than its neighbour, Florence. Dante complained of 'that ungrateful and malignant people of old who came down from Fiesole'. Settled around 800BC, it became an Etruscan town about 600BC, emerging as a leading member of the Etruscans' 12-city federation. As Faesulae under Roman occupation it became capital of Etruria but, despite its relatively secure strategic position, it fell to Florence in 1125. Since then Fiesole's attractive site and reputedly healthy climate have made it a favoured rural retreat, patronised by everyone from the *Decameron*'s fictional storytellers, who came here to escape the plague, to the army of British expatriates who swarmed through its villas and gardens in the 19th century.

Today, reached by an easy bus ride and promising cooling breezes and wonderful views, Fiesole is promoted as the perfect antidote to the sweltering heat and constant crowds of central Florence, only 6km to the southwest. In reality, while Fiesole's green surroundings may make it appear cooler, temperatures here on a hot August day are barely a degree lower than those of the city below. As for the crowds, Fiesole has its fair share of worthwhile sights, and is now so well established as *the* day trip from Florence that it tends to be as cluttered as the city itself. This said, the streets retain something of the atmosphere of a small village, and tracts of rolling Tuscan countryside lie close by if you are prepared for some modest walking. In high summer, Fiesole is the focus for one of Tuscany's major arts festivals, the Estate Fiesolana, when concerts are held in the Badia Fiesolana and the Teatro Romano (see page 183).

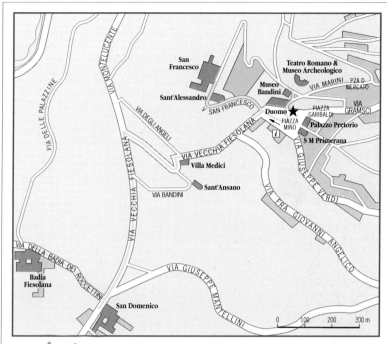

Walk Fiesole

A walk around Fiesole and its surroundings, taking in the main sights and offering extensive views of Florence (2.5km; allow a morning).

Start in Piazza Mino, Fiesole's central square and site of the Roman forum. The dull 19th-century exterior of the **Duomo** conceals a more appealing interior. The Cappella Salutati has two fine works by Mino da Fiesole: the tomb of Bishop Salutati and an altar frontal of the Madonna and Child.

The 3,000-seat, 1st-century BC **Teatro Romano►►** and the **Museo Archeologico** lie off Via Marini. The other ruins – two Etruscan temples, baths and defensive walls – are set amid olive groves with pleasant shady spots. *Open*: daily 9–7 (9–6 in winter). Closed Tuesday. Admission charge (moderate). The **Museo Bandini►** (Via Dupre 1) contains a collection of terracottas, ivories and Florentine paintings. *Open*: daily 9:30–1, 3–7 (10–1, 3–6 in winter).Closed Tuesday. Admission charge (inexpensive).

Go up the steep Via San Francesco to visit two churches. **Sant' Alessandro►** was built in the 6th century over Etruscan and Roman temples. Inside, its ancient *cipollino* (onion-ring) columns help make it one of Fiesole's loveliest buildings. **San Francesco►►** occupies the site of the ancient acropolis and contains an important 15th-century painting, *The Immaculate Conception* by Piero di Cosimo. There are also cloisters, good views of Florence and a small museum.

Either retrace your steps or take the wooded path from San Francesco back to Piazza Mino. Walk down Via Vecchia Fiesolana, past the **Villa Medici**, built by Michelozzo in 1458 and one of the earliest Renaissance villas (not open). **San Domenico►**, once home to Fra Angelico, contains his *Madonna and Angels* (*c*.1430).

Walk down Via della Badia dei Roccettini. The lovely Romanesque façade of the **Badia Fiesolana►** is a jewel of coloured marble incorporated into a larger 15th-century frontage.

The Fontana del
Bacco

Forte di Belvedere

The fort above the Giardino
di Boboli was built for
Ferdinand I by Buontalenti
(1590–5) to defend the city
and remind errant citizens
of Medici muscle. It is
crowned by a three-
storeyed *palazzina*, built in
the style of the Medici villas and now used for exhibitions. Views over
Florence from here are
some of the best in the
city. Access is from Via di
Belvedere and the Costa di
San Giorgio (see page 156).
Open: daily 9–8 or dusk, if
earlier. Admission free
except during exhibitions.

Grotta di Buontalenti

This cave is the most
bizarre of the Boboli's
Mannerist monuments
(constructed 1583–8). A
pebble-mosaic menagerie
of limestone animals struggles to escape from its
froth of carved stone and
fake stalactites. Copies of
Michelangelo's *Slaves*
(see page 52) occupy its
four corners, whilst a statue of Pan peeps from the
walls. Beyond lies a lasciv-
ious statue, *Paris
Abducting Helen of Troy.*
Further back still stands
Giambologna's scarcely
less erotic statue, *Venus
Emerging from her Bath.*

► ►   **Giardino di Boboli**   *IFCC2*
Entrance via the Palazzo Pitti

Five million people annually used to visit the Giardino di
Boboli (making them Italy's most visited gardens). Among
the visitors were thousands of mothers and children, for
whom this magnificent open space in the Oltrarno was
the only green retreat in a hot and dusty city. Imagine,
then, the fury when the Rome-based Ministry of Culture
insisted (in 1992) that the city should start charging for
admission to what had previously been a free public park.
Florentines took to the streets, demonstrating in Piazza
della Signoria, and with right on their side: after all, Anna
Maria Luisa, sister of the last Medici Grand Duke, had
bequeathed the entire Medici estate – palaces, paintings,
parks and all – to the people of Florence in perpetuity. It
was not for Rome to dictate to them what they should do
with their own property. Since then a compromise has
been reached: Florentines can now buy a reduced-price
season ticket to the gardens, while the rest of us have to
pay a substantial sum for each visit. One hopes (but
probably in vain) that the Italian government might one
day be shamed into reversing a decision which does it no
credit.

Initiated in 1549, when the Medici took over the Palazzo
Pitti, the gardens were completed in the 17th century and
first opened to the public in 1766. Today, sightseeing
possibilities include dozens of Mannerist and antique
statues and fountains, beautiful views, and all manner of
charming incidental details. Bring a picnic, or find a shady
nook for an hour's siesta.

The main path leads from the entrance, in the Palazzo
Pitti's courtyard, to the Amphitheatre, at the rear of the
Palazzo Pitti. This was laid out for Medici entertainments
in the manner of a Roman *circo* over the quarry used to
provide the Palazzo's building stone. The basin at the

centre is from Rome's Terme di Caracalla; the obelisk comes from Luxor and dates from 1500BC.

The best views are from the terrace beside the rococo *Kaffeehaus* (which serves as a bar in summer) or from the secluded and unkempt Giardino del Cavaliere (perched on a bastion created by Michelangelo). Further afield, stroll the Viottolone, a statue-lined cypress avenue aimed at the Isolotto, a moated island dominated by a copy of Giambologna's famous *Oceanus* fountain.

As you leave the gardens, look for the famous chubby statue of Cosimo I's favourite dwarf, depicted riding on a turtle, on the Fontana del Bacco (Bacchus Fountain) to the right. Some 50m before it lies the extraordinary Grotta di Buontalenti (see panel opposite).

Open: daily 9–dusk or 6:30, whichever is earlier. Closed Monday. Admission charge (moderate).

▶ ▦ **Giardino dei Semplici**   *IFCE5*

Via Micheli 3

Open space, however modest, is to be treasured in Florence, where it is a rare commodity. The Semplici gardens provide a convenient bucolic bolthole after the sightseeing rigours of the Accademia, the Museo di San Marco or Santissima Annunziata.

Founded in 1545 by Cosimo I, the Giardino dei Semplici was created – like much else in Florence – to keep up with rival cities, in this case Pisa and Genoa, both of whom possessed botanical gardens. Cosimo's creation embraced – and still embraces – a wide range of medicinal plants and Tuscan shrubs, trees and miscellaneous flora (as well as greenhouse exhibits). Be sure also to spend some time in the less scholarly and more relaxing surroundings of the garden's original lawns and avenues.

Open: Monday, Wednesday, Friday and Saturday 9–12. Admission free.

University museums
A visit to the Giardino dei Semplici could easily be combined with a look at three of the city's smaller museums, all at present entered from a courtyard cluttered with temporary huts, bikes and student mopeds at Via Giorgio La Pira 4, but destined to move eventually to a new site on Via Circondaria.

The **Museo Botanico** is Italy's foremost botanical collection. Its 4 million exhibits include some beautiful wax and plaster models, and plants collected by Charles Darwin on his first major voyage. The museum also contains one of the world's oldest herbariums. *Open*: Monday, Wednesday and Friday 9:30–12:30. Admission free.

Pride of place in the dowdy **Museo di Mineralogia** goes to a Brazilian topaz weighing 151kg or 755,000 carats, a monster that overshadows Tuscany's endemic minerals (mainly from Elba) and the Medici's worked-stone trinkets – vases, snuff boxes and the like. *Open*: daily 9–1. Closed Sunday. Admission free.

The **Museo di Paleontologia** contains one of Italy's best fossil collections, but is probably not for the casual visitor – unless you want to see prehistoric elephant skeletons dredged up from the Arno Valley. *Open*: Tuesday, Wednesday, Thursday and Saturday 9–1; Monday 2–6. Admission free.

Forget the city hubbub in the green retreat of the Boboli gardens, Florence's most famous park

LOGGIA DEI LANZI

Cellini's Perseus
*holds aloft the head
of Medusa*

Perseus
A passage in Cellini's
swashbuckling
Autobiography (1558–62)
describes the casting of
Perseus (a feat many
thought impossible). On the
appointed day, Cellini
stoked the furnaces so
high he caught a fever.
Retiring to bed, he left an
assistant in charge. Not
only did the bronze begin
to cool too soon, but the
foundry (in Cellini's house)
caught fire. Resurfacing as
the inferno raged, Cellini
hurled all available metal
into the furnace (including
his cutlery and the family
pewter). Two days later,
when the bronze had
cooled, the figure was
revealed, complete except
for three toes on the right
foot which were added
later.

Loggia lounging
In the 15th century Alberti
wrote of the 'Portico under
which the old men may
spend the heat of the day',
adding that, 'the presence
of the fathers may deter
and restrain the youth,
who are sporting and
diverting themselves in the
other part of the place,
from the mischievousness
and folly natural to their
age.' In 1896 Augustus
Hare wrote that 'hundreds
of men stand here for
hours, as if they had
nothing else to do, talking
ceaselessly in deep
Tuscan tones [and]
wrapped in long cloaks
thrown over the shoulder'.

▶▶ **Loggia dei Lanzi** *IFCE3*
Piazza della Signoria

The area occupied by this triple-arched loggia was long
used as Florence's *arringhiera*, a platform from which officials harangued the city's hapless *Parlemento* (see page
35). Florence began to consider the comfort of its politi-
cians only in 1376, a year in which numerous public cere-
monies were washed out by heavy rain (San Gimignano's
worthies, by contrast, had been protected from the
weather by a loggia since 1338). Masons were transferred from the Duomo to work on the new loggia –
hence the similarities between its arched vaulting and the
cathedral's nave. The artist Orcagna may have drawn up
its plans, for in its early days the Loggia della Signoria, as
it was later called, was known as the Loggia dell'Orcagna.
The present name dates from the 16th century, when the
Swiss lancers (Lanzichenecchi) of Cosimo I's personal
bodyguard were garrisoned in nearby Via Lambertesca.

For the past 200 years, a collection of statues has
enjoyed the protection of the loggia (currently cordoned
off for restoration and draped in rusting scaffolding).
Along the back wall are six antique pieces, said to be the
figures of Roman empresses. In the centre row, from left
to right, are Pio Fedi's *Rape of Polyxena* (1866); *Ajax and
Patroclus*, a Greek work; and Giambologna's *Hercules
and the Centaur* (1599). To the left of the lions flanking the
stairs stands Cellini's *Perseus* (1545), one of the supreme
masterpieces of the Renaissance, made for Cosimo I. A
bravura piece of casting (see panel), it shows Perseus
(son of Zeus and Danae) standing over Medusa and
clutching her snake-covered head (a glance from which
turned men to stone). To the right is Giambologna's *Rape
of the Sabines* (1583), carved from one of the largest
pieces of marble ever brought to Florence. In extracting
three powerful figures, in violent spiral motion, out of its
awkward shape, Giambologna created one of
Mannerism's masterpieces. Originally the artist had no
ambition other than to carve figures representing an old
man, a young man and a young woman. The statue's present name was coined later.

► **Museo Archeologico** *IFCF5*

Palazzo della Crocetta, Via della Colonna 36

Even non-specialists, such as Oscar Wilde, who spent 'two delightful hours' here in 1874, should find much to admire in Florence's archaeological museum, still the best of its kind in northern Italy despite appalling damage inflicted during the 1966 flood. The Etruscan collection is especially good – a perfect introduction to Tuscany's Etruscan sites – whilst the Greek and Roman sections provide a graphic illustration of the wells from which Renaissance art drew much of its inspiration. Although some rooms remain closed, and various works are still unrestored, most of the museum's real highlights are usually on display.

The ground floor is devoted to Greek and Etruscan art. The star turn of the first room is the François Vase, a huge Attic *krater* made in Athens around 570BC and used to mix water and wine. Its 638 pieces were painstakingly stuck together after being dropped by a hapless custodian in 1900. Room II contains examples of Etruscan tomb sculpture recovered from around Chiusi and Chianciano in southern Tuscany.

The Egyptian displays fill eight rooms on the first floor. Though some consider this one of the museum's less captivating areas, it contains some unique exhibits such as 3,000-year-old hats, baby clothes and other everyday items. There is even a 14th-century BC wooden chariot, almost complete – the only one known in the world.

More Greek, Roman and Etruscan pieces follow, notably the Hellenic *Horse's Head* (Room XIII), removed from the courtyard of the Palazzo Medici–Riccardi, where it was studied by Verrocchio and Donatello in anticipation of their own equestrian statues in Venice and Padua. The same room boasts the famous *Idolino*, a young athlete in bronze, probably a Roman copy of a 5th-century BC Greek original. The Long Gallery (Room XIV) displays some equally accomplished Etruscan bronzes, notably the *Chimera* (see panel) and the toga-clad *Arringatore* (Orator), whose naturalism had a profound influence on Renaissance sculptors. The second floor is often closed – not usually a cause for disappointment, as the rooms here are given over almost entirely to an endless succession of dusty Greek and Etruscan urns.

Open: daily 8:30–2 (Sunday 8:30–1). Closed Monday. Admission charge (moderate).

Head of a coffin lid in the Egyptian rooms

The *Chimera*
This mythical beast with its three heads (lion, ram and snake) was an ancient religious icon that symbolised the three seasons of the Mediterranean's agricultural year. When it was found in 1555, however, Cosimo I imbued it with fresh meaning, declaring it a symbol of the state's enemies and the peace he had brought to Florence. This interpretation suited his favourite political claim: that in assuming power over Tuscany he was reuniting a region (Etruria) that had existed in the Etruscan age.

87

CANTINETTA
DEI
VERRAZZANO

CANTINETTA DEI VERRAZZANO
VIA DEI TAVOLINI 18/20R - TEL. 055/268

MUSEO BARDINI

▶▶   **Museo Bardini**   *IFCE2*

Piazza de' Mozzi 1

One of Florence's unsung museums, the Museo Bardini remains unknown to many visitors. It is still not fully catalogued, and receives little or no publicity, but its wide-ranging collection is nonetheless fascinating, and more enjoyable than the similar Museo della Fondazione Horne across the river (see page 93).

Like the Horne, this museum was created by a 19th-century private collector, Stefano Bardini (see the panel on this page), who – by occasionally dubious means – acquired hundreds of historic architectural details and miscellaneous artefacts. When the collection became too extensive for his home, parts of it were incorporated into the made-to-measure medieval *palazzo* that Bardini had built for himself. A 13th-century church that stood on the site was simply pulled down. For all its modernity (it was built just a hundred years ago in 1883), the *palazzo* still feels thoroughly medieval – not least because its doors, ceilings and fireplaces (some of them salvaged from medieval buildings that were demolished in order to create Piazza della Repubblica in the 1860s) lend it the requisite authenticity.

The ground floor The museum as described may sound complicated, but in practice you should have few problems in finding your way around. All the rooms are numbered, and the more valuable exhibits have been labelled. Fragments of stone frieze and other architectural carvings in the vestibule immediately set the tone for what is to come. More of the same follows in Rooms 1 and 2 (to the right of the vestibule in the open-plan arrangement). In Room 2, look for the large decorative fresco, made to appear as a curtain tapestry, especially the woman painted peeping from its left-hand corner. (Rooms 3–5 are closed.)

Room 8, straight on from the vestibule, is dominated by a worn well-head of red Veronese marble, and opens out into Room 7, formerly an open courtyard. This contains several beautiful objects, notably the stone emblems on the wall on the right and the Cosmati-work pulpit (inlaid with glass and precious stones) on the wall opposite. The tiny (labelled) head in the centre of the right wall is attributed to Nicola Pisano (*c.*1220–84?). The room's finest piece is also one of the museum's highlights – a Gothic aedicule (frame) and statue of Charity by Tino da Camaino, on the rear wall. The aedicule, incidentally, is a pastiche, cobbled together from disparate reliefs and statuettes.

Room 9 lies to the left of the vestibule and is entered through a worn but beautifully carved doorway. It contains two impressive fireplaces and a monumental porphyry basin from the reign of Diocletian (AD284–305). Climb the stairs to the first landing to reach Room 10. The exhibits in this room include an enamelled terracotta altarpiece by Andrea della Robbia as well as pavement tombs which have been gathered together from as far afield as Venice.

The first floor Rooms 11–13, to the left at the top of the stairs, bulge with all manner of death-dealing medieval weaponry – pikes, pistols, crude mortars, crossbows, daggers and a rather effete-looking collection of swords and rapiers. Room 14 (straight ahead at the top of the stairs) boasts two of the museum's most precious treasures: a polychrome terracotta of the Madonna and Child by Donatello (on the right-hand wall) and the same artist's extraordinary *Madonna dei Cordai*, an almost modern-looking collage of glass, stucco and mosaic.

Room 16 offers a vast, anonymous *Crucifix*, chests, furniture and several Florentine paintings of the Madonna and Child – an image of which Bardini seems to have been inordinately fond. The bright orange-tiled floor of Room 15 (which follows 16) sets off half-a-dozen magnificent carpets. The remaining five rooms are crammed with a miscellany of reliefs, furniture, majolica and paintings among which Antonio Pollaiuolo's *St Michael* in Room 18 stands out. Room 20 (steps down from 18) contains one of the city's most sumptuous wooden ceilings, as well as two exquisitely inlaid choir stalls.

Open: daily 9–2 (Sunday 8–1). Closed Wednesday. Admission charge (moderate). *Biglietto Cumulativo* (combined ticket) available, also covering the Palazzo Vecchio, the Museo di Firenze com'era and the Museo di Santa Maria Novella.

A roomful of statues and sculptures – just part of Stefano Bardini's eclectic collection

Opposite page: Adoration of the Christ Child with the Young St John the Baptist, *by Pseudo Pier Francesco Fiorentino (fl. 1475–1500). The Madonna and Child was a favourite image of Bardini's*

A façade for all purposes
Barely hinting at the luxury within, the dour façade of the Palazzo Davanzati is topped by a fifth-storey loggia, a replacement for battlements removed in the 16th century. The medley of metalwork on the lower facade served for tying up animals, suspending bird-cages, supporting festive banners, or hanging out wool and washing to dry. The vaulted entrance hall (now the ticket office) was once a loggia, used originally to close off the house in times of danger. Later it hosted family parties, while later still it became a mall of medieval wool shops.

▶▶▶ **Museo della Casa Fiorentina Antica (Museum of the Old Florentine House)** IFCD3

Palazzo Davanzati, Piazza Davanzati, Via Porta Rossa

You should perhaps see this beautiful medieval house before visiting almost anything else in Florence. In offering an insight into how the city's artists, merchants and noble families might once have lived, it both makes up for the medievalism missing from the streets of today and provides a welcome context for the paintings and sculptures that can sometimes seem rather lifelessly displayed in the museums and galleries. Few Florentine museums are as captivating.

The courtyard Amid the courtyard's redoubtable stonework only the modern lighting strikes a false note: this perfect medieval vignette might be the stage-set for some swashbuckling B-movie epic. The private well served the whole house, operating by means of a complex system of pulleys – something of a luxury at a time when most people drew their water from public fountains. Store-rooms to the rear were replenished directly from side and back alleys, stocked with up to a year's supply of oil and grain to insure against the threat of siege, famine or runaway inflation. Notice the courtyard's rear right-hand pillar, carved with heads thought to be portraits of the Davizzi family (see panel). The glorious wood and stone staircase is the only one of its kind left in Florence.

The first floor Turn right at the top of the stairs into the Sala Madornale, originally used for family gatherings, when the wall hooks would have supported decorative drapes. In less happy times the floor's four wood-covered holes were used to bombard attackers in the entrance hall below. The ceiling, like most in the house, is magnificent, but smaller details – such as the powerful set of bellows – are equally captivating. Two small rooms to the right have been set aside for displays of lace and embroidery. More beguiling, however, is the Sala dei Pappagalli to the left, named after the tiny parrots (*pappagalli*) decorating its wall frescos (whose *trompe-l'oeil* folds and tucks have been artfully made to resemble textile hangings). Such wall-paintings were once common in contemporary houses: these are now some of the last surviving examples in the city. The leaded windows were originally covered with turpentine-soaked rags, stretched across the frames in order to repel water, even though they admitted only a tiny amount of light.

A small passage leads to the plain-walled Sala Piccola, probably a child's bedroom, with another fine ceiling, a fantastically elaborate safe and four parts of a painted wedding chest (*cassone nuziale*). The house's most covetable room, however, is the neighbouring Sala Pavoni or Camera Nuziale (Wedding Room). Under a beautiful ceiling runs a frescoed frieze of trees, peacocks (*pavoni*) and exotic birds, interwoven with the coats of arms of all the families related to the Davizzi. The two-winged tabernacle has an *Angel and Saints* by Neri di Bicci, while the linen bedspread is a rare piece of 14th-century Sicilian work decorated with the story of Tristan. Only the en-suite bathroom strikes a disconcertingly rudimentary note (see panel opposite).

A family home
The Palazzo Davanzati was built around 1330 for the Davizzi, a family of wealthy wool merchants. In 1578 it was sold to the Davanzati, with whom it remained until 1838, when the clan's last member committed suicide by jumping from an upper window. After being divided into apartments the palace was restored (1904) to its 14th-century appearance by Elia Volpi, a painter and antiquarian, who furnished the rooms with artefacts appropriate to the period. Opened as a museum in 1910, it was bought by the State in 1951.

The second floor The layout of this floor is the same as that of the first, and all its rooms are similarly filled with furniture, tapestries, ceramics, paintings and decorated wedding chests. Notice the shoe-shaped hand-warmers and the Davanzati family tree in the main *salone*, the dining room's bizarre salt-cellars, and the bedroom's faded frescos, their narrative lifted from a medieval French romance.

The third floor This is given over to the kitchen, a room often situated at the top of medieval *palazzi* to minimise damage in the event of fire. The house's cosiest corner, this was where the women would spend most of their time, using the sorts of kitchen utensils displayed around the room. Many of these look like medieval instruments of torture. Notice, in particular, the *girapolenta*, a polenta stirrer, and the *impastatori*, used for mixing dough for bread or pasta. Be sure to look out of this delightful room's windows for views over Via Porta Rossa.
Open: daily 9–2. Closed Monday. Admission charge (moderate).

Bare necessities
Palazzo Davanzati's lavatories might look crude today, but in the 14th century they were the best that money could buy. Drains were a recent innovation, a law of 1325 having forbidden the disposal of sewage directly into the streets. An earlier statute had required three loud warning cries to be given before a chamber-pot was emptied. Florence may have had public latrines (San Gimignano certainly had them), but for most people the arrangement was as described in Boccaccio's *Decameron* – two planks of wood perched over a small pit.

Pots and pans in the Palazzo Davanzati's medieval kitchen on the third floor

*One of van Utens'
lunettes of the
Medici villas*

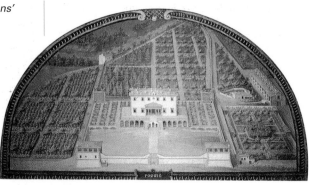

Santa Maria Maddalena dei Pazzi

This church, at Borgo Pinti 58, is only a few minutes from the Museo di Firenze com'era. It is well worth a visit to see its chapter house, home to a beautiful three-part *Crucifixion* (1496) by Perugino, one of the painter's masterpieces. The church, built in 1257 (but with a baroque interior), was reputedly named after a 'mad' (*pazzo*) Florentine nun who habitually covered herself in boiling wax as a mark of devotion. Now run by French Augustinians, the church is a favourite of Florence's French community. *Open*: daily 9–12 and 5–7. Admission by donation.

►   **Museo di Firenze com'era (Museum of Florence as it was)**   *IFCE4*

Via dell'Oriuolo 4

One sad aspect of Florence today is the lack of public parks and grassy squares, something easily overlooked until – with some surprise – you stumble across somewhere like the Museo di Firenze com'era, whose small garden of lawns and mature trees reminds you how more of the city must once have looked. It is a fitting introduction to a museum which, with engravings and topographical paintings, documents the Florence of days gone by. Unashamedly modest, it is nonetheless a charming and – to its benefit – a relatively under-visited spot.

Turning right at the entrance into the first room you are confronted with the museum's prize piece – the *Pianta della Catena* – a bewitching medieval view of Florence stretched across an entire wall. Painted in 1887 from a 1470 original (now in Berlin), it offers a fascinating panorama of the city walls, towers and buildings. It was painted by an unknown artist, perhaps the red-cloaked figure in the right-hand foreground. The Arno, a lovely blue, is particularly vivid, and is depicted complete with swimmers, fishermen and a punt-like ferry. Many of the churches shown still lack their present façades; the Uffizi and the Cappelle Medicee have yet to be built; and the Medici and Pitti palaces are still a fraction of their later size.

The room to the right contains lunettes of the Medici villas (1599) by the Flemish painter van Utens, reproductions of which are on sale all over the city in the form of cards and posters. The originals – 12 aerial views of neatly arranged woods, houses and gardens – are among the loveliest things in this or any other Florentine museum. More maps, pictures and engravings follow, the highlights being a painting of Savonarola's execution and the engravings of Telemaco Signorini (1874). Return to the entrance; the vaulted room to the left is filled with covetable engravings of the city's major buildings, the most interesting of which are the exploded diagrams (dated 1755) of the Duomo, the Battistero and the Campanile on the right-hand wall.

Open: daily 9–2 (Sunday 8–1). Closed Thursday. Admission charge (inexpensive). *Biglietto Cumulativo* (combined ticket) available, also covering the Palazzo Vecchio, the Museo di Santa Maria Novella and the Museo Bardini.

► **Museo della Fondazione Horne** *IFCE3*

Palazzo Corsi-Alberti, Via de' Benci 6

Like the nearby Museo Bardini (see pages 88–9), the Museo Horne was founded by a private collector, in this case the Englishman Herbert Percy Horne (1864–1916), known in his day for a pioneering biography of Botticelli. The collection is more modest than Bardini's (Horne was not a wealthy man), but also a touch more intimate and discerning than its rival. It is worth seeing the two museums in conjunction.

Exhibits are numbered rather than labelled, but a free catalogue is available at the ticket desk. The ground floor has just one room, whose highlight is Jacopo Sansovino's *Madonna and Child*, its protagonists' haloes delicately picked out in gold against the coarser carved stone. Andrea Sansovino's workshop was responsible for the capitals of the courtyard's two central pillars, which are among the finest in the city.

The first floor contains the core of the collection's paintings and furniture. Room I's highlights are a faded *Crucifix* by Filippino Lippi (between the second and third windows); a tiny, bowed panel by Masaccio depicting St Julian (on the far wall); a group of Saints by Pietro Lorenzetti (centre of the far wall); and the adjoining wall's age-darkened *Deposition* by Benozzo Gozzoli. Room II contains the museum's star turn, Giotto's *Santo Stefano*, part of a polyptych (centre of the right-hand wall), and the face and upper torso of a *Redeemer* by Luca Signorelli. Room III offers Beccafumi's important tondo of the Holy Family, a glorious frame enclosing a group of tousle-haired, red-headed children.

The second floor follows the same three-room plan. The main room boasts a tiny *Pietà* by Filippo Lippi (behind glass on the left of the end wall) and Filippino Lippi's almost infantile *Esther*, part of a marriage chest, its simple background no more than a scratch of paint. The two book-size panels in the centre of the room are attributed to Simone Martini.

Open: daily 9–1. Closed Sunday. Admission charge (moderate).

Palazzo Corsi-Alberti
The palace housing the Museo della Fondazione Horne was built in 1489 for the Corsi, a family of cloth manufacturers attracted to the area around Santa Croce, then the heart of Florence's textile industry. A typical house of the period, it included a large cellar for dyeing vats and an open-air upper gallery in the courtyard for drying skeins of wool.

93

One man's collection: part of the Museo Horne's display of paintings, decorative arts and furniture

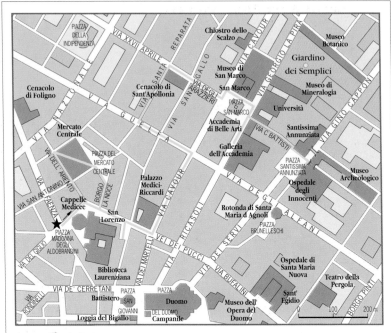

Walk The north of the city – Michelangelo and Fra Angelico

A walk taking in Florence's main market area and the most important churches and galleries in the north of the city (3km; start early and allow at least half a day to visit all the sights mentioned, noting that most of them close by 2pm).

Start in Piazza Madonna degli Aldobrandini by visiting the **Cappelle Medicee (Medici chapels)►►►**, the remarkable last resting place of many of the Medici family (see pages 64–5). The church of **San Lorenzo►►** itself (entered from Piazza San Lorenzo) is a masterpiece of Renaissance church design. The interior boasts bronze pulpits and other works by Donatello. Do not miss Brunelleschi's Sagrestia Vecchia or Michelangelo's Biblioteca Laurenziana (see pages 132–5).

Explore the market north of San Lorenzo (see pages 114–15), cut through the lively covered Mercato Centrale and return to Piazza San Lorenzo. On the north side of the square is the **Palazzo Medici–Riccardi►►**, worth a visit to see Benozzo Gozzoli's frescos depicting the journey of the Magi (see page 113). Follow Via Cavour, Via degli Alfani, Via San Reparata and Via XXVII Aprile to reach the former convent of **Sant'Apollonia►**, whose large fresco of the Last Supper is by Andrea del Castagno (see panel on page 100).

Walk east to Piazza San Marco, perhaps pausing to view Michelangelo's *David* in the **Galleria dell' Accademia►►►** (see pages 52–3). The ex-convent on the north side of the square houses the **Museo di San Marco►►►**, devoted to the frescos and paintings of Fra Angelico (see pages 100–2). Continue eastwards to Piazza della Santissima Annunziata, one of the city's most distinctive squares. Its church, **Santissima Annunziata►►**, is known for its frescos by Andrea del Sarto and others (see page 155). Across the square is the **Ospedale degli Innocenti►** (see page 112). If time permits, go inside to see the modest museum and two Brunelleschi cloisters.

► ### Museo Nazionale di Antropologia ed Etnologia (National Museum of Anthropology and Ethnology) *IFCE4*

Palazzo Nonfinito, Via del Proconsolo 12

Few museums could be as out of place in a Florentine setting as the Museum of Anthropology and Ethnology. Founded in 1869, it was the first such museum in Italy, and is still the best of its kind in the country. In Florence, however, it suffers badly by comparison with its illustrious and better-known neighbours, and is little-visited, both for that reason and because would-be visitors are frustrated by its very restricted opening times (see below). Nevertheless, it is free and centrally placed, and is worth a quick visit in passing – perhaps if you are on the way from the Duomo to the Bargello.

The collection is housed in the 35 rooms of a palace (1593) which was left unfinished (*nonfinito* – hence its name) after the death of its architect, Buontalenti. The museum includes a range of artefacts and folk art from as far afield as Japan, Peru and Tibet. The Peruvian mummies and endless rows of desiccated skulls are ghoulishly fascinating, but of most anthropological interest is the collection relating to the Kafiri tribe of Pakistan (amassed between 1955 and 1960). Of more general appeal are the many musical instruments and the Pacific Basin exhibits collected by Captain Cook during his last voyage in 1776–9.

Open: Thursday to Saturday 9–1; third Sunday of every month 9–1 (except July to September). Admission free.

95

In a city devoted to fine art, the Anthropological Museum has something a little different to offer the visitor

The entrance to the Museo dell'Opera del Duomo: within it, many of the city's sculptural treasures are given protection from the elements

Michelangelo's *Pietà*
A late work begun around 1550, this sculpture was intended for Michelangelo's tomb. According to Vasari the head of Nicodemus was a self-portrait. The sculptor became so disenchanted with the marble, however, and with his own poor craftsmanship, that he took a hammer to Christ's left arm and leg. The resulting damage is still clearly visible. A pupil, Tiberio Calcagni, repaired the limbs and finished the (clearly inferior) figure of Mary Magdalene after Michelangelo's death.

Holy relics
Florence has relics that other cities would covet, but rather than parade them in her churches, prefers to hide them away in the Opera del Duomo museum. The museum's saintly fragments include nails from the True Cross, a finger of John the Baptist, the jaw of St Jerome, St Philip's arm, and one of the arrows that killed St Sebastian.

► ► ► **Museo dell'Opera del Duomo
(Cathedral Works Museum)**   *IFCE4*

Opera di Santa Maria del Fiore, Piazza del Duomo 9
The Opera del Duomo ('Work of the Cathedral') was created in 1296 to look after the Duomo. In 1331 it was placed under the care of the Arte della Lana (Wool Weavers' Guild). Its present home, built alongside Ghiberti's workshop, was established in the 15th century. Since 1891 it has housed works of art removed for safe keeping from the Duomo, the Battistero and the Campanile – usually those endangered by pollution.

The ground floor Michelangelo's *David* was carved in the *cortile* (courtyard) of the Opera del Duomo, a fitting prelude to a museum whose sculpture collection is second only to that of the Bargello (see pages 56–9). Now stacked with Roman sarcophagi and lesser sculpture, the *cortile* provides one or two artistic tasters before the gallery proper. On the left after the entrance is a room full of ropes, winding gear, giant pincers and other instruments used by Brunelleschi during construction of the Duomo. Another small room to the left contains Brunelleschi's grinning death-mask, plus a lop-sided and woodworm-damaged model of the dome (possibly made for the 1418 competition to settle the dome's design).

Room I contains a multitude of statues, most of them 14th-century works salvaged from Arnolfo di Cambio's quarter-finished Duomo façade before it was demolished by Ferdinand I in 1587. *Santa Reparata*, one of Florence's patron saints, sits on the left, together with a stiff-backed

Boniface VIII, one of the most vicious of popes (distinguished here by stump-like hands and a comically elongated hat). Straight ahead the heavily jowled *Madonna of the Glass Eyes* fixes her famously unsettling gaze (note the lovely pink marble and gold-backed mosaic to the rear). Donatello carved the figure of St John, one of the room's four stone Evangelists.

Room II presents a distinct contrast to Room I's stony austerity. Darker and warmer in tone, its prize exhibits are four wooden models entered in a 1588 competition to design the Duomo's new façade. Alongside stand several huge *codici,* some of the 58 sumptuously illustrated books of choral music used in the cathedral until as recently as 1930. All have been immaculately restored after being damaged in the 1966 flood. The modern octagonal chapel contains precious reliquaries and a lovely altarpiece of the Madonna and Saints Catherine and Zenobius (1334) attributed to Bernardo Daddi. A corridor of sculptural fragments leads to stairs and Michelangelo's *Pietà* (see panel opposite).

The first floor Room I contains a pair of exquisitely carved *cantorie* (choir lofts), both masterpieces of the Renaissance. They languished in storage for almost two centuries, all but forgotten after their removal from the Duomo in the 17th century. Luca della Robbia's beautifully lyrical piece on the left (1431–8) was his first major commission. It bursts with life as deliriously happy children dance and sing in line with Psalm 33's instruction: 'Praise the Lord with harp and sing unto Him …' (the psalm is inscribed in the choir's frame). The loft opposite is by Donatello (1433–9), a far more turbulent and free-spirited character. These qualities are reflected in the wild abandon of its figures – 'A rowdy lot of winged street urchins', in the words of one critic.

Below the loft stands Donatello's *Mary Magdalene* (removed from the Battistero), a hollow-eyed wooden figure of extraordinary intensity. Of the 16 figures ranged around the room (all removed from Giotto's Campanile), the most eye-catching is Donatello's bald and madly staring *Abacuc* (the Old Testament prophet Habbakuk), to which the artist himself gave the nickname *lo zuccone* (the marrow). Room II, to the left, is studded with bas-reliefs removed from the Campanile, most of them the work of Andrea Pisano. Although worn and age-blackened, their stories and allegorical content remain eminently intelligible (see also page 63).

Room III has as its centrepiece a case containing four panels from Ghiberti's Baptistery doors (see panel), now displayed here following painstaking restoration (the others will follow in due course). Do not miss the tiny Byzantine mosaic on the right wall as you enter, so finely detailed as to resemble the pages of an illuminated manuscript. Giovanni del Biondo's triptych on the long left wall depicts perhaps the most heavily arrowed St Sebastian in the canon of Italian art. The vast altar is a miracle of 14th-century Florentine goldwork, decorated in infinitesimal detail, as is the silver cross (1459) on top, crafted principally by Antonio Pollaiuolo.

Open: daily 9–7:30 (winter 9–6). Closed Sunday. Admission charge (moderate).

Detail from a Roman sarcophagus

97

Baptistery doors
All ten panels from Ghiberti's east doors will eventually be displayed in the Museo dell'Opera del Duomo. At present only four are on show:
1. The creation of Adam and Eve, original sin and the expulsion from Paradise
2. Cain the shepherd, Abel the tiller of the land, Cain slays Abel and the wrath of God
3. Joseph pulled from a pit and sold, Joseph explains the Pharoah's dreams
4. Saul and David, the battle with the Philistines, David kills Goliath.

■ **From the 14th century onwards, the most important type of wall painting in Italy was known as *fresco* (because the artist painted on to wet – or fresh – plaster). Frescos are such a familiar feature of churches and galleries in Florence and elsewhere that it is easy to forget the artistic and technical difficulties that accompanied their creation......■**

Top: frescos in the Palazzo Vecchio, Sala di Gigli

Essential frescos in Florence
Museo di San Marco (pages 100–2): Fra Angelico; Ghirlandaio (Refettorio).
Ognissanti (page 109):Ghirlandaio (Convento).
Palazzo Medici-Riccardi (page 113): Gozzoli.
Sant'Apollonia (panel, page 10): Andrea del Castagno.
Santa Croce (pages 138–43): Giotto.
Santa Maria del Carmine (pages 145–7): Masolino, Lippi, Masaccio (Cappella Brancacci).
Santa Maria Novella (pages 148–53): Masaccio, Ghirlandaio, Filippino Lippi; Andrea da Firenze (Cappellone degli Spagnoli); Uccello (Chiostro Verde).
Santa Trinita (page 154): Ghirlandaio.
Santissima Annunziata (page 155) Andrea del Sarto (Chiostrino dei Voti).

The chemistry At the heart of fresco technique is a chemical reaction, aided by the drying and fixing qualities of plaster (a mixture of lime, water and fine sand). As plaster dries, carbon dioxide is absorbed from the air, converting the lime (calcium hydroxide) to calcium carbonate. This crystallises around the sand particles, binding them to the wall. If powdered pigments (usually mineral clays and silicates) are mixed with water and applied to the wet plaster, then the carbonisation process also fixes the particles of pigment. In this way a durable surface is created in which the pigment is permanently fixed and becomes resistant to further action by water. Only the subsequent crumbling of the plaster, or chemical deterioration of the pigment itself, can then affect a fresco's colours.

The preparation Layers of plaster, or 'ground', were applied to a bare wall in several stages. The first was a thick base coat known as the *arrichio* (one part lime to three parts sand). On to this the artist incised lines to indicate the scene's main outlines. He then drew a sketch of the whole composition in red ochre. This sketch is known as the *sinopia* after the red pigment used in the drawings (many Florentine churches contain such preliminary sketches).

A daily limit Wet plaster was the key to fresco, so each day an artist could only work on an area of a painting small enough to be completed in that day, before the plaster dried. Paintings were therefore divided into sections called *giornate* (days). Each morning the artist or his assistant added a thin coat of fine white finishing plaster, or *intonaco*, to the chosen portion of *arrichio*. This obscured part of the *sinopia*, which was redrawn in *verdaccio*, a mixture of lime and black pigment. Only then was the surface ready for painting.

A race against time Artists had to work quickly, and know exactly the final effect they desired. Once the plaster had dried there was no room for correction or improvisation. Mistakes could be altered only by cutting away the day's *intonacco* and starting again. Changes of colour also proved a constant headache. The range of pigments available, for example, was initially limited, and only natural pigments were considered suitable. These tended to lighten, or lose subtleties of tone, as they dried. Surface crystals also gave an added lustre to the dry

plaster. The blending of colours was also difficult, making depth of tone difficult to achieve. Final effects were therefore accomplished with hatching, or the deft use of base coats. Parts of a fresco that were to represent flesh, for example, were given an undercoat of *terra verde,* a green earth pigment, whilst the skin tone itself was achieved using *cinabrese,* a red pigment composed of *sinopia* and lime-white.

Short cuts Although great advances were made in fresco technique during the 15th century, artists always remained in thrall to the tyranny of wet plaster. Many innovations, in any case, came too late for Florence's most famous frescos. Certain pigments, however, were introduced which could not be applied wet, and were painted instead on to dry plaster using *tempera* (where egg yolk is used to fix the pigment). Leonardo da Vinci, for example, frustrated by fresco's limitations, painted the whole of his famous but badly deteriorated *Last Supper* in Milan on dry plaster, using many new pigments of his own invention – with disastrous results. Colours added in this way were much less durable and easily flaked off the surface if subjected to external moisture. Vasari, with some justification, considered such processes 'a vile practice'.

Cartoons
These were used as detailed aids to composition as frescos became more complicated. The design was transferred to the walls by a variety of methods. The outlines were either scratched on to wet plaster, or enlarged from a small drawing on to a wall squared up for the purpose. Alternatively, small holes were made on a full-sized cartoon along the lines of the drawing and charcoal or chalk dusted through them on to the wall behind.

Andrea del Sarto's **Assumption of the Virgin,** *in the Chiostrino dei Voti of Santissima Annunziata*

MUSEO DI SAN MARCO

San Marco
If the church next to the museum is open, go in to see Fra Bartolomeo's *Madonna and Saints* (1509; second altar on the right) and the *Madonna in Prayer* (third altar on the right), a superb 8th-century mosaic which had to be cut in half during its journey from Constantinople. The join across the Virgin's midriff is still obvious. *Open*: daily 7–12:30 and 4–8.

Sant'Apollonia
Quite close to San Marco, this former convent on Via XXVII Aprile is worth seeing. Little survives of the old building save a vestibule with paintings by Paolo Schiavo and Neri di Bicci, but one entire wall of the room beyond, the former monastic refectory, is covered by a fresco of the Last Supper (1450), the unsettling masterpiece of Andrea del Castagno. Above are much-ruined murals of the Crucifixion, Deposition and Resurrection. The sinopie underlying these frescos (see pages 98–9), were discovered during restoration and are displayed at the opposite end of the room. *Open*: daily 9–2 (Sunday 9–1). Closed Monday. Admission free.

▶▶▶   **Museo di San Marco**   *IFCE5*
Piazza San Marco

Busy with traffic roaring to and from the city centre, and usually thronged by students from the nearby university buildings, Piazza San Marco is a long way from anyone's idea of monastic calm. On its north side, however, stands the baroque-fronted church of San Marco (see panel) and its erstwhile convent which is now well known as a museum devoted almost entirely to the paintings of Fra Angelico. Owned first by Vallombrosan and then by Sylvestrine monks, the convent was given to the Dominicans in 1436 after a word to Pope Eugenius IV from Cosimo de' Medici. The monks moved from their previous home in Fiesole, and the following year Cosimo assumed financial responsibility for the convent, deciding, in the words of Vasari, that it should be 'rebuilt on a larger and more magnificent scale … with all the conveniences which the friars could desire.' Cosimo's largesse was partly to assuage the guilt stirred by his banking successes (usury was still a sin in the eyes of the Church). 'Never', he announced to the monks, unnerved by his generosity, 'shall I be able to give God enough to set him down as my debtor.'

The Medici's pet architect, Michelozzo, was commissioned to design the building, described by Vasari as 'the best appointed, finest and most convenient convent in Italy.' It was consecrated in 1444, with theologian Antonino Pierozzi (1389–1459) as its founding Dominican prior (he was later to become Archbishop of Florence). Subsequent priors were to include Fra Angelico and, even more famously, Savonarola (1491), who was eventually besieged and captured in the convent before being tried and executed in Piazza della Signoria (see pages 40–1).

The ground floor After buying your ticket you enter the **Chiostro di Sant'Antonino** (Cloister of Sant'Antonino), designed by Michelozzo and named after the convent's first prior. Most of the faded frescos here, panels on the life of Sant'Antonino, date from the 16th century. Fra Angelico's contribution consists of four small frescos in the four corners of the cloister.

Turn right in the cloister and immediately on your right you enter the **Ospizio dei Pellegrini**, the spot where visiting pilgrims were offered hospitality. Now it is home to most of the museum's free-standing paintings, most of them brought from elsewhere when the convent was suppressed and turned into a museum. Its two most famous works occupy the opposing end walls. On your right as you enter stands Fra Angelico's *Deposition* (c.1440), an altarpiece removed from Santa Trinita. It was originally commissioned by the Strozzi family from Lorenzo Monaco, who completed only the top three triangular pinnacles before his death. On the opposite end wall hangs the *Madonna dei Linaiuoli*, commissioned by the *linaiuoli*, or flax-workers' guild, for their headquarters. Angelico came to painting comparatively late in life, and this tabernacle, painted in 1433 (when he was 33) was among his earliest major commissions. The magnificent frame was designed by Lorenzo Ghiberti.

Other masterpieces to look out for include panels from the *Life of Christ*, originally used as cupboard doors in

Santissima Annunziata, and an altarpiece of the Last Judgement (1431) in which the saved are shown in their finery, and the damned stripped bare in readiness for the tortures of hell.

Located off the far right-hand corner of the cloister, the small **lavatorium** contains two works by Uccello and three by Fra Angelico. Off to the right is the **Refettorio Maggiore** (Great Refectory), dominated by an eye-catching *Last Supper* (but otherwise filled with insignificant paintings). Off to the left are two smaller rooms, the first with seven winsome 'portraits' by Fra Bartolomeo and a large sepia fresco around the walls, the second graced by a narrow panel by Benozzo Gozzoli, a pupil of Fra Angelico.

Back out in the courtyard the entrance to the **Sala Capitolare** (Chapter House) lies to the right of the huge convent bell. The single vaulted room contains a large but rather over-restored *Crucifixion and Saints* (1442) by Fra Angelico. The convent bell also marks the entrance to the museum's shop and the first floor. Before taking the stairs up to the Dormitory Cells, however, turn left into the **Refettorio**, home to a large *Last Supper (Cenacolo)* by Domenico Ghirlandaio (an almost exact facsimile of his similar work in Ognissanti – see page 109). Beyond lies the **Foresteria** (Guest Rooms), reached along a gloomy corridor of unintelligible stone fragments, worth visiting mainly for the views it offers of the (closed) Cloister of San Domenico.

> **The Annunciation**
> This was a favourite theme with Florentine painters, partly because, according to the Florentine calendar, New Year's Day fell on 25 March, the Feast of the Annunciation. The city dated the start of its year *ab incarnazione* – from the conception or incarnation of Christ (nine months before Christmas). Parallels with pagan spring fertility rituals, and with the Roman New Year, which started with the spring equinox (21 March) are inescapable. The Florentine calendar survived until 1750, when the reforming Dukes of Lorraine, inheriting Florence from the Medici, adopted the papal calendar.

101

The first floor One of the loveliest masterpieces of the Renaissance stops you in your tracks at the top of the stairs – Fra Angelico's simple but sublimely beautiful *Annunciation* (see panel). Notice the inscription, a reminder to monks to say a Hail Mary as they pass the painting. Beyond, under a huge-beamed roof, the rest of the first floor is taken up by the **Dormitory Cells**, 44 small

Fra Angelico's Annunciation

MUSEO DI S MARCO

Visitors admire the paintings of Fra Angelico in the Museo di San Marco

The Chiostro dello Scalzo
Knock on the door a minute from San Marco at Via Cavour 69 for admission to this small cloister containing 16 skilful monochrome frescos of the Cardinal Virtues and scenes from the life of John the Baptist, both early works by Andrea del Sarto. The cloister is all that remains of a convent once owned by the Brotherhood of St John, an order whose monks walked around *scalzo* (barefoot). *Open*: Monday and Thursday 9–1. Admission free.

monastic cells, most of them frescoed by Fra Angelico and his assistants between 1439 and 1445. The cells on the left side of the corridor ahead of you (nos 1–11) contain the frescos most confidently attributed to Fra Angelico (notice cells 17 and 22, whose floors conceal 'secret', recently discovered medieval frescos). The expressive *Madonna and Saints* on the corridor's right-hand wall is by Fra Angelico.

Turn right at the end of the corridor, and at the far end of the next (south) corridor are three cells once occupied by Savonarola (nos 12–14). His erstwhile presence is commemorated by an unexceptional memorial and two powerful portraits (the bloodied head in one of the portraits is an allusion to Peter the Martyr, an eminent Dominican martyred by having a cleaver sunk in his skull). Also here is a copy of a painting depicting Savonarola's execution, and fragments of the stake to which he was tied when the bonfire was lit.

Turn right at the *Annunciation* to pass Europe's first public library, instigated by Cosimo de' Medici in 1441 (and designed by Michelozzo). A short way beyond are two cells (nos 38 and 39) used by Cosimo personally, both significantly larger than the others, and each decorated with two frescos, as opposed to the one allocated to each of the monks.

Open: daily 9–2. Closed Monday. Admission charge (moderate).

►   **Museo Stibbert**   *IFCE6*
Via Federico Stibbert 26
Were it not so far from the city centre, the Museo Stibbert would doubtless have achieved cult status long ago. As it is, few people make the trek into Florence's northern suburbs to sample its bizarre collection. Remarkable for its 50,000 exhibits – which range from buttons to bronzes – it is almost as alluring for the eccen-

MUSEO STIBBERT

Practicalities
The Museo Stibbert is 1.5km north of San Marco. Buses 31 or 32 run here from the railway station.

Stibbert's park
Stibbert created a small park alongside his house which is open to visitors daily, 9–dusk.

tric decoration of its 64-room labyrinth (part of a 14th-century mansion).

Half-Scottish, half-Italian, Frederick Stibbert (1838–1906) was born in Florence, distinguishing himself in Garibaldi's army before inheriting a fortune and becoming an artist, traveller, intimate of Queen Victoria and inveterate collector. After being left the house as part of his inheritance, he bought an adjoining *palazzo* and adapted the two to serve as a joint home and museum. Alterations made after his death are now being removed, returning the rooms to the wonderfully gloomy Gothic state in which Stibbert left them.

Stibbert's passion was militaria, and the museum contains what many consider one of the world's greatest collections of armour, much of it arranged on a phalanx of mannequins, magnificently drawn up as if ready for battle, in the mansion's Great Hall. Etruscan, Roman, oriental and medieval pieces are all here, as well as novelties such as the costume worn by Napoleon when he was crowned King of Italy (in Room 50, the *Sala Impero*).

Even if armour fails to appeal, you will find something to captivate, be it tapestries, gilded candelabra, malachite fireplaces, snuff-boxes, Murano glass chandeliers, flags from the Sienese Palio, pre-Raphaelite paintings (some by Stibbert himself), stained glass, small bronzes, French furniture, Oriental porcelain, bronze washbasins, family photographs, and even Stibbert's dress kilt – altogether an eclectic assemblage, representing the fruits of Stibbert's many magpie-like obsessions. The museum's best paintings, incidentally, are those by Carlo Crivelli and Botticelli (attributed) in the *Sala delle Bandiere* (Room 32), and Pietro Lorenzetti's *Crucifixion* upstairs in Room 36. *Open*: daily 9–1; guided tours only (hourly, on the hour), except Sunday, when visitors may wander at will, though usually no more than a dozen rooms are open. Closed Thursday. Admission charge (moderate), except Sunday.

Detail of Fra Angelico's Deposition, in the Museo di San Marco

MUSEO DI STORIA DELLA SCIENZA

104

The Accademia del Cimento

The world's first academy for scientific experiment was founded in 1657 by two former pupils of Galileo, Grand Duke Ferdinand II and his brother Prince (later Cardinal) Leopold. *Cimento* means 'trial' or 'experiment'. The Academy's motto was 'Try and try again', testimony to Galileo's empirical methods of inquiry, deduction and proof by experiment. First housed in the Palazzo Pitti – where the kiln in the Giardino di Boboli was used to produce scientific glassware – the *Cimento* now has its home in the museum's Palazzo dei Castellani, previously home to the Accademia della Crusca, founded in 1582 to study the Italian language.

Galileo's telescope

▶▶ **Museo di Storia della Scienza (Museum of the History of Science)**   *IFCE3*

Piazza dei Giudici 1

Although Florence's artistic star waned in the 16th and 17th centuries, the achievements of men like Galileo, working under the patronage of sympathetic rulers such as Ferdinand II and Cosimo II, ensured that the city remained at the forefront of science and learning. Something of the flavour of the times is captured in this fascinating museum which, as befits a gallery given over to science and rational thought, is one of the most carefully presented in the city. Although it is devoted to science (each room deals with a different scientific theme), it would be a mistake to think its appeal is for specialists only. As well as revealing a different historical side to the city (distinct from art and architecture), its old instruments and miscellaneous exhibits are endlessly fascinating and often extremely beautiful.

The first floor Rooms 1–3 display cases full of astronomical, mathematical and navigational instruments. Like many of the museum's displays, these require close scrutiny for a full appreciation of their intricate beauty. In Room 1, the left-hand case on the right-hand wall contains compasses that belonged to Michelangelo. In Room 2 look out for the quadrant (no 42), studded with beautiful enamel vignettes, and Sir Samuel Morland's early calculating machine. In Room 3 the large Tuscan astrolabe (no 27) and coloured polyhedrons command most attention. Room 4 is devoted to Galileo's instruments, notably a large inclined wooden plane used to demonstrate the acceleration of bodies. Slightly less prosaic are the bones of the middle finger of Galileo's left hand, kept on the top shelf of a case on the room's left. They were removed when his body was transferred to the church of Santa Croce. Also here is the lens used by Galileo to discover the moons of Jupiter. The scientist deliberately cracked the lens before he presented it to Ferdinand II.

Room 5 contains telescopes, including two belonging to Galileo (in a case on the left). Many are covered in leather or marbled paper, graphic illustrations of the Florentines' ability to turn even utilitarian objects into works of art. Highlights in Room 6 are some amusing optical games, though you are quickly tempted to Room 7, whose glorious displays of maps and globes make it perhaps the museum's most impressive room. Notice, in particular, the detailed but hopelessly impractical map on the left wall, which shows the known world radiating from the Holy Land. Take in, too, the eccentric coffee table, also on the left, etched with a marble map (1694) depicting the course of the Danube. Microscopes in Room 9 lead into a room devoted to the Accademia del Cimento (see panel), the body that, along with the Medici, amassed most of the museum's exhibits. A menagerie of barometers and telescopes follows (Room 11), looking for all the world like a battery of medieval cannons.

The second floor The lovely timepieces in Room 12 probe the mysteries of the mechanical clock, investigating the finer points of escapement, mainspring, pendulum, and striking mechanism. Room 13 records the advances made in mathematical instruments in the 18th and 19th centuries, a theme continued in Room 14, where the accelerating pace of scientific discovery is reflected in the increasing variety of magnetic, electro-static and electro-magnetic instruments. Succeeding rooms of pneumatic and hydrostatic exhibits are less arresting, though Room 18 brings you up short with some alarming surgical instruments and a collection of horrify-ing anatomical models made of wax. Expectant mothers should pass these up, for they deal mainly with obstetric complications, breech births and all manner of less than straightforward passages into the world. As a literal account of where babies come from, however, few exhibits could be as graphic or as compelling.

Things calm down again in Room 19, which analyses the role of the alchemist and medieval pharmacist. Notice the jars and vases which advertise such unlikely medicines as *Coca Boliviana* (Bolivian cocaine), *Sangue del Drago* (dragon's blood) and *Confetti di Seme Santo* (confections made of blessed seed).

Open: daily 9:30–1; Monday, Wednesday and Friday also 2–5. Closed Sunday. Admission charge (expensive).

Practicalities
The science museum is arranged over two floors, each room being devoted to a particular branch of science or technology. On each floor be sure to pick up the excellent free guides, available in four languages, which not only describe each room's con-tents, but also explain the exhibits' historical and sci-entific background.

The History of Science Museum will fascinate all visitors, scientists and non-scientists alike

■ **Physicist, astronomer and mathematician, Galileo Galilei was the first modern scientist. He revolutionised the study of astronomy and mechanics, insisting on an empirical approach to all scientific enquiry. Unfortunately for him, his objectivity was not welcomed by the Church, and his beliefs could easily have seen him executed by the Inquisition as a heretic......■**

Galileo Galilei

Galileo was born in Pisa in 1564, the son of a musician. He moved, with his family, to Florence in 1574. After a period with the monks of Vallombrosa, his education involved a short spell at the University of Pisa, where lack of funds prevented him from completing his degree (in medicine). An iconoclast from the outset, he dissented from even basic orthodoxies, refusing, for example, to wear the university's toga outside the classroom. After returning to Florence, he published a paper describing the hydrostatic balance, an invention which made his name throughout Italy. He then moved to a university post in Pisa, where – famously – he is said to have dropped weights from the Leaning Tower to disprove Aristotle's assertion that bodies of different masses fall at different speeds. In 1592 he secured the chair of mathematics at Padua, a post he was to hold for 18 years.

The moons of Jupiter
'I have discovered four planets, neither known nor observed by any one of the astronomers before my time, which have their orbits around a certain bright star, one of those previously known, like Venus and Mercury round the sun, and are sometimes in front of it, sometimes behind it, though they never depart beyond certain limits. All which facts were discovered and observed a few days ago by the help of the telescope devised by me, through God's grace first enlightening my mind.' *The Starry Messenger* (1610)

Galileo's discoveries Dutch glass-makers, not Galileo, invented the telescope (in 1608), but within a year Galileo had taken the Dutch original and produced a model 10 times as powerful, which was soon in demand all over Europe. Equipped with this new tool Galileo made a series of astronomical discoveries, expounded in a ground-breaking paper of 1610, *Sidereus Nuncis* (*The Starry Messenger*). The first to observe the moon's surface, he was also the first to realise that the Milky Way consisted of stars. He discovered Jupiter's four principal moons, which he named the Sidera Medicea (Medicean Stars), after his former pupil and future patron, Grand Duke Cosimo II. He went on to make observations of the moons of Saturn, the phases of Venus, and sunspots travelling across the sun's surface, suggesting the sun was not a perfect sphere, as traditional philosophy had maintained.

Science and religion In the summer of 1610 Galileo left Padua to become 'first philosopher and mathematician' to Grand Duke Cosimo II. Freed by the move to spend more time on research, he confirmed, in his own mind at least, the Copernican heliocentric view of the heavens – that the Earth and other planets orbited the sun. This was contrary to the Ptolemaic assertion, long supported by the Church, that the Earth was at the centre of the universe. Seeing its vested interests threatened, the Church rose against him, the Jesuits asserting he would do more damage in the fight against Protestantism 'than Luther and Calvin put together.' The crunch came in 1616 with the Inquisition's decree declaring Copernicus 'false and erroneous'. Galileo was told he could neither 'hold nor defend' the doctrine. In private, however, Cardinal Bellarmine, the pope's chief theologian, told Galileo his ideas could be discussed as 'mathematical supposition.' In doing so he tacitly acknowledged Galileo's genius, underlining at the same time the gulf that was to separate religious faith and scientific 'truth'.

Papal support Galileo then lay low at his house in Bellosguardo for seven years. A paper he published during this time contained the famous assertion that the 'Book of Nature … is written in mathematical characters.' A virtuoso treatise of 1632 reopened old wounds, and this time the Jesuits were determined to bring the scientist down. Galileo's supporters, however, included Pope Urban VIII, who (as Maffeo Barberini) had been his lifelong friend and protector. Though he could not prevent a trial, the pope was able to ensure Galileo was tried on lesser charges, which, if upheld, would at least not lead to the scientist's execution. In June 1633, the Inquisition forced Galileo to kneel in the church of Santa Maria sopra Minerva in Rome and agree that he 'abjured, cursed and detested' his errors. Imprisonment was waived on condition that he remained in Florence under the protection of Ferdinand II. Overcoming house arrest and the onset of blindness, Galileo continued with scientific work until his death in 1642.

Laws of motion

Galileo's work on the movement of bodies was as important as his more famous astronomical discoveries. In establishing mechanics as a science, he paved the way for the theories of the English physicist and mathematician Isaac Newton, born in the year of Galileo's death. He defined the laws governing pendulum motion, and in 1640 wrote a treatise on which the Dutch scientist, Huygens, based his own invention of the first mechanical pendulum clock. He formulated the laws of parabolic motion (the curving path followed by a ball thrown in the air as it falls to the ground). He also studied the natural acceleration of bodies in free fall; discovered the nature of percussive force; devised a rudimentary thermometer; patented a device to raise water; and discovered the brachistochrone (the shortest path taken by any object describing a curve as it moves).

Galileo's tomb in Santa Croce

►► **Museo Zoologico – La Specola**
(Zoological Museum) *IFCC2*

Via Romana 17

Most people come to the zoological museum not for its stuffed animals but to revel in Florence's strangest museum collection, the Cere Anatomiche, a wonderfully stomach-turning assemblage of anatomical waxworks. Finding this little house of horrors, however, is something of a battle, for it is not signposted either from the street or within the dour *palazzo* (formerly an astronomical observatory, 'La Specola') at Via Romana 17. To find it, walk straight on at the threshold, keeping the courtyard car park on your right, and at the statue of Torricelli climb the stairs to the third floor.

The ghoulish show opens with hundreds of identical glass cases, filled with some 1,400 lovingly constructed models of arms, legs and internal organs. It culminates in several splayed and dissected wax corpses, each sinew, nerve fibre and blood vessel sculpted in the most careful detail. All around, the museum's worn, rather lurid red tiles serve to heighten the charnel-house atmosphere, which is emphasised still more by the sickly yellow hue

The plague
The poet Longfellow musing on the character of Zumbo, creator of the plague tableau, wrote: 'a man of the most gloomy and saturnine imagination, and more akin to the worm ... thus to have revelled night and day in the hideous mysteries of death, corruption, and the charnel-house. It is strange how this representation haunts one ... with its loathsome corpses, with "the blackening, the swelling, the bursting of the trunk – the worm, the rat, and the tarantula at work." You breathe more freely as you step out into the open air ... the bright sunshine ... the crowded busy streets.' *Outre-mer: A Pilgrimage Beyond the Sea* (1833–4)

One of the hundreds of anatomical waxworks on view in Florence's most macabre museum

pervading many of the ageing models. Created as a teaching aid, the collection dates from 1775–1814.

There are, however, several more highlights (if they can be called that), notably the chastening obstetrics section and a famous four-piece tableau of Florence during the plague. The latter – not for the squeamish – is tucked away in a small room on the left side of the museum (through the rooms devoted to dissected animals). Made by a Sicilian cleric, it comprises four three-dimensional vignettes worthy of Dante's *Inferno*. All are very obviously the product of a disturbed imagination (see panel opposite). The corpses of men, women and children are shown piled high, each in various stages of colourful putrescence. Smaller details, though, prove even more blood-curdling – such as the rats gnawing at curled intestines, and the tiny clumps of mushrooms growing from the mulch of human and animal detritus.

Open: Waxworks: Tuesday, Saturday and the last Sunday in the month 9–12. Admission free.

▶ **Ognissanti** *IFCC4*

Piazza d'Ognissanti

Florence's early mercantile dynamism owed much to the Umiliati, a skilled Benedictine order brought from Lombardy in the 13th century to help foster the city's nascent woollen industry. On land leased by the *Comune* in 1239, much of it near the Arno, they built workshops and the church (completed in 1259) that was to become Ognissanti (All Saints). Under their sway the area became a focus of the city's carding, weaving and dyeing industries. Some idea of the Order's stature can be gained from the fact that it commissioned the great Giotto to paint an altarpiece for its church – the stupendous *Maestà* that now forms a majestic introduction to the Uffizi.

In 1561 the church passed to the Franciscans, who instigated two centuries' worth of 'improvements'. These spared the old campanile but produced a baroque façade (one of the city's earliest) which outraged Florentines by flouting what they considered to be Tuscany's architectural traditions.

Inside, amid the gloom of murky baroque decor and grey stone altars, lie several points of artistic and historical interest. The second altar on the right contains two early works by brothers Davide and Domenico Ghirlandaio. In the lower, *The Madonna of Mercy*, the Virgin's cloak protects the Vespucci, a merchant family who hailed from the surrounding area. Between the Virgin and the dark-cloaked man is the young boy who was to give his name to a continent, – Amerigo Vespucci. The woman beneath her left hand is Simonetta Vespucci, mistress to Giuliano de' Medici and reputedly the most beautiful woman of her age. Legend has it that she was the model for Botticelli's famous *Venus*, in the Uffizi.

The claim may not be too far-fetched, for Botticelli also came from the parish of Ognissanti. It was he who painted the fresco between Ognissanti's third and fourth altars, *St Augustine's Vision of St Jerome*, mirrored by Ghirlandaio's *St Jerome* on the opposite side of the nave. Moreover, Botticelli is buried in the church, beneath a round pavement tomb in the south transept.

The Last Supper
Ognissanti's convent refectory, entered through a cloister to the left of the church, contains a superb fresco of the Last Supper (1480) by Ghirlandaio, a variation on his similar painting in the Museo di San Marco (see pages 100–2). It is thought to have inspired Leonardo da Vinci's famous *Last Supper* in Milan. *Open*: Monday, Tuesday and Saturday 9–12. Admission free.

Ponte alla Carraia
To the south of Ognissanti stood the city's second oldest bridge after the Ponte Vecchio. The original, built around 1218, was entrusted to Ognissanti's Umiliati, who built a new bridge in 1269. That bridge collapsed in 1304, buckled by the weight of spectators who had gathered to watch the Calendimaggio (Maytime) celebrations. Today's Ponte alla Carraia is a modern copy of the bridge's 16th-century replacement. Its name derives from the *carri* (carts) used at one time to carry raw and finished wool across the Arno between the cloth-making districts of Ognissanti and San Frediano.

Miraculous Madonna
'The sick were healed, the lame walked again, and the possessed were liberated,' wrote chronicler Giovanni Villani of Orsanmichele's miraculous Madonna fresco. '... people came there on pilgrimage from all over Tuscany ... bringing many wax images to record the miracles wrought.'
Cronache Fiorentine (1300)

Andrea Orcagna
Although few works survive, Orcagna (1308–68) was the most important Florentine painter, sculptor and architect after Giotto's death during the mid-14th century. There are damaged frescos in S Croce and S Spirito, but Orsanmichele's tabernacle is his best Florentine work.

Palazzo dell'Arte della Lana
This is the lovely building opposite the entrance to Orsanmichele, decorated with a tabernacle and exterior fresco and a fine set of wooden eaves. The decoration is ersatz 19th-century medievalism, however. A covered passage on the first floor gives access to Orsanmichele's medieval upper storeys.
Open: Monday to Saturday 9–2; Sunday 9–12.30. Admission free.

Statues
Starting on Via dei Calzaiuoli and working left to right, Orsanmichele's surviving statues and copies are:1. *John the Baptist*, Ghiberti; 2. *Quattro Coronati*, Nanni di Banco (for the Masons' and Carpenters' Guild – notice the workmen in the lower relief); 3. *St George*, Donatello (original in the Bargello); 4. *St Matthew*, Ghiberti; 5. *St Stephen*, Ghiberti; 6. *St Eligius*, Nanni di Banco; 7. *St Mark*, Donatello; 8. *Madonna and Child*, Lamberti; 9. *St John*, Baccio di Montelupo.

▶▶ **Orsanmichele**   *IFCD3*

Via dei Calzaiuoli

Few churches are as calm and beguiling as Orsanmichele, whose deceptively gaunt bulk punctuates the walk between the Duomo and Piazza della Signoria. The first church on the site appeared around 750, an oratory nestled in the kitchen garden of a Benedictine monastery. The present name derives from these humble roots – a contraction of San Michele ad Hortum and then San Michele in Orto (*orto* still means 'vegetable garden' in Italian). The oratory was destroyed in 1239 to make way for a grain market, completed around 1280, possibly to a design by Arnolfo di Cambio. Religious associations, however, continued to cling to the site. The most notable was a fresco of the Virgin (painted on one of the market's pillars), an image whose supposed miracle-working powers attracted countless pilgrims to the area (see panel). In the end the Madonna's popularity led to the building of a small chapel and the founding of a religious confraternity.

Both market and Virgin, however, were victims of a great fire that swept Florence in 1304, destroying some 1700 buildings. Rebuilding started in 1336, probably to designs by Francesco Talenti, who constructed an open loggia on the market's ground floor (the upper storeys were set aside for emergency supplies of grain). In 1380, however, the market was relocated and the loggia's open arches bricked up. By this time it had been decided to retain the granary but turn the lower floor into a church – the present Orsanmichele.

Decoration of Talenti's new trade hall assumed an importance never before seen in Florence. As early as 1339 it was decided to provide each of the loggia's pillars with a statue, responsibility for the decoration being assigned to the city's leading guilds. Each was to commission a statue of its patron saint to fill the appropriate niche. Over the next 60 years, however, only one statue materialised (the Arte della Lana's *St Stephen*). In the meantime, most of the loggia – by now a church – had already received most of its interior decoration (see below). In 1408, exasperated by the delay, the city council set a 10-year deadline for completion of the outstanding statues, reserving the right to allocate niches to other guilds if the commissions remained unfulfilled.

In the long run the guilds' foot-dragging was to posterity's benefit. Instead of statues executed at a time when Florentine sculpture was in the doldrums, the niches were filled with work from the first wave of great Renaissance artists – Verrocchio, Ghiberti, Donatello, Luca della Robbia and others. Not all the statues have remained in their intended places: some of the 14 niches are now either empty or filled with copies (though you can still admire the beautifully carved surrounds). The originals have been removed to a variety of galleries for safe keeping (see panel).

Orsanmichele's entrance is at the rear, tucked away from the razzamatazz of Via dei Calzaiuoli. Inside is a dusky and peaceful oasis studded with indistinct patches of fresco peeping from shadowy, dark-stone walls. Most of the fragments depict the guilds' patron saints, painted to complement the statues outside. As your eyes become accustomed to the gloom, notice the bricked-up arches of the old loggia, its arcaded outline still clearly visible. Notice, too (not that it is easily missed), the glorious Tabernacle to the rear, a glittering glass and marble masterpiece bathed in the soft yellow glow of candlelight. Created by Andrea Orcagna, and 11 years in the making (1348–59), it is the most beautiful work of its kind in Italy. It was financed by donations that flooded into Orsanmichele's religious confraternity. (In its first year – 1348, the year of the great plague – these offerings amounted to more than the total sum raised by the city in taxes.) At its heart lies a lovely *Madonna and Child* (1347) by Bernardo Daddi, said to have inherited miraculous powers from the fresco of the Virgin that was destroyed by the fire of 1304.

Open: daily 9–12 and 4–6. Admission free.

High praise
'Orsanmichele … is the complete, unravaged child of the Renaissance. There more than anywhere one can feel the continuity of the Florentine spirit, with all its seriousness, its humanity and its unexpected level of beauty.'
Kenneth Clark, *The Other Half* (1977)

Orcagna's Tabernacle

111

Spedale degli Innocenti ling Hospital and its Museum

12739

N. 12739

▶ ▬▬ **Ospedale degli Innocenti**   *IFCE5*

Piazza Santissima Annunziata

The Ospedale degli Innocenti (Foundling Hospital) is but one component (with the church of Santissima Annunziata – see page 155) of **Piazza Santissima Annunziata▶**, widely reported to be the most beautiful square in Florence. In reality, it does not quite live up to its billing, its Renaissance lines no match for some of Tuscany's medieval squares. Worse still, today its harmony is compromised by traffic and backpackers.

Begun by Brunelleschi in the 1420s, the piazza was then saddled with 200 years of minor modifications by architects from Ammannati to Antonio da Sangallo. Their additions did remarkably little to upset its overall unity, however. The equestrian statue at its heart is Giambologna's *Ferdinand I*, the sculptor's last work (1608). Less eye-catching, but more bizarre, are the two smaller fountains by Giambologna's pupil, Pietro Tacca – a pair of water monkeys spraying two bearded sea-slugs.

The Ospedale degli Innocenti, along the piazza's eastern edge, was established in 1419 by the *Arte della Seta*, the Silk Weavers' Guild, and designed and built over the next seven years by Brunelleschi. Europe's first orphanage (and still operating as such), its function is advertised on the façade by Andrea della Robbia's medallions (1487) of blithe children wrapped in swaddling clothes. Under the nine-arched loggia (1432), one of the earliest creations of the Renaissance, notice the *rota* on the far left. Built in 1660, it contained a small revolving door used to receive abandoned children. This was bricked up in 1875.

Inside, you pay to see Brunelleschi's central Chiostro degli Uomini (Men's Cloister) and its narrow neighbour, off to the right, the Choistro delle Donne (Women's Cloister). The ticket also admits you to the Ospedale's small gallery, reached by stairs from the cloisters' left-hand corner. Among the paintings, only Domenico Ghirlandaio's *Coronation of the Virgin* and Botticelli's *Madonna and Child* stand out, together with a simple terracotta *Madonna and Child* by Luca della Robbia. *Open*: daily 8:30–2 (Sunday 8:30–1). Closed Wednesday. Admission charge (inexpensive).

Brunelleschi's loggia frames Pietro Tacca's fountain

Gozzoli's Journey of the Magi *includes portraits of prominent Medici*

Rustication
According to Michelozzo the purpose of rustication (building with huge, rough-hewn blocks of stone – to be seen all over Florence) was to 'unite an appearance of solidity and strength with the light and shade so essential to beauty under the glare of an Italian sun.'

▶▶ **Palazzo Medici-Riccardi**   *IFCE5*

Via Cavour 1

Amid the cacophony of Via Cavour, the seat of the city's greatest dynasty could easily be overlooked as just another grime-covered *palazzo*. Most people come here to see Benozzo Gozzoli's sublime fresco cycle, the *Journey of the Magi* (1459). Before seeing it, however, spare a moment for the palace itself, built by Michelozzo for Cosimo de' Medici in 1444. The design, with its heavy rusticated ground-floor exterior (see panel), was to influence numerous buildings in the century of palace-building that followed (notably the Palazzo Pitti and Palazzo Strozzi). It remained the Medici's principal residence until 1540, when Cosimo I moved to the Palazzo Vecchio.

Gozzoli's tiny frescoed chapel comes as a beautiful surprise after traipsing through the palace's bureaucratic gloom. Its frescos, commissioned by Piero de' Medici, were painted in honour of the Compagnia dei Magi, one of the city's most prestigious religious confraternities (of which the Medici were members). The oriental splendour of the figures in the paintings may also reflect the appearance of Greek and Ottoman visitors to the ecumenical Council of Florence, held in 1439. Several of the Medici are portrayed as kings and attendants, whilst the Magi's journey itself recalls the pageantry of the confraternity's annual procession through Florence.

Ignore, for a moment, the frescos on either side of the altar (the landscapes are by Gozzoli) and concentrate on the chapel's three main walls. Each deals with one of the three kings. The first, on the right wall, depicts an immense procession, headed by a courtly figure on horseback – probably an idealised portrait of Lorenzo the Magnificent. Cosimo rides behind on another white horse, followed by his brother Lorenzo (in conical hat, riding a mule). Piero de' Medici, hatless, is between them. Head-on, behind the bowman, is Piero's younger son, Giuliano. The scene on the rear wall contains a lovely pastoral background of green hills and tower-filled villages. In the final scene the maroon-cloaked king astride a mule is surrounded by colourful details of the kind that make Gozzoli's work so appealing – leopards, monkeys, ducks, giraffes and falcons with their bleeding prey.

Open: daily 9–1 and 3–6 (Sunday 9–1). Closed Wednesday. Admission charge (moderate).

Finding the way
Finding Gozzoli's frescos can be tricky. Walk through the first courtyard to the walled side garden (a rare survival of what was once a common feature of medieval *palazzi*). Buy your ticket and return to the courtyard. With your back to the entrance, take the first doorway on the right and climb the stairs to the second floor. To see the chapel's former altarpiece, take the second door on the right in the main courtyard as you enter from the street, and climb to the first floor. The picture, by Filippo Lippi, is in the triangular container off the windowed gallery.

Self–portrait
Gozzoli has painted himself on the left of the crowded procession that follows the king in the fresco on the right-hand wall of the chapel. He stands a couple of rows from the rear in the ranks of red-hatted figures. His hat bears the words OPVS BENOTII ('Benoti's Work') in a gold-lettered band. This particular type of hat was favoured by scholars of the day.

■ **Markets often lend heart and character to a city, and those of Florence are no exception. Choose between the Mercato Centrale's superb food stalls and the souvenir–oriented stalls of San Lorenzo, or between the rougher-edged bustle of Sant'Ambrogio and the more Bohemian atmosphere of the markets in the Cascine and Piazza dei Ciompi......■**

114

Porcellino
'Little Pig' is the affectionate name given by Florentines to the bronze statue of a huge wild boar alongside the Mercato Nuovo. If you rub his polished snout and throw a coin in the fountain, tradition has it that you will return to Florence (all the money, incidentally, goes to charity). A copy of an ancient Roman statue now in the Uffizi, it was cast (*c*.1612) by Giambologna's pupil Pietro Tacca, the sculptor responsible for the eccentric sea-creatures in Piazza Santissima Annunziata (see page 112).

The Cascine
Florence's largest and busiest general market spreads through the gardens of the Cascine every Tuesday morning (7–1; see page 73).

San Lorenzo Florence's most central market, San Lorenzo is the one you will probably stumble on first. Usually thronged with visitors, including many foreigners, the sprawl of stalls fills the streets north of Piazza San Lorenzo. With its predictable panoply of fakes, clothes and leatherware, this market is more a spot to wander and soak up the atmosphere than a place for serious purchases (though there are bargains to be had). The open-air crowds make a welcome change from sightseeing, but beware of pickpockets.
Open: daily 8–7. Closed Sunday and Monday in winter.

Mercato Centrale Situated at the heart of San Lorenzo's labyrinthine market, the Mercato Centrale is one of Europe's largest covered food halls. Built in 1874 and given an extra floor in 1980, it is a fantastic and flamboyant medley of colour and activity, crammed with fruit, vegetables, bread, meat, cheese, herbs, pasta and seasonal specialities such as figs, truffles, wild boar, cherries and plump *porcini* mushrooms. Some of the city's best delicatessens are gathered here, notably *Il Forteo* and *Baroni*, not to mention numerous bars, and cheap hole-in-the-wall *trattorie* like *Ottavino*, *Zà-zà* and *Da Nerbone*. Whether you come to buy picnic supplies, or to revel in the atmosphere and sheer entertainment value, this is as essential a spot to visit as any of the city's museums and galleries.
Open: Monday to Saturday 7–2, additionally Saturday 4–8.

Sant'Ambrogio Located to the northeast of Santa Croce in Piazza Lorenzo Ghiberti, Sant'Ambrogio is a more rumbustious and more down-at-heel version of the Mercato Centrale. Aimed at Florence's working population, it feels much more like a rural, small-town market. Wander the food stalls, watch the people and enjoy the atmosphere – and the prices, which are among the lowest in the city. The lunch counter and coffee bar inside make handy refreshment stops.
Open: Monday to Friday 7–2.

Piazza dei Ciompi Big-city flea markets these days rarely offer bargains, and Piazza dei Ciompi's modest *Mercato delle Pulci*, a couple of minutes' walk to the north of Sant'Ambrogio, is unfortunately no exception. Prices for its medley of books, coins, uniforms and bric-a-brac are often as high as those in the city's antique shops. Nonetheless you can pick up the odd bargain and, as ever,

it is fun to browse. If you do intend to haggle seriously, come to the much larger second-hand market held in the square on the first Sunday of every month (except July).

On the north side of the piazza is the Loggia del Pesce, built by Vasari for the fishmongers (*pesce* means 'fish') of the Mercato Vecchio when their market was moved in 1568.

Open: Tuesday to Saturday 8–1 and 3:30–7; first Sunday of the month (except July) 9–7.

Mercato Nuovo The name may mean 'New Market', but a market has existed here, at the junction of Via Calimala and Via Porta Rossa, since the 11th century. Originally a covered market for silk and gold, it became a favoured meeting place for shipping merchants with boats at Pisa and Livorno. (Notice the stone set in the floor, marking the spot where bankrupts and confidence tricksters were exposed before being pilloried.) Now sheltered beneath a 16th-century loggia, the market deals in raffia goods, paper, leather, silks and cheap souvenirs.

Don't miss the famous *Porcellino* statue (see panel opposite).

Open: daily 9–6. Closed Sunday and Monday in winter.

Mercato delle Piante
Florence's Flower Market is held weekly except in July and August (Thursday 8–6) under the post office loggia in Via Pellicceria (just off Piazza della Repubblica).

115

Craft market
Piazza Santo Spirito has a small general market during the week but comes alive during the special craft market held here on the second Sunday of every month (except August).

Choose your market and then put together your picnic lunch

▶▶▶ Palazzo Pitti IFCD2

Piazza dei Pitti

Few palaces or galleries come much larger than the Palazzo Pitti, home to the Medici for almost 200 years and now an eight-museum complex devoted to the family's insatiable (and sometimes tasteless) passion for paintings and fine art. Although intimidating on first acquaintance, the palace in fact boasts only two museums that definitely demand attention: the Galleria Palatina, home to a magnificent collection of paintings, and the Museo degli Argenti, a lavish assortment of Medici silverware and precious *objets d'art*.

The palace Few people linger to admire the Pitti's overbearing façade, variously described as a 'rusticated Stalinist ministry' (Dana Facaros), 'a rather expensive barracks' (Arnold Bennett) and a 'union of Cyclopean massiveness [and] stately regularity' (George Eliot). Commissioned in 1457 by Luca Pitti, a wealthy banker, the palace's purpose was partly to put one over on the Medici (then the Pitti's implacable rivals). It was probably designed by Brunelleschi, who brought the plans to Pitti in a huff, having had them rejected by Cosimo de' Medici as too ostentatious. When Pitti died, in 1472, the palace remained unfinished, consisting of just seven central

The Parting of Venus from Adonis *(1707–8), a ceiling fresco by Sebastiano Ricci*

bays. Even at this modest juncture, however, its scale and grandeur were already attracting murmurs of admiration from the likes of Vasari and Machiavelli.

Poor old Pitti was doubtless turning in his grave by 1549, when the family – now fallen on hard times – were forced to sell out to their old enemies, the despised Medici. Cosimo I bought the palace on his wife's prompting (she hated the Palazzo Vecchio, their previous home). Vasari was commissioned to unite the Medici holdings, the palace being linked to the Uffizi (the Medici's 'offices') by way of the Corridoio Vasariano (see page 129). Once installed, the family remained in residence for almost two centuries. In 1549 the palace was only one room deep (hemmed in by the slope of the Giardino di Boboli). This proved too modest for Cosimo's wife, Eleonora of Toledo, who engaged Ammannati to extend the palace in all directions. This was followed by several bouts of building in the 17th and 19th centuries, after which the façade had grown to three times its original width and the palace looked more or less as it does today.

The Galleria Palatina An unrivalled collection of 16th- to 18th-century paintings, the Palatine Gallery is packed with masterpieces by Raphael, Titian, Tintoretto, Giorgione, Velázquez, Murillo, Perugino, Rubens, Andrea del Sarto and many others (as great a range of painters, in fact, as the Uffizi). Many complain, however, that the works, though well labelled, are badly displayed – wedged as they are from floor to ceiling with no attempt at classification by period or provenance. In truth, the stacked arrangement was the way in which the Medici Grand Dukes chose to display their artistic possessions. It is also a vivid illustration of the collection's sheer scope.

Only the absolute highlights are given below, so be sure to put down the guide and spend time in front of paintings which simply catch the eye. (The gallery's own catalogue numbers are included below in square brackets.) Orientation can be confusing, both around the palace generally and within the Galleria Palatina in particular. To find the gallery, buy your ticket (see panel), walk to the rear right of the main courtyard, and climb the grand staircase to the Palatina's entrance. Beyond a stupendous chandelier, a hint of the splendour to come, walk straight on through the first two rooms (belvederes with lovely views of Ammannati's courtyard and the Giardino di Boboli). In the third room turn left. From here on, work down the six state rooms, all labelled, and then return down the seven parallel rooms to your starting point.

Room 1 (Sala di Venere) Note first the ceiling frescos, the first of four masterpieces (continued in the following rooms) by Pietro da Cortona depicting allegorical and mythological scenes inspired by the Medici. Below them, look for [185] *The Concert* (c.1510–12), [18] *Portrait of a Lady (1536)* and [54] *Portrait of Pietro Aretino* (1545) by Titian; two vast seascapes [4, 15] by Salvator Rosa; and a pair of lovely landscapes [9, 14] by Rubens (c.1637).

The statue at the centre of the room is the *Venus Italica*, commissioned from Canova by a guilty Napoleon in 1812 to replace the famous *Venus de' Medici* which he removed to Paris (see the panel on page 164).

Room 2 (Sala di Apollo) This room's largest work is

117

PALAZZO PITTI

One of Titian's best-known portraits, but the identity of the subject is unknown

Hospitality abused
Many writers left accounts of the high life to be enjoyed at the Pitti's Medici court – usually at the hosts' expense: 'Guests', observed Trollope, 'used to behave abominably. The English would seize plates of *bonbons* and empty the contents into their coat pockets. The ladies would do the same with their pocket handkerchiefs ... I never saw an American pillaging ... though I may add that American ladies would accept any amount of *bonbons* from English blockade runners ... I have seen large portions of fish, sauce and all, packed up in newspaper, and deposited in a pocket. I have seen fowls and ham share the same fate, without any newspaper at all. I have seen jelly carefully wrapped in an Italian countess's laced *mouchoir*...'

[237] Rosso Fiorentino's *Madonna and Saints* (1522), removed from Santo Spirito, but the masterpiece is [92] Titian's *Portrait of a Gentleman* (1540), one of the painter's most famous portraits. The sombre, dignified sitter is unknown, but was long believed to be the English Duke of Norfolk. To his left is [67] Titian's golden-hued and ripely sensuous *Mary Magdalen* (c.1531). Van Dyck's portrait *Charles I and Henrietta Maria*, tucked behind the door, may well be familiar. Henrietta, a Medici scion, was married to the English king.

Room 3 (Sala di Marte) Notice the balls of the Medici symbol on the ceiling, one of which, in an expression of the utmost conceit, has been painted as the Earth. The most eye-catching canvas is Rubens' huge [86] *Consequences of War* (1638), an allegory of the Thirty Years War. The whole painting seems dragged to the right by its immense compositional force. Rubens explained that 'the grief-stricken woman in black [is] the unfortunate Europe, who, for so many years now, has suffered plunder, outrage, and misery.' Tintoretto's [83] *Portrait of Luigi Cornaro*, one of his finest works in the gallery, is outshone by [201] Titian's *Cardinal Ippolito de' Medici* (1532).

Room 4 (Sala di Giove) In its day this was the grand-ducal throne room. Now it is home to one of Raphael's finest portraits [245], the *Donna Velata* (Veiled Woman, c.1516). The model was a Roman baker's daughter and, according to Vasari, the painter's mistress. By the exit door are [272] Andrea del Sarto's *John the Baptist* (1523), one of the most familiar paintings of the subject; [219] a

Perugino *Madonna*; and [64] Fra Bartolomeo's *Deposition* (1516), one of his last and greatest works.

Room 5 (Sala di Saturno) Although [164] Perugino's luminous *Deposition* (1495) dominates, this room bulges with paintings by Raphael. His [151] *Madonna della Seggiola* (1515), encased in a gargantuan frame (all the gallery's frames are on an epic scale), has long been among the Pitti's most famous works (see panel). Raphael also painted [61] *Agnolo* and [59] *Maddalena Doni* (both 1505–6), portraits executed after their marriage (Michelangelo's only Uffizi painting, the Doni Tondo, celebrates the same union). Maddalena's pose is copied directly from that of Leonardo's *Mona Lisa*. Another half-dozen Raphaels line the walls, the most beautiful of which are [165] the *Madonna del Baldacchino* (1507–8) and [178] the sublime *Madonna della Granduca* (1504–5), so called because its owner, Ferdinand III of Lorraine, took it with him wherever he travelled.

Room 6 (Sala dell'Iliade) Elizabeth I of England makes a surprise appearance in [273] an anonymous portrait by a 16th-century English school (at one point the Medici attempted to make a collection of all the crowned heads of Europe). Also here are [229] Raphael's unusual *La Gravida* (Expectant Mother, 1504–8), showing the discreet bulge of pregnancy, and three works by Andrea del Sarto (well represented in the gallery), including [191, 225] two noted depictions of the Assumption (both *c*.1527).

Rooms 7-11 These rooms on your return are smaller and less packed with obvious masterpieces. Again, however, certain paintings deserve special attention. The Sala della Stufa (7), formerly a bathroom, boasts an exquisite tile floor. The Sala dell'Educazione di Giove (8; entered before Room 7), boasts [96] Cristofano Allori's famous *Judith and Holofernes* (see panel) and [183] Caravaggio's *Sleeping Cupid* (1608), sporting a wonderfully ugly Cupid. Room 9 is a lovely bathroom. The Sala di Ulisse (10) has a late Raphael [94], the *Madonna dell'Impannata* (1514), a vivid display of the painter's range, and [338] a quiet, almost out-of-place *Death of Lucrezia* by Filippino Lippi (on the right wall). The Sala di Prometeo (11), last of the rooms, ends the gallery in style with a remarkable tondo [343], the *Madonna and Child* by Filippo Lippi (1452).

If you turn left here you enter a maze of rooms crammed with more minor paintings. Walk straight on, however, through the Galleria del Poccetti and the Sala della Musica, to return to your starting point.

Museo degli Argenti The entrance to this museum is on the left of the main courtyard (separate ticket required). The so-called Silver Museum contains not only silverware but also any sort of precious object – whether exquisite or execrable – on which the Medici could lay their hands. Overwhelming as it is, the collection is only a fraction of that once owned by the family. Although Anna Maria, the sister of the last Medici, left the entire family collection to Florence, some of the most valuable pieces were sold to finance the wars of her family's Austrian relatives.

The lavish salons on the ground floor, used as reception rooms for important guests, boast exuberant and surprisingly charming baroque frescos devoted – inevitably – to the Medici's unflagging prowess. Off to the left of the

The *Madonna della Seggiola*
According to legend the *tondo* (round panel) for this painting came from the end of a wine barrel. Raphael, it appears, was keen to master the demands of tondo technique, a traditional Florentine form. For centuries the work was one of the most popular depictions of the Virgin in Italian art. Would-be copyists in the 19th century had to join a five-year waiting list to study the painting. The bulging figures appear as if seen in a slightly convex mirror – one of the earliest conscious uses of illusionism in the Renaissance.

Judith and Holofernes
This was one of the most universally admired Florentine paintings of the 17th century. The figures are portraits of the artist Cristofano Allori, his mother and his mistress. Despite the violence of the subject, few executions can have been so bloodless. Judith, a seductive, erotic figure dressed in spotless silks and gold satin, is immaculately coiffured, remaining sublimely indifferent to Holofernes' severed head.

Galleria d'Arte Moderna
This gallery boasts over 30 rooms of Tuscan painting from about 1800 to 1945. Its undoubted highlights are the sunny Italian landscapes of the so-called Italian Impressionists (the Macchiaioli), a group who broke with the tradition of the day to produce colourful and realistic paintings after the manner of Corot and Courbet. Also on show are some immensely morbid and perverse sculptures, notably Room 19's *Suicide* and *Pregnant Nun*. Unless you have a special interest, however, you may feel that this part of the Pitti is not worth its high admission charge.

Cappella Rucellai
Alberti designed this superb chapel (entrance at Via della Spada 18) for Giovanni Rucellai's tomb. It represents Alberti's idea of how Jerusalem's Holy Sepulchre might have looked when it was first built by Emperor Constantine. The design also borrowed ideas from Florence's Battistero, then believed to be a Roman building. *Open*: Saturday 5:30 only, for Mass.

Museo Marino Marini
The Marini Museum lies behind the Palazzo Rucellai in Piazza San Pancrazio and houses 200 works by the modern sculptor Marino Marini (1901–66). *Open*: daily 10–1 and 4–7 (winter 3–6). Closed Tuesday. Admission charge (moderate).

first salon, in the Sala Buia, resides one of the museum's unquestioned masterpieces – a collection of 16 *pietre dure* vases owned by Lorenzo the Magnificent. They range from Roman and Byzantine pieces to medieval Venetian works. In an act of minor vandalism Lorenzo engraved his monogram on each of the vases: 'LA V.R.MED'. Lorenzo believed that such items, along with gemstones, made better investments than paintings. Many precious stones in his collection, for example, were valued at over 1,000 florins, while a Botticelli painting could be had for less than 100.

Some of the collection's most magnificent and magnificently awful highlights reside on the museum's mezzanine and first floors. Everything is here – caskets, embroidery, rugs, ivory, painted glass, reliquaries, cutlery, furniture and a host of articles to which you would be hard pushed to give a name. Make first for the superb jewellery exhibits on the mezzanine, then marvel at exotica such as tortoise butter-dishes, ostrich-egg chalices, mosaic stone portraits, Mexican feather mitres, buffalo-horn goblets, carved cherry stones and sensationally tacky seashell figurines.

The **Galleria del Costume** (same ticket) is one for devotees of clothes and fashion. It illustrates the history of costume from the 18th century up to the 1920s. Displays are frequently changed, and the gallery hosts many special exhibitions.

Open: Galleria Palatina, Museo degli Argenti, Galleria del Costume, Appartamenti Monumentali and Galleria d'Arte Moderna daily 9–2. (Last admission 45 minutes before closing time.) Closed Monday. Admission charges (moderate). See the panel on page 117 for ticket information.

▶ **Palazzo Rucellai** *IFCD4*
Via della Vigna Nuova
Rucellai was a wealthy merchant and scholar, whose fortune was made from *oricello*, the famous Florentine red dye (from which the family took its name). Proud of his patronage, he liked to say he earned more honour 'by having spent money well than by having earned it'. Much honour, then, must have accrued from his palace, built between 1446 and 1451, probably to a design by Leon Battista Alberti. A great theorist, Alberti was an architect with firm ideas of what constituted good architecture. He particularly abhorred the fortress-like rustication championed by the Medici and Strozzi palaces (see below and page 113). 'Only the house of a tyrant can look like a fortress,' he chided, adding that palaces should be 'open to the world outside, beautifully adorned, and delicate and finely proportioned rather than proud and stately.'

His palace, still owned by Rucellai's descendants, was the first in the city to use the old classical orders. The pilasters on the ground and top floors are decorated – like Rome's Colosseum – with Doric and Corinthian capitals, while the pilasters of the middle floor sport a Corinthian hybrid designed by Alberti himself. Alberti created only the façade's five left-hand bays: Rucellai added the other two, and might have added more but for a financial crisis brought on by the loss of two of his ships at sea. Notice the family's emblem on the façade – Fortune's sail – entwined with trios of Medici diamond rings, an allusion to

the marriage of Rucellai's son to the granddaughter of Cosimo de' Medici.

The Palazzo Rucellai's ground floor now houses the **Museo di Storia della Fotografia Fratelli Alinari**, host to temporary photographic exhibitions and a collection tracing the history of the Alinari firm (founded in 1852), famous for its black-and-white photographs.
Open: daily 10–7:30 (Friday and Saturday closing 11:30pm). Closed Wednesday. Admission charge (moderate).

Palazzo Strozzi   IFC4D
Piazza Strozzi
The style of palazzo so abhorred by Alberti (see above) is well exemplified in the nearby Palazzo Strozzi. Built for Filippo Strozzi, a powerful banker and head of Florence's anti-Medici faction, it was the last and largest of the 100 or so palaces raised in the city during the 15th century. It copies the **Palazzo Medici-Riccardi** (see page 113), offering almost nothing in the way of architectural nicety or innovation. Size is all here, the immeasurably ugly façade topped by a classically inspired cornice and faced in cyclopean blocks of rusticated stone. Only the inner courtyard might betray any hint of intimacy or delicacy – had it not been spoilt by the addition of an incongruous metal fire-escape.
Closed for restoration at time of writing.

Spotlight on the Loggia dei Rucellai

Loggia dei Rucellai
The loggia opposite the palace was the last of 26 such arcades built in medieval Florence. Noble families built a loggia in or close to their *palazzo* for weddings, meetings and family entertainments. Alberti probably designed the Rucellai loggia (1460–6) for the marriage of Rucellai's son to Nannina Medici. Six properties were destroyed to create the site. Such profligacy was the death of loggias, which declined as building land became more expensive.

Guardian of the city

The *Signoria*
The nine *Priori* of the Priorate or *Signoria* (founded 1282) were responsible for government, law and diplomacy. After a two-month term of office each was ineligible for re-election for three years. While in office the *Priori* received only official visitors, and left the palace only for matters of the gravest importance. They were paid a modest wage.

▶▶ **Palazzo Vecchio**   IFCE3
Piazza della Signoria

'A stark ... incarnation of the stern realities of medieval times' was Stendhal's description of the Palazzo Vecchio which, with its doughty tower and bristling crenellations, dominates Piazza della Signoria and a swathe of the Florentine skyline. The city's seat of government for seven centuries (and still the town hall), it was first mooted in 1285, three years after the creation of the *Signoria* (see panel and pages 34–5). Work started under Arnolfo di Cambio, who at that time was also employed on the Duomo, and was completed around 1302. Over the years the building underwent several changes, the most notable in 1540, when Cosimo I transferred the Medici court here from the Palazzo Medici. Ten years later, when Cosimo moved again – this time to the 'new' Palazzo Pitti – the palace took its present name (*vecchio* means 'old').

Between 1865 and 1871, while Florence was briefly Italy's capital, the palace housed the country's foreign ministry and parliament.

The courtyard The palace's grand *cortile* (1453), designed by Michelozzo, was later subjected to Vasari's dubious interior design talents. The result, as elsewhere in the palace, was a wearisome paean to Medici prowess. Some of the frescos, rather oddly, depict views of Austrian cities; they were added to celebrate the marriage of Francesco, Cosimo's son, to Joanna of Austria.

The first floor Vasari's staircase leads to the palace's centrepiece, the cavernous but strangely soulless Salone dei Cinquecento. Built in 1495, it was designed to accommodate the 500-strong meetings of the *Consiglio Maggiore*, then the city's ruling assembly. In what might have been a Renaissance *tour de force*, Michelangelo and Leonardo da Vinci were lined up to fresco the walls, but they were called away to Rome and Milan respectively, so neither progressed much beyond preliminary sketches. Vasari was commissioned instead, the result being six immense paintings (1563–5) of Florentine triumphs over Pisa and Siena. Few works of art can have been painted with such militaristic relish. More decorative excess washes over the ceiling (again courtesy of Vasari) where an orgy of paint and gilt celebrates the apotheosis of Cosimo I.

The second floor Steps opposite the Studiolo (see panel) lead to the palace's second floor. Half-way up, notice the fireworks fresco (1558), a view of Piazza della Signoria during the feast-day celebrations of St John the Baptist. Turn left at the top and you enter five rooms known as the Quartiere degli Elementi, each frescoed by Vasari and assistants. Beyond them is the more appealing Terrazza di Saturno, an open loggia with views over the rooftops to Santa Croce, San Miniato and the hills beyond.

Return to the stairs and turn right: an open balcony gives a view over the Salone below. Next comes the Quartiere di Eleonora di Toledo, the six-roomed apartment of Cosimo I's wife. The star turn here is the chapel (immediately on the right as you enter), a masterpiece of vivid Mannerist decoration by Bronzino (1540–5). Beyond it you emerge into the larger Sala d'Udienza, with a beautiful ceiling and superb views of the Piazza della Signoria. Next door is the still larger Sala dei Gigli, its walls and tremendous ceiling swathed in the gold lilies that give the room its name (*giglio* means 'lily'). The palace's key work of art is here – Donatello's statue *Judith and Holofernes* (1456–60). The one frescoed wall is by Domenico Ghirlandaio. The two final rooms are the Cancelleria (off to the left), once used as an office by Machiavelli, and the lovely Sala delle Carte (or Guardaroba) to the right, filled with globes and 57 beautiful maps (painted on leather) of the known world in 1563.

Open: daily 9–7 (Sunday 8–1). Closed Saturday. Admission charge (expensive). Combined ticket (*Biglietto Cumulativo*) available, covering the Palazzo Vecchio, the Museo Bardini, the Museo di Firenze com'era and the Museo di Santa Maria Novella.

Victory
Michelangelo's statue *La Vittoria* (c.1525), intended for the tomb of Julius II, is to be found almost opposite the entrance door of the Salone dei Cinquecento. It shows a heavily muscled youth kneeling on a barely realised bearded figure. It was given to Cosimo I by the sculptor's nephew and set up here in 1565 to celebrate Florence's victory over Siena 10 years earlier. At some point, and for reasons unknown, Michelangelo changed the main figure from a woman to a man. The figure of the defeated adversary may be a self-portrait.

Studiolo di Francesco I
Built for Cosimo I's gloomy son, Francesco I, the 'study' (1569–73) is a tiny, windowless room off the Salone dei Cinquecento, to the right of the entrance. It was decorated by 30 of Florence's leading Mannerist painters with scenes that reflected his scientific and alchemic interests. Each wall depicts allegorical episodes connected with Earth, Water, Air and Fire. The vault's facing figures are portraits by Bronzino of Francesco's parents. Francesco kept his more treasured knick-knacks hidden behind the oval-shaped lower paintings.

Room with a view
The tiny room at the top of the Palazzo Vecchio's tower was known ironically as the *alberghettino* ('little guest-house'). It was used for eminent prisoners such as Cosimo de' Medici (before his brief exile) and Savonarola, who stayed here between torture sessions gazing down over the piazza where he was later to be executed.

■ **The name of Niccolò Machiavelli (1469–1527) has become a byword for intrigue and political cynicism. A look at his life and works, however, suggests that posterity has served him ill, for in reality he was a great political theorist, a superb stylist and one of the foremost historians of his age.....■**

Only one portrait of Machiavelli survives: an oil painting by Santi di Tito in the Palazzo Vecchio. From it 'Old Nick' gazes out with an expression that is anything but Machiavellian. Instead he looks simultaneously quizzical and sardonic, his features thin, neat and ascetic, his thinning hair swept back from a high forehead.

Deprivation and diplomacy Machiavelli came from noble stock, albeit from a family that – having once held high Florentine office – had recently fallen on hard times. 'I learnt to do without', he wrote, 'before I learnt to enjoy.' Poverty was to limit his education, leaving him to his own devices, a hardship that perhaps honed, rather than hindered, his style and original thinking.

Entering political service after Savonarola's execution (1498), he became chancellor and secretary to the ruling council of the Florentine Republic. Entrusted with diplomatic missions, he spent five months at the French court (1500), receiving an object lesson in how a strong nation might be united under a single prince. The lesson was reinforced by visits to Switzerland and Germany, and by observing Cesare Borgia's attempts to carve out a principality in central Italy. Recording his observations, he noted – with the realism that was to become his trademark – that 'the world has always been inhabited by human beings who have always had the same passion.'

A smiling Niccolò Machiavelli, the only surviving portrait

Republic and Medici Rising through the ranks, Machiavelli became right-hand man to Piero Soderini, *gonfaloniere*, and chief magistrate under the city's Republican constitution. Having the ear of Florence's effective ruler (the Medici having been temporarily deposed), he persuaded Soderini to create a militia in 1505, having seen at first hand the untrustworthiness of traditional mercenary armies. It was to be supervised by the Council of Nine (1506), with Machiavelli – who also led troops in the field – as its chief secretary.

Nemesis arrived in 1512 with the return of the Medici. Soderini was deposed and Machiavelli barred from the Palazzo della Signoria. When an anti-Medici plot was uncovered in 1513, Machiavelli, already under suspicion, was accused of complicity and imprisoned. Although tortured, he maintained his innocence and was eventually released. Limits were placed on his freedom, however, and without employment he was soon faced with destitution.

Machiavelli's writings It was at this point that he retired to write *The Prince* and the *Discourse on the First Ten Books of Livy* (both completed in less than six months). The books were masterpieces of political analysis, linking political science (the 'reason of state') with the study of human nature. They also proposed the idea of historical cycles, based on the premise that human behaviour remains immutable.

Reading the books today it is essential to see them as products of their time. Machiavelli loved Florence 'more than his own soul', and to see his beloved city descend into chaos inevitably coloured his thinking. His books and their proposed remedies, therefore, must be seen as the attempts of a patriot desperate to rescue his city, while doing so in a way that was compatible with human nature and with the vicissitudes of the age. His diabolic reputation and the moral backlash only came later (see panel).

After years in the political wilderness, Machiavelli gradually crept back into favour, serving as an advisor to Giuliano de' Medici and becoming the republic's official historian in 1520 (the *Istorie Fiorentine* were the result). When the Medici were again usurped in 1527, however, Machiavelli failed to regain his old post as chancellor – one final twist in the life of a man who raised the political twist to an art form.

Machiavelli's tomb in Santa Croce, by Innocenzo Spinazzi

Backlash
Machiavelli first came in for a critical mauling during the Counter-Reformation, when his ideas were singled out by the Inquisition for particular opprobrium. 'Machiavellianism', however, was originally a French term, coined to denigrate not Machiavelli, but all things Italian.

PIAZZA DELLA SIGNORIA

Ammannati's **Neptune**

▶▶▶   **Piazza della Signoria**   *IFCE3*

Florence kept the two chief pillars of medieval society
well apart. While the Church busied itself in Piazza del
Duomo, civic proceedings were confined to Piazza della
Signoria. Lacking in architectural harmony, the latter is a
less beautiful square than many in Italy. It has, however,
witnessed key events in the city's history – Savonarola's
execution in particular – and remains one of Florence's
prime social meeting places. Of only modest size until the
14th century, the square was enlarged in 1307 as a setting for the Palazzo dei Priori (now the Palazzo Vecchio).
Enlarged still further, it acquired more or less its present
size when it was paved in 1385.

The piazza has always been a stage for political rallies
and crowd-pleasing spectacles. Wild boar and lions, for
example, were often released here for hunting and entertainment. On one occasion three men were killed by ram-
paging buffaloes. On another, a stallion was set loose
among mares: the ensuing high jinks were described by
one onlooker as 'the most marvellous entertainment for
girls to behold', and by another as a spectacle that 'much
displeased decent and well-behaved people'.

Political proceedings took place on the raised dais in
front of the Palazzo Vecchio. It was known as the
arringhiera – the origin of the English word 'harangue'.

Rallies often became heated. One meeting in 1343, for example, ended with a man reputedly being eaten by the inflamed mob. Cannibalism notwithstanding, high standards of behaviour were expected in the piazza. Carts and traffic were banned (as they are today), as were begging, gambling and prostitution. Crimes committed within its precincts were punished more severely than those committed elsewhere.

The piazza's key components are self-evident: the towered bulk of the **Palazzo Vecchio** (see pages 122-3) and the triple-arched **Loggia dei Lanzi** (see page 86). Between them lies the entrance to the **Uffizi** (see pages 160–5). Ranged across the piazza is a series of fountains and statues, some familiar, others – deservedly – more obscure. Most were erected during the 16th century to accentuate the approach to the Uffizi. (Michelangelo once proposed extending the Loggia's arches around the entire piazza to achieve the same effect.) From left to right as you face the Palazzo Vecchio the statues are as follows:

1. *Cosimo I* (1587–94) by Giambologna. This equestrian statue – the only one of its kind cast in the late Renaissance – was designed to emulate Rome's ancient statue of Marcus Aurelius, thus linking the 'glory' of Florence (and Cosimo) with that of classical Rome. The base reliefs describe three key events in Cosimo's career: the conquest of Siena (1555); his becoming Duke of Florence (1537); and Pope Pius V conferring on him the title of Grand Duke of Tuscany (1569).

2. *Neptune Fountain* (1565–75) by Ammannati. Neptune symbolises Cosimo I's ambitions for Florence as a naval power. Florentines call it *Il Biancone* (The Big White One), a river god turned to stone for spurning the love of women. When struck by the light of a full moon, it is said to wander the piazza conversing with other statues. It prompted a famous put-down (attributed to Michelangelo) 'Ammannato, Ammannato, che bel marmo hai rovinato' (what a beautiful piece of marble you have ruined). The better bronzes around the base are by Giambologna and others. A porphyry disc in front of the fountain marks the spot of Savonarola's execution.

3. *Il Marzocco*. A copy of Donatello's sculpture of Florence's heraldic lion (see panel). The original (1418–20) is in the Bargello (see page 59).

4. *Judith and Holofernes*. A copy of an original (1456–60) removed to the Palazzo Vecchio in 1980 (see page 123). Taken from the Medici palace after the family's fall in 1494, its role in the piazza was to symbolise the defeat of tyranny.

5. *David*. An 1873 copy of Michelangelo's original in the Accademia (see pages 52–3).

6. *Hercules and Cacus*. Bandinelli's statue, carved to partner *David*, simultaneously symbolises Cosimo I, Florentine fortitude and the conquest of domestic enemies. The marble was originally offered to Michelangelo. Having been awaited with great expectation, Bandinelli's version was unveiled in 1534 to much disappointment. Cellini described it as a 'sack of melons'.

7. *Male Herm* by Vincenzo Rossi (1535).

8. *Female Herm* by Bandinelli (1535). The identity of the two herms is unknown. They served as posts for a chain across the entrance to the Palazzo Vecchio.

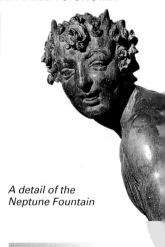

A detail of the Neptune Fountain

The Marzocco
Florence's heraldic lion may have its origins in a mutilated Roman equestrian statue of Mars (*Martocus*) that stood at the end of the Ponte Vecchio until the 1333 flood. Or it may come from lions kept in the dungeons of the Palazzo Vecchio, whose behaviour was watched for auguries in times of crisis. From the 13th century onwards, the symbol was raised in Tuscan towns conquered by Florence. Captured prisoners were customarily required to kiss its posterior. Donatello's lion was carved for a papal apartment in Santa Maria Novella and moved to the piazza in 1812 to replace a 14th-century version.

Men only
'I saw the pale crouching Duomo and in the thick moon-mist the Giotto tower … the Palazzo Vecchio with Michelangelo's *David* and all the statues of men we passed. "This is a men's town," I said, "not like Paris, where all the statues are women."'
Frieda Lawrence, *Not I, but the Wind* (1935)

PONTE VECCHIO

Emblem of the city, and miraculous survivor

A bridge too far
The Ponte Vecchio was the only Florentine bridge spared by the Nazis during the retreat of 1944. Harried by the American 5th Army, the Germans reneged on a promise to demilitarise the city and spare its artistic heritage (as had happened in Rome). All the Arno bridges were blown up, on 4 August, to hamper the Allied advance. Medieval quarters at either end of the Ponte Vecchio were also razed in order to block access to the bridge. Only the bridge itself survived, spared by Field Marshal Kesselring, possibly on Hitler's direct orders.

▶▶▶ Ponte Vecchio   *IFCD3*

With its evocative huddle of shops, the Ponte Vecchio is as much a symbol of Florence as the cathedral's dome or Michelangelo's *David*. As symbols go, however, it is one of the city's more crowded – so be prepared for hordes, hawkers and souvenir-sellers.

Pitched close to the Arno's narrowest point and earliest crossing, the Ponte Vecchio is the last in a succession of bridges on the site that dates back to Roman times. Until 1218 it was the only bridge across the river, providing a vital lifeline between the old city and the Oltrarno. A wooden bridge, recorded here in 970 and reinforced in 1170, was swept away in the floods of 1333, some of the worst in the city's history. The bridge built to replace it in 1345 is the one that visitors flock to see today – a unique and miraculous survivor both of World War II (see panel) and (just) of the 1966 flood. Its name – the Old Bridge – was coined to distinguish it from the city's other medieval bridge, the Ponte alla Carraia (originally built in 1218).

Shops clung to the Ponte Vecchio from as early as the 13th century. Butchers and fishmongers were among its first occupants, attracted by the proximity of the Arno, a convenient sewer for their offal and other waste. Tanners were the next arrivals, a no less noxious bunch. They added to the communal stench by soaking hides in the river before tanning them in horse's urine. With the bridge awash in such delights, it was not long, inevitably, before a gap was made between the shops so that debris could be swept off the pavements into the river (the space is still there). Smells and detritus notwithstanding, the commercial pot-pourri was enriched over the years by barbers, blacksmiths, cobblers, hosiers, surgeons and greengrocers.

The Ponte Vecchio is one of the best places to admire Vasari's much-vaunted **Corridoio Vasariano**, a covered aerial passageway built for Cosimo I in 1565 to link the Uffizi (the Medici offices) with the newly acquired Palazzo Pitti across the river. The corridor also served as a monument in celebration of the marriage of Cosimo's son, Francesco, to Joanna of Austria. It was built in just five months, and Vasari liked to boast that it might have taken others five years to complete. He also liked to allude to its classical antecedents, citing as his inspiration the passageway that reputedly linked the palaces of Priam and Hector in ancient Troy. (He kept quieter about the five men killed as a result of the hasty construction work.)

For Cosimo's part, the Corridoio allowed him to roam his domain without having to meet the Florentine *hoi-polloi*. After crossing the Ponte Vecchio, for example, it snakes towards Santa Felicita (see page 144), passing over the church's portico in such a way that Cosimo could follow services without setting foot on a public street.

The corridor did not, however, offer enough protection to spare the nostrils and sensibilities of Cosimo's still more fastidious successors. By 1593 Ferdinand I had had his fill of the noxious odours and evicted the bridge's butchers and tanners – practitioners of what he termed 'vile arts'. In their place he introduced eight jewellers and 41 goldsmiths, practitioners of a traditional Florentine skill in which some of the finest Renaissance artists had been trained. This more decorous breed of craftsmen (more to the point, perhaps) allowed themselves to be cajoled into paying double the previous rents. To this day, jewellers have continued to monopolise the bridge's legitimate trade, hence its central bust (1900) of the most celebrated of Florence's goldsmiths, Benvenuto Cellini.

Dickens's view
'... the Ponte Vecchio ... is [a] most enchanting feature of the scene. The space of one house, in the centre, being left open, the view beyond is shown as in a frame; and that precious glimpse of sky, and water, and rich buildings, shining so quietly among the huddled roofs and gables on the bridge, is exquisite ...
Charles Dickens, *Pictures from Italy* (1846)

The flood of 1966

■ **The Arno is a fickle creature. In one breath Dante called it 'il bel fiume' (the beautiful river), in another 'la maladetta e sventurata fossa' (the cursed and luckless ditch). Its most malevolent side was certainly to the fore on 4 November 1966, when it unleashed a deluge that created a human and artistic tragedy of unprecedented proportions.....■**

The 1884 flood

Writers love a disaster. It makes good copy. Looking down from the Campanile at the submerged city in 1884, Anthony Trollope marvelled at the 'truly terrible and magnificent sight'. The river, he wrote, was 'one turbid, yellow, swirling mass ... bringing down with it fragments of timber, carcasses of animals, and large quantities of hay and straw.' Later, Trollope had to travel by barge to his lodgings in a submerged Piazza Santa Croce. *What I Remember* (1887)

Top and below: wake of the flood – the morning after

Floods in Florence were nothing new. Early chroniclers traced the city's foundation back to Noah. A deluge in 1269 washed away the Carraia and Santa Trinita bridges. In 1333 the old Ponte Vecchio was destroyed after a four-day tempest – a storm so violent that the city's bells were tolled to exorcise the devils believed to be causing the cyclone. In 1557 flash floods submerged the city to a depth of 6m, moving so quickly that all but two children in a crowd on Ponte Santa Trinita were drowned before they could dash to safety. Stranded on a lone pillar, the surviving pair were fed for two days via a rope slung from the Palazzo Strozzi.

A city in the wrong place Surveying the Arno's muddy trickle in midsummer, it is easy to sympathise with Mark Twain's view that this 'great historical creek with four feet in the channel ... would be a very plausible river if they would pump some water into it' (*The Innocents Abroad*, 1869). Had Twain made his observation in a different season, however, he would have realised that the Arno is more usually a torrent that holds Florence a watery hostage. Part of the fault lies with the city's position. Surrounded by hills, it sits helpless on a broad plain, the first flat ground downstream of the point where the Arno has been joined by the Sieve, its major tributary. Worse still, of course, the Arno rises in the Apennines, so is

The flood of 1966

Cleaning up: the restoration of damaged treasures

A city in crisis
The 1966 flood plunged Florence into chaos. Women and children were rescued from the rooftops by helicopter; men were left until the waters subsided. Food was short, and electricity and fresh water were cut off for days. Milk and bread were distributed from the Palazzo Vecchio. Total darkness enveloped the city at night, forcing the police to run patrols to discourage looting.

Ruinous waters
'A tumultuous mass of water stretches from bank to bank … a snarling brown torrent of terrific velocity, spiraling in whirlpools and countercurrents that send waves running backward; its colour is a rich brown, a boiling *caffè-latte* brown streaked with crests the colour of dirty cream. This tremendous water carries mats of debris: straw, twigs, leafy branches, rags, a litter that the river sucks down and spews up again in a swelling turbulence.' K K Taylor, *Diary of Florence in the Flood* (1966)

Cimabue's *Crucifix*
In 1971 on the anniversary of the flood Mayor Bargellini wrote in Florence's daily paper: 'When Cimabue's *Crucifix* was carried past, fatally wounded, on a tank going to Limonaia, even the most hardened men, the loudest blasphemers, stopped in their muddy labours and took off their hats in silence; every woman, however tough or dishonest, crossed herself with sincerity … It was as still and silent as on Good Friday.' *La Nazione*

seasonally swollen by heavy rains and the meltwaters of countless mountain streams. Moving Florence, as has been said many times, is the only way to prevent Florentine floods.

The fateful morning By 4 November 1966, it had been raining for 40 days and nights. Around 48cm of rain had fallen on Florence in the last 48 hours. Yet, as dawn broke on that fateful morning, and as the Arno rose, few people seemed aware of the imminent danger. Only upstream, where a reservoir threatened to burst, were the sluices opened. In the city itself only the Ponte Vecchio's jewellers stirred, warned in the small hours by a lone nightwatchman of the bridge's trembling. Two solitary policemen, apparently, watched in the darkness as they cleared their shops. Asked why they failed to raise the alarm they reputedly replied 'We have no orders.' In the words of the American writer, Francis Steegmuller, half the shops were soon 'gaping open – gutted by the tremendous force of a torrent that passed right through them' (*Stories and True Stories*, 1972).

The wake of the flood The Ponte Vecchio itself, miraculously, survived. The Arno's embankments were not so lucky. Shortly before dawn some 500,000 tons of mud and water tore through the sleeping city, moving with such ferocity that early-rising commuters in the station underpass were drowned where they fell. In all, 35 people lost their lives. Hundreds of homes and 16,000 cars were destroyed. In places the waters rose 6m above street level, filling cellars and flushing out heating oil that had just been delivered for the approaching winter. Five of Ghiberti's famous panels were torn from the Baptistery doors and later found 2km away. Slurry filled the cellars of the Uffizi, home to some 8,000 paintings. It lapped at Michelangelo's *David* and damaged 1½ million volumes in the Biblioteca Nazionale, a million of them beyond repair. It filled palaces, museums and churches, devastating Santa Croce, whose ravaged *Crucifix* by Cimabue (see panel) has become a symbol of that terrible morning.

Planning your visit
The San Lorenzo complex can be confusing. First see Brunelleschi's church and the Sagrestia Vecchia. Then visit Michelangelo's Biblioteca Laurenziana. Move on to the Cappelle Medicee behind the church and Michelangelo's Sagrestia Nuova (see pages 64–5). Note carefully the opening times of the Biblioteca Laurenziana and the Sagrestia Vecchia (see page 135).

San Lorenzo and the street market alongside it

▶▶ **San Lorenzo**   *IFCD4*

Piazza San Lorenzo

An unfinished façade and San Lorenzo's market distract attention from what is one of Florence's oldest and most important churches. The first chapel here was consecrated in 393 by St Ambrose, Bishop of Milan, just 13 years after Christianity had been proclaimed the Empire's official religion. Dedicated to San Zenobius, it served as Florence's first cathedral until around the 7th century, when the bishop's seat was moved to Santa Reparata (itself later replaced by the present Duomo). A Romanesque church was built in 1060.

In 1419 eight parishioners led by Giovanni de' Medici offered to help finance a new church. The design went to Brunelleschi, who embarked first on the Sagrestia Vecchia (Old Sacristy), and in 1421 was given responsibility for the entire project (a distraction from the Duomo, on which he was also working). Twenty years of financial and political upheavals, however, meant that work faltered, recovering only when Giovanni's son, Cosimo de' Medici, provided 40,000 florins for the church's completion (at a time when 150 florins would keep a family for a year). In return the building became a Medici fiefdom and mausoleum (see also **Cappelle Medicee**, pages 64–5).

The church interior Praise is always heaped on Brunelleschi's downbeat interior, a landmark of early-Renaissance architecture (clearly influenced by the architect's study of classical buildings in Rome). A system of *creste e vele* (waves and sails) was used, with broad 'sails' of creamy wall stretched between expanses of grey *pietra serena*.

The two bronze pulpits (*c.*1455–66), raised on marble pillars, were designed and partly executed by an elderly Donatello. Neither of these betrays any slackening of the artist's powers, each bristling with energy and rough-cast figures (particularly on the right-hand dais, where Donatello's hand is more evident). The scenes on this pulpit depict the Resurrection, while those on its neighbour show events from the life of Christ up to and including the Crucifixion. Sadly, however, the pulpits are too high for much detail to be easily discernible (the pillars were added in the 17th century). In his day, Savonarola used to thunder his sermons from these pulpits. Today, in keeping with their decorative theme, they are traditionally only used in Holy Week.

Close by, at the end of the right nave, stands the *Pala del Sacramento* (1458–61) by Desiderio da Settignano. This was a highly influential work in its day: notice the perspectival tricks of its upper tabernacle (an echo of Masaccio's famous *Trinità* in Santa Maria Novella).

Rosso Fiorentino
Seven years after painting San Lorenzo's *Marriage of the Virgin*, Rosso abandoned Florence for France 'to raise himself', in Vasari's words, out of the 'wretchedness and poverty which is the common lot of those who work in Tuscany.' In France he became one of the country's most influential painters.

133

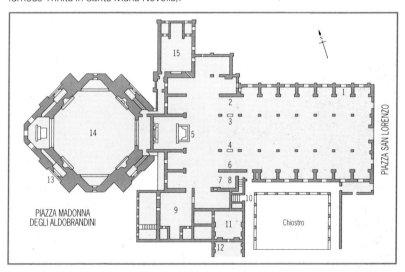

PIAZZA MADONNA DEGLI ALDOBRANDINI

PIAZZA SAN LORENZO

Chiostro

1. *Marriage of the Virgin* (1523) by Rosso Fiorentino (see panel).
2. *Pala del Sacramento* (1458–61) by Desiderio da Settignano.
3. and 4. Two bronze pulpits (*c.*1455–66) by Donatello.
5. Tomb of Cosimo de' Medici.
6. *Martyrdom of San Lorenzo* (1565–9) by Bronzino.
7. Altarpiece *The Annunciation* (1440) by Fra Lippo Lippi.
8. Cenotaph to Donatello.
9. Sagrestia Vecchia (Old Sacristy).
10. Entrance to Biblioteca Laurenziana.
11. Ricetto (Vestibule), designed by Michelangelo.
12. Reading Room of Biblioteca Laurenziana.
13. Entrance to Cappelle Medicee (Medici Chapels).
14. Cappella dei Principi (see pages 64–5).
15. Sagrestia Nuova (New Sacristy – see page 65).

One of Donatello's pulpits

Lorenzo
San Lorenzo (St Lawrence), one of Florence's patron saints, was a 3rd-century deacon of some character. When the Romans ordered him to hand over the treasures of the Church he gathered all the sick and poor people he could find. The gesture was not appreciated and he was roasted alive on a grid-iron, telling his executioners at one point they could turn him over: 'I am done on this side.' The scene is depicted in Bronzino's colourful fresco in the church (see the plan on page 133).

St Cosmos and St Damian
These early Christian martyrs feature prominently in Florentine art. They were the patron saints of doctors (*medici*) and, as the Medici were descended from doctors, the family adopted them as its own patron saints. By chance, Cosimo de' Medici was born on the saints' feast day, 27 September, so the pair are often seen in paintings commissioned by him.

Three brass grilles in front of the high altar mark the tomb of Cosimo de' Medici. The all-powerful city ruler, who died in 1464, is commemorated by the simple epitaph *Pater Patriae* (Father of the Fatherland). In the chapel just to the south is a cenotaph to Donatello, who died two years later and was buried, in accordance with his last wishes, close to Cosimo de' Medici who had been his friend and patron.
Open: daily 7–12 and 3:30–5:30.

Sagrestia Vecchia A companion to Michelangelo's Sagrestia Nuova (see page 65), the Old Sacristy (1421) was the only structure designed by Brunelleschi to be completed during his lifetime. Dignified and simple – a perfect cube and hemispherical dome – it is far more satisfying than the church from which it is entered (note opening times below). On the left of the door stands the bronze and porphyry tomb of Giovanni and Piero de' Medici (Cosimo's sons), commissioned from Verrocchio by Lorenzo the Magnificent (1472). As a tomb, however, it is overshadowed by the marble table in the centre of the room, the tomb of Giovanni and Piccarda de' Medici (Cosimo's parents and founders of the Medici fortune). Otherwise the decoration around the room is mostly by Donatello (1434–43), and was executed some 20 years before the church's pulpits.

Above the chapel's cherub frieze lie Donatello's eight tondi, four orange-pink in colour and four white against grey, the former striking for their surreal compositional effect. Between them they depict the Evangelists and scenes from the life of St John (Giovanni de' Medici's patron saint).

Over the two doors on the end wall are a pair of large reliefs, one showing St Lawrence and St Stephen (twin protectors of Florence), the other St Cosmos and St Damian, the Medici saints (see panel). Donatello's lively bronze doors below portray disputing martyrs to the left, Apostles and Church Fathers to the right. The starry ceiling frescos of the blue-painted dome depict the heavens as they were on 6 July 1439, when the short-lived union of the Eastern and Western churches was declared at the

Council of Florence. The bust on the right as you enter is that of St Lawrence.

Open: Monday, Wednesday, Friday and Saturday 10–11:45; Tuesday and Thursday 4–5:45. Admission free.

Biblioteca Laurenziana To reach the Laurentian Library leave the church beside the Bronzino fresco and in the cloister (having paused to enjoy the lovely views), take the stairs immediately on your right. Begun in 1524 on the orders of Pope Clement VII (Giulio de' Medici), the building was designed to house the 100-year-old Medici library (see panel). Michelangelo's Mannerist Ricetto (Vestibule) provides the entrance, a deliberately strange and revolutionary use of space designed to amuse, perhaps even unsettle, his Medici patrons. Its lava-black staircase (completed by Vasari and Ammannati in the 1550s) contrasts with a fine wooden ceiling and the room's rough-cast rendering. Among the eccentricities are pillars which carry no weight, and decorative brackets that support nothing but air.

The Reading Room, by contrast, is deliberately conventional. This, too, was designed by Michelangelo, who was responsible for virtually every detail. Notice the Medici symbol in every window, the date (1571) above the door (the year the library was opened to the public), and the fact that the only part of the Vestibule visible from the Reading Room is a blank wall. Four rooms beyond contain glass cases displaying a handful of the library's thousands of volumes. The collection's oldest item is a 5th-century Codex of Virgil, but the oldest work on show is on the left as you enter the first room – a papal bull (dated 20 January 1060) issued by Pope Niccolò II (formerly Bishop of Florence) authorising the reconsecration of San Lorenzo. *Open*: daily 9–1. Closed Sunday. Admission free.

Books and the Medici

A 1418 inventory of Giovanni de' Medici's possessions mentions just three books. His son Cosimo, however, and Cosimo's son and grandson (Piero and Lorenzo), were avid bibliophiles and tireless collectors. Agents in search of books and manuscripts scoured Europe (notably Germany, whose monks had little idea of their value) and the Middle East on their behalf. The Medici also founded libraries for the friars of San Marco and the Badia. The family library was confiscated in 1494 and moved (on Savonarola's advice) from the Palazzo Medici to San Marco. It was reclaimed and transferred to Rome in 1508 by the Medici Pope Leo X. Another Medici, Clement VII, restored it to Florence in 1534.

135

Michelangelo's lost contract

Michelangelo certainly knew how to mess up a contract. Having fought off competition from Sansovino and Giuliano da Sangallo to design San Lorenzo's façade (his winning model is in the Casa Buonarroti), he then argued with Pope Leo X over the choice of marble, wasted two years on building roads to carry stone from Carrara, antagonised his workmen and finally found the quarrymen unwilling to co-operate. 'I am dying of grief,' he wrote, tortured by the project: 'it is as though Fate is against me.' Exasperated by the delays, the pope cancelled the contract in 1520 and the façade was never built.

Carved detail from the statue of a Medici duke, Giovanni delle Bande Nere, in Piazza San Lorenzo

SAN MINIATO AL MONTE

Getting there
The best approach to San Miniato is on foot (see page 156). Failing that, take bus 13 to Piazzale Michelangelo, a fine but invariably crowded viewpoint from where the church is a short walk. Alternatively, take bus 12 (Via Porta Romana) to the steps on Viale Galileo Galilei leading to the church. Both services pick up at the Duomo and near the railway station.

Cappella del Cardinale del Portogallo
This chapel is dedicated to the 25-year-old Jacopo di Lusitania, the cultured nephew of King Alfonso V of Portugal. Sent to study law in Perugia, he became ambassador to Florence. After he died here in 1459, humanist admirers commissioned his tomb. Notice the angels flanking his tabernacle, one holding a virgin's crown (symbolising the cardinal's chastity), the other a palm (a symbol of his subjugation of earthly passion).

A 13th-century mosaic of Christ and the Evangelists

▶▶▶ **San Miniato al Monte**   *IFCF1*

Viale Galileo Galilei

San Miniato is Florence's most beautiful and (after the Battistero) most venerable church. Its multicoloured façade is a dazzling fixture on the green heights above the Oltrarno.

St Minias was a merchant from the East (possibly a son of the Armenian king), who became a Christian and left his native land to seek penance in Rome. Moving to Florence around AD250, he was caught up in the anti-Christian purges of the Emperor Decius. Being a member of royalty, however, he was offered numerous inducements to renounce his faith. He would accept none, and was executed on a spot close to the present-day Piazza della Signoria. Then, however, 'by a miracle of Christ', to quote chronicler Giovanni Villani, he picked up his severed head 'and set it again on his trunk, and on his feet passed over the Arno, and went up the hill where now stands his church.' The hill, the Mons Fiorentinus, was then crowded with pagan temples, and a 'little oratory in the name of the blessed Peter the Apostle, where many bodies of holy martyrs were buried.' Here Minias 'gave up his soul to Christ' and was buried.

The present church and convent were started in 1013 by Alibrando (Hildebrand), Bishop of Florence, on the orders of Emperor Henry II, who endowed it 'for the good of his soul'. Most of the building from this period is what is seen today. Initially run by the Benedictines, the church later became a Cluniac monastery, passing in 1373 to the Olivetans, its present incumbents.

The exterior It is hard to know which to admire first – San Miniato's exquisite façade or the magnificent view of Florence that unfolds below the church's lofty terrace. Like the Battistero, whose patterned marbles it recalls, the façade (1090–1270) was often mistaken during the Renaissance for a Roman edifice. The mosaic of Christ, Mary and San Miniato was added in 1260 (notice Christ's rather jolly oriental blue bolster). A gilded copper eagle (1401) clutching a bale of wool crowns the façade – the symbol of the Arte di Calimala, the guild responsible for

A close-up view of the façade showing the mosaic added to the green, grey and white marble in the 13th century

the church fabric since 1228. This may explain some of the decorative similarities between San Miniato and the Battistero, a building also looked after by the Calimala.

The interior Few Florentine sights are as lovely as the first glimpse of San Miniato's Romanesque interior (1018–63). The famous inlaid pavement (1207), reputedly inspired by Sicilian fabrics, is patterned with lions, doves and the signs of the zodiac (the floor's date is inscribed in the zodiac panel). The painted wood ceiling dates from 1322 but was restored in the 19th century, along with the nave's columns, victims of some rather heavy-handed resurfacing. The capitals, however, are Roman and Byzantine originals.

Further highlights include the free-standing Cappella del Crocifisso (1448), designed by Michelozzo to house a miraculous *Crucifix* (now in Santa Trinita). It was one of the few commissions managed by Piero de' Medici during his short period at the city's helm. Steps beside the chapel lead up to the raised choir, dominated by a magnificent carved pulpit and screen (1207). The mosaic in the apse to the rear dates from 1297. Off to the right the sacristy contains a fine fresco cycle by Spinello Aretino, *Scenes from the Life of St Benedict* (1387).

Back in the lower body of the church see the Cappella del Cardinale del Portogallo (1460-8), a masterpiece of Renaissance collaboration off the left-hand aisle. It was designed by Manetti, a pupil of Brunelleschi (see panel opposite). The tomb is by Antonio Rossellino, the painting of the Annunciation (left-hand wall) by Baldovinetti, and the terracotta (and tiled) ceiling by Luca della Robbia. The altarpiece is a copy of a work by Antonio and Piero Pollaiuolo (now in the Uffizi).

Open: daily 8–12 and 2–7 (winter 2:30–6).

Saved by mattresses
San Miniato's bell-tower collapsed in 1499 and was replaced in 1523 by the present unfinished tower. During the siege of Florence in 1530 it was used as an artillery post, thus attracting the attentions of enemy gunners. Michelangelo, helping to organise the city's defence, had the tower covered in mattresses to protect it from cannon balls.

The crypt
San Miniato's relics were transferred to the church's lovely crypt in the 11th century. The sanctuary is supported by four rough-hewn pillars and a forest of more delicate Roman columns. It also has a magnificent carpet of worn pavement tombs.

The first Santa Croce

Santa Croce's origins are slightly mysterious. It seems Franciscan friars preached in the vicinity at an oratory dedicated to the Holy Cross (Santa Croce). Florence was an early Franciscan centre, among the first towns after Assisi in which the Order established a foothold. In 1218 the Franciscans founded the hospital of San Gallo. In the same year, according to legend, St Francis personally founded the first Santa Croce. Fragments of a 13th-century chapel found after the 1966 flood lend the legend some credence.

The dignified lines of Santa Croce soar above the rooftops

▶▶▶ Santa Croce   IFCF3

Piazza Santa Croce

'In Santa Croce's holy precincts', wrote Lord Byron, 'lie/ Ashes which make it holier, dust which is/ Even in itself an immortality.' Some 270 eminent Florentines lie buried in the church, including such illustrious corpses as Galileo, Ghiberti, Michelangelo and Machiavelli. Alongside them are frescos by Giotto and his followers, a small museum with Cimabue's famous flood-damaged *Crucifix*, and Brunelleschi's Cappella dei Pazzi, widely acknowledged as a masterpiece of the early Renaissance. Taken together, these attractions make Santa Croce the city's most important church.

History The church (1294–1450) was probably designed by Arnolfo di Cambio, architect of the Duomo and the Palazzo Vecchio (both begun at about the same time). Its Franciscan sponsors – theoretically members of an Order dedicated to poverty – were determined from the outset to create one of Christendom's largest churches (equal in size to Rome's old St Peter's). In pursuing size for its own sake, the Franciscans were anxious not to be outdone by the Dominicans, then in the process of building the equally grandiose **Santa Maria Novella** (see pages 148–53). They were also being pressured by the *Comune* to create a church which, as well as 'benefiting the soul', would also 'do credit to the city'.

Both the city of Florence and private families sank vast sums into the project. Foremost among the latter were the members of banking dynasties, unsettled by their usurious practices and eager to ease their consciences by trying to purchase redemption. Clans like the Bardi, Peruzzi and Baroncelli, in particular, sought spiritual deliverance by commissioning chapels around the church. It was also considered an act of humility – ironically, given the church's grandeur – to be buried amidst the 'humble' Franciscans (hence Santa Croce's large number of tombs).

The interior A glance around Santa Croce's enormous interior suggests an intimidating sightseeing prospect. Work methodically around the church, however, and the labour is not as daunting as it appears. The main features of interest are identified on the plan on pages 140–1.

The nave Before doing anything, be sure to sit and take in the atmosphere. The barn-like sense of space, not unlike that of the Duomo, is accentuated by high and graceful Gothic arches, leading the eye to a glorious and delicately strutted wooden ceiling. Patches of fresco adorn the walls, tantalising suggestions of how the church might once have appeared (fresco cycles by Orcagna in the nave were destroyed by Vasari in the 16th century to make way for side altars).

A façade at last
Even after 150 years of building, Santa Croce was left without a façade. One was added only in the 19th century, paid for by the Englishman Sir Francis Sloane. Even then it was a fake, designed by a charlatan who claimed to have discovered the long-lost plans for the 'original' façade. In fact it is based on Orcagna's Tabernacle in Orsanmichele (see pages 110–11).

139

A plea for humility
St Francis would have been none too happy with Santa Croce. 'Small churches should be built,' he once wrote, 'for they ought not to raise great churches for the sake of preaching to the people or for any other reason, for they will show greater humility and give a better example by going to preach in other churches.'

Dubious duties
Despite St Francis's pacific principles, the Franciscans of Florence took over the duties of the papal Inquisition from the Dominicans in 1254. The Head Inquisitor was based at Santa Croce. Two armed friars roamed the city in the company of a lawyer hunting down heretics. 'Confessions' were often extracted with torture, and malefactors could be fined or burnt at the stake. One-third of the fines went to the papacy (and the Inquisition), one-third to the city (they were spent on the city walls), and one-third towards building Santa Croce and Santa Maria Novella.

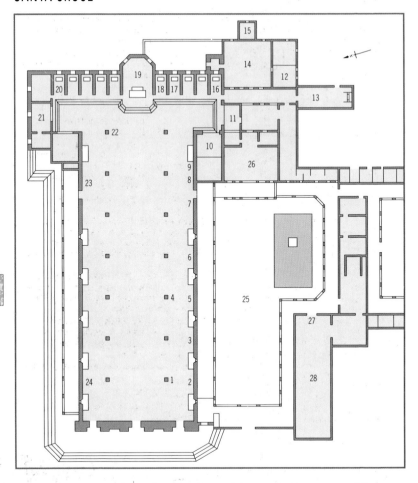

As you walk round the nave looking at some of the many monuments, it soon becomes clear that the finest memorials and the most famous names seldom go together. For example, Dante (though he died and was buried in Ravenna) is remembered here, but his memorial is an undistinguished affair dating from 1829 – even though Michelangelo had offered to carve a monument to the poet some three centuries earlier. Galileo, Michelangelo himself and Machiavelli are all here, but their monuments are unexceptional in comparison with the magnificent Renaissance tombs of Leonardo Bruni and Carlo Marsuppini, eminent 15th-century scholars and humanists who are given places of honour at the head of the aisles. Bruni was a Chancellor of the Republic, author of the city's first history (a copy of which he is shown holding), and a translator of Plato, Aristotle and Plutarch. He was also responsible for organising the competition to design the Baptistery doors. His tomb, by Bernardo Rossellino (see panel), was one of the most influential funerary monuments of the Renaissance. The human figure dominates for the first time in a secular tomb, lacking the figures of saints or virtues, with the Madonna and

Monumental sculptors
The tomb of Leonardo Bruni in Santa Croce is the best-known work of Bernardo Rossellino (1427–79), an architect who was also responsible for planning the 'new town' of Pienza. His brother Antonio (1409–64) made the tomb of the Cardinal of Portugal in the church of San Miniato al Monte.

1. *Madonna del Latte* (1478), a relief by Antonio Rossellino above the tomb of Francesco Nori, a victim of the violent aftermath of the Pazzi Conspiracy (see pages 74–5).
2. Tomb of Michelangelo (1570). (See the panel on page 143.)
3. Cenotaph to Dante (1829).
4. Pulpit (1472–6) by Benedetto da Maiano.
5. Monument to Vittorio Alfieri (1810) by Antonio Canova.
6. Tomb of Niccolò Machiavelli (1787; Machiavelli died in 1527).
7. *The Annunciation* (c.1435) by Donatello.
8. Tomb of Leonardo Bruni (1446–7) by Bernardo Rossellino.
9. Monument to the composer Gioacchino Rossini (1792–1868) by Giuseppe Cassioli.
10. Cappella Castellani, with frescos by Agnolo Gaddi (c.1385)
11. Cappella Baroncelli, with frescos by Taddeo Gaddi (1332–8).
12. Santa Croce's shop. Beyond the shop is a small leather workshop.
13. Cappella Medici, commissioned from Michelozzo by Cosimo de' Medici. The terracotta altarpiece is by Andrea della Robbia. *Note*: this chapel is usually closed for services.
14. Sacristy. Noted for its 16th-century wood panelling and for three fine frescos on the south (back) wall: the *Crucifixion* (Taddeo Gaddi, c.1340–55), the *Way to Calvary* (Spinello Aretino, c.1400) and the *Resurrection* (Pietro Gerini, c.1400).
15. Cappella Rinuccini. This tiny, grille-covered chapel is covered with frescos of the lives of the Virgin and Mary Magdalene (c.1365) by Giovanni da Milano, one of Giotto's more pioneering followers.
16. Cappella Velluti. The browny frescos, by a follower of Cimabue, are overshadowed by Giovanni del Biondo's polyptych altarpiece.
17. Cappella Peruzzi, with frescos by Giotto (c.1326–30).
18. Cappella Bardi, with frescos by Giotto (c.1315–20).
19. Chancel. The extensive frescos here depict the Legend of the True Cross. They and the stained glass are both by Agnolo Gaddi (c.1380). The high altar polyptych is a composite of panels by different artists. *Note*: the chancel is often closed to visitors.
20. Cappella Bardi di Vernio. This chapel is superbly frescoed with scenes from the life of St Sylvester painted by Maso di Banco, one of Giotto's most sophisticated followers.
21. Cappella Bardi. The wooden *Crucifix* here, byDonatello, was reputedly denigrated by Brunelleschi for making Christ look 'like a peasant on a Cross'.
22. Monument to Leon Battista Alberti by Lorenzo Bartolini (early 19th century).
23. Tomb of Carlo Marsuppini (1453) by Desiderioda Settignano.
24. Monument to Galileo by Stefano Ricci (1737).
25. First cloister.
26. Cappella dei Pazzi.
27. Museo dell'Opera di Santa Croce.
28. Refectory.

141

The Sacristy frescos, dated to the 14th century

Santa Croce contains dozens of monuments, some to famous people (above, detail from Michelangelo's tomb) and some by famous sculptors

Stendhal at Santa Croce
The tourist who tries to see too much, warned the French novelist Stendhal, 'will develop a furious headache, and presently satiety and pain will render him incapable of any pleasure.' He appears to have had a turn of sorts himself after visiting Santa Croce: 'I was moved almost to tears,' he wrote, 'I've never seen anything so beautiful … Painting has never given me so much pleasure. I was tired, my feet swollen and pinched in new boots – sensations which would prevent God from being admired in His glory … but I overlooked it … Emerging from Santa Croce I was seized with a fierce palpitation of the heart: I walked in constant fear of falling to the ground.' *Diaries* (1811)

Child banished to a position high in the lunette. Desiderio da Settignano (see panel, page 59) took Bruni's tomb as his inspiration for that of Marsuppini, who lies in an equally prominent place, despite the fact that Marsuppini is said to have died without taking confession or communion. Near Bruni's tomb, note Donatello's outstanding *Annunciation*, an unusual work in gilded *pietra serena*.

Further down the nave, close to Benedetto da Maiano's lovely pulpit (see panel, page 59), with its five expressive panels intimately carved with scenes from the life of St Francis, another monument recalls the famous Italian poet and dramatist Vittorio Alfieri (1749–1803). Sculpted by Antonio Canova, the tomb was paid for by Alfieri's mistress, the Countess of Albany, erstwhile wife of Bonnie Prince Charlie. The countess modelled for the tomb's figure, a symbol of Italy bereaved by Alfieri's death.

The chapels Santa Croce's chapels were decorated with the lives of religious figures of particular relevance to the Franciscans. The **Cappella Castellani's** patchy frescos (*c.*1385), by Agnolo Gaddi and assistants, depict (on the right) the stories of St John the Baptist and St Nicholas of Bari (the patron saint of children – he is shown saving girls from prostitution and reviving three murdered boys). On the left are episodes from the lives of St John and St Antony Abbot (Antony gave away his wealth in keeping with the Franciscan tradition of proverty). The frescos (1332–8) in the nearby **Cappella Baroncelli** are by Agnolo's father Taddeo Gaddi, a pupil of Giotto. They depict scenes from the life of the Virgin. The panels contain the first night scenes in Italian painting. This chapel's altarpiece, *The Coronation of the Virgin*, is probably by Giotto, with Taddeo Gaddi and assistants.

Giotto was also responsible for the frescos in the **Cappella Peruzzi** and the adjoining **Cappella Bardi** – two chapels which together form the church's artistic highlight. Motifs and scenes from both chapels were to be copied again and again by subsequent painters. Many of

the panels are in poor condition, the result of Giotto having painted some scenes on dry plaster (see pages 98–9). Their condition was worsened in the 18th century when both chapels were whitewashed and then badly repainted. Restoration in the 1950s repaired some of the damage. The frescos in the Cappella Peruzzi (*c*.1326–30) show scenes from the life of St John on the right wall and scenes from the life of St John the Baptist on the left. The Cappella Bardi's frescos (*c*.1315–20) are in better condition. Like Giotto's great Assisi cycle they depict scenes from the life of St Francis. The left wall has: *Francis Renouncing his Worldly Goods; Francis Appearing to St Antony of Arles; The Death of St Francis*. On the right wall are *Francis Issuing the Franciscan Rule; Francis's Ordeal by Fire before the Sultan; Francis Appearing to Friar Augustine and the Bishop of Assisi*. The vaults show allegories of Poverty, Chastity and Obedience, the three qualities on which Francis founded his Order. The entrance arch depicts *Francis Receiving the Stigmata*. Figures on the rear wall are Franciscan saints. Notice, in particular, *The Death of St Francis*, vividly portraying the touching and deeply felt emotions of the grieving friars. Around 150 years later Ghirlandaio used this as a model for his own version of the scene in **Santa Trinita**'s Cappella Sassetti (see page 154).
Open: daily 8–6:30 (closed 12:30–3 in winter and on Sunday; also closed Sunday morning in winter).

Cappella dei Pazzi and Museo dell'Opera di Santa Croce

Outside Santa Croce to the south are the church's convent buildings, home to two beautiful cloisters, the Cappella dei Pazzi and the Museo dell'Opera di Santa Croce. The **Cappella dei Pazzi** is perhaps the finest of Brunelleschi's smaller works, an even more complete encapsulation of Renaissance architectural ideals than San Lorenzo's Sagrestia Vecchia. Begun in 1430, its exterior remained unfinished at the time of the Pazzi Conspiracy (none of the Pazzi family is buried here). All is calm within, the interior based on the harmonious interaction of circle and square. Simple geometric forms are matched by simple decoration, with the repetition of similar elements. The 12 terracotta tondi of the Apostles are by Luca della Robbia (as is the decoration in the portico). The polychrome roundels in the upper corners have been attributed to Donatello and Brunelleschi.

Off the cloister on the right is the entrance to the small **Museo dell'Opera di Santa Croce**. Piazza Santa Croce is the city's lowest point: church and museum languished under 6m of water in the 1966 flood. Cimabue's damaged *Crucifix* hangs in the Refectory, together with a superlative fresco by Taddeo Gaddi of the Last Supper. Along the walls are fragments of fresco by Orcagna saved from Vasari and removed from the main church. Centrestage stands Donatello's redoubtable *St Louis of Toulouse*, commissioned for a niche in **Orsanmichele** (see pages 110–11).
Open: daily 10–12:30 and 2:30–6:30 (winter 3–5). Closed Wednesday. Admission charge (inexpensive).

Florence Nightingale
In Santa Croce's first cloister is a monument to Florence Nightingale, who was born in Florence in 1820 and named after the city.

Michelangelo's tomb
Michelangelo's body was returned to Florence from Rome in 1574, 10 years after his death (and 34 years after he left the city). He wished to be buried near Santa Croce's entrance, it is said, so that on the Day of Judgement (when tombs would fly open), the first thing he set eyes on would be Brunelleschi's cathedral dome. Originally the tomb was to have included pieces of his own sculpture (such as the *Pietà* in the Museo dell'Opera del Duomo – see page 96). In the end posterity had to make do with a memorial by Vasari.

143

Figure from Vasari's 1570 tomb of Michelangelo

SANTA FELICITA

Jacopo Pontormo

Pontormo (1494–1556) was one of Florence's more Bohemian painters. Disturbed, reclusive and terrified of disease, he lived in the top room of a house, which could only be reached by the ladder that he pulled up when he wished to be alone. His diary records both his parsimonious meals and the daily state of his bowels and kidneys. One writer claimed he 'kept dead bodies in troughs of water to make them swell' (in order to study them). Vasari said Pontormo had a morbid fear of death, and described his room as a 'beast's lair'. The artist worked only when the mood took him, which was infrequently, but he devoted the last 18 years of his life to a fresco cycle in San Lorenzo. It was totally destroyed in the 18th century.

▶ **Santa Felicita** *IFCD3*

Florence's second oldest church (after San Lorenzo), Santa Felicita may have been founded as early as the 2nd century, perhaps by Syrian or Greek merchants who settled in the area and who may have been responsible for introducing Christianity to Florence. A 4th-century church certainly existed on the site, dedicated to St Felicity, an early Roman martyr. That building was replaced by new churches in the 11th and 14th centuries. Vasari added a portico in 1564 (to accommodate his *corridoio* – see page 129), and in 1736 all but the façade received a thorough remodelling.

In view of all these changes it is small wonder that little in the interior of Santa Felicita suggests the church's antiquity. Instead the inside is a miniature version of the grey-stone *pietra serena* interiors found all over the city. Only the **Cappella Capponi** (immediately to the right of the entrance) provides a compelling reason to go inside. Designed in 1420 by Brunelleschi (but later altered), the small chapel is famous for Jacopo Pontormo's extraordinary *Deposition* (1525–8), one of the supreme masterpieces of Mannerist painting (located above the main altar).

The painting's chief impact is in its remarkable colours: vivid purples, puce, candy-floss pinks, and luminous Wedgwood blues. Christ, a pallid corpse, is the only realistically coloured figure. He is also the only conventional element in this *Deposition*. The thieves, cross and Roman soldiers are all missing. In fact the only extraneous characters are a set of strange, androgynous figures, whilst the only background detail is a solitary ghostly cloud. Pontormo may have included himself in the picture – the brown-cloaked figure on the extreme right is said to be a self-portrait.

The chapel's right-hand wall displays another work by Pontormo, an *Annunciation*, but it is tame by comparision, almost as if painted by another artist. The tondi of the Evangelists on the ceiling are also by Pontormo, with the exception of *St Mark*, which is a copy of an original by Bronzino.

The Cappella Capponi in Santa Felicita was designed by Brunelleschi

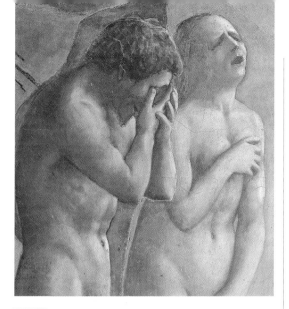

Masaccio's Adam and Eve banished from Paradise: a scene from the seminal series of frescos in the Cappella Brancacci, Santa Maria del Carmine

►►► Santa Maria del Carmine   *IFCC3*

Piazza del Carmine

For itself, Santa Maria del Carmine would rank low in the roll of honour of Florentine churches. Built between 1268 and 1422, it was almost completely rebuilt after a disastrous fire in 1771. Among the areas that survived, however, was the **Cappella Brancacci**, which is decorated with one of the most important and influential fresco cycles in Western art (see pages 146–7). It was commissioned in 1424 by Felice Brancacci, a powerful patrician figure, shortly after his return from a period as Florence's ambassador to Egypt.

The painter Masolino da Panicale (1383–1447) set to work on the chapel in 1424, fresh from a stint working with Ghiberti on the bronze doors for the Battistero. With him was a 22-year-old pupil, Tommaso di Ser Giovanni di Mone Cassai, better known by his nickname Masaccio (Mad Tom). The youngster's talent received fuller rein in 1426 when Masolino was recalled to Budapest, where he was painter to the Hungarian court. Left to his own devices, Masaccio demonstrated a mastery of perspective, narrative drama and bold naturalism not seen in Florence since the days of Giotto. 'In a career of but a few years,' wrote Bernard Berenson (in *Italian Painters of the Renaissance*, 1930), 'he gave to Florentine painting the direction it pursued to the end.' The frescos became, in Berenson's words, 'the training school of Florentine painters.'

Masolino – now revealed as his pupil's inferior – returned to the chapel in 1427. He was called away again in 1428, this time to Rome. Masaccio followed him a few months later. Neither was to work on the frescos again; the brilliant Masaccio died in the Holy City in 1428, aged just 27. After 1436, when Brancacci was exiled by Cosimo de' Medici, the frescos remained untouched until 1480–5, when they were completed by Filippino Lippi in a style so carefully copied from that of the original artists that Lippi's work was only recognised in 1838.

Cappella Brancacci open: daily 10–4:30 (Sunday 1–4:30). Closed Tuesday. Admission charge (moderate).

Narrow escapes
The Brancacci frescos have survived against considerable odds. In 1680 Francesco Ferroni, the chapel's new patron, sought to remove 'these ridiculous men in their cassocks and old-fashioned outfits'. His attempt was thwarted only by the Accademia del Disegno and Vittoria della Rovere, wife of Ferdinand II. In the 1771 fire the frescos' gilt frames caught fire, damaging their fringes and compounding damage inflicted by centuries of candle wax and revarnishing. By the time Bernard Berenson saw them in 1930, the frescos were 'dust-bitten and ruined'.

145

■ **All but two scenes of Santa Maria del Carmine's great fresco cycle – the work of Masaccio, Masolino and Filippino Lippi – portray episodes from the life of St Peter, to whom the chapel is dedicated. The original plan for the series of paintings was probably drawn up by Masolino......■**

Plan of the frescos in the Cappella Brancacci

146

Practicalities
The entrance to the Cappella Brancacci is through the cloister to the right of the church. During busy times a maximum of 30 people are allowed in the chapel for 15 minutes. For opening times see page 145.

1. The expulsion of Adam and Eve (Masaccio). One of the most powerful images in Renaissance art, this traumatic fresco shows Adam and Eve distraught at their banishment from Paradise. Eve is half-hugging herself in grief and Adam – plunged into despair – trudges forward with his head in his hands. Notice the angel above them, an almost avenging figure brandishing the sword of righteousness. Compare this harrowing depiction of Adam and Eve with Masolino's far gentler and jollier portrayal of the pair opposite, in panel 6.

2. The tribute money (Masaccio). Three episodes are depicted here in the same scene. In the centre, Christ is asked by an official outside the gates of Capernaum to pay the tribute money owing to the city. He orders the apostles to: 'Render unto Caesar that which is Caesar's'. To the left, St Peter takes coins from the mouth of a fish for the tribute. To the right, St Peter hands over the money to the tax collector.

3. St Peter preaching at Jerusalem on Whit Sunday (Masolino).

4. St Peter baptises the Neophytes (Masaccio).

5. St Peter heals the cripple and raises Tabitha (Masolino). St Peter, in the company of St John, heals a cripple and brings Tabitha back to life. Note the background view of 15th-century Florence, and the pair of well-dressed Florentines, blithely ignoring the miracles taking place to either side.

6. The temptation of Adam and Eve (Masolino).

7. St Paul visits St Peter in prison (Filippino Lippi).

8. St Peter enthroned and the raising of Theophilus' son (Masaccio and Filippino Lippi). Theophilus was the son of the Prefect of Antioch. St Peter raises him after he has been dead for 14 years. The people of Antioch, looking on, are converted to Christianity by the miracle. They build Peter a throne from which to preach. The three figures to the right of the throne are said to represent Masaccio, Alberti and Brunelleschi.

9. St Peter healing the sick with his shadow (Masaccio). The lame are healed one by one as Peter's shadow passes over them. St John follows in St Peter's footsteps.

10. The distribution of alms and the death of Ananias (Masaccio). St Peter tells the people to give up their possessions to be distributed among the poor. Ananias retains some of his wealth and gives up his soul instead. Notice touching details such as the bottom of the child peeping out under its white smock.

11. St Peter and St Paul before the Proconsul, and the Crucifixion of St Peter (Filippino Lippi).

12. St Peter freed from prison by an angel (Filippino Lippi).

147

Restoration
Unsullied patches of the Cappella Brancacci's frescos, showing what might lie beneath the grime, were found in 1932 under an altar installed in the 18th century. Restoration, however, only started 50 years later. Olivetti paid for the clean-up, which was completed in 1988.

An inspiration to others
'All the most celebrated sculptors and painters since Masaccio's day have become excellent and illustrious by studying their art in this chapel.' Vasari, *Lives of the Artists* (1550)

Left and top opposite: in Filippino Lippi's fresco, St Paul visits St Peter in prison

The polychrome Romanesque façade of Santa Maria Novella

▶▶▶ Santa Maria Novella IFCC4

Piazza Santa Maria Novella

A certain squalour pervades Piazza Santa Maria Novella, a square where young people congregate during the day, and the scene of some seedy goings-on at night. It therefore comes as a relief to enter Santa Maria Novella, a church to rival Santa Croce in its scale and in the beautiful variety of its decoration. Originally a simple 9th-century chapel, it was rebuilt in 1094 as Santa Maria delle Vigne. In 1221 it was given to the Dominicans, who started a new church on the site in 1246. A series of Dominican architects saw the project through to its conclusion in 1360 (among them brothers Sisto and Cami, probably also responsible for much of the work on the Bargello).

The Romanesque façade remained half-finished until 1456, when Leon Battista Alberti completed it in a harmonious Renaissance fashion for Giovanni Rucellai. Note Rucellai's name, picked out in Roman capitals, and his family emblem, the billowing sail of Fortune, woven into the façade's decorative friezes (as it is in the façade of his nearby Palazzo – see pages 120–1).

The interior A classic Gothic shell belies the fact that this was one of the first Italian churches of its kind to depart from the Cistercian model previously copied from France. Much of the original decoration was ruined in the 16th century by Vasari, who bleached numerous frescos, removed the choir and rood screen, and shortened several aisle windows to accommodate new side chapels (he performed similar acts of vandalism in Santa Croce). Some of the damage was undone in the 18th century.

In a trick of perspective, the nave's columns become closer together as you approach the high altar, making the already huge interior seem larger still. While in the nave, be sure to peep out of the doors on the east wall to see the lawns and Gothic-arched arcade of the *avelli*, a communal cemetery for the city's well-to-do medieval families. It is the only one of its kind in Florence.

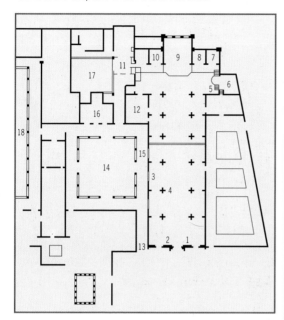

1. *Annunciation* by Santi di Tito.
2. Fresco (Florentine School, late 14th century).
3. *Trinità* (*c*.1428) by Masaccio.
4. Pulpit. It was from this pulpit (1443–52), designed by Brunelleschi, that Galileo was first denounced by the Inquisition for espousing the Copernican theory of the heavens.
5. Three Gothic tombs. The simple classical tomb which precedes (6) is that of Paolo Rucellai.
6. Cappella Rucellai. This raised chapel contains a marble *Madonna and Child* by Nino Pisano, and Lorenzo Ghiberti's bronze tomb (1425) of Dominican General Leonardo Dati. *Note*: the chapel is often closed to visitors.
7. Cappella dei Bardi. The patchy 14th-century frescos here are imprisoned behind a grille. The lunette murals of the Madonna Enthroned have been attributed to Cimabue, Giotto's first teacher.
8. Cappella di Filippo Strozzi, with frescos by Filippino Lippi (completed 1502).
9. Chancel, with frescos by Ghirlandaio (1485–90).
10. Cappella Gondi. The chapel contains Brunelleschi's famous *Crucifix*, his only surviving work in wood. It was reputedly carved in response to Donatello's Santa Croce *Crucifix* (see page 141). Donatello is said to have been so struck on seeing his colleague's work that he dropped a basket of eggs.
11. Cappella Strozzi, with frescos by Nardo di Cione (1351–7).
12. Sacristy. A Giotto *Crucifix* usually hangs here, but it has been under restoration for many years.
13. Entrance to Museo di Santa Maria Novella.
14. Chiostro Verde.
15. Frescos by Paolo Uccello including *The Universal Deluge*.
16. Cappellone degli Spagnoli.
17. Chiostrino dei Morti.
18. Chiostro Grande.

A detail from Masaccio's Trinità: *the kneeling figure on the right is the wife of judge Lorenzo Lenzi, the painting's donor*

SANTA MARIA NOVELLA

Part of the avelli, *Santa Maria's communal cemetery*

Plague victims
Fear generated by the plague prompted the commissioning of many chapels in Santa Maria Novella. At the beginning of his *Decameron*, Boccaccio describes his protagonists in Santa Maria Novella discussing the plague. 'Many dropped dead in the streets, both by day and night, whilst many others, though dying in their houses, drew their neighbours' attention to the fact by the smell of rotting corpses ... How great a number of splendid palaces, fine houses and noble dwellings, once filled with retainers, with lords and ladies, were bereft of all who had lived there, down to the tiniest child. How many gallant gentlemen, fair ladies and sprightly youths, who would have been judged hale and hearty ... having breakfasted in the morning with their kinsfolk ... supped that same evening with their ancestors in the next world.'

Masaccio's *Trinità* Perhaps the single most important work of the early Renaissance, Masaccio's *Trinità* was one of the first paintings successfully to incorporate the ideals of perspective and classical proportion. Florentines queued to see it on its unveiling, flabbergasted by a painting that appeared to create a three-dimensional chapel in a solid wall. The theme of the painting was suggested by the fact that the Dominican calendar began with the Feast of the Trinity.

A skeleton lies below the main picture bearing the none too cheerful motto: 'I was that which you are, you will be that which I am.' The fresco's sponsors, judge Lorenzo Lenzi and his wife, are the figures flanking the pair of painted pillars. Note how the painting's perspective and triangular composition deliberately underline the path of Christian redemption, drawing your eye from the Lenzi through the figures of the Virgin and John the Baptist (humanity's mystical link with the Holy Trinity) to Christ and God the Father at the triangle's apex. The coffered chapel behind owes much to Brunelleschi, whose architecture already applied the principles of perspective mastered here by Masaccio.

Frescos Generations of visitors have come to Santa Maria Novella not only to marvel at the architecture but also to enjoy the many fine frescos that escaped Vasari's whitewash. Filippino Lippi was commissioned to paint the **Cappella di Filippo Strozzi**, bought by the wealthy banker (see page 121) in 1486. Lippi's subject was the life of his saintly namesake, St Philip the Apostle. The cycle, different from anything in Florence at the time, was only finished in 1502, several years after Strozzi's death. Both its awkward style and its classical allusions looked ahead to the Mannerists. St Philip's crucifixion and his miracle in front of the Temple are depicted on the right wall. In the miracle, Philip kills the king's son by summoning forth an unholy stench, wonderfully depicted as orange smoke billowing from a monster's maw. The king's son, stricken and green-faced, collapses into the arms of his followers.

On the left wall are *The Raising of Drusiana* and *The Martyrdom of St John* (he was martyred by being dipped in boiling oil); the vaults depict Adam, Noah, Jacob and Abraham. Lippi also executed the chapel's stained glass and beautiful white *trompe-l'oeil*. The superb tomb of Filippo Strozzi (1491–3) behind the altar is by Benedetto da Maiano.

Several of Santa Maria Novella's chapels were commissioned in the aftermath of the 1348 Black Death (notably the Cappella Strozzi; see page 152). The zealous Dominicans used the terror provoked by the pestilence, seen by many as a sign of divine ire, to cultivate a wave of religious fervour. It was in this chapel (before its frescos were painted) that Boccaccio set the opening of the *Decameron*, a medieval literary masterpiece set in the period during and after the plague (see panels on this page and opposite).

During the period when Lippi was carrying out his commission for the Cappella di Filippo Strozzi, seven vast and very different frescos were being painted on either side of the neighbouring **chancel**. They are the masterpiece (1485–90) of Domenico Ghirlandaio, who numbered the young Michelangelo among his many assistants. They replaced frescos on the same theme by Orcagna, destroyed a century earlier by a bolt of lightning. Ostensibly scenes from the life of the Virgin (left wall) and the life of John the Baptist (right wall), they actually provide magnificent vignettes of daily life, costume and customs in 15th-century Florence. They were commissioned by another banker, Giovanni Tornabuoni, and members of the Tornabuoni family are liberally sprinkled throughout

Boccaccio's *Decameron*
Boccaccio's 100-tale epic (1349–51), told over 10 days, opens in Santa Maria Novella's Cappella di Filippo Strozzi. It was here, one Tuesday morning after Mass, that 'seven ladies young and fair' decided to leave a city ravaged by the plague for the safety and tranquillity of the countryside. Here they would tell stories, 'hear the birds sing, and see the green hills, and the plains, and the fields covered with grain and undulating, like the sea, and trees of species manifold …'

Nice and vulgar
Ghirlandaio's chancel frescos in Santa Maria Novella have often been criticised by serious art critics as superficial. John Ruskin believed 'if you are a nice person, they are not nice enough for you; and if you are a vulgar person, not vulgar enough.' *Mornings in Florence* (1875–7)

St Thomas Aquinas, to whom the Cappella Strozzi is dedicated, depicted in a stained-glass window by the di Cione brothers

SANTA MARIA NOVELLA

Something for the sharp-eyed visitor to seek out in Piazza Santa Maria Novella: a tortoise creeps out from the base of the obelisk

Look-out
The bell-tower of Santa Maria Novella (*c.*1330) was used for years as a watch-tower for spotting fires around the city.

A detail from Ghirlandaio's late 15th-century chancel frescos, in which biblical scenes are depicted in a contemporary context

most scenes. Such flattering glorification singled the paintings out for special vitriol during the sermons of Savonarola a few years later. Ghirlandaio (amid helpers) is shown in a red hat in the scene of the expulsion of St Joachim from the Temple (left wall, lower register). The painter, incidentally, is buried in one of the *avelli* outside the church (see page 149).

Much earlier frescos, ruined but still highly appealing, adorn the **Cappella Strozzi**, whose patrons were Filippo Strozzi's ancestors. Stairs climb to this chapel, on the site of Santa Maria delle Vigne's earlier raised chancel. It is dedicated to St Thomas Aquinas, one of the Dominicans' top-ranking saints, and its frescos (1351–7) are by Nardo di Cione. Most arresting is the crowded *Paradiso* on the left wall. The right wall depicts a map-like *Inferno*, a faded commentary on Dante's epic. Aquinas and the Virtues are shown in the vaults. Dante is one of the saved in the *Last Judgement* behind the altar (third row, second from the top). Signor and Signora Strozzi are also among the saved: they are shown being led by an angel into Paradise. The magnificent altarpiece is by Nardo's brother, Andrea di Cione, better known as Orcagna, and shows Christ giving the keys to St Peter and the Book of Knowledge to St Thomas Aquinas (1357). Both brothers together were responsible for the stained glass.
Open: daily 7–11:30 and 3:30–6.

Museo di Santa Maria Novella With its lovely cloister, Uccello frescos and magnificent chapel, this museum is much more than a mere afterthought to the main church. From the entrance (outside the church to the left of the façade), you reach the Romanesque **Chiostro Verde** (Green Cloister), named after the green *terra verde* pigment of its badly deteriorated fresco cycle. The best-preserved panels are on the right-hand (east) side, notably Panel 4, Paolo Uccello's *Universal Deluge* (*c.*1430), one of Florence's strangest Renaissance paintings. Its lurching compositional vortex vividly illustrates Uccello's obsession with perspective. Notice the arks on either side, before and after the Flood, and the wicker-ring hats, or *marzocchi*, whose 72-faceted structure allowed the painter to indulge his perspectival fixation to the full.

Off the cloister is the **Cappellone degli Spagnoli** (Spanish Chapel), so called because it was used by the Spanish entourage of Eleanor of Toledo (wife of Cosimo I). It was funded by one Lapo Guidalotti, whose wife died in the 1348 plague. At one time it was the headquarters of the Inquisition (later transferred to Santa Croce). Inside lies one of the city's least-known but most extensive fresco cycles (*c.*1365), a sequence described by Ruskin as 'the most noble piece of pictorial philosophy in Italy'. It is the work of the little-known artist Andrea da Firenze. The left wall shows *The Triumph of Doctrine*, exemplified by Thomas Aquinas, who sits enthroned amidst the winged Virtues and Doctors of the Church. The 14 figures below represent the Arts and Sciences: the figures at their feet are their historical embodiments.

The spectacular right wall shows *The Work and Triumph of the Dominican Order*. Note Florence's pinky-purple Duomo (imagined 80 years before its completion) and (bottom right) St Dominic unleashing the 'hounds of the Lord' (*Domini canes*), a pun on the Dominicans' name. Above the kneeling pilgrims are portraits of Cimabue, Giotto, Boccaccio, Dante, Petrarch and others. The four winsome women are the Four Vices, surrounded by scenes of dancing and other examples of unholy debauchery. A nearby friar gathers the saved, hearing confession before sending them heavenwards towards St Peter.

Be sure also to walk into the Chiostrino dei Morti, the oldest part of the church convent, and peep into the Chiostro Grande, used as a police parade ground.

Open: daily 9–2 (Sunday 8–1). Closed Friday. Admission charge (inexpensive). *Biglietto Cumulativo* (combined ticket) available, also covering the Museo Bardini, the Palazzo Vecchio and the Museo di Firenze com'era.

Farmacia di Santa Maria Novella
This famous pharmacy lies just northwest of the church at Via della Scala 16. Founded in 1612, it is well known for its lovely 19th-century neo-gothic interior and its range of old-fashioned soaps, scents and pot-pourris. *Open*: daily 8:30–12:30 and 3–7. Closed Sunday and Monday morning.

153

Old-world remedies in the Farmacia di Santa Maria Novella

▶▶ **Santa Trinita** IFCD3

Piazza Santa Trinita

Santa Trinita appeals not only by virtue of its superb fresco cycle, a masterpiece by Domenico Ghirlandaio, but also because of its oddly harmonious mixture of Gothic austerity and baroque exuberance. Founded in 1092 by Giovanni Gualberto (see panel), the church was rebuilt between 1258 and 1280, possibly by Nicola Pisano. The façade, by Buontalenti, dates from 1594.

In the atmospheric interior, make first for Domenico Ghirlandaio's frescos (1483) in the **Cappella Sassetti** (the right-hand of the two chapels to the right of the altar). A series of scenes from the life of St Francis, they were commissioned by Francesco Sassetti to match those of his rival, Giovanni Tornabuoni, in Santa Maria Novella (also by Ghirlandaio). *St Francis Receiving the Rule*, in the lunette above the altar (the upper of the frescos' three levels) is set in Piazza della Signoria and contains (right foreground) portraits of Sassetti between his son, Federigo, and Lorenzo the Magnificent (Sassetti worked for the Medici bank). On the stairs are the humanist Poliziano and three of his pupils, the sons of Lorenzo the Magnificent.

The chapel's altarpiece, *The Adoration of the Magi*, is also by Ghirlandaio. The epitome of a Renaissance painting, it fuses classical and Christian motifs, setting Mary and the Magi among ancient pillars, a Roman sarcophagus and a triumphal arch transplanted from Rome's ancient forum. Sassetti and his wife are shown on either side, and it is they who occupy the black tombs under the side arches.

The chapel to the left of the Cappella Sassetti contains the *Crucifix* that bowed its head to Gualberto (see panel). On the church's right wall (fourth chapel) are eye-catching frescos by Lorenzo Monaco. To the left of the high altar, the second chapel on the left is graced by the tomb of Benozzo Federighi (a bishop of Florence who died in 1450), executed by Luca della Robbia. Finally, note Neri di Bicci's fresco of Gualberto pardoning his brother's assassin (fourth altar, left wall) and his lovely free-standing *Annunciation* (third altar).

Open: daily 7–12 and 4–7.

Giovanni Gualberto
One Good Friday, so the story goes, Gualberto, an 11th-century Florentine nobleman, set out to avenge the murder of his brother, Ugo. On finding the murderer, however, Gualberto pardoned him in honour of the holy day. Entering San Miniato, he then knelt to pray. As he did, a *Crucifix* (now in Santa Trinita), miraculously bowed its head in approval of his merciful act. Gualberto went on to become a Benedictine monk and founded the Vallombrosan Order. In the 14th century a 40,000-strong brotherhood dedicated to his memory, the Compagnia dei Bianchi, preached forgiveness in an effort to end acts of revenge.

Ghirlandaio's altarpiece, The Adoration of the Magi, *in the Cappella Sassetti*

▶▶ **Santissima Annunziata** *IFCE5*

Piazza Santissima Annunziata

As a church celebrating the Annunciation, Santissima Annunziata has long played a special role in the life of the city, whose New Year, in the old Florentine calendar, started on the Feast of the Annunciation (25 March). It is also the mother church of the Servi di Maria (Servite Order), with whose history it is inextricably linked (see panel).

The Order's fortunes changed dramatically in 1252, when a painting of the Virgin, started by one of the monks, was miraculously completed by an angel. By 1450 so many people were coming to venerate the image that a new church, paid for by the Medici, was commissioned from Michelozzo (the brother of the Servites' head prior). Via dei Servi was built at the same time to link Santissima Annunziata and the Duomo, the two most important churches in the city dedicated to the Virgin.

More changes ensued in 1516, when San Filippo Benizzi, a leading Servite saint, was canonised. To celebrate the event the church's entrance atrium, the covered **Chiostrino dei Voti**, was decorated with superb frescos by Andrea del Sarto, Jacopo Pontormo and Rosso Fiorentino. The church's interior decoration is among the city's most sumptuous – though there is little of real substance beyond the gilt-smothered ceiling and Michelozzo's magnificent Tempietto (to the left of the entrance), which was built (1448–61) to shelter the church's miraculously painted *Virgin*. The second chapel on the left contains Andrea del Castagno's noted *Holy Trinity with St Jerome*. Another more sombre work by the same artist, the *Vision of St Julian*, occupies the first chapel on the left. Outside the church, visit the **Chiostro dei Morti**, entered through a portico on the left of the façade. Over the door in the far right-hand corner is Andrea del Sarto's *Madonna del Sacco*, one of his most famous works.

Open: daily 7:30–12:30 and 4–7.

Andrea del Sarto's work in the Chiostrino

The Servites
In 1234, so the story goes, seven noblemen abandoned Florence to live in poverty on nearby Monte Senario. Here they dedicated themselves to the cult of the Annunciation, taking the name Servants of Mary. On the site of the present church, then a field outside the city walls, they built a small oratory.

Offerings to the Virgin
It became a tradition for pilgrims to leave wax votive offerings in honour of the the Annunziata's *Virgin*. Initially placed around the walls, the images became so numerous that they were eventually hung from the nave ceiling and placed in the Chiostrino dei Voti. Most were life-size statues of the donors, many of them portrayed fully clothed and riding wax horses. The collection of 600 statues was renowned throughout Europe until 1786, when the images were melted down to make candles.

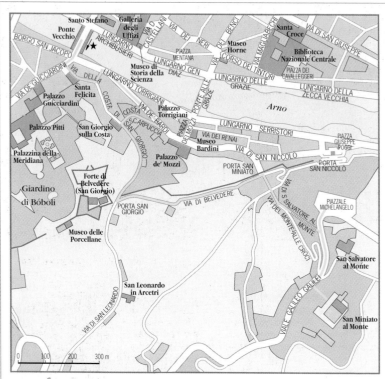

Walk To San Miniato al Monte

An uphill walk in the Oltrarno, worth the effort for fine views of the city walls, across open countryside and over Florence (2km; allow 2 hours if you plan to visit the churches).

Start at the **Ponte Vecchio**►►► (see pages 128–9). Visit the church of **Santa Felicita**►, known for its Pontormo frescos (see page 144), before starting a steady climb on Via de' Bardi and Costa Scarpuccia – a pleasant alternative to the more direct route along Costa di San Giorgio.

Turn left uphill on Costa di San Giorgio. The house on the right at No 19 was the home of Galileo before he was condemned by the Inquisition (see pages 106–7). At Porta San Giorgio, the city's oldest surviving gate (1258), turn right into the **Forte del Belvedere** for views over Florence and the Giardino di Boboli (see the panel on page 84).

Turn left down Via di Belvedere, which follows the line of the city walls, with views of olive groves and distant hills. At the bottom turn right for 150m until you see the stepped lane of Via di San Salvatore del Monte on your left. Walk up the avenue of cypress trees and Calvary crosses, turning right at the top to visit **San Miniato**►►► (pages 136–7). Return downhill to Piazzale Michelangelo for more views. The no 13 bus will take you back from here to the city centre.

► **Santo Spirito** *IFCC3*

Piazza Santo Spirito

You can have too much of a good thing. The piazza fronting Santo Spirito may be among the city's most pleasant – its shady trees and cobbles a welcome whiff of old Italy – but the church itself is one Brunelleschi-designed barn too many (even if Bernini did call it 'the most beautiful church in the world'). Behind its barren façade lies an interior of grey pillars, dour arches and an almost impenetrable gloom. Although the effect is calming, it barely tempts you to explore the 38 side chapels in search of their hidden treasures (which, in fact, are very few).

Brunelleschi designed the building in 1434 to replace an earlier Augustinian church (1250–92). Work on the project commenced in 1444, two years before the architect's death, just one column in the nave being raised during his lifetime. Fire, financial shortfalls and arguments over the design delayed final completion until 1487. The sandy-coloured façade dates from the 18th century, its plaster obscuring earlier and, by all accounts, more prepossessing decoration. The interior, however, remains true to Brunelleschi's design, only the baroque high altar disturbing its bland unity of tone.

The church's artistic highlight is Filippino Lippi's age-blackened *Madonna and Child with Saints*, located in the right transept (second chapel from the left of the four chapels on its south wall). Across in the left transept, your eye is caught by an anonymous *Madonna and Saints* (first chapel on the right as you stand with your back to the altar). In the chapel to its left is the unmistakable *St Monica and Augustinian Nuns*, an unusual and strangely composed painting attributed to Andrea del Verrocchio. Paintings in this transept's other chapels are worth a quick look.

To the left is the entrance to the much-praised (but actually rather dowdy) Vestibule (1489), where 12 columns are crammed into a tiny space. It was designed, like the adjoining Sacristy, by Giuliano da Sangallo.

Open: daily 8–12 and 4–6.

The peaceful piazza

Cost-cutting
The building of Santo Spirito cost so much money that its Augustinian monks gave up one meal a day as a fund-raising example to others. The money saved went towards the church.

Refectory frescos
The refectory of Santo Spirito's vanished 13th-century Augustinian monastery contains damaged but important frescos attributed to Orcagna. One depicts the Last Supper, the other a large Crucifixion. The entrance is to the left of the main church at Piazza Santo Spirito 29. *Open*: daily 9–2 (Sunday 10–1). Closed Monday. Admission charge (inexpensive).

Thwarted
Medieval architects had only limited influence. Brunelleschi wanted Santo Spirito to enjoy a view of the Arno, but was thwarted by the rich families whose homes would have had to be demolished.

■ **The Florentine Renaissance of the 15th century was preceded by more than a century of artistic development across Tuscany and central Italy. Artists such as Giotto and Nicola Pisano steered art away from the stilted conventions of Byzantium, moving it gradually towards the more naturalistic style of the Renaissance......■**

158

Giotto di Bondone (c.1266–1337)
Born of peasant stock in the hills above Florence, Giotto spent his early life tending his father's flock. According to legend it was thus that Cimabue found him, scratching pictures of his sheep on pieces of stone. He became a friend of Dante and Petrarch, the other great iconoclasts of the age. Fresco cycles in Rome and Naples are lost, while the true authorship of his famous work on the life of St Francis in Assisi is disputed. The frescos in Santa Croce and in Padua's Cappella Scrovegni are his only universally attributed cycles.

Dante on Giotto
Dante described how Giotto surpassed his erstwhile teacher: 'Cimabue thought he held the field in painting, but now his fame is obscured and the cry is Giotto.' *Divine Comedy* (1321)

Top: a Giovanni Pisano pulpit, Pisa. Below: Sienese work – popes in the Duomo

New world, old art Byzantine art dominated Italy until the 12th century. Its reverential approach was typified by beautiful but highly stylised Madonnas which eschewed real life, lacking naturalistic detail and almost any sense of movement, shadow or depth. Imagine, then, how its exponents would have reacted to Renaissance paintings, whose attributes were outlined two centuries later in Alberti's treatise *Della Pittura* (Of Painting, 1436). 'Copiousness and variety', it suggested, should characterise a work of art, whose brief should embrace 'old, young, maidens, women, youths, young boys, fowls, small dogs, birds, horses, sheep, buildings, provinces ...'

Much had obviously changed in 200 years. City states, increased prosperity and a wealth of new learning had all produced an increasingly sophisticated society. In the early part of the period, however, art still lagged behind the changes. It seemed to require some new or reinvented artistic language to match – and express – the advances in the civic domain.

Sculpture The first stirrings of this new language came with the sculptural work of Nicola Pisano (1220–84), whose great pulpits in Pisa's Baptistery and Siena's cathedral took as their inspiration the realistic reliefs of Roman sarcophagi brought to Pisa from the Holy Land. Such reworking of classical forms was to be a cornerstone of Renaissance art, and one which Pisano's pupil, Arnolfo di Cambio (1245–1302), and his son, Giovanni Pisano (1248–1314), were to develop further. Giovanni's work on the façade of Siena cathedral, along with his pulpits in Pisa and Pistoia, incorporated startling new positions for figures – designs and forms never before seen in sculpture – and brought new vigour to formalised images: the Mother and Child ensemble, for example, began to

STEPHANVS M   PASCHALIS I   EVGENIVS II   VALENTIN

Santa Croce frescos

suggest an emotional relationship in which maternal love received artistic expression.

Painting After lagging behind sculpture's advance, painting also began to shake off the strictures of Byzantine art. The transformation began in the late 13th century in Rome, where painters like Pietro Cavallini turned from mosaic – very much a Byzantine tradition – to fresco, a medium more able to match sculpture's new realism and more complex compositions. His lead was taken up by the Florentine Cimabue (1240–1302), called by Vasari the 'father of Italian painting', who furthered the move towards naturalism with work in Assisi's Basilica di San Francesco. Here he was soon joined by his pupil, Giotto, born in about 1266.

Giotto Giotto revolutionised Italian art, forging a new style independent of both Byzantine and Gothic convention. Simply put, he introduced realism and naturalism into painting. His works had light and shade, depth and foreshortening. Events, now infused with narrative drama, turned to the real world for subject and inspiration. For the first time, people capable of movement and emotion were set in backgrounds informed by naturalistic details. In time Giotto's disciples – Maso di Banco, Agnolo di Gaddi and others – were painting in their master's style around Florence's churches. Sienese painters, who had long adapted Byzantine motifs to their own brilliant use of colour and design, now fused the influence of Duccio, their school's founding father, with the space and realism of Giotto. The style that resulted, exemplified by men like Simone Martini, Lippo Memmi and Pietro Lorenzetti, was of immense influence, not only in Italy but also in France, Holland and England.

Giotto in Florence
Giotto probably painted Santa Croce's Bardi and Peruzzi chapels between 1315 and 1330. He owned property in the city, and occupied a prominent position in the Arti Maggiori. He also requested a seat on the *Signoria*, even though he did not meet the two-year residency condition. A second spell in the city saw him appointed city architect and *capomaestro* of the Duomo (1334). He designed the Campanile, and may have planned some of its reliefs.

Boccaccio on Giotto
'Giotto's art was of such excellence that there was nothing in nature that his pen or paintbrush could not exactly reproduce, not simply to make a likeness, but to be the very thing itself. His work was so perfect that a man standing before it would often find his visual senses confused, taking for real what was only painted.'
Decameron (1349–51)

*Waiting in line for
the Uffizi's art*

▶▶▶ **Uffizi, Galleria degli** *IFCD3*

Piazzale degli Uffizi

One of the world's great art galleries, the Uffizi contains in its 45 rooms not only the best Florentine paintings of the 14th and 15th centuries, but also masterpieces from elsewhere in Italy (Venice and Siena in particular) as well as four centuries' worth of works from the leading artists of Holland, Spain and Germany. The gallery's building, begun by Vasari in 1560, was originally designed as a suite of offices (*uffizi*) from which to administer the Grand Duchy. In 1743 they were left to the city, along with the Medici art collection, by Anna Maria Luisa, sister of the last Medici Grand Duke, Gian Gastone.

Serious art-lovers will want to visit the Uffizi at least twice, the high admission notwithstanding. If you are so tempted, your first visit should cover Rooms 1–15, dedicated to the Florentine Renaissance (and home to the most famous paintings). A second visit might deal with Rooms 16–27, devoted to the High Renaissance and Mannerism in Florence. Rooms 28–45 move out from the city to encompass later Italian and European paintings (the rooms are arranged in chronological order throughout). Only highlights are given below, especially in later rooms, but do not be tempted to skim through the gallery's final stages. Its last three rooms, for example, contain masterpieces by Caravaggio, Rembrandt and Canaletto respectively. The collection proper starts on the third floor (lift or stairs). Downstairs, in rooms that formed part of an earlier church, are detached frescos including portraits of illustrious Florentines by Andrea del Castagno and an *Annunciation* by Botticelli.

Room 1 (Roman statues; often closed) Statues were considered the Uffizi's main attraction until the last century, when many were removed to the Bargello. Shelley, for example, ignored the paintings altogether when he visited, and Gibbon made 12 tours of the gallery before even looking at a painting.

Room 2 The Uffizi opens in majestic style, with three altarpieces of the Madonna Enthroned by Italy's greatest

The Uffizi bomb
The terrorist car bomb that exploded in an alleyway behind the Uffizi in the early hours of 27 May 1993 left five people dead and nearly 40 works of art damaged – some beyond repair. Miraculously, the Renaissance masterpieces are located on the eastern side of the gallery, away from the blast, and escaped the worst effects. Much of the collection was open again within a month, but many months of rebuilding and restoration were needed to repair wrecked rooms and staircases on the west side of the gallery. Rooms 26–33 and 41–5 were still closed at the time of writing.

13th-century artists – Giotto, Duccio and Cimabue. Each reflects a stage in the development of Italian art away from the influence of Byzantium. Duccio's version (c.1285), while rooted in the older tradition, suggests hints of what was to come in the folds of the Virgin's cloak and her delicately painted throne. Byzantium is uppermost in Cimabue's version (painted around 1280 for the church of Santa Trinita), though touches of perspective are used to create a sense of depth and volume. The throne, however, is cruder than Duccio's, and gold is used instead of light and shadow to pick out folds in the Madonna's cloak (a Byzantine device).

Compare both with Giotto's version, painted around 1310 for the church of Ognissanti. Light and shade (*chiaroscuro*) give body to the Madonna's clothing and, in a deft piece of realism, the Virgin even has the suggestion of breasts. Both the Madonna and her throne have solidity and depth, while the relationship between Mother and Child suggests genuine human tenderness. The surrounding angels and saints are standing, rather than floating rootlessly as they do in the works by Duccio and Cimabue.

Room 3 (14th-century Sienese School) Siena's art has been called 'poetry' to Florence's 'prose'. In this room are displayed some of the greatest Sienese paintings, including *The Annunciation* (c.1333) by Simone Martini (the two flanking saints are by Martini's brother-in-law, Lippo Memmi), and works by the brothers Pietro and Ambrogio Lorenzetti, both of whom died in the 1348 plague. Ghiberti called Ambrogio a 'most famous and unique master,' preferring him to Martini, whom the Sienese considered their finest painter.

Room 4 (14th-century Florentine School) Painters from this period shown here, such as Orcagna, Taddeo Gaddi and Bernardo Gaddi, are better represented by the fresco cycles of Santa Croce and Santa Maria Novella.

Room 5-6 (International Gothic) Florence's leading exponent of the courtly, highly embellished International

Visiting the Uffizi
The Uffizi is the most visited museum in Italy (1.5 million visitors a year). Queues are almost inevitable. Weekends and between 11am and 3pm are the busiest times, so arrive early or late in the day if possible. For opening times see page 165.

Domenico Veneziano
This Venetian artist is one of the rarest of painters. There are only 12 known paintings by him in the world (only two of them signed), three of which are in Florence (though the Uffizi's is the only one on public view). He spent most of his life in Venice, but died destitute in Florence.

161

Giotto's Madonna di Ognissanti

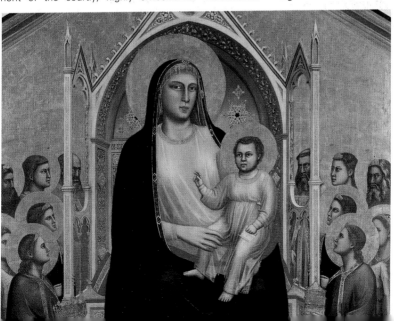

UFFIZI

Federico da Montefeltro

Duke Federico's court at Urbino was renowned throughout Europe for its culture and learning. His hooked nose is also one of the most familiar profiles of the Middle Ages. He is always depicted in left profile, for the right side of his face was badly disfigured in a jousting accident. The allegorical triumphs on the reverse of Piero's portraits depict the Cardinal Virtues (the Duke) and the Theological Virtues (the Duchess) carried on carts drawn by unicorns. The town in the Duchess's portrait is Gubbio (in Umbria), where she died giving birth to her ninth child and first son, Guidobaldo. The portrait was painted two years after her death.

Primavera

The meaning of Botticelli's painting has been debated for centuries. The central figure is Venus, goddess of spring and love. On the right, Zephyr, god of the west wind, chases the nymph Chloris, who is metamorphosed into the flower-decked Flora. On the left, Mercury wards off the clouds of winter while the Three Graces perform a dance under the threat of Cupid's arrow. The work may be an allegory of spring (*primavera*) or of all four seasons. Most critics believe, however, that it represents the Triumph of Venus, the Graces representing her beauty, Flora embodying her fruitfulness.

There is no escaping Botticelli's Birth of Venus

Gothic style of painting was Lorenzo Monaco, though his *Coronation of the Virgin* (c.1413), which dominates the room, is overshadowed by an exquisitely detailed *Adoration of the Magi* (1423) by Gentile da Fabriano, a painter from the Marches.

Room 7 (Early Renaissance) Renaissance pioneers here include Masaccio, Masolino and Fra Angelico, but the most famous works are Veneziano's *Sacra Conversazione* (see panel on page 161) and Piero della Francesca's well-known portraits (see panel) of Federico da Montefeltro, Duke of Urbino, and his wife Battista Sforza (c.1460). Piero was a pupil of Veneziano. Also here is one panel of Paolo Uccello's *Battle of San Romano*, painted 24 hours after the actual event in 1456 (its other two panels are in the Louvre in Paris and in London's National Gallery). It used to hang in Lorenzo de' Medici's bedroom in the Palazzo Medici. The painting displays an obsession with perspective shared by both Uccello and Piero della Francesca.

Room 8 Most paintings here are by Filippo Lippi who, though brought up by monks, was consumed by earthly passions. Seduced nuns were among his models. His *Madonna and Child with Two Angels* (c.1465) here is one of the loveliest depictions of the Madonna in the gallery.

Room 9 Much of this room is devoted to the brothers Antonio and Piero Pollaiuolo, better known as sculptors, engravers and goldsmiths than as painters. The gallery's most infamous forgery is also here: *Man in a Red Hat*, long believed to be a self-portrait of Filippino Lippi, but actually a fraud perpetrated by an 18th-century English art dealer.

Room 10–14 Botticelli was virtually ignored until this century. Now this room (four smaller rooms run together) is the most popular in the gallery. The painter's most renowned works are collected here, notably *Primavera* (1478) and *The Birth of Venus* (1485), both profoundly influenced by humanist ideas (see panels). Members of the Medici family feature in his *Adoration of the Magi*, Cosimo il Vecchio as the first king, his sons Piero and Giovanni as the other Magi. Lorenzo the Magnificent occupies the far left foreground. Botticelli has painted himself in a yellow robe on the right.

Bronzino's portrait of Cosimo I

Birth of Venus
This was the first 'pagan' nude of the Renaissance, and the last of Botticelli's mythological paintings. It was probably inspired by a poem by Poliziano, humanist, scholar and friend of Lorenzo de' Medici. According to myth Venus rose from the sea after it had been impregnated by the castration of Uranus. The painting's allegorical meaning, therefore, suggests that beauty arose from the meeting of the spirit world (represented by Uranus) and the physical world. The supporting figures are the nymph Chloris and Zephyr, who, in the myth, blows the risen Venus to shore on a half-shell, where Hora hurries to robe her.

In later life Botticelli became increasingly religious, refusing to accept anything but devotional or 'improving' subjects. This more severe later period is reflected in less lyrical works such as *The Calumny of Apelles* (c.1496). The room's large triptych by Hugo van der Goes was bought in 1488 by an agent of the Medici bank in Bruges. Its naturalism was to have a profound impact on Florentine painters.

Room 15 Florence has few confidently attributed works by Leonardo da Vinci. This room contains his sublime *Annunciation* and exotic *Adoration of the Magi*, the latter left unfinished when Leonardo left Tuscany for Milan in 1482 to paint *The Last Supper*. As an 18-year-old pupil he also painted the angel in Verrocchio's *Baptism of Christ* (begun c.1470). Verrocchio confessed he himself could paint nothing as beautiful as his pupil's angel. Also in the room are wonderful works by Luca Signorelli and Perugino. The latter trained with Leonardo in Verrocchio's workshop.

Room 16 is a map room, the Sala delle Carte Geografiche.

Room 17 is often closed but contains a famous statue, *Hermaphrodite*, a 2nd-century BC copy of a Greek original.

Room 18 (The Tribune) This specially built octagon was designed in 1584 as an inner sanctum for the Medici's finest works of art. It also marks a convenient break in the gallery, ushering in the artists of Italy's High Renaissance. Paintings here include works by Bronzino and Raphael, and Pontormo's *Cosimo il Vecchio* (1519), one of the gallery's premier portraits. For centuries, however, the room's most famous work was the *Venus de' Medici*,

Detail from Filippo Lippi's Madonna and Child with Two Angels

Venus de'Medici

The Medici Venus is a Roman copy of a 1st-century BC *Aphrodite of Cnidos*, considered to be antiquity's most erotic statue. Cosimo III kept it in Rome's Villa Medici, but removed it to Florence to prevent it from corrupting the city's students.
Drawings and reproductions flooded Europe, and visitors grappled in prose with its sensual charge. Even the habitually miserable Smollett was moved by its famous buttocks: 'the back parts are executed so happily', he wrote, 'as to excite the admiration of the most indifferent spectator.'

Byron on the Venus

'We gaze and turn away, and know not where,/ Dazzled and drunk with beauty, till the heart/ Reels with its fullness ... Chain'd to the chariot of triumphal Art/ We stand as captives and would not depart.'
Childe Harold's Pilgrimage (1812)

The Doni Tondo

Michelangelo considered easel painting to be drudgery in comparison with fresco or the still more elevated art of sculpture. This is the only such painting he brought close to completion. Executed at the time of *David*, it was commissioned to celebrate the marriage of Angelo Doni and Maddalena Strozzi. Much of the content is still not understood, but the acid colours, contorted composition and deliberately opaque meaning greatly influenced Mannerist painters such as Rosso Fiorentino.

long considered to be Europe's most salacious sculpture (see panel). It was the only statue in Florence to be called to Paris after Napoleon's invasion of Italy.

Room 19 The paintings here include works by Perugino, Raphael's teacher, and Luca Signorelli, a pupil of Piero della Francesca.

Room 20 Among this room's pictures, mainly by German painters, is Albrecht Dürer's earliest work, *A Portrait of the Artist's Father* (painted when he was 19, in 1490). Dürer worked for a time in Venice, commenting: 'Here I am a lord, but at home I live as a sponger.'

Room 21 (Venetian School) Among works here by Giorgione, Carpaccio, Tura and others, the most famous is Giovanni Bellini's baffling *Sacred Allegory* (c.1495), whose strange symbolism has never been fully explained.

Room 22 (German and Flemish Schools) Works here include portraits by Memling, Joos van Cleve and Hans Holbein the Younger.

Room 23 Correggio dominates the room, but the finest paintings are three pieces by Andrea Mantegna, notably the three-panelled *Epiphany, Circumcision and Ascension* (1489).

Room 24 is given over to miniatures.

Room 25 Only when you are well over half-way round the Uffizi do you reach its only work by Michelangelo, *The Holy Family* (1504), or the Doni Tondo (see panel). Note the remarkable contrast with Raphael's *Madonna of the Goldfinch* (in Room 26), a quintessential late-Renaissance work painted at almost the same time, around 1505. Close to hangs Rosso Fiorentino's violently energetic *Moses Defending the Daughters of Jethro* (1523–4), one of the key works in the Mannerist canon. It was commissioned by a patron known for his violent temper.

Room 26 Here are to be found most of the Uffizi's Raphaels, notably his luminous *Madonna of the Goldfinch* (1506), a self-portrait, and a penetrating study (1518) of Medici prelates, *Pope Leo X and Cardinals Giulio de' Medici and Luigi de' Rossi*. Andrea del Sarto is also well represented.

Room 27 Mannerism's leading lights – Bronzino, Pontormo and Rosso Fiorentino – dominate this room. Pontormo's *Supper at Emmaus* (1525) stands out, filled with artificial light, macabre shadows, and the virulent colours beloved of painters in this genre.

Room 28 Raphael's Medici portrait (Room 26) influenced Titian, whose portraits decorate this room. More notorious, however, is Titian's famous *Venus of Urbino* (1538), one of the best-known and most highly charged nudes in Western art. Byron thought her the definitive Venus. Mark Twain thought this 'the foulest, the vilest, the obscenest picture the world possesses.'

Room 29 Several devices which have given the Mannerist style a bad name are displayed in Parmigianino's famous *Madonna and Child with Angels* (1534–40) – the Virgin's unnaturally long neck, her peculiar posture (somewhere between sitting and standing), the column behind her, supporting nothing but thin air, and the compositional overloading of the left-hand side of the painting while the right-hand side is almost empty.

Rooms 30–35 Paintings from Emilia Romagna, Venice

and the Veneto hang here, notably works by Dosso Dossi, Lorenzo Lotto, Veronese, Tintoretto and Sebastiano del Piombo.

Room 41 Rubens and Van Dyck claim this room, which is dominated by the former's sizeable *Triumphal Entrance of Henri IV into Paris* (c.1620) Henri's presence in the Medici collection is explained by his marriage to Maria de' Medici.

Room 43 Three paintings by Caravaggio make their mark here: an alarming *Medusa* (1596–8), a self-satisfied *Bacchus* (1593–4) and a violent *Sacrifice of Isaac* (1594–6).

Room 44 Two Rembrandt self-portraits, young (1634) and old (1664), and his *Portrait of an Old Man* stand out in the gallery's penultimate room.

Room 45 Canaletto and 18th-century paintings bring the tour to a close. The Uffizi's welcome cafeteria awaits beyond.

Open: daily 9–7 (Sunday 9–2). Closed Monday. Admission charge (expensive)

Looking through the Arno façade of the Uffizi, designed by Vasari. The top floor was used by the Medici to display their works of art

165

■ **The artistic reawakening of almost two centuries came to glorious fruition in Florence during the 15th century when the Renaissance (*Rinascimento*) was born against a background of wealth, patronage and the artistic, social and intellectual ferment of a great and cosmopolitan European city......**■

166

Why 'rebirth'? A combination of cultural and economic circumstances paved the way for the Renaissance. Initially the rediscovery of classical texts and humanist scholarship, of the type promulgated by Lorenzo de' Medici's Platonic Academy, helped free art from its purely religious obligations. This led quite naturally to renewed interest in the classical ideals of art: form and harmony. Secular patronage – by successful laymen such as the Medici – fostered these new ideas in art and architecture, replacing a world in which art was sponsored by the Church – with all the rigidity and conservatism that that implied.

It was no accident that the mood of artistic and intellectual innovation came to fruition in Florence. By the 15th century banking and commerce, particularly textiles, had turned it into one of Europe's most prosperous cities. Creativity and individual genius flourished in its free-thinking atmosphere, enriched by the exchange of ideas among artists drawn together by its burgeoning artistic reputation.

Three angels visit Abraham – a detail from one of Lorenzo Ghiberti's panels for the east doors of the Battistero, the 'Gates of Paradise'

The big three The Renaissance did not spring out of thin air (see pages 158–9). Nonetheless, it can be said to have been ushered in by three artists in three key disciplines. **Filippo Brunelleschi** (1377–1446) was its first great architect. Today he is chiefly remembered as the designer of Florence's cathedral dome, but his ideas were also vital to the new thinking on matters such as the ideals of design and the science of perspective. **Donatello** (1386–1466), perhaps the greatest of the early-Renaissance sculptors, overturned tradition with his extraordinarily life-like figures; he also reintroduced the nude to the mainstream of artistic expression. **Masaccio** (1401–28), third of the triumvirate, was revolutionary in his use of perspective, producing paintings that stunned his contemporaries. His frescos in the Cappella Brancacci became a point of pilgrimage for nearly every Florentine artist of their day.

Year one A date for the start of the Renaissance, as far as a date can be set, is often fixed at 1401, the year of a competition to design a second set of doors for Florence's Battistero. As a result, **Lorenzo Ghiberti** (c.1378–1455) was to produce two pairs of doors permeated with the essentials of Renaissance style (allusions to classical sculpture, realistic portrayal of the human form, and the use of perspective to position figures in a naturalistic setting). Another notable sculptor, **Luca della Robbia** (c.1400–82), perfected the art of glazed terracotta, a medium which his family spread, over the course of the century, throughout much of Tuscany. Other contemporary sculptors adopted the more joyful aspects of Donatello's often severe style – men like **Benedetto da Maiano**, **Bernardo Rossellino** and **Desiderio da Settignano**.

The painters Nowhere does the Renaissance avalanche of hallowed names become more overwhelming than amongst the painters. Many, like Masaccio, were innovators, some only accomplished copyists, but all made their contribution to the body of beautiful work with which the Florentine *quattrocento* (15th century) is most commonly associated. One of the earliest, **Paolo Uccello** (1397–1475), was also one of the most taken with the new possibilities of perspective, driving himself to personal and artistic eccentricity with his new-found obsession. Challenging, almost visionary work was the result, best seen in Santa Maria Novella's *Universal Deluge* and the Uffizi's *Battle of San Romano*.

Equally intense, but more spiritually elevated, was the

Top: detail from one of Ghirlandaio's frescos on the life of St Francis in Santa Trinita church Below: Taddeo di Bartolo's Assumption of the Virgin, *a glittering early-Renaissance work in the Duomo in Montepulciano*

167

Michelozzo di Bartolommeo
After collaborations with Ghiberti and Donatello, Michelozzo (1396–1472) turned to architecture. He worked mainly for Cosimo de' Medici designing a tribune for Santissima Annunziata, the Villa Medici at Fiesole, the library in the monastery of San Marco, and the highly influential Palazzo Medici-Riccardi.

Leon Battista Alberti
A complete Renaissance man, Alberti (1404–72) was a scholar, writer, architect and theoretician, whose tracts on painting and architecture – *Della Pittura* and *De Re Aedificatoria* – greatly influenced his Florentine contemporaries.

Agostino di Duccio
Possibly a pupil of the Sienese sculptor Jacopo della Quercia, Agostino (1418–81) worked on projects all over central Italy. His best work in Florence can be seen in the Bargello.

One of Michelangelo's Four Slaves *in the Accademia*

heavenly inspiration of **Fra Angelico** (*c*.1395–1455), a devout Dominican monk. His sublime work, intended as an aid to devotion, introduced innovative use of colour and composition. Few matched the ethereal blue of his palette, best seen in the frescos of his own monastery, San Marco. Less profound, but no less beautiful, was Angelico's pupil, **Benozzo Gozzoli** (1420/22–97), who left examples of his highly decorated work in the Palazzo Medici-Riccardi (as well as in hill towns across Tuscany and Umbria).

More in keeping with Angelico's mystery and depth, if not his religious devotion, was **Filippo Lippi** (*c*.1406–69, an errant friar who made a habit of seducing young women). A pupil of Masaccio, he soon instigated innovations of his own, introducing complex compositional groups, detailed colouring and mystical paintings of poetic landscapes and wistful Madonnas. Another of Masaccio's pupils, **Andrea del Castagno** (1417/19–57), rigorously applied the rules of perspective, but added heroic figures to his striking, boldly painted frescos (most notably in the Duomo's *Niccolò da Tolentino* and Sant'Apollonia's disturbing *Last Supper*). **Domenico Ghirlandaio** (1449–94) was perhaps the most prolific of Florence's painters (he offered at one point to cover the entire city wall with frescos). His huge religious narratives set against classical and contemporary backgrounds epitomised the Renaissance approach (notably in Santa Trinita, Santa Maria Novella and the Palazzo Vecchio's Sala dei Gigli).

Another spur to artistic progress came from **Antonio Pollaiuolo** (1433–98), painter, engraver, sculptor and goldsmith. Dedicated to the study of anatomy and movement, he also undertook a wide range of commissions, typical of the ever-widening interests developed by artists and patrons as the 15th century progressed. Also part of this trend was **Andrea del Verrocchio** (1435–88), a multi-talented artist in his own right, but better known, like Pollaiuolo, as a teacher and the head of a flourishing workshop (Leonardo was among his pupils). As the century spawned more artists, so it moved towards its artistic climax, heralded by **Sandro Botticelli** (1444–1510), whose mythological paintings and graceful mastery of line and colour are the epitome of Renaissance endeavour.

The High Renaissance Just as a trio of artists dominate the early years of the Renaissance, so three figures stand out at the climactic end of the era, the so-called High Renaissance. *The Last Supper*, painted at the beginning of the 16th century in Milan by **Leonardo da Vinci** (1452–1519), marks the start of the period, also underlining the fact that the glory of the Renaissance does not belong to Florence alone. Leonardo, born in Vinci (east of Florence) and trained in Verrocchio's workshop, now has only three works in the city, all of them in the Uffizi (see page 163).

Rome, too, saw its share of Renaissance greatness – not least in the work of **Michelangelo** (1475–1564), the consummate genius of his age. Though he spent the earlier part of his career in Florence, he was

frequently lured to Rome, where papal patronage began to replace that of the Medici. Concerned primarily with sculpture, and with the nude in particular, Michelangelo's work is represented in Florence by the *David*, the Museo dell'Opera del Duomo's *Pietà*, the Medici tombs and the Biblioteca Laurenziana. But it was Rome, ironically, that saw Michelangelo's greatest and most famous work – the frescos in the Sistine Chapel. Urbino-born **Raphael** (1483–1520) was another Florence-trained genius lured to Rome – though he painted numerous masterpieces in Florence, many of them now in the Uffizi and the Palazzo Pitti.

Mannerism After the sack of Rome in 1527, Renaissance self-confidence gave way to the more self-conscious art that became known as Mannerism. Partially inspired by Raphael and Michelangelo, artists of the genre followed some of the techniques, but not the spirit, of their masters, in a way which perhaps allowed artifice to dominate over art. Established conventions of scale, colour and composition were ignored. Mannerism was a style in which home-grown artists continued to excel, its leading lights being **Rosso Fiorentino** (1495–1540) **Jacopo Pontormo** (1494–1556), **Andrea del Sarto** (1486–1531) and **Agnolo Bronzino** (1503–72). In sculpture the style was embraced by **Bandinelli** (1493–1560) and **Ammannati** (1511–92), and by the more accomplished **Giambologna** (1529–1608) and **Benvenuto Cellini** (1500–71). Examples of their work decorate the Bargello and the open spaces of the Piazza della Signoria.

The atrium of Santissima Annunziata has a series of Mannerist frescos. Above: an Andrea del Sarto

Renaissance talent outside Florence
Piero della Francesca (1416–92), from the Tuscan town of Sansepolcro, painted mysterious pictures which combined ethereal beauty with compositional precision. In Cortona, his pupil Luca Signorelli (c.1441–1523) began a career later distinguished by the powerful *Apocalypse* in Orvieto cathedral in Umbria. Umbria also had Perugino (1446–1523), Raphael's teacher, known for his harmonious religious paintings. Siena boasted sculptors like Jacopo della Quercia (c.1374–1438), and painters such as Sassetta (c.1392–1450) and Giovanni di Paolo (c.1403–82).

Gargoyle from the Villa della Petraia

The perfect villa
Alberti's *De Re Aedificatoria* (*About Building*) described the perfect villa: it sat on a hill to enjoy the best views, its rooms radiated from a central atrium, and its windows were large and numerous to admit light and air. Its garden – considered more important than the house – was based on geometric formality and was linked to the villa by a central path. Secondary paths crossed it to create a grid, and squares, arcs and circles were introduced as complementary motifs. In short, said Alberti, 'the harmony and concord of all the parts [should be] achieved in such a manner that nothing could be added or taken away or altered except for the worse.'

The king's tree-house
The upper terrace of the Villa della Petraia's garden contains a famous 400-year-old ilex. It was King Vittorio Emanuele II's favourite tree, and he built the tree-house which is still here today.

▶ **Villa Medicea di Careggi** *IBCD5*

Viale Pieraccini 17 (5km north of city centre)
Bus: no 14c from railway station
The Villa di Careggi is now a nurses' home, but in its day it was the first and most famous of the Medici's several villas – elegant country homes, within easy reach of Florence but offering a rural alternative to the family *palazzo*. Acquired by the Medici in 1417, and altered by Michelozzo in the 1430s, it was to the Villa di Careggi that Cosimo de' Medici returned after his Venetian exile (1434), and here that Cosimo, his son Piero and his grandson Lorenzo (the Magnificent) all came to die. Under Lorenzo the house also became the meeting place of the Platonic Academy, the informal gathering of poets, scholars and philosophers that promulgated Florence's humanist movement. When the Medici left Florence in 1494, the villa was ransacked and badly destroyed by fire. It was restored by Cosimo I and later by the Englishman Sir Francis Sloane.
Open: grounds only, daily 9–dusk. Closed Monday. Admission charge (moderate).

▶▶ **Villa Medicea di Castello** *IBCD5*

Via di Castello 47 (7km northwest of city centre)
Bus: no 28 from railway station
The Villa di Castello's attraction is its gardens, among the finest in Tuscany. The building was bought in 1477 by Giovanni and Lorenzo di Pierfrancesco de' Medici, second cousins of Lorenzo the Magnificent and principal sponsors of Botticelli (the Uffizi's *Primavera* and *Birth of Venus* hung here until 1761). Sacked during the siege of Florence in 1530, it was restored by Cosimo I. It was given to the state in 1919, and now houses the Accademia della Crusca, founded in 1582 to promote the study of the Italian language.
  The gardens were laid out for Cosimo I in 1537 by Niccolò Tribolo, a pupil of Michelangelo. Although his work was continued by Buontalenti, who also restructured the villa, the planned arrangement of over 50 sculptural tableaux was never realised. The gardens dazzled visitors nonetheless, among them Montaigne, who described them as the most beautiful in Europe. Among their lemon trees, labyrinths and geometrically arranged hedges, the centrepiece is the marvellous Grotto degli Animali (*c.*1570), encrusted with false stalactites, shell mosaics and a teeming menagerie of birds and plaster animals (Giambologna's bronze animals in the Bargello were removed from here). Walk to the upper terrace for some fine views, and search out the large orangery, Tribolo's triple-bowled fountain and Ammannati's chilly statue, *January*.
Open: gardens only, daily 9–dusk. Closed Monday. Admission charge (inexpensive; includes Villa della Petraia).

▶ **Villa Medicea della Petraia** *IBCD5*

Località Castello (7km northwest of city centre)
Bus: no 28 from railway station
One of the last Medici villas, the Villa della Petraia was originally a castle owned by the Brunelleschi family. Only its tower was retained when Ferdinando I bought and rebuilt the property in 1575. Today the area suffers badly

from its proximity to Florence. Matters are made worse by the interior, reappointed in poor taste by King Vittorio Emanuele II in 1864. Only a handful of 17th-century frescos (tracing the Medici's history), the odd tapestry and a statue of Venus by Giambologna make a visit worthwhile. The beautiful park and gardens are more enticing, however. *Open*: villa and gardens, daily 9–dusk (villa closes 1 hour before dusk). Closed Monday. Admission charge (inexpensive; includes Villa di Castello).

A Medici rural retreat: the Villa della Petraia

►► Villa Medicea di Poggio a Caiano   *IBCC5*

Piazza dei Medici 12 (18km west of city centre)
Bus: COPIT bus (every 30 minutes) from Piazza Santa Maria Novella to Poggio a Caiano village
Poggio a Caiano – the best-preserved of the Medici retreats – is the place to visit if you have time for only one villa. Bought as a farmhouse by Lorenzo the Magnificent in 1480, it was converted by Giuliano da Sangallo, becoming the first purpose-built villa since antiquity (and Lorenzo's only architectural commission). Despite later additions (notably the entrance loggia added by Lorenzo's son, Giovanni, later Pope Leo X) the villa retains a classical elegance which owes much to Alberti's blueprint for the ideal country house (see panel).

The interior is magnificent, its *pièce de résistance* being a two-storey *salone*, described by Vasari as the most beautiful room in the world. Among its frescos are Andrea del Sarto's *Caesar Receiving Egyptian Tribute* and Pontormo's sunny *Vetumnus and Pomona*. The Romans in the latter are the Medici in disguise, whilst the historical scenes of the former depict events parallel to those connected with the family. The villa also has pleasant English-style gardens which are open to the public.
Open: daily 9–7:30 (winter 9–2). Closed Monday. Admission charge (inexpensive).

Strange deaths
Poggio a Caiano contains the apartment of Bianca Cappello, second wife of Francesco I. She left her Venetian lover to be with Francesco, but was banned from Florence by Francesco's first wife. As his second wife she became a social outcast, shunned by Florentine society. In 1587 both she and Francesco died within hours of each other at the villa, possibly from a virulent illness, or possibly as a result of being poisoned.

Accommodation

Doing Florence in style: one of the city's top-class luxury hotels

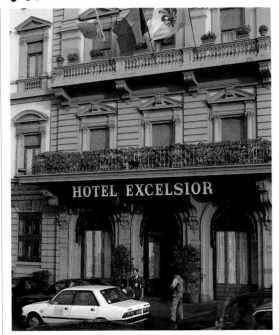

Noise
The only way to escape Florence's cacophony – car horns, wailing sirens, motor scooters, domestic discord, buses, early-morning street cleaners, late-night bars – is to stay in a sound-proofed hotel or flee the city altogether. You could spare yourself some of the racket, however, by avoiding the main streets and piazzas, and by asking for rooms either away from the front of the hotel or facing into a central courtyard. Better still, invest in earplugs.

Last-minute bookings
If you arrive without a room booked, try the ITA (Informazioni Turistiche Alberghiere) office on the railway station concourse (*open*: daily 9–9; tel: 282 893). They charge a fee of L2,000–L5,000 for finding a room, depending on the category of hotel. Other ITA offices (open April to November) are located at the Chianti Est service station (on the A1 motorway) and the Agip service station at Peretola (on the A11 motorway to the coast).

Florence's limitless stream of tourists has spoilt its hoteliers. Certain of custom, they are often able to pass off lacklustre rooms at premium prices. Exceptions to this rule are well known, so to be sure of a bargain, or even of value for money, you need to book well in advance. Location is not of prime importance, except in the budget bracket, where most of the options cluster in the dowdy streets around the station. Cheaper *pensioni* also lurk close to the Duomo, however. Smarter hotels dot most neighbourhoods.

Noise, as in any Italian city, is invariably a problem. So, too, is summer heat. Opting for a quieter hotel in Fiesole or the Florentine hills is an alternative possibility. You might look even further afield if hotels are full: train journeys of less than an hour make day trips to Florence feasible from Arezzo, Pistoia, Prato and Pisa.

Booking That much-vaunted commodity, a room with a view, is not usually to be found at the last minute – unless you are very lucky or very rich. Florence's peak season is between Easter and the end of October, but the city's 400 or so hotels are always well booked. The bargain establishments and the better hotels are well known, so reservations are essential whatever you are paying. Some hotels will accept a credit card reservation over the phone, but to be absolutely sure of a booking aim to send some sort of deposit. The Italian State Tourist Office in your home country will help with booking. Eurocheques (made out in Italian lire) or International Money Orders (available from post offices) are both useful.

A day or two before your planned arrival, always telephone to confirm a reservation (most receptionists speak some English). If you arrive without a booking, try one of the agencies on the spot (see panel), but make sure you are not given a room a long way from the city centre. If you have no reservation, be certain to arrive early in the morning, for most spare rooms will have gone by mid-afternoon. Do not accept offers from touts at the railway station.

Prices Italy's hotels are classified into five categories from one-star (basic) to five-star (luxury). The prices charged in each category are set by the local tourist office and must, by law, be displayed in each room. Although this arrangement clearly protects the visitor, an EU directive of June 1993 has now, unfortunately, outlawed the legal obligation as unfair 'price-fixing'. Whether this will lead to runaway prices remains to be seen, but for the moment most hotels seem to be adhering to the old system.

Prices for different rooms can vary within a hotel, so if one room is too expensive do not be afraid to ask for another, cheaper one (the chances are you will be offered the most expensive rooms first). Single rooms cost about two-thirds the price of doubles, and to add an extra bed to a room increases the rate by 35 per cent. Even smarter hotels may have a few cheaper rooms without bathrooms. Some hotels will offer reduced rates between November and March, though few admit to a low season. Taxes and service charges should be included in the room rate, but hotels can charge supplements for showers (in cheaper places) and for air-conditioning (as much as L25,000 a day). Places with restaurants invariably demand you take half-pension and many hotels insist you pay for breakfast, whether you want it or not.

Prices
Hotel rates are high in Florence. For hotels listed as 'Expensive' in the Hotels and Restaurants section (pages 273–81), expect to pay between L250,000 and L500,000 for two people in a double room. 'Moderate' rates are roughly L125,000–L250,000; 'Budget' L70,000–L125,000.

173

A riverside setting and rooms with a view

Food and drink

Most city–centre restaurants in Florence are crowded. Something is probably badly wrong with any that are not. The food served by some of them, however, is little more than tourist fodder. The better places are all well known, so either book or arrive early to be sure of a table. (See pages 277–8 for recommendations.)

Only the most expensive restaurants require a jacket and tie, but Italians invariably dress up more than most. Dress code for most places can best be summarised as casual elegance.

Types of restaurant Little difference exists these days between a *ristorante* and a *trattoria* (a *ristorante* used to be smarter). An *osteria*, once extremely basic, now often indicates somewhere smart and expensive. A *pizzeria*, of course, is what it says, though it will usually offer pasta and the odd main course as well as pizzas. The *tavola calda* and the *rosticceria* are now something of a rarity, but both serve hot snacks throughout the day, usually to take away. *Enoteca*, *vinaio* and *fiaschetteria* are all names for a wine bar. A *gelateria* serves ice-cream, a *pasticceria* cakes and pastries.

Main meals Breakfast (*prima colazione*) is a straightforward stand-up affair of *cappuccino* and plain, cream- or jam-filled croissants (*brioche or cornetti*). Stocks of *cornetti* in the best bars last until about 10am. Lunch (*pranzo*) – from around 12:30 – is no longer the overblown affair of days gone by. You may find it best to buy a picnic or bar snack at midday (see page 175) and save the main meal until evening. Dinner (*cena*) starts around 7:30.

Menus Traditionally lunch and dinner run through *antipasto* (starters) of ham, salami and *crostini* (toasts); a course consisting of soup, risotto, polenta or pasta (*il primo*); a meat or fish course (*il secondo*); salad or vegetables (*insalata* or *contorni*); and dessert (*dolce*), cheese (*formaggio*) or fruit (*frutta*). Coffee, liqueurs and *digestivi* round things off. Naturally you need not wade through all the courses. Smarter restaurants, however, will take a dim view if you order only a salad and a glass of wine. Note that the main course (*il secondo*) will not be garnished: salad and vegetables are served and billed separately. When ordering fish and the famous *bistecca alla fiorentina* you usually pay by the *etto* (100g) or *hectogram* (400g). Items thus priced are usually marked *S. Q.* or *hg*. (See also pages 210–11.)

Le volpi e l'uva

Piazza De' Rossi - 50125 Firenze
Tel. e Fax 055/2398132

Paying The bill (*il conto*) invariably includes a per person cover charge (*pane e coperto*) and a 10–15 per cent service charge (*servizio*). Tip around this amount if service is not included. Remember that bars and restaurants are required by law to give you a proper receipt (*una ricevuta*). Illegible scrawl on a scrap of paper may mean someone is on the fiddle. Always check the bill carefully. You can

Taking it easy in a Florentine café

Holidays and closing
Most restaurants close for their annual holidays in August. They may also be closed on public holidays. All must, by law, close one statutory day (*chiusura settimanale*) each week, often Monday. Many also close on Sunday evening. First orders for lunch are at about 12:30, for dinner around 7. Few places stay open for late-night dining (after 11), and to have an unhurried meal you must be at the restaurant by 9:30, especially weekdays.

175

Vegetarians
Florence has only a handful of vegetarian restaurants. Many *antipasti*, pizzas and pastas, however, will suit vegetarians (though soups may be made with meat stock). Salads, cheeses and vegetables are usually of high quality. If you eat neither meat nor fish, your main course may have to be an omelette (*una frittata*).

keep costs down by skipping *antipasti* and desserts (go to a *gelateria* for an ice-cream instead). Alternatively, opt for a fixed-price *menù turistico*, usually a basic pasta, main course, fruit and half-bottle of wine and water per person. The food will be filling rather than exciting. The slightly different *prezzo fisso* is a set-price menu that usually excludes cover, service and beverage charges.

Snacks Head for markets, corner shops or supermarkets for picnic supplies. Most bars serve a variety of sandwiches (*tramezzini*) or filled rolls (*panini*). Slices of pizza (*pizza taglia*), sold everywhere, are good value, but check the quality of the topping first: some have nothing but a smear of tomato. A *rosticceria* will provide you with anything from chips to a whole roast chicken, whilst a *tavola calda* confines itself to a few soups and basic pastas. Wine bars also offer snacks and cold cuts to accompany a glass or bottle of wine.

Caffè Gilli

FOOD AND DRINK

Tea

Tea with lemon (tè al limone) is common in Italy. Tea with milk is a combination that still raises eyebrows, so be sure to ask for it specifically (un tè con latte). Make sure the milk is cold (latte freddo). Camomile (camomilla) is common and popular before bed, and iced tea (tè freddo) is widely available in summer.

Aperitifs

Fortified wines such as Martini, Cinzano and Campari are common aperitifs. Campari Soda comes ready mixed in its own bottle. The artichoke-based Cynar is also popular.

Brandy

The best Italian brandies, both widely drunk, are Vecchia Romagna and the second-ranked Stock.

Fast food, Italian-style

Bars Florence has a bar on nearly every street corner. Many are functional places for coffee, snacks and an after-work *aperitivo*. You pay a premium to sit down, inside or out, though a single purchase allows you to sit and watch the world go by almost indefinitely. Sitting down usually implies waiter service. The normal procedure otherwise is to pay for what you want at the cash desk (*la cassa*) and take your receipt (*lo scontrino*) to the bar. A L100 tip slapped down when repeating your order usually guarantees prompt service. It is a good idea to take breakfast in bars (cheaper and better than hotels), and they are also ideal for lunchtime snacks.

Coffee A good cup of coffee is a certainty almost anywhere in Italy. Breakfast means a milky *cappuccino*, named after the brown robes and white cowls of Capuchin monks. At other times the *espresso*, a short kick-start of caffeine, is the coffee of choice (usually known as *un caffè*). Decaffeinated coffee is *caffè Hag*, iced coffee *caffè freddo*, and American-style coffee (long and watery) *caffè Americano*. Other varieties include *caffè corretto* (with a dash of grappa or brandy), *caffè latte* (a longer *cappuccino*), and *caffè macchiato* (an espresso 'stained' with a drop of milk). If you are really particular, the mark of a good bar is one that uses fresh (not UHT) milk. Italians, incidentally, never drink tea or coffee with meals, and rarely touch *cappuccino* after midday (and *never* after a meal).

Wine Most middle- to upper-price-bracket restaurants should have a good selection of Tuscan wines (see pages 212–13). Cheaper places may only have a house wine (*vino della casa*), usually a Chianti or one of its close cousins. Ask for a bottle (*una bottiglia*), half-bottle (*mezzo litro*) or quarter flask (*un quartino*). Better restaurants should also have a variety of other Italian wines, and in some cases, a few of French or German origin as well.

The famous Enoteca Pinchiorri, one of Europe's greatest cellars (see page 278), has 80,000 bottles of French and Italian vintages. At the other extreme, you can sample wine by the glass in any bar (*un bicchiere di vino*).

Beer The cheapest way to buy beer (*birra*) is from the keg (*una birra alla spina*). Be sure to specify the size you want – *piccola* (25cl) or *media* (50cl). A *grande* (litre) is getting serious. Usually you will be served yellow, lager-like beer, though dark British-type ale (*birra scura*) is becoming more common. Italian bottled beer (*birra nazionale*) is reasonably priced. Peroni, Dreher and Nastro Azzurro are the most common brands. Again, specify the size you want. The 25cl Peroncino ('little Peroni') is a good thirst-quencher. Foreign beers are fashionable, and consequently expensive.

Water Florence's tap water is perfectly safe (*acqua normale* or *acqua dal rubinetto*). Nonetheless Florentines usually reserve it for washing-up or watering the flowers. In its place they drink mineral water (*acqua minerale*), either fizzy (*gassata*) or still (*liscia*, *naturale* or *non gassata*). Ask for a litre (*un litro*), half a litre (*mezzo litro*) or a glass (*un bicchiere*).

Soft drinks Freshly squeezed orange juice (*una spremuta*) in spring or early summer (when Sicily's oranges are in season) is the best accompaniment to breakfast. Lemon (*limone*) and grapefruit (*pompelmo*) juice are usually also available. Alternatively ask for bottled fruit juices (*un succo di frutta*), available in flavours such as pear (*pera*), peach (*pesca*) and apricot (*albiccoca*). Lemon Soda, a bitter lemon drink, is popular and widely available. Also be sure to try a fresh milk shake (*un frullato* or *un frappé* if made with ice-cream). *Granita* is crushed ice covered in a syrup (usually coffee). Colas, of course, are ubiquitous. *Crodino*, a non-alcoholic aperitif, has also recently become popular. Ice is *ghiaccio*; a slice of lemon is *uno spicchio di limone*.

Grappa
Usually drunk after a meal, Italy's most famous spirit is a clear fire-water made from the mulch of skins and stalks left over after wine-making. The best known come from Bassano del Grappa in the Veneto. Fruit- and herb-flavoured versions are common, but frowned on by purists.

177

Liqueurs
The best-known Italian liqueurs outside Italy are Sambuca, a sweet aniseed-based drink, and Amaretto, a sweet almond-flavoured concoction. In Italy itself, however, the most common after-dinner tipple is *amaro*, a bitter medicinal brew of herbs, wines and secret ingredients. The best brands (in ascending order of bitterness) are Montenegro, Ramazotti, Averna and Fernet-Branca.

Shopping

Florence ranks second only to Milan as a source of Italian high fashion, also scoring highly for its range of luxury and leather goods (shoes, bags and gloves). Craft items and antiques are other specialities, together with art books and the marbled paper for which the city is famous. Quality does not come cheap, but reproductions of many goods can be found in supermarkets and street markets (see pages 114–15).

The city centre forms the heart of shopping country – Piazza della Repubblica, Via de' Tornabuoni, Ognissanti, and around the Duomo. Shops of certain types, however – leather and antique shops in particular – can be found dotted throughout the city.

Clothes The top names in Italian design cluster in the city's most fashionable shopping street, Via de' Tornabuoni – which has **Versace**, **Gucci**, and **Ferragamo** – and its surrounding streets, such as Via della Vigna Nuova, home of **Valentino**, **Armani** and **Pucci**. Notable exceptions include **Luisa**, first choice for *alta moda* (high fashion), which can be found at Via Roma 19–21. More affordable **Max Mara** is at Via de' Pecori 23r, while mainstream **Krizia** operates from Piazza Strozzi 12–13r.

Other streets with less exalted names and more reasonably priced shops include Via de' Cerretani, Via del Corso, Via Roma and Via Calimala. Also worth a look are the department stores **Coin** (Via dei Calzaiuoli 56r) and **Principe** (Via degli Strozzi 21–9r). **Upim**, on Via Speziali (off Piazza della Repubblica) is more down-market, but good for basic clothes and accessories.

Leather goods Florence has hundreds of shops and market stalls selling leather handbags, gloves, belts and other accessories. For quality and real craftsmanship you have

Head-turning Florentine fashion

A better class of souvenir on sale in the Oltrarno

to make for the big names, of which **Ferragamo**, (Via de' Tornabuoni 2) and **Gucci**, (Via de' Tornabuoni 73r) are the best known. A better-kept secret, beloved of Florentines, is **Cellerini**, (Via del Sole 37r), generally considered the best shop of its type in the city. Everything from gloves to lizard-skin handbags is made on the premises, closely supervised by the firm's family founders. Items here are as stylish, as skilfully made and as steeply priced as they come. Close behind comes **Raspini**, as renowned in Florence as Gucci but with the difference that they have no foreign outlets, only licensees. They boast three branches (Via Roma 25–9r, Via Martelli 5–7r and Via Por Santa Maria 72r).

As ever, you can cut costs by visiting the markets (San Lorenzo in particular) or one of the better chains, amongst which **Beltrami** (for shoes, clothes and accessories) receives most plaudits (branches at Via dei Calzaiuoli 31r and 44r, Via de' Pecori 16, Via Calimala 9 and Via de' Tornabuoni 48r).

Antiques 'Antique' in Italy does not always mean what it says. Under Italian law an antique need not be old. In the case of furniture, for example, it needs only to be made from wood that is old. Much of what you see in Florence, therefore, is reproduction work – albeit very beautiful reproduction work, for this is a craft at which Florentines have excelled for centuries. Good buys, over and above furniture, include picture frames, jewellery, ceramics, statues and paintings. Specialist shops congregate on Borgo Ognissanti (and its side streets Via dei Fossi and Via della Porcellana) and in the Oltrarno around Borgo San Jacopo and Via Santo Spirito (and their side streets). Via Maggio, also in the Oltrarno, is known for its small-scale dealers, and for the auction house **Casa d'Aste Pitti** at Via Maggio 15.

Jewellery Jewellers have had a virtual monopoly on trade across the Ponte Vecchio for almost four centuries. Still the most famous source of jewellery in Florence, shops

Leather workshops
To see leather goods being made visit the workshops in the church of Santa Croce or the Santo spirito district and Peruzzi's shop and factory at Borgo dei Greci 8r.

Fabrics
Florence's most beautiful and expensive fabrics come from Lisio Tessuti d' Arte (Via dei Fossi 45r).

Terracotta pots
Visit Sbigoli (Via Sant' Egidio 4r) for Florence's best selection of that most Tuscan of garden ornaments, the orange terracotta pot.

SHOPPING

Window-shopping in Via de' Tornabuoni

Art and architecture

Centro Di (Piazza dei Mozzi 1r), despite its hidden basement location, is one of Italy's most important art bookshops and publishers. Salimbeni (Via M Palmieri 14–16r) is another highly reputable art and antiquarian bookshop.

Perfumes and toiletries

No shopping trip in Florence is complete without visiting the Farmacia di Santa Maria Novella (Via della Scala 16). Founded in 1612, its lovely antique interior is as famous as its products, which include soaps, face creams and medieval herbal remedies. Less well known but equally beautiful is the Antica Farmacia di San Marco (Via Cavour 146r), best known for its colognes, rose-water and medieval remedies.

Herbs and flowers

De Herbore (Via del Proconsolo 6a) sells over 400 different herbs and a wide selection of dried fruit, vegetables, herbal teas and dried flowers.

Porcelain

Tuscany's most famous porcelain is made by Ginori in the town of Sesto Fiorentino. The firm has a shop in Florence at Via Rondinelli 17r.

on the bridge offer reliable quality and an impressive range of specialities. **Melli** (Nos 44–6r), **Piccini** (No 23r) and **Manelli** (No 14r) are among the top names. The gold jewellery, in particular, is outstanding, a legacy of Florence's long tradition in the craft (Cellini, Ghiberti, Brunelleschi and Verrocchio all trained as goldsmiths). Prices, however, are somewhat over the odds.

Top names elsewhere include the Milanese firm of **Buccellati**, (Via de' Tornabuoni 71r) and **Settepassi** (Via de' Tornabuoni 25r), one of the grandest and longest-established Italian jewellers. **Bijoux Casciou** (Via de' Tornabuoni 32r and Via Por Santa Maria 1r) has a reputation stretching back over 30 years for good costume jewellery. **COI**'s upstairs showroom at Via Por Santa Maria 8r, deals in high-volume, low-cost gold jewellery.

Food Markets such as the **Mercato Centrale** (San Lorenzo) and **Sant'Aŝmbrogio** (Piazza Lorenzo Ghiberti) provide excellent starting points in the hunt for edible souvenirs such as olive oil, truffles and dried *porcini* mushrooms. Street-corner food shops (*alimentari*) sell perfectly good olive oil, brands such as Monini (from Umbria) being the staple of most Italian households. Alternatively you could go for 'designer-label' oils (such as Antinori, sold at Piazza degli Antinori 3) or buy directly from open terracotta pots at **Vino e Olio** (Via de' Serragli 29r).

Leading delicatessens include **Alessi** (Via delle Oche 27–9r), **Vera** (Piazza Frescobaldi 3r) and **Pegna** (Via dello Studio 28r). The top restaurant **Cibrèo** also has a shop selling fine foodstuffs on its premises at Via dei Macci 118r. Among the more specialised shops, **Porta del Tartufo** (Borgo Ognissanti 133r) is the place to find truffle products, while **Dolce Dolcezze Corti** (Piazza Beccaria 8r) is the last word in high-calorie sweets (cream, pastries, butter, chocolate and cheesecake are the top specialities). At the other extreme, supermarkets like **Standa** sell Italian basics at keen prices (branches at Via dei Mille 140 and Viale Pietrapiana 42–40).

Wine Wine can be bought at most grocery stores (*alimentari*) and at the old-fashioned *Vino e Olio* stores (a dying breed). Other specialist shops are known as *cantine*, *fiaschetterie* or *mescite* (from *mescere*, which means 'to pour'). In most places you should be able to buy snacks and wine by the glass to taste before buying. **Alessi** (Via della Oche 27–9r) has the best selection of Tuscan wines (with one room devoted to nothing but varieties of Chianti). **Zanobini Fratelli** (Via Sant'Antonio 47r) is also well known for its Tuscan selection (and has the advantage of being close to the Mercato Centrale). For northern Italian vintages and further local varieties go to **Biagini** (Via de' Banchi 55–7r) and the **Cantinone del Gallo Nero** (Via Santo Spirito 5r), a Chianti specialist. If you are serious about purchases, and have a car, head for the huge **Cantina Guidi**, located at Viale dei Mille 69r in the city's northeastern suburbs. **RF** (Via Ghibellina 142) is the place for grappa and other Italian spirits.

Paper Florence is renowned for its marbled paper, the product of a craft first brought to Venice from the Orient in the 12th century. The city's most venerable outlet (and *the* place to buy) is **Giannini e Figlio** (Piazza Pitti 37r), a beautiful little shop founded in 1856. **Pineider** have stores all over Italy, but the one at Piazza della Signoria 14r was the first. As well as hand-made papers, they sell fantastically expensive pens and miscellaneous stationery. Other outstanding but more reasonably priced shops include **Il Torchio** (Via dei Bardi 17) and **Il Papiro**, which has branches at Via Cavour 55r, Piazza del Duomo 24r and Lungarno degli Acciaiuoli 42r. Look out, too, for market stalls selling marbled paper products.

Artists' materials
Zecchi (Via dello Studio 19r) sells a huge range of artists' materials, many of them unavailable anywhere else in Europe.

181

Shopping al fresco *in Piazza Santo Spirito*

Main concert halls

Teatro Comunale (Corso Italia 16; tel: 277 9236; buses 1, 9, 12, 26 or 27); Teatro della Pergola, Via della Pergola 12 (tel: 247 9651; buses 6, 12, 14 or 23); Teatro Verdi (Via Ghibellina 101; tel: 239 6242).

Florence has all the nightlife you would expect of a medium-sized city. Cinema and theatre will probably be beyond non-Italian speakers, but classical concerts, nightclubs and a quiet dinner *al fresco* are within everyone's grasp.

The city centre may appear staid at times, but a large student population ensures some lively venues. If your dancing days are behind you, a stroll across the Ponte Vecchio or a summer evening's drink may be all the nightlife you need. Further afield lies Fiesole (see pages 82–3), a favourite spot at night to admire the lights of the city below.

Information Listings of all daily events (music, theatre, cinema etc) can be found in Florence's daily newspaper, *La Nazione*, or monthly magazines such as *Time Off* and *Firenze Spettacolo*. The main tourist office (Via Cavour 1r; tel: 290 832 or 276 0381) also has numerous pamphlets and posters detailing events. So, too, does the city council information kiosk inside the Palazzo Vecchio. Tickets can be bought directly from box offices or ordered through travel agents and the larger hotels. There are also

The Teatro Comunale, Florence's main concert venue

several central ticket agencies, notably **Box Office** (Via Faenza 139r; tel: 210 804) and **Agenzia Globus** (Piazza Santa Trinita 2r; tel: 214 992).

The sun sets behind the Ponte Santa Trinita

Music festivals Florence's big classical music event is the annual **Maggio Musicale Fiorentino**, perhaps the most important such event in all Italy. Held between May (*Maggio*) and early July, it embraces opera and ballet as well as classical concerts and smaller recitals. It has its own orchestra, chorus and ballet troupe, but performances are also given by visiting international companies. Most big events take place in the **Teatro Comunale** (Corso Italia 16; tel: 277 9236). This is also the festival's main box office. More modest recitals use the Teatro's smaller auditorium, the **Ridotto** (or *Piccolo*); the **Teatro della Pergola** (Via della Pergola 12; tel: 247 9651); and the **Teatro Verdi** (Via Ghibellina 101; tel: 239 6242).

The other big festival is Fiesole's **Estate Fiesolana**, a series of chamber and symphony concerts held between June and late August. Like the Maggio Musicale it also offers peripheral opera, ballet, theatre and film presentations. Most events take place in Fiesole's **Badia Fiesolana** or in the open-air **Teatro Romano** (the old Roman theatre). Others are staged in Florence, usually in **Santa Croce** or the courtyard of the **Palazzo Pitti**. (Bus no 7 will take you to Fiesole.)

Theatre
Florence's main classical theatre is the Teatro della Pergola, host to leading Italian companies between October and May. One of the city's oldest theatres, the Teatro Niccolini (Via Ricasoli 3; tel: 213 282 or 239 8333), comes a close second. For cabaret or more experimental work try Teatro Variety (Via del Madonnone 47; tel: 677 937) and Teatro di Rifredi (Via Vittorio Emanuele 303; tel: 422 0361).

Classical music As well as the summer festivals, Florence hosts several seasonal concert cycles. The **Amici della Musica** organise concerts every Saturday afternoon from October to April at the **Teatro della Pergola**. Their office is at Via Sirtori 49 (tel: 608 420 or 607 440). **Musicus Concertus** (Piazza del Carmine 19; tel: 287 347) present recitals between October and June at various locations, usually in the auditorium of the **Palazzo dei Congressi** (on Viale F Strozzi, east of the railway station). As well as the Maggio Musicale's big events, the **Teatro Comunale** stages its own cycle of concerts. These take place

Cinemas are plentiful, but most films are dubbed into Italian

Dance

Florence's best ballet and modern dance is to be found at the two summer festivals – the Maggio Musicale and Estate Fiesolana. Visiting companies also perform at the Teatro Comunale and the Teatro della Pergola.

between mid-September and December, in tandem with the city's main opera season, which finishes in mid-January. From January to April the **Teatro Verdi** mixes opera and ballet with its theatrical productions. Finally, members of the **Orchestra Regionale Toscana** present regular chamber concerts at the church of **Santo Stefano** (near the Ponte Vecchio).

Cinema In Italy, almost every film is dubbed into Italian – new or old, and whatever its provenance. The only cinema showing English-language films is the **Cinema Astro**, a rather dowdy operation at Piazza San Simone (near Santa Croce and opposite Gelateria Vivoli, the famous ice-cream parlour). It is closed on Mondays. Film clubs occasionally show original-language films; these include **Spazio Uno** (Via del Sole 10; tel: 283 389) and **Atelier Alfieri** (Via dell'Olivo 6; tel: 240 720). For a one-off experience, try films in the open air at the **Pianeta Cinema** in the Forte del Belvedere (summer only). More devoted film buffs might be interested in Florence's three international film festivals. The **Festival dei Popoli**, based at Via Castellani 8 (tel: 294 353), is the best known, but the **Florence Film Festival**, established in 1983, is gaining ground, as is the festival of women's films in cinema and television, the **Incontro Internazionale Cinema Donne**. For details of the three festivals contact the Atelier Alfieri (see above).

Rock, pop and jazz The reputations of places offering rock music change from year to year. The names that follow include the clubs of the moment, together with some of the larger and longer-established venues. (Nearly all are in the suburbs, involving a bus ride there and possibly a long walk back late at night.) Big international acts use the **Palasport** stadium at Viale Paoli (reached by bus no 10). Bands or solo singers who draw slightly smaller crowds use the **Teatro Verdi** (Via Ghibellina 101; tel: 212 320) and the **Teatro Tenda** (Lungarno Aldo Moro; tel: 650 4112; bus no 14). Indie bands have an annual festival, the 'Meeting', held during the summer at the **Palazzo dei Congressi** (Viale F Strozzi). Best known of the more intimate venues, featuring bands of all persuasions, is **Auditorium Flog** (Via Mercati 24; tel: 490 437; bus no 4).

Jazz fans are not so well served as in Milan or Rome, but Florence's Auditorium Flog (see above) still manages to attract many of the top international names. More specialised clubs include the **Jazz Club** (Via Nuova dei Caccini 3; tel: 247 9700; buses 6, 12, 14 or 23) and **Salt Peanuts** (Piazza Santa Maria Novella 26r; buses 13, 14 or 23). Both these clubs host events organised by the Toscana Jazz Pool, a jazz festival held in several Tuscan cities. For information on this and other jazz events contact **Arci Nova di Firenze** (Via Montebello 6; tel: 295 007; buses 1, 9, 12 or 26).

Clubs and discos Like music venues, nightclubs drop in and out of fashion. Again, these are some of the longer-running and currently popular locations. Four of the city's older discos have achieved almost historic status. **Tenax** (Via Pratese 46a; tel: 308 160) is the biggest and most popular, attracting locals and foreigners alike; it also presents new and established live bands (*open*: nightly Wednesday to Saturday). **Manila** (Piazza Matteucci–Campi Bisenzio; tel: 894 121) is perhaps trendier and almost as big (*open*: afternoons and evenings Friday to Sunday). The other two are more central and more intimate: **Andromeda** (Piazza de' Cerchi 7a; tel: 292 002; *open*: nightly except Sunday) and **Space Electronic** (Via Palazzuolo 37; tel: 293 082; *open*: nightly).

Smaller and more sedate clubs and piano bars which have been around for a while include **Jackie O** (Via dell'Erta Canina 24a; tel: 234 2442/3) and **Full Up** (Via Vigna Vecchia 21r; tel: 293 006), both popular with older punters. At the other extreme, try the Brazilian-influenced **Maracanà** (Via Faenza 4; tel: 210 298) and the well-known alternative hang-out, **Caffè Voltaire** (Via della Scala 9r; tel: 218 255; closed August). Small annual membership fees are payable for most nightclubs.

Gay and late-night bars
Gay clubs include the Crisco, a men-only pub (Via Sant'Edidio 43r.
If you want to burn the midnight oil, the following bars and cafés stay open later than most:
Il Rifrullo (Via San Niccolò 55r)
La Dolce Vita (Piazza del Carmine)
Sant'Ambrogio Caffè (Piazza Ambrogio 7).

Florence is full of small, smart clubs and discos

A good map is always a worthwhile investment

Main bus routes
Most buses can be picked up either at the bus station (right next to the railway station) or in Piazza del Duomo.

1 Duomo, Stazione, Viale Talenti
6 Duomo, San Marco, San Frediano
7 Stazione, Duomo, San Marco, Fiesole
10 Stazione, Duomo, San Marco, Settignano
11a Duomo, Porta Romana, Poggio Imperiale
12 Duomo, Porta Romana, San Miniato al Monte
13 Stazione, Duomo, Piazzale Michelangelo (San Miniato al Monte)
14 Duomo, Stazione, Careggi
17b Cascine, Stazione, Duomo, Salviatino (for the youth hostel)

Circular bus
Bus no 15 follows a circular route through the city centre and Oltrarno that doubles as a cheap sightseeing tour: Fortezza da Basso, San Marco, Via del Proconsolo, Ponte alle Grazie, Palazzo Pitti, Piazza Santo Spirito, Piazza del Carmine, Porta Romana, Ponte Santa Trinita, Via de' Tornabuoni, Via de' Servi, Fortezza da Basso.

Information Before setting foot in a museum visit one of Florence's **tourist offices** to collect a free city map, a list of events, and a full list of gallery opening times and up-to-date admission prices. The most convenient is at **Via Cavour** 1r (tel: 276 0381 or 290 832), close to the Palazzo Medici-Riccardi and the Duomo. Equally handy is the office at **Chiasso Baroncelli** 17r (tel: 230 2124 or 230 2033). This is off Piazza della Signoria, in a small alley to the right of the Loggia dei Lanzi (on the piazza's south side). A third office has opened outside the **railway station**; it is at the bottom of the bus rank on your left as you leave the station building (tel: 238 1226 or 212 245).

All three are open from Monday to Saturday (summer 8.15–7.15, winter 8.15–1.45); the Via Cavour and station offices are also open on Sunday in summer 8–1.45). For accommodation bookings see the panel on page 172.

Buses Much of what visitors come to see in Florence is easily reached on foot. However, you may wish to take a bus when visiting San Miniato al Monte and Piazzale Michelangelo, the Cascine and the Museo Stibbert. Longer trips to Fiesole and to the Medici villas (see pages 82–3 and 170–1) can also be made by bus from the city centre. General public transport information is given in **Travel Facts** (see pages 257–9).

The city bus company is called ATAF. There are four basic ticket types: one valid for any number of journeys within an hour; a similar one valid for two hours; a similar one valid for 24 hours; and a 'carnet' of 10 one-hour tickets. Tickets must be purchased before boarding the bus, and are available from bars, news-stands or tobacconists displaying an orange ATAF sticker (saying '*Biglietti Abbonamenti Qui*'). Automatic ticket machines also dot the city, notably at the bus station itself, the Fortezza da Basso and Piazza San Marco (where there is also an ATAF kiosk). You can enter buses through either the front or the rear doors, where there is a machine to validate tickets. Leave by the central doors.

Buses run to and from Florence's Peretola airport roughly every hour, seven days a week. The journey time is about 15 minutes, and buses leave from Via Santa Caterina da Siena (just west of the railway station).

Crime and safety No large city is entirely free of crime. Florence is no exception, its many tourists a source of rich potential pickings for the unscrupulous. Like other large Italian cities, Florence also has a drugs problem, though it remains less evident to the casual visitor than in Rome and Milan. This said, Florence is hardly a den of vice, and basic precautions combined with common sense should ensure a trouble-free trip.

Avoid certain areas late at night, notably the Cascine, Piazza Ognissanti and the back streets around the station: all are red-light areas of dubious repute. The same goes for the *Viali*, the busy roads on the city outskirts (though there is little reason for visitors to be here at night). Women on their own can expect kerb-crawlers in quieter city streets.

Use common sense to guard against pickpockets. Buses and street markets (especially San Lorenzo) are the thieves' favourite hunting grounds. Never keep money or valuables in a back pocket. Carry them in a pouch or money belt. Carry bags and cameras across your chest, not over your shoulder, and never put them down on café tables. Reduce temptation by leaving anything that can be snatched, such as necklaces and bracelets, in the hotel safe. Never leave luggage or radio-cassette players in cars.

Addresses Florence has a slightly confusing double-number address system. Business addresses (which usually include bars and restaurants) are followed by the letter 'r' for *rosso* (red), as in 'Via Confusione 32r'. Numbers are usually marked in red on a white background. Most hotels and residential addresses simply have a number, occasionally followed by a blue or black 'b'. Matters are further complicated by the fact that the two sets of numbers are independent of each other. Via Confusione 32r, therefore, will probably be some distance from Via Confusione 32b, or 31r for that matter.

Tourist pass
Non-residents can buy a special *Carta Arancio*, a seven-day pass valid for all trains and buses within the province of Florence (which does not include Siena). It must be used with valid identification such as a passport, and is available from ATAF (Piazza della Stazione) or SITA (Via Santa Caterina da Siena 15) or CAP (Via Nazionale 13) or COPIT (Piazza Santa Maria Novella 22).

187

An ATAF bus: workhorse of Florence's public transport system

TUSCANY

TUSCANY

Veterinary services advertised on an old Tuscan street sign

For many people, Tuscany *is* Italy. Its vineyards and soft-edged hills, its red wines and balmy summers, its quiet villages and cypress-ringed villas weave a spell that can be hard to resist from Florence's traffic-clogged streets. Resist it, however, many visitors do – some simply because they are short of time, others perhaps because they are loath to leave the city's protective cocoon. It takes a courage of sorts, after all, to tackle public transport or face the perils of Latin drivers and Italian roads. You should not, however, be faint-hearted. Most Tuscan towns of note, including nearly all those featured in this A to Z section, can be reached in no more than an hour from Florence. In the case of the big three – Siena, Lucca and Pisa (not to mention Arezzo, Prato and Pistoia) – this journey requires no more than the simplest of train rides. If Florence is your base, all such towns can be seen as day trips; if not, many make ideal springboards for the type of leisurely exploration that will ultimately reveal the best of the region.

Towns The attractions of most Tuscan towns make each one worthy of a whole day's sightseeing. **Siena** deserves at least that, its calm medieval ambience the perfect antidote to Florence. Little-known **Lucca** comes next, as graceful and civilised a town as any in Italy. **Pisa** attracts by virtue of its Campo dei Miracoli (but can be curiously disappointing thereafter). **Arezzo** might be similarly lacklustre but for Piero della Francesca's great fresco cycle. Nearby **Cortona**, by contrast, seduces with its views, its galleries and its quiet medieval streets. Much the same goes for **Montepulciano**, as attractive for its own sake as for any surfeit of art and architecture. **Volterra**, too, has its views and its medieval moments, as well as a wealth of Roman and Etruscan remains. **Pistoia** and **Prato** are perhaps too industrialised for immediate visitor appeal, but each has a sprinkling of masterpieces within easy reach of Florence.

Essential sights
Arezzo: San Francesco (frescos of Piero della Francesca).
Cortona: Museo Diocesano (Fra Angelico paintings), views.
Lucca: Duomo, San Michele, San Frediano, walls, town.
Monte Oliveto Maggiore: abbey (Il Sodoma frescos; see pages 232–3).
Pienza: Duomo, village.
Pisa: Leaning Tower, Duomo and Battistero.
San Gimignano: village.
Siena: Campo, Duomo, Museo dell'Opera del Duomo, Pinacoteca.

The façade of San Michele in Foro, Lucca

TUSCANY

Vineyards chequer the hills of Chianti, Tuscany's most famous region

Escape
'I'd had my fill of Florence, lovely but indigestible city. My eyes were choked with pictures and frescos, all stamped one on top of the other, blurred, their colours running. I began to long for those cool uplands, that country air, for the dateless wild olive and the uncatalogued cuckoo.' Laurie Lee, 'I Can't Stay Long' (1975).

191

Villages The siren call of Tuscany's towns could well leave little time for its villages. No trip to the region, however, would be complete without a visit to **San Gimignano** and its famous towers. Fewer people find their way to **Pienza**, a tiny Renaissance jewel, or to **Montalcino**, heart of the famous Brunello wine region (see pages 212–13 and 242–3). More are discovering **Monteriggioni**, a short hop from Siena, and perhaps the most perfect of Tuscany's fortified villages (see panel on page 239). Close by stand three beautiful abbeys – **Sant'Antimo**, **San Galgano** and **Monte Oliveto Maggiore** (see pages 232–3) – all fascinating monuments to Tuscany's long monastic tradition.

Landscapes Try to visit **Chianti**, of course – the most famous of Tuscany's landscapes – but try also to see the similar but less lauded areas of the **Mugello**, the **Pratomagno** and the **Casentino**. All three are mountainous regions smothered in huge forests, each a far cry from the pastoral images often associated with other parts of the Tuscan heartland. Departing further from Tuscany's gentler side are the marble-streaked summits of the **Alpi Apuane**, part of the great mountain range that rears up behind Pisa, Lucca and the Versilian coast. Too distant, perhaps, for many visitors to Florence, this spectacular country still deserves exploration, particularly the green **Garfagnana Valley** and the flower-strewn meadows of the **Orecchiella**. Less immediately appealing is the **Maremma**, a rather melancholy coastal plain, but nonetheless one of Italy's more unspoilt shores, offering the **Parco Naturale della Maremma** as well as a couple of Tuscany's best beaches. South of Siena and closer to home are the **crete**. Here will be found some of the region's strangest landscapes – bare clay hills chequered with dusty fields and prairies of rippling wheat.

Scenic drives
Tuscany has numerous drives worth following for their own sake. These are a few of the best:
• SS146/451 Montepulciano, Pienza, San Quirico, (Montalcino), Buonconvento, Monte Oliveto Maggiore.
• SS222 (the *Chiantigiana* wine road) Siena, Castellina, Greve, Florence.
• SS68 Volterra, (San Gimignano), Colle di Val d'Elsa.
• SS70/208 (Florence), Pontassieve, Poppi, Camaldoli, Bibbiena, Chiusi di Verna.
• SS324 Castelnuovo di Garfagnano, San Pellegrino, Pievepelago, San Marcello, Pistoia. (See also pages 198–9 and 242–3.)

The sloping Piazza Grande

Tourist information
Arezzo's tourist offices are outside the station at Piazza della Repubblica 22 (tel: 0575/377678) and one block to the north of the station at Piazza Risorgimento 116 (tel: 0575/23 952).

Casa di Vasari
Giorgio Vasari was born in Arezzo in 1511. Best known for his *Lives of the Artists* (1550), he was also the court painter and architect to Cosimo I. Few of his works have stood the test of time, and churches such as Santa Croce and Santa Maria Novella in Florence lost numerous earlier frescos through his ill-considered interventions. His house (1540), at Via XX Settembre 55, is decorated with some of the better examples of his work. *Open*: daily 9–6:30. Admission free.

▶▶ **Arezzo**   *IBCF4*

Arezzo would probably have few fans, were it not the home of one of Tuscany's most celebrated fresco cycles. Largely modern in appearance, the town relies for its prosperity on furniture-making and on one of Europe's largest gold and jewellery industries. In days gone by it was a leading member of the Etruscans' 12-city federation. Trans-Apennine trade routes maintained Arezzo's importance under the Romans and it became an independent city state during the Middle Ages before falling to Florence in 1384.

The church of San Francesco and its frescos (see below) will probably take most of your time, but leave an hour or so to see the precipitous **Piazza Grande**▶, flanked by Vasari's 1573 loggia and the **Palazzetto della Fraternità dei Laici**. The latter, built for a lay confraternity, sports a Gothic ground floor (1377) and a Renaissance upper storey by Bernardo Rossellino (1434). To its right stands the arcaded apse of the **Pieve di Santa Maria**▶▶, among the region's finest Romanesque churches. The Pisan-inspired façade looks on to Corso Italia, its portal decorated with touching reliefs (1210) illustrating the months of the year. Inside, the high altar has a grandiose polyptych by Pietro Lorenzetti. Wander past the Casa di Petrarca (Petrarch's House) to take in the **Duomo**▶, with its small fresco of Mary Magdalene by Piero della Francesca (end of the north aisle) and, alongside it, the superb tomb of Bishop Guido Tarlati (d. 1327), possibly built to a design by Giotto. The nearby church of **San Domenico** has fresco fragments, an *Annunciation* by the local artist Spinello Aretino and a *Crucifix* painted by the 20-year-old Cimabue.

San Francesco▶▶▶ Although it was built in 1320, Arezzo's Franciscan church only received its great fresco

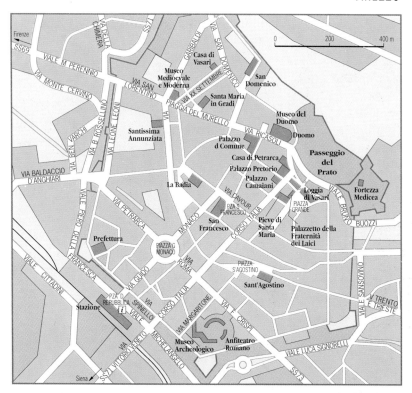

cycle in the 1450s. Commissioned by the Bacci, one of the town's leading families, the paintings were started by Bicci di Lorenzo, who, at his death, had completed only the choir's vaults (decorated with scenes of Hell, Heaven and Purgatory). Piero della Francesca, who continued the cycle, adopted a new theme taken from *The Legend of the True Cross*, a series of stories first collected in the 13th century by Jacopo da Voragine, Archbishop of Genoa. By Piero's time the tales had become an

Getting there
Arezzo is a major stop on the Rome–Florence rail line. Journey time from Florence is 40 minutes.

Museo Archeologico
This museum (Via Margaritone 10) offers lovely examples of the Roman *coralline* ceramics for which Arezzo was famed throughout the ancient world. *Open*: daily 9–2 (Sunday 9–1). Admission charge (moderate).

Antique fair
One of Italy's foremost antique fairs, the Fiera Antiquaria, is held in Arezzo's Piazza Grande over the weekend of the first Sunday in the month.

Three wise men: Arezzo locals

Part of Piero della Francesca's True Cross *cycle*

The Piero Trail
Arezzo is one stop on a trail of masterpieces by Piero della Francesca. His *Madonna del Parto*, the only pregnant Madonna in Italian art, stands in Monterchi's museum, 25km east of Arezzo. Further east, the Museo Civico in Sansepolcro, Piero's birth-place, contains two minor and two major works by the artist, a *Resurrection* and the *Madonna della Misericordia*.

international bestseller, reprinted in countless editions in all the major European languages. Cleverly linking the story of Adam and Eve and original sin with the story of humanity's redemption, this narrative charts an unlikely series of events in which the tree from which Eve plucked the forbidden fruit becomes the cross of Christ's crucifixion.

The story had already been painted, notably by Agnolo Gaddi in Florence's Santa Croce and by Cenni di Francesco in Volterra's San Francesco. Piero's version, however, is more complicated – not to say more accomplished – than its predecessors. This is partly because he was a better painter, and partly because he takes his story from two versions of the *Legend*. It was further complicated by Piero's insistence on artistic rather than narrative logic. Two battle scenes, for example, are placed opposite one another, their positions designed for compositional impact rather than narrative explanation. Similar symmetries are repeated in the Queen of Sheba's courtly retinue, which appears twice, and in the identical portraits of the Queen and the Empress Helena.

194

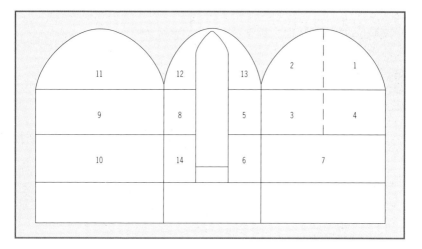

The narrative sequence of the frescos is as follows:

1. Adam announces his death and implores his son, Seth, to seek the 'oil of mercy' from the Angel of Paradise.
2. The Angel instead sends a twig from Paradise's Tree of Knowledge, which Seth plants in his father's mouth.
3. The twig has become a tree over Adam's grave. Solomon intends to use it in his temple, but instead orders a bridge to be built from its wood. The Queen of Sheba, visiting Solomon, kneels in prayer, sensing the bridge's divine importance.
4. The Queen foresees the Crucifixion and the fate of the Jews, whose realm 'shall be defaced and cease'. She tells Solomon of her prophecy.
5. Solomon orders the beam's burial (the scene deliberately echoes Christ's carrying of the cross).
6. The Roman emperor, Constantine the Great, asleep on the eve of battle, has a vision telling him to look for the sign of the cross. An angel announces 'Under this sign shall you be victorious'.
7. The victory of Constantine over his rival emperor, Maxentius. Constantine asks the meaning of the cross and is baptised.
8. Under torture, the Levite Judas (kept in a well for six days) reveals to the Empress Helena, mother of Constantine (and an inveterate collector of relics), the location of Calvary's three crosses.
9. The crosses are found: the True Cross is revealed when it touches a dead man and brings him back to life. The city in the background (meant to be Jerusalem) is Arezzo.
10. Thirty years later the Persian King Chosroes steals a portion of the cross, using it to build a throne on which he sets himself up as a god. Chosroes is defeated by Heraclius, emperor of the Eastern Empire.
11. Heraclius returns the cross to Jerusalem.
12. Prophet (by an assistant to Piero).
13. Prophet.
14. Annunciation.

Open: daily 8:30–12 and 1:30–6:30 (Sunday 8:30–12 and 2–6:00). Admission free.

Plan of the San Francesco frescos

Passeggio del Prato
Arezzo's public garden, next to the Duomo, is the nicest place in town for a walk or picnic. The ruined Fortezza Medicea, above the park, offers magnificent views over the surrounding countryside.

Giostra del Saracino
After a morning of processions in medieval costume, a pair of knights from each of Arezzo's four quarters take it in turns to charge at the *Buratto*, a figure recalling the days when Saracen pirates menaced Tuscany and the Tyrrhenian coast. In one hand the *Buratto* bears a numbered shield (scores depend on where the knights' lances strike), in the other a cat-of-nine-tails that swings when the shield is struck. The winner receives a golden lance. The event is traditionally held on the first Sunday in September in Piazza Grande. Recently it has become so popular that repeat performances are held throughout the summer. Contact the tourist office for dates.

■ **Tuscany's rural patchwork of hills and valleys offers many pockets of beautiful countryside. Some are less well-known versions of Chianti's classic scenery; other, wilder places are areas of outstanding natural beauty which enjoy protection as regional or national parks......■**

Birdwatching

Tuscany's best birdwatching sites are the Ombrone estuary in the Parco Naturale della Maremma; the Worldwide Fund for Nature (WWF) oasis at Albinia, on the Orbetello lagoon; the WWF reserve at Lago di Burano, 10km southeast of Orbetello; and the WWF reserve at Bolgheri, near Cecina about 40km south of Livorno. WWF reserves are usually open only from September to May on Thursday and Sundays, but many birds can be seen in these areas outside the reserves.

196

Sunflowers and vines in the Chianti hills: part of the gentler face of Tuscany

Mugello, Pratomagno and Casentino It can only be a matter of time before this great arc of countryside east of Florence begins to share the popularity of the more famous (but scenically inferior) Chianti hills to the south of the city. A tour of the **Pratomagno**, a great bowed dome of meadow-topped hills, should start at Vallombrosa, whose mighty forests were immortalised in the opening book of Milton's *Paradise Lost*. Milton describes the rebel angels, fallen from Heaven, lying 'Thick as autumnal leaves that strow the brooks/ In Vallombrosa, where th'Etrurian shades/ High over-arched, embow'r'. In 1638 the poet stayed at the village's famous monastery, now largely modern in appearance but still at the heart of some magnificent scenery.

Further west, another old monastery village, Camaldoli, makes a good focal point in the **Casentino**, an area famed since antiquity for its mountains and huge, wind-blown forests. The biggest region of all, the **Mugello**, offers enough by-ways for days of exploration, best accomplished – as elsewhere in these regions – on the scenic mountain roads well away from the towns and semi-industrialised valleys.

Alpi Apuane and Orechiella Tuscany's most spectacular scenery – and its best walking country – gathers north of Pisa in two mountain ranges flanking the Garfagnana Valley. To the west the **Alpi Apuane** rise from the sea with almost Alpine splendour, dotted with marble quarries whose snow-like streaks glisten on the slopes above Massa and Carrara. Countless marked trails criss-cross the hills, well-worn tracks weaving through thick chestnut forests or cresting the panoramic and craggy-topped summit ridges. The mountains are well mapped (unlike much of Italy) and refuges provide picnic supplies and overnight stops (maps and refuge information are available from Massa, Carrara and most coastal towns). As a result, day hikes in this area, and several long-distance paths, are some of the easiest in Tuscany to tackle without too much forward planning. The best starting points are the villages of Stazzema and Levigliano on the western flanks. If you wish to drive instead, a network of tiny roads criss-crosses the mountains, providing superb views.

The **Orecchiella**, east of the Garfagnana – higher and wilder than the Alpi Apuane – offers almost equally good scenery and walking country. Visit Barga for its honey-coloured cathedral, and the well-managed Parco Naturale, whose park centre at Orecchiella (a hamlet 15km north of Castelnuovo di Garfagnana) is the starting point of several easy marked trails. Castelnuovo di Garfagnana and

Corfino are the best bases for the area. Excellent and readily obtainable maps allow you to explore under your own steam. Driving, too, is a delight, a particularly good target being the excellent folk museum at San Pellegrino in Alpe (16km northeast of Castelnuovo).

Maremma A stretch of fertile coastal lowlands under the Etruscans and the Romans, the Maremma deteriorated into a malaria-ridden swamp during the Middle Ages. It remained that way – and all but uninhabited – until reclamation began in the 18th century. Today the region's finest sweep of unspoilt landscape is protected by the Parco Naturale della Maremma (a proposed national park). The hills of the park, the Monti dell'Uccellina, are topped by coastal watch-towers and boast caves that have yielded some of Italy's oldest prehistoric remains. The shores are the least spoilt in Tuscany, while forests of umbrella pine, coastal dunes, marshes and Mediterranean *maquis* provide cover for a fantastic assortment of flora and fauna. Only the superb beach at Marina di Alberese is open to cars. Otherwise you have to park at Alberese, 20km south of Grosseto and take the park bus (see panel). Alternative access is on foot from Talamone, an appealing village at the park's southern edge.

Park bus
For access to the Parco Naturale della Maremma, leave your car at Alberese and buy a bus ticket from the main square's park kiosk (hourly, Wednesday and weekends only). This drops you in the heart of the park (there are no other roads). From here you can walk almost at random; the lovely beach is about 20 minutes' walk away. The last bus out is at 5:30.

197

Top: the Maremma. Below: the jagged peaks of the Alpi Apuane near the marble town of Carrara

Drive **The heart of Chianti**

A circular tour from Siena (see pages 234–41) through Chianti's hills, villages and most famous vineyards (approximately 110km).

Chianti is a name to conjure with, not only the home of Italy's most famous red wine, but also a region whose vineyards and wooded hills evoke the quintessential image of Tuscany. Visitors in their thousands swarm to its villas and farmhouses. Some villages are tarnished by the influx: others, like Radda and Gaiole, are spoilt by a surprising amount of light industry. The region's real pleasures, therefore, lie in driving its winding back roads, exploring the smaller hamlets, and sampling wine at any one of the hundreds of vineyards open to the public.

Leave Siena by the SS408 (signed to Montevarchi), joining it beyond Siena's railway station. Turn right after 10km on to the minor road past San Giusto alle Monache and San Felice. **Castello di Brolio**►► offers tours around one of Chianti's best vineyards. The estate has been in the Ricasoli family since 1167, and it was Barone Bettino Ricasoli, Italy's second prime minister, who established Chianti Classico's formula in 1870.

Rural and rambling: a typical Chianti farmhouse

For marvellous views of the Chianti hills take the SS484 south of Brolio. Continue north past the hamlets of San Gusmé, Campi and Linari before rejoining the SS408 beyond the castle of Meleto. (This loop adds 27km. If you are short of time, drive west from Brolio for 5km to meet the SS408 2km south of Meleto.)

Continue to **Gaiole**► – not the prettiest of Chianti villages, though its single main street is pleasant enough, and there is the novelty of a stream (often dry) through the village centre. Further on, a short detour from the main road (worthwhile for the views alone) leads to **Badia a Coltibuono**. The lovely (but rarely open) Romanesque church, San Lorenzo, is part of an abbey complex owned by one of the more commercially minded Chianti estates. Its wine, honey and oil are exported to delicatessens all over Europe, but you can also buy produce directly from Da Gianetto, the estate's stylish restaurant.

The road west to **Radda in Chianti** is particularly panoramic, and though Radda's outskirts are offputting, the

village's medieval centre, Piazza Ferrucci, is more picturesque. If you have time to spare, drive the 15km loop north to the fortified hamlet of **Volpaia**, whose evocative towers and castle are the legacy of its role as a vital military lookout in the 16th century.

Continue west to **Castellina in Chianti▶**, another walled village whose main concern these days is wine production. Be sure to visit the Bottega del Vino Gallo Nero at Via della Rocca 13, a showcase for the region's wine and olive oils. They will also advise on local vineyards offering tours and tastings.

Return to Siena on the SS222, or turn right off the SS222 1km south of Castellina at Malafrasca to visit the superbly preserved village of **Monteriggioni** (see page 239), off the SS2 (10km southeast of Poggibonsi).

▶▶ **Cortona** *IBCF3*

Cortona may become one of your favourite Tuscan hill-towns. Magnificently situated, with olives and vineyards creeping up to its walls, it commands enormous views over Lake Trasimeno and the plain of the Valdichiana. Its two fine galleries and scattering of churches are relatively unvisited, whilst its delightful medieval streets are a pleasure to wander for their own sake. Last but not least, pleasant hotels and restaurants make the town a good overnight base.

Cortona may be one of Italy's oldest towns – 'Mother of Troy and Grandmother of Rome', in popular parlance. Tradition claims it was founded by Dardanus, the founder of Troy (after whom the Dardanelles are named). He was fighting a local tribe, so the story goes, when he lost his helmet (*corythos*) on Cortona's hill. In time a town grew up that took its name (Corito) from the missing headgear. By the 4th century the Etruscans had built the first set of town walls, whose cyclopean traces can still be seen in the 3km sweep of the present fortifications. A member of the Etruscans' 12-city Dodecapolis, it became one of the federation's leading northern cities. An important consular road, the Via Cassia, which passed the foot of its hill, maintained the town's importance under the Romans. Medieval fortunes waned, however, as the plain below reverted to marsh. After holding out against neighbours like Perugia, Arezzo and Siena, the *comune* was captured by King Ladislas of Naples in 1409 and sold to the Florentines two years later.

Cortona's steep streets make you pay for your pleasure, but any amount of puffing and panting is worth it to enjoy their views and medieval vignettes. Only one lane is level: the main Via Nazionale (linking Piazza Garibaldi and Piazza della Repubblica), referred to by locals as the *Ruga Piana* (Flat Street). Areas well worth seeking out include Via Guelfa and Via Ghibellina, the main streets of the old town, both sprinkled with a mixture

Getting there
Trains to Cortona from Florence (90 minutes) stop at Terontola or Camucia-Cortona. Both stations are several kilometres from the town. Shuttle buses connect them roughly every 30 minutes to Piazza Garibaldi. The town centre is closed to cars, so use car parks near San Domenico or at Porta Colonia and Piazza del Mercato. LFI buses run from Piazza Garibaldi to Arezzo and Castiglion Fiorentino.

Special events
Cortona's lively weekly market takes place on Saturday. An annual antiques and furniture fair is held in late August and September.

Santa Margherita is the highest church in this lovely hill-town

of medieval and Renaissance architecture; Via Janelli, a picturesque thoroughfare of 14th-century timber-framed houses below Piazza del Duomo; and Via Maffei, lined with a parade of 16th-century Renaissance *palazzi*. Also in this last street is the church of **San Francesco**, the first church established by the Franciscans outside Assisi. The third altar on its left (north) wall has an unfinished *Annunciation* (1669) by Pietro da Cortona, a poor substitute for the painter's best work, which is divided between Rome's baroque churches and the Palazzo Pitti in Florence, whose state rooms feature the ceiling frescos

Time on his hands: a Cortona watchmaker

Tourist Information
Cortona's tourist office is at Via Nazionale 70–2 (tel: 0575/630 356 or 630 357).

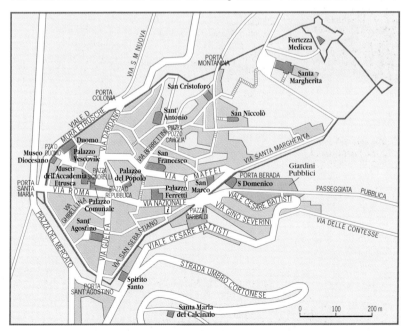

Washday and a pause for thought – a timeless scene in Cortona

Views
Visit the Fortezza Medicea and the public gardens near San Domenico for Cortona's best views. Come at dusk, when lights twinkle across the huge plain below the town.

Hannibal
At Tuoro sul Trasimeno, just a few kilometres east of Cortona, you can visit the site of one of antiquity's most famous battles. In 217BC Hannibal and his army defeated a Roman army under the Consul Flaminius. Some 16,000 Romans were killed after a cunningly planned ambush. A drive and a marked trail have been laid out around the site.

that brought the artist fame (see page 117). The church's crypt is believed to contain the tomb of Cortona's other famous painter, Luca Signorelli (1441–1523).

Northeast of the town centre, be sure also to visit the cypress-shaded **San Nicolò**, known for an unusual double-sided painting by Signorelli. One face shows a fine *Deposition*, the other a *Madonna and Child*. Ask the custodian to operate the intriguing pulley system that turns the painting around. Fra Angelico's old church, **San Domenico**, has a faded fresco by the painter over its portal. A chapel to the right of the high altar contains a *Madonna and Saints* (1515) by Signorelli and a detached fresco of San Rocco by Bartolomeo della Gatta. The striking altarpiece, *The Coronation of the Virgin* (1402), is by Lorenzo Gerini. To the east of the church the **Giardini Pubblici** (public gardens) offer lovely walks with superb views (see panel).

Museo dell'Accademia Etrusca►► Cortona's civic museum offers a fascinating and eclectic collection that goes beyond the Etruscan limits suggested by its name. (The *Accademia*, a historical institute founded in 1727, numbered Voltaire amongst its early members.) The museum occupies one of the town's more impressive medieval palaces, the 13th-century Palazzo Casali (or Palazzo Pretorio), former home to Cortona's leading medieval family.

The main hall contains a famous and unusual 5th-century BC chandelier. The largest object of its kind ever found, it consists of a gorgon's head surrounded by dolphins and stylised waves, its 16 small oil lamps formed by alternating male and female figurines. Attic vases, bronze figures and Roman statuettes line the walls, together with paintings by Pietro da Cortona and Luca Signorelli, both natives of Cortona (as well as works by Pinturicchio,

Cristofano Allori and more minor artists). Rooms off the hall include further paintings, notably a triptych by Bicci di Lorenzo, as well as (poorly labelled) fans, ivories, weapons, porcelain, miniatures, coins and jewellery. Best of this miscellany are several medieval ceramics and an Egyptian collection amassed in 1891 by the Vatican's Egyptian legate. *Open*: daily 10–1 and 4–7 (winter 9–1 and 3–5). Closed Monday. Admission charge (moderate).

Museo Diocesano ▶▶▶ Piazza del Duomo's main draw is not so much its lacklustre Duomo as the museum opposite, a rather gloomy former church whose interior is enlivened by a small but prestigious collection of Renaissance paintings. Perversely, however, it opens with a 2nd-century Roman sarcophagus, whose carved centaurs and battle scenes were apparently much admired by Donatello and Brunelleschi. The fresco fragments here include *The Way to Calvary* by the Sienese master, Pietro Lorenzetti.

Two paintings by Fra Angelico dominate the gallery proper – a sublime *Annunciation* (1428–30) and a triptych of the Madonna and Child with Saints. Both were painted during the artist's 10-year sojourn in Cortona's Dominican monastery (the triptych's predella depicts scenes from the life of St Dominic). The room also contains three works that would be outstanding in any other company: a *Crucifix* by Pietro Lorenzetti; Sassetta's *Madonna and Child*; and Bartolomeo della Gatta's *Assumption of the Virgin*. Lorenzetti has another beautiful painting in the room beyond, a *Madonna Enthroned*. Local painter Luca Signorelli is also well represented by a *Deposition* and *Communion of the Apostles*. *Open*: daily 9–1 and 3–6:30 (winter 9–1 and 3–5). Closed Monday. Admission charge (moderate).

Santa Maria del Calcinaio
This outstanding 15th-century Renaissance church is located on the winding approach road to Cortona (3km from Porta Sant'Agostino). It was built on the site of a tannery (known as a *calcinaio* after the lime used in the tanning process) to house an image of the Virgin that had miraculously appeared on the tannery walls. Similar High Renaissance churches, built on the Greek cross plan and with a central dome, are to be found at Prato, Montepulciano and Todi (in Umbria).

203

Part of a Roman sarcophagus in Cortona's Museo Diocesano

LUCCA

The city's Roman grid of streets, glimpsed from the Torre Guinigi

Getting there
Lucca is easily reached by bus or train from Pisa (30 minutes). Hourly trains from Florence on the Viareggio line take 70–90 minutes. The railway station is in Piazza Ricasoli, just outside the walls to the south of the city. Local and long-haul CLAP and Lazzi buses use the terminal in Piazza G Verdi, in the west of the city. There are regular fast buses to Florence (1 hour). Cars are severely restricted in the city centre. The best car park is Le Tagliate, outside Porta San Donato.

▶▶▶ Lucca   *IBCB5*

No city in Italy is as quietly urbane as Lucca. Its ring of walls encloses dozens of tiny Romanesque churches, quiet paved streets, doughty defensive towers, and numerous museums and monuments – the sort of place, in the words of Henry James, that is 'overflowing with everything that makes for ease, for plenty, for beauty, for interest and good example' (*Italian Hours*, 1909). The city centre is closed to traffic, and the local people, prosperous and courteous, have responded by taking to bicycles (though you can walk across the city in less than 20 minutes). If you are pressed for time the essential sights are the Duomo; San Michele and San Frediano; the Museo Nazionale Guinigi; and the Torre Guinigi and Piazza Anfiteatro. If possible, leave time also to walk at least part of the way round the city's magnificent walls.

Lucca prospered as a Roman colony, whose grid-iron plan is still reflected in the city's streets. It became Tuscany's first Christian town (the city's first bishop, Paulinus, was a disciple of St Peter) and then capital of Tuscany (Tuscia) under the Lombards and the Franks. Later it was ruled by the Margraves, who eventually moved to Florence. Its medieval wealth, second only to that of Florence, was based on banking and a thriving silk industry (underwear is still a major money-earner). Under the dashing Castruccio Castracani the town dominated western Tuscany, capturing Pisa and Pistoia: only Castracani's untimely death prevented the capture of Florence as well. Lucca remained independent until 1799 under successive noble families (notably the Guinigi). Nemesis came in 1805 in the shape of Napoleon (see panel), who presented the city to his sister, Elisa Baciocchi. In 1817 it passed to Marie Louise de Bourbon, becoming part of the Tuscan Grand Duchy in 1847.

Tourist information
Lucca's main tourist office is in the northern corner of Piazza G Verdi (tel: 0583/419 689). There is another small office off Piazza Napoleone at Via Vittorio Veneto 40 (tel: 0583/493 639).

Lucca in literature
Lucca's surrender to Napoleon features in the opening lines of the great Russian novel, Tolstoy's *War and Peace*: '*Eh bien, mon prince*, so Genoa and Lucca are now no more than private estates of the Bonaparte family.' (Anna Pavlovna Scherer to Prince Vasili, July 1805)

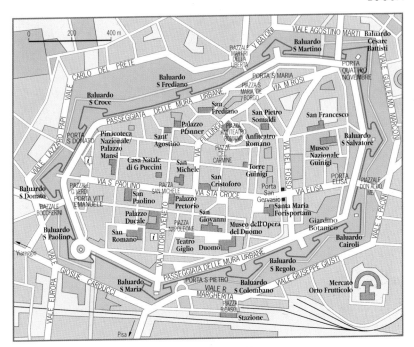

Duomo di San Martino ▶▶▶ Lucca's cathedral was consecrated in 1070 by Pope Alexander II (previously the city's bishop), and built in fits and starts over the next 400 years. The delays were to present several problems. When the 13th-century façade was added, for example, it had to be married uncomfortably with the existing bell-tower, whose lower half was built in 1060 as a defensive tower. The result was a decidedly lopsided frontage (the tower's upper section was added in 1261). Asymmetry notwithstanding, the façade remains dazzling, the

Such summer tasks as threshing, fruit-picking and wine-making are depicted in the Labours of the Months *relief sculptures beside the Duomo's central doorway*

Jacopo della Quercia's tomb of Ilaria del Carretto

Jacopo della Quercia
This greatest of Sienese sculptors was working at the same time as Donatello and Ghiberti and was one of the unsuccessful entrants in the competition to design Florence's Baptistery doors. Other works are to be found in Siena and San Gimignano.

Volto Santo
According to myth, Lucca's prized holy relic came to the city in 782 of its own volition, journeying by boat from the Holy Land before being guided to Lucca, on an ox-cart, by divine will. In truth it is probably a 13th-century copy of an 11th-century work, copied in turn from an 8th-century Syrian original. It is perhaps no coincidence that it brought huge wealth to the church of the time, or that it appeared during the reign of Lucca's Bishop Anselmo, later to become pope. Revered for centuries, its fame was enormous. King William Rufus of England swore by it – '*per sanctum vultum de Lucca*', and in France the mythical St Vaudeluc grew from a contraction of its French name – St Vault de Lucques.

apotheosis of Pisan-Romanesque architecture – all arches, arcades and decorated columns – for which the city is renowned. Note in particular the stunning entrance colonnade and its three portals (1233), the carvings on the left door – notably an *Annunciation* and an *Adoration of the Magi* – probably early works by Nicola Pisano (and possibly his first works in Tuscany). Reliefs beside the central door depict the life of St Martin and the Labours of the Months (note, in particular, the wonderfully graphic pig-sticking scene).

The interior is dominated by Matteo Civitali (1435–1501), a barber-turned-sculptor almost unknown outside his native Lucca. He was responsible for the inlaid pavement, the pulpit, a pair of water stoups, two beautiful tombs (in the south transept) and for the huge gilt-and-marble *Tempietto* mid-way down the nave. The last was built to house the famous *Volto Santo* (Holy Face), a cedar-wood Crucifix, reputedly a true effigy of Christ carved by Nicodemus after the Crucifixion (see panel). Beyond it on the left, and considerably more beautiful, is the tomb of Ilaria del Carretto (1410), the masterpiece of Sienese sculptor Jacopo della Quercia (justifiably described by John Ruskin as 'the loveliest Christian tomb in Italy'). It consists of a raised dais and the sculpted body of Ilaria, second wife of Paolo Guinigi (one of the city's medieval overlords). Note the touching addition of the family's favourite dog at its mistress's feet. The large statue of St John near by is by the same sculptor.

The church's surprisingly good paintings include a *Madonna and Child* (1509) by Fra Bartolomeo (immediately before the Carretto tomb); Bronzino's *Presentation of the Virgin* (first chapel on the left); a garish *Last Supper* by Tintoretto (third altar on the right); and a *Madonna Enthroned* by Domenico Ghirlandaio (on the left wall of the sacristy). Outside the Duomo a small Museo dell'Opera del Duomo has opened, worth seeing for its collection of medieval silverware.

San Michele in Foro▶▶▶ With its poetic confection of tiny arcades and delicately twisted columns, San Michele's sublime façade – surely one of Tuscany's most beautiful – draws you time and again to Piazza San

Michele (once the city's Roman forum, or *foro*). The church took some 300 years to build, during which time money for the project ran out, a shortfall that left the interior bereft of its projected splendour. Its only works of note are a della Robbia *Madonna and Child* and Filippino Lippi's *Saints Jerome, Sebastian, Roch and Helena* (at the end of the right nave).

Whilst in the area, make for **Via Fillungo**, the city's appealing main street. Be sure to visit the **Caffè di Simo** (Via Fillungo 58), a café famous for its beautiful turn-of-the-century interior. It is close to the Torre delle Ore, the city's clock-tower since 1471. The whole of Via Fillungo is full of other lovely art nouveau shop fronts and interiors. Also worth a brief stop is the church of **San Cristoforo**, burial place of Matteo Civitali and a monument to Lucca's war dead (whose names are etched into the walls). The church is now used as an art gallery.

San Frediano►► The third of Lucca's big three churches, San Frediano (1112–47) substitutes a glorious 13th-century mosaic for the columns and arcades of the city's other Romanesque façades. An evocative twilight bathes the interior, the gloom half-concealing the Fonta Lustrale, a stupendous 12th-century font decorated with

Giacomo Puccini
The composer Puccini (1858–1924) was born in Lucca, at Corte San Lorenzo 9 (off Via di Poggio). His family were organists in the Duomo for four generations, and he himself was a chorister at San Michele. His house now contains a small museum of memorabilia – scores, piano, photographs and even his overcoat. *Open*: daily 10–1 and 3–6 (winter 11–1 and 3–5). Closed Monday. Admission charge (inexpensive).

The magnificent Fonta Lustrale in San Frediano

207

LUCCA

A detail of the mosaic from the façade of San Frediano

Olive oil
Much of Lucca's prosperity derives from its rich agricultural plain – 'half-smothered in oil and wine and corn and all the fruits of the earth', in the words of Henry James, who was much taken with Lucca (*Italian Hours*, 1909). Consider buying its famous olive oil, regarded as some of the best in Italy.

Markets
Lucca's main market takes place in Piazza Anfiteatro every Wednesday and Saturday (8–1).

reliefs of the Apostles, the months of the year, the Shepherds, the Prophets and scenes from the life of Moses (note the relief depicting the crossing of the Red Sea, its Egyptian soldiers depicted as medieval knights). Behind the font is an *Annunciation* by Andrea della Robbia, festooned with garlands of glazed terracotta fruit. The adjoining Cappella di Santa Zita holds the body of St Zita (patron saint of servants), who was given to smuggling bread from her household to give to the poor. Challenged one day as to what was in her apron, she replied 'only flowers and roses', into which the bread was miraculously transformed.

The Cappella Trenta (the fourth chapel of the north aisle) contains two pavement tombs and a carved altarpiece (1422) by Jacopo della Quercia. The north aisle's second chapel boasts Lucca's best frescos (1508–9) – Amico Aspertini's *Life of St Augustine*, *The Arrival of the Volto Santo* (see panel on page 206) and *The Legend of San Frediano* (Frediano was a 6th-century Irish monk who saved Lucca from flood).

Piazza del Anfiteatro►► This piazza's oval of tall, rather ramshackle buildings reflects the shape of the Roman amphitheatre that stood here until the 12th century. Stone from the theatre was used to build the city's churches and palaces, but some still remains embedded in the piazza's buildings, particularly on its north side. This part of the city, quiet and interesting, is a pleasure to explore. Its worthwhile targets include Sant' Agostino. Palazzo Pfanner and the Romanesque façade of San Pietro Somaldi. Also try to pop into the cavernous San Francesco on your way to the Museo Nazionale.

Museo Nazionale Guinigi► Although Lucca's museums pale beside those of Florence or Siena, the 20 rooms of this gallery in the Via della Quarquonia offer a pleasingly eclectic collection. The lower floor is given over largely to archaeology and sculpture. Highlights are finds from Roman Lucca (Room 1), a tomb slab by Jacopo della Quercia (Room 2) and several works by the ubiquitous Matteo Civitali (Room 5). Upstairs the paintings of relatively anonymous Lucchese masters dominate, leavened by Sienese works and Fra Bartolomeo's *Madonna della Misericordia* and *God the Father with Mary Magdalene* and *St Catherine* (both in Room 14). *Open*: daily 9–7 (winter 9–2). Closed Monday. Admission charge (inexpensive).

Torre Guinigi▶ Lucca's eastern margins are duller than the rest of the city, so cut back from the Museo Nazionale to Via Sant'Andrea, where the Torre Guinigi constitutes one of the city's more eccentric landmarks. The 14th-century tower, part of the Guinigi's rambling red-brick palace, is topped by a grove of ilex trees whose roots have grown into the room below. Climb the tower to see this oddity and to enjoy some tremendous views of the city and surrounding countryside. *Open*: daily 9–7:30 (winter 10–4:30). Admission charge (moderate).

Leave time to take in **Santa Maria Forisportam** just to the south, so called because until 1260 it was outside the walls of the medieval and Roman city. The façade is captivating, while the interior has a couple of good works by Guercino (in the north transept and on the north aisle's fourth altar).

City walls▶▶ No visit to Lucca is complete without walking at least part of the way round its impressive ramparts (the total circuit measures 4km). Tree-lined and closed to traffic, the walls were built between 1500 and 1650, prompted by advances in weapon technology that had rendered the old (1198) walls obsolete. The moats are 35m wide, with 11 bastions defending ramparts 12m high and 30m wide. A surrounding swathe of green, 200m wide, created to deprive an enemy of cover, now serves to keep the worst aspects of the modern world at bay. The defences, among the finest in Europe, were never defended in anger; the only time they were used was in 1812, when the three original gates were shut to protect against a flood. Napoleon's sister, Elisa Baciocchi, had to be winched over the ramparts by crane. Her successor, Marie Louise de Bourbon, transformed the rampart walks into tree-shaded gardens shortly afterwards.

Special events
A large antiques market takes place in the streets around the Duomo over the third weekend of every month. September sees the Settembre Lucchese, a month-long festival of music and the performing arts. An outdoor festival of Puccini's opera, the Festival Pucciniano, takes place in July and August in Torre del Lago Puccini, 18km west of Lucca. The Festival di Marlia (opera and classical music) is held at the Villa Reale near Marlia, 8km east of the city.

Make time to enjoy the tree-shaded walk round Lucca's city walls

Tuscan food

■ **Poverty was the mother of culinary invention through the long centuries of peasant tradition that have shaped Tuscany's contemporary cuisine. As a result the region's cooking – like most Italian cooking – relies on simple ingredients and a refreshingly down-to-earth approach to preparation and presentation......**■

210

Cheese
All sorts of national and regional cheeses are available in Tuscany. Some of the most typical are the many varieties of pecorino, a sheep's cheese that comes in soft (*dolce*) or matured (*stagionato*) versions. Another sheep's cheese, ricotta, is a delicious soft cream cheese. It can be eaten either savoury (with olive oil, salt and pepper) or sweet (with honey and cinnamon).

Antipasti The simplicity of Tuscan cooking is apparent from a meal's first mouthful. *Antipasti* (starters) are nothing if not straightforward. Ham and salami are both common *antipasti*, with specialities such as *finocchiona* (fennel-flavoured salami) and *prosciutto di cinghiale* (air-cured wild boar ham). Ordinary hams are also commonly served – perhaps with melon or figs – either *crudo* (raw) or *cotto* (cooked). Equally widespread are *crostini* – small pieces of toast dripped with warm oil and covered with a savoury paste made from anchovy, or pine nuts with cheese and basil, or liver and capers. *Bruschetta* (or *fettunta*) is similar, but tends to be plainer – just toasted slices of bread rubbed with garlic and brushed with warm olive oil.

Primi First courses traditionally consist of pasta, rice, soup or polenta – originally a means of filling up before the main meat or fish dishes to follow. Tuscany naturally has its pasta dishes – the most famous being *pappardelle alla lepre* (noodles with a hare sauce) – but it puts more enthusiasm into its soups. Most ubiquitous of these is *ribollita* (literally 'reboiled'), a hearty mix of vegetables, beans, cabbage and bread, so reduced as to be more like a thick casserole than a liquid soup. Equally warming and also vegetable-based is the well-known *minestrone*. *Pappa al pomodoro* is a rich tomato soup, thickened with bread and seasoned with basil. Egg is whisked into *acquacotta* (literally 'cooked water') – an onion, celery and mushroom soup served over toasted bread. Bean soup (*zuppa di fagioli*) and onion soup (*carabaccia*) are other favourites. On the coast, every restaurant has its own version of *cacciucco*, a fish soup with more than a passing resemblance to the French *bouillabaisse*.

A risotto flavoured with Tuscany's prized porcini mushrooms

Tuscan food

Tuscan appetisers: a mouthwatering selection of antipasti

Tuscan appetisers: a mouthwatering selection of antipasti

If pasta is your preference, most Italian staples are usually available. Try to venture beyond the old favourites – meat and tomato sauces (pasta *al sugo* or *al pomodoro*) – and experiment with local specialities like *pici* (handmade pasta found around Siena) or *tortelli* (ricotta- and spinach-stuffed pasta from the Maremma).

Secondi Meat and fish provide the centrepiece of any Italian meal. Nowhere in Italy is the meat grander than in Tuscany, whose best-known dish is the redoubtable *bistecca alla fiorentina*. These days you have to pay a lot for the real thing – a vast T-bone steak from the white cattle of the Valdichiana near Montepulciano. Cooked in the traditional way it is unbeatable – dripped with olive oil, seasoned with herbs, and grilled over the perfumed embers of a chestnut-wood fire. Grilled meats (*alla griglia*) are generally a Tuscan staple, whether lamb (*agnello*), pork (*maiale*) or chicken (*pollo*). The same meats are also served roasted (*arrosto*), often presented together as a mountainous mixed roast (*arrosto misto*). They may also be prepared *alla cacciatore*, a rich casserole of meat, tomatoes and olives 'in the style of the hunter'. Tuscan *scottiglia* is similar, a stew of poultry, white wine and veal (*vitello*). Less immediately appealing to many visitors, but one of the great Florentine specialities, is *trippa alla fiorentina* – tripe in a tomato sauce. A notch more appetising, perhaps, are *baccalà* (salted cod in a tomato sauce) and *cibreo* (chicken liver and egg stew). All types of fish and seafood are available on the coast (and occasionally inland). Vegetables and salads, it goes without saying, are almost invariably excellent.

Dolci Restaurants often disappoint over puddings, too many of which are made off the premises and over-sweetened with some virulent liqueur. Fruit can be a wiser choice – especially grapes, cherries and strawberries in season. Better still, indulge in an ice-cream from a *gelateria* during an after-dinner stroll. Special desserts worth a try are *cantuccini*, almond biscuits dipped in dessert wine (*Vin Santo*), or more readily available specialities such as Siena's tooth-rotting *panforte* (a cake of nuts and candied fruit).

Seasonal fare
Autumn adds game to the Tuscan menu, usually boar (*cinghiale*), but also hare, rabbit, pheasant, partridge and guinea fowl. Other seasonal delicacies include truffles (from Umbria) and mushrooms, especially the highly prized *porcini*, eaten grilled or added to pasta and risottos.

211

■ **Tuscan wine no longer means a straw-covered flask of old-fashioned Chianti. Attention these days is more likely to focus on Brunello and Vino Nobile, central Italy's finest reds, and on the cultish 'Super Tuscans' of the region's more forward-thinking producers......■**

A hard sell for San Gimignano's well-known white wine

The DOC system
Italy's DOC (*Denominazione di Origine Controllata*) classification system, modelled on the French *Appellation Contrôlée* equivalent, is now largely outdated and discredited. A radical overhaul is currently under way. A DOCG (*Denominazione di Origine Controllata e Garantita*) label, for example, is being awarded to the finest wines. Many producers, however, ignore both systems, producing excellent wines under the humblest classification of all – *vino da tavola* (table wine).

A new breed Tuscan wine is enjoying a renaissance, rejuvenated by the adoption of French grape varieties and by the grafting of foreign techniques on to traditional production methods. Foremost among the resulting vintages has been Sassicaia, a wine that eschews Tuscany's traditional grape, the red Sangiovese, in favour of 100 per cent Cabernet Sauvignon. In its wake have come imitators like Antinori's Tignanello and the reliable Carmignano, both blends of native grapes with foreign varieties such as Merlot, Cabernet and Pinot Noir. Whites have wedded Chardonnay and Sauvignon to Tuscany's indigenous Trebbiano. Many of the new wines have jumped on to what is proving to be a lucrative bandwagon, and prices for some are out of all proportion to their quality (though Italians have proved willing to pay for novelty and for being fashionable). The innovations overall, however, have been a good thing, enhancing the range and quality of the region's wines.

Chianti Tuscany's most famous wine has been forced to look to its laurels by the region's viticultural revolution. No wine was previously in greater disarray, its 700 or more varieties ranging from the sublime to the substandard. Chianti's name, perhaps derived from an Etruscan family, first appears in the 14th century when it referred to a group of nobles known as the Chianti League. Its first mention as a wine comes in 1404, in the diaries of Francesco Datini, the entrepreneurial subject of Iris Origo's famous biography *The Merchant of Prato*. In 1716, under a Grand Ducal decree, Chianti became part of Europe's first wine zone. These days its wines are grouped into seven areas, the best by far the original Classico area, whose bottles bear the distinctive *Gallo*

Nero (Black Cockerel) symbol. Rufina is the second-ranking zone, but such is Chianti's variety that there are few hard and fast rules to help you pick a reliable wine.

Brunello Montalcino's vineyards produced what was – before the advent of brash new rivals – Tuscany's most majestic wine. The best Brunello is still outstanding, though you occasionally pay an unnecessary premium for the top names. Over and above the prestigious Biondi Santi (the earliest producers), the tiny Case Basse estate receives high plaudits, so too Lisini, Altesino, Carpazo, Il Poggione and Villa Banfi. The Fattoria dei Barbi is also well known (as much for its restaurant as for its wine). For more leisurely quaffing, Brunello's younger cousin, Rosso di Montalcino, is an increasingly good buy.

Vino Nobile Montepulciano's ancient Vino Nobile – the 'king of wines' – is also riding the crest of Tuscany's wine revival. Standards are rising (in what was, in most cases, already a fine wine). Top names, both new and old, to look out for here include the mass-produced but excellent-value Vecchia Cantina (a co-operative), Poliziano, Cantucci, Bindella and Le Casalte.

White wines Tuscany's big reds have long overshadowed its more humble whites. In days gone by the region's most famous *bianco*, the Vernaccia di San Gimignano, might have stood comparison with its *rosso* rivals. Now, over-production and slipshod standards have besmirched its once lofty reputation (in 1966 it was the first wine to be awarded a DOC classification). Several producers do retain an excellent name, notably Roberto Guicciardini's 1,000-year-old Cusona estate, producers of Vernaccia since the 15th century. Even better (and more expensive) are Teruzzi & Puthod's Carmen and Terra di Tufo, closely followed by Falchini's Casale and Vigna a Solatio. (Be warned that most of the wine available in San Gimignano's shops is insipid tourist fodder, made in one of several large co-operatives.) Other reasonable whites include the ubiquitous Galestro and Bianco di Pitigliano.

Noble lineage
Many Tuscan wine producers come from ancient noble families. The Ricasoli trace their association with wine-making to 1141, the Frescobaldi to 1300. Antinori, one of the region's finest estates, has been in operation for 600 years.

Poetry and wine
Poet Fulvio Testi paid effusive tribute to the 'Etruscan Chianti that kisses you and bites you and makes you shed sweet tears'.

213

Tuscan wine in history
Viticulture in Tuscany blossomed under the Etruscans, but fell away under the Romans, who preferred the heavier wines of southern Italy. Monks guided its re-emergence in the Middle Ages, quickly making wine a staple part of their daily diet.

Tuscany produces some of Italy's finest red wines

Getting there

Montepulciano's nearest railway station is 11km away at Chiusi-Chianciano, from where hourly buses run to the town's Porta al Prato. Regular buses run to Pienza and there is a twice-daily service to Siena. By car, the quickest approach is on the A1 motorway (leave at the Chiusi exit, 16km from Montepulciano). Park outside the town walls.

Tourist information

Montepulciano's tourist office is at Via Ricci 9 (tel: 0578/758 687).

San Biagio

This cool and harmonious Renaissance church (1518–45) stands in open country about 2km south-west of Montepulciano. It is the masterpiece of Antonio da Sangallo the Elder, and compares with similar chuches in Prato, Cortona and Todi (in Umbria).

Tempted by home-made produce

▶ ▓▓▓ **Montepulciano** *IBCF2*

Montepulciano, like nearby Pienza, represents an attempt to impose Renaissance architectural ideals on an ancient Tuscan hill-town. It also offers magnificent views (it is one of the region's highest towns), the chance to wander quaint medieval streets, and opportunities to taste and buy its famous red wine, Vino Nobile di Montepulciano (see page 213), or sample the home-made preserves that are a local speciality.

Historically, the town was bandied around between Siena and Florence during the Middle Ages. Siding with Florence for good in 1511 was the cue for its Renaissance overhaul, an orgy of building that employed some of the era's leading architects – Antonio Sangallo the Elder, his nephew Sangallo the Younger, and (a little later) the Mannerist master, Vignola.

Montepulciano sits along the ridge of a long, narrow hill. The best way to explore it – and take in the town's best Renaissance palaces – is to clamber up the **Corso▶▶**, a serpentine main street that follows the hill's north-to-south axis. (Be sure to duck into the smaller lanes along the way.) Effectively a single street, it nevertheless changes its name three times (from Via di Gracciano to Via di Voltaia and Via dell'Opio).

The Porta al Prato, Sangallo's first commission, marks the town entrance and the start of the Corso. Immediately inside the gate is a statue of the Marzocco, Florence's heraldic emblem (see the panel on page 127) – an 1856 copy of a 1511 original (now in the Museo Civico). The best of the Corso's many palaces include the Palazzo Cocconi (No 70), attributed to Antonio Sangallo, and the Palazzi Tarugi (No 82) and Avignonesi (No 91), both attributed to Vignola. Palazzo Bucelli (No 73) is unmistakable, its lower walls inset with numerous ancient Etruscan funerary urns.

The church of **Sant'Agostino▶** stands 150m up from the Porta al Prato on the right. Designed by Michelozzo, one of the Medici's favourite architects, it contains a high altar *Crucifix* attributed to Donatello and a couple of good paintings – by Lorenzo di Credi (third altar on the north

The church of San
Biagio, a Renaissance
masterpiece

wall) and the Sienese painter Giovanni di Paolo (second altar on the south wall).

(At the Loggia del Mercato, 150m beyond Sant' Agostino, a right turn into Via di Poggiolo will take you directly to the tourist office and offers a short cut to Piazza Grande. The churches of **Santa Lucia** and **San Francesco** en route are both worth a look, the former home to a superb *Madonna* by Signorelli.)

The longer route to Piazza Grande, along the Corso, brings you to the church of the Gesù (150m up on the left), a baroque conversion created by Andrea del Pozzo, the architect of many similar renovations in Montepulciano and elsewhere. More palaces line the street, which bends around the Fortezza at the town's southern flank to enter Montepulciano's oldest and most interesting quarter.

At the summit of the Corso the main square, the **Piazza Grande►►**, is dominated by the 13th-century **Palazzo Comunale►**. Its façade was added by Michelozzo, and its tower commands views that stretch to Siena in one direction and over Lake Trasimeno in the other. (*Open*: daily 8–2. Closed Sunday. Admission free.) Sangallo designed a couple of palaces here, one of which, the **Palazzo Cantucci**, has a *cantina* where you can taste and buy Vino Nobile di Montepulciano (similar outlets are dotted around the town).

The plain-faced **Duomo►►** is redeemed by Taddeo di Bartolo's high altar *Assumption*, and by fragments of the dismantled tomb of Bartolomeo Aragazzi (1427–36) by Michelozzo. Reliefs and statues from the tomb are scattered to the right of the door and around the high altar: two of its angels even found their way to London's British Museum. The nearby **Museo Civico** (Via Ricci 11) is disappointing, its best pieces being some della Robbia terracottas and a handful of Sienese paintings.

Special events
August in Montepulciano is one long festival. The well-known Cantiere Internazionale d'Arte (early August) specialises in the performance of new works in theatre, dance and music, often coinciding with Montepulciano's highly regarded jazz festival, which attracts top performers. Exhibitions of local handicrafts and the Baccanale wine festival are also held in August, along with performances of *Bruscello*, a local form of masked street theatre, over Ferragosto (14–16 August). The oldest festival is the Bravio delle Botti, in which pairs of men from the town's eight quarters race uphill, pushing 80kg barrels, from Piazza Marzocco to Piazza Grande (last Sunday in August). The town's patron saint, St Agnes, is celebrated with a fair on her feast day, 1 May.

PIENZA

Getting there
Buses run to Pienza from Montepulciano (nine daily), Siena and Buonconvento (seven daily). By bus or car you arrive at Piazza Dante, outside Porta al Murello, from where Corso Rossellino leads to Piazza Pio II, the main square.

Tourist information
Pienza's tourist office is in the Palazzo Civico, Piazza Pio II (tel: 0578/748 502).

Museo della Cattedrale
Housed in the Canonica (Piazza Pio II), the cathedral museum contains illuminated manuscripts, Flemish tapestries, Pius II's famous *Opus Anglicanum* (a cope made in England) and several fine paintings by Duccio, Sassetta, Fra Bartolomeo, Vecchietta, Bartolo di Fredi and Pietro Lorenzetti.
Open: daily 10–1 and 3–5. Closed Tuesday. Admission charge (inexpensive).

Pieve di Corsignano
This lovely little Romanesque church stands alone in an olive grove 1km west of Pienza's Porta al Ciglio. It has an unusual tower, fine views of Pienza, and an old font used to baptise Pius II.

▶▶   **Pienza**   *IBCE2*

Pienza owes its appearance to Aeneas Sylvius Piccolomini who, as Pope Pius II, had grand plans to transform his home village into a model Renaissance town. Born in 1405 of an exiled Sienese family, Piccolomini set about the reconstruction of Corsignano – as it then was – a year after his election to the papacy in 1459. The man entrusted with the transformation was Bernardo Rossellino, a protegé of the great Renaissance theorist Leon Battista Alberti. His brief was to create a cathedral, a papal palace and a town hall (plus miscellaneous buildings) which adhered to his master's principles. Gothic and Renaissance styles were to be fused, and the buildings were to be decorated with Sienese and Florentine paintings, as well as incorporating ideas picked up by Pius II during his travels overseas. The net result was to be a project that expressed Renaissance ideals of art, architecture and civilised good living in a single scheme.

After the completion of the Duomo and its flanking palaces (in just three years), Pius renamed the town in a papal bull, adding the caveat that not a single detail of the cathedral should be changed (he considered it the 'finest in all Italy'). The plan was then for a city to sprout of its own accord, nurtured by sycophantic cardinals who would be encouraged to build their own palaces. In the event Pius died just two years later, relieving his successors of the responsibility for a 'city' that was a monument to one man's dreams (only Pius's nephew, Pius III, showed any further interest in the project). As a result, the planned metropolis scarcely extended beyond the village's piazza.

Pienza's main square remains a Renaissance jewel – despite its occasionally empty and windswept appearance – and, with lovely countryside on its doorstep, makes an ideal place to spend a quiet morning. Start a tour at the Duomo▶▶▶ (Piazza Pio II), the heart of Pius's planned folly. Its classically inspired frontage, one of Tuscany's earliest, features Pius II's garlanded coat of arms in the upper pediment. Pius's hand is further evident in the interior, whose barn-like appearance was inspired by the *Hallenkirchen* (hall churches) he had admired during visits to Germany. The tall windows were also a papal whim, commissioned to produce a *domus vitrea* (house of glass), a symbol of the age's humanist enlightenment.

Five specially commissioned 14th-century altarpieces by Sienese masters dot the interior, all depicting the Madonna and Child with a variety of saints: the artists concerned are Giovanni di Paolo (south aisle); Matteo di Giovanni (north aisle); and Matteo di Giovanni, Vecchietta and Sano di Pietro (in the apse's first, fourth and fifth chapels respectively). Note the lovely stalls (1462) and the crypt's baptismal font (carved by Rossellino). The various fragments of Romanesque sculpture come from Santa Maria, an earlier church on the site. Note, too, how the church has been shored up at its eastern end. The cramped site meant that Rossellino had to build on sandstone underpinned only by an unstable substratum of clay. Cracks, now widening alarmingly, appeared in the building even before its completion.

The **Palazzo Piccolomini**▶▶, Pius II's palace (finished by his nephew, Pius III), stands to the right of the Duomo. Rossellino's masterpiece, it owes much to Alberti's Palazzo Rucellai in Florence (see pages 120–1) – though its rear three-tiered loggia was an inspired innovation. The first floor apartments (entered from the right of a magnificent courtyard) were occupied by Piccolomini's descendants until as recently as 1962. *Open*: guided tours every half-hour, daily 10–12:30 and 4–dusk. Closed Monday. Admission charge (inexpensive).

An entrance to the left off the courtyard leads to the hanging gardens, a beautiful medley of box hedges and small trees unaltered since the days of Pius. They offer sweeping views over the Val d'Orcia towards the distinctively shaped Monte Amiata – a dramatic embodiment of Alberti's idea that gardens should provide a link between architecture and nature.

Cheat
Rossellino cheated Pope Pius during the building of Pienza, embezzling funds and spending three times his original budget. The pope forgave him because he had 'built these glorious structures which are praised by all except those consumed by envy'.

Pienza lords it over the hills of southern Tuscany

217

Part of Nicola and Giovanni Pisano's Gothic Baptistery

Getting there
Trains leave Florence hourly for Pisa Centrale (for the city) and Pisa Aeroporto (1 hour). From outside Pisa station bus no 1 goes directly to the Campo dei Miracoli (tickets from the forecourt kiosk). Allow about 25 minutes if you prefer to walk.

Tourist information
Pisa's tourist offices are outside the station at Piazza della Stazione 11 (tel: 050/42 291) and in the corner of the Campo dei Miracoli (tel: 050/560 464).

►► **Pisa**   *IBCB5*

There is more to Pisa than its Leaning Tower – but not much more. The city offers surprisingly little temptation to linger after the tower and its companion pieces the Duomo, the Battistero (Baptistery) and the Camposanto. Nearby Lucca is more deserving of your time. Access from Florence is straightforward, however, so a trip to Pisa need take no more than a morning.

Though settled around 1000BC, the city first flourished under the Romans and the Lombards. By the 11th century it was one of Italy's four great maritime republics (with Amalfi, Venice and Genoa). War with the Saracens won Pisa Corsica, Sardinia and the Balearic islands (1050–1100). The 12th century saw a building boom and the emergence of pioneering sculptors such as Nicola and Giovanni Pisano. This was also the heyday of Pisa's Romanesque architecture, whose Moorish-inspired hybrid of columns, blind arcades and coloured marbles influenced churches as far afield as Arezzo and Sardinia. War with Genoa and defeat at the Battle of Meloria (in 1284) marked the city's fall from grace. By 1421 both the port – by then silting up – and the city had fallen to Florence. Pisa's modern and frequently ugly appearance is the result of bomb damage in 1944, when much of the great medieval city was lost.

Leaning Tower►►► Pisa's foremost monuments gather together in the **Campo dei Miracoli** (The Field of Miracles), a remarkable swathe of meadow in the city's northwestern corner. Few medieval ensembles are as beautiful, and few so beautifully framed by their surroundings. Only the sprawl of souvenir stands detracts. The key component is the Campanile, better known as

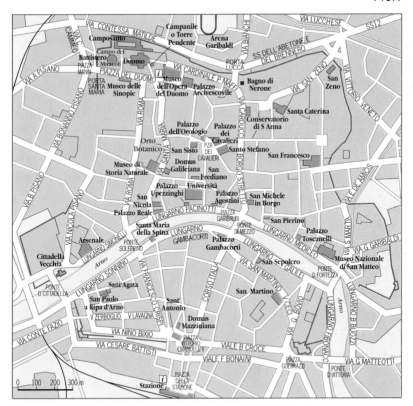

the Leaning Tower (*Torre Pendente*). Begun in 1173, the tower started to lean almost immediately precipitated by the area's sandy subsoil (this part of the coast, once beneath the sea, is mostly sand and silt). Successive architects attempted to correct the tilt, all to no avail, and since the tower's completion (around 1350) the lean has reached a giddy 5m from the vertical.

The tower these days is so dangerous that it has been closed to visitors (though only after considerable opposition from Pisans worried at losing valuable tourist revenue). A tilt which was increasing by 1mm a year for decades has now started to lurch by the same amount every few weeks. With the tower's 14,000 tonnes showing alarming cracks, an international commission is struggling to agree on a possible remedy. Steel cables anchored by lead weights, inserted at the base in 1992, are likely to be only a short-term measure.

Duomo►►► Even without the Leaning Tower, visitors would flock to Pisa simply for its cathedral. Begun in 1063, it represents the archetype of all Pisan Romanesque churches (and was the first to be decorated in the black and white stripes typical of the style). The entrance is usually through the south transept's Portale di San Ranieri, whose celebrated bronze doors (1180) were cast by Bonanno, the Leaning Tower's first architect. Much of the interior was restored after a disastrous fire in 1595 (hence its rather lacklustre decoration) though

Candlelight inside Pisa's Duomo

A detail of the Duomo's interior, heavily restored after a fire at the end of the 16th century

Santa Maria della Spina
A thorn (*spina*) from Christ's crown sits at the heart of this lovely Romanesque-Gothic church near the Ponte Solferino. In 1871 the whole building was moved brick by brick from a site nearer the Arno to protect it from floods.

Palazzo dell' Orologio
The palace stands on the north side of Piazza dei Cavalieri, Pisa's main medieval square. In 1288 Count Ugolino, a Pisan military leader, was starved to death in the palace's old tower (along with his sons and grandsons), falsely accused of treachery during the Battle of Meloria. Dante consigned him to the Eighth Circle of Hell for eating his children in a vain attempt to ward off starvation.

several masterpieces survived the conflagration. Most noteworthy are the tomb of Emperor Henry VII (1315), by Tino da Camaino (in the south transept's left corner); an ornately framed *St Agnes* by Andrea del Sarto (on the choir's right-hand entrance pier); and Giovanni Pisano's stupendous pulpit (1302–10), decorated with reliefs of New Testament scenes (top of the left aisle). *Open*: daily 7:45–1 and 3–7 (winter 3–5).

Battistero (Baptistery)▶▶▶ Begun in circular Romanesque mode in 1152, Italy's largest baptistery received its Gothic finishing touches from Nicola and Giovanni Pisano between 1270 and 1290 (the 120-year delay was caused by a financial shortfall). The echoing interior contains a lovely octagonal font by Guido da Como (1246) and a ground-breaking pulpit (1260) by Nicola Pisano, carved 50 years earlier than his son's pulpit in the Duomo. The work was the sculptor's first major commission, and its departure from Romanesque convention marked a step towards more recognisably Renaissance forms. Pisano was inspired by classical models, notably the Roman sarcophagi brought by Pisan ships from the Holy Land and re-used as tombs by Pisa's more *recherché* citizens. Many examples are still to be seen in the Camposanto. *Open*: daily 8–8 (winter 9–5). Admission charge (moderate); joint ticket with Camposanto.

Camposanto►► Before it was severely damaged by incendiary bombs in 1944, John Ruskin described the Camposanto as one of Italy's three most precious buildings (the Sistine Chapel and Venice's Scuola di San Rocco were the others). Begun in 1278 and completed in the 15th century, the marble-walled cemetery was reputedly filled with soil brought from the Holy Land (which, it was claimed, could rot down a corpse to a skeleton in less than 24 hours). At one time the vast internal cloister was covered in some 2,000sq m of fresco. Now only a few fragments of fresco survive, fossils of works by Gozzoli, Taddeo Gaddi and Spinello Aretino. A few surviving sketches have been displayed in the new, rather dull Museo delle Sinopie nearby. For all its vanished splendour, however, the cemetery is still worth a visit, if only to enjoy its myriad tomb sculptures, an illuminating insight into the Pisan way of death. *Open*: daily 8–8 (winter 9–5). Admission charge (moderate); joint ticket with Battistero.

Museo dell'Opera del Duomo►► The Duomo's old chapter house displays works removed from the cathedral, the Battistero and the Camposanto. The 23-room collection is variable, but the highlights more than justify the admission charge. Look out for the 11th-century Islamic bronze griffon (Room 1); Nicola Pisano's *Christ, Madonna and St John* (Room 2); Giovanni Pisano's ivory *Madonna and Child* (Rooms 9–10); and the colossal figures of the Prophets, Evangelist, Madonna and Child by Nicola and Giovanni Pisano (at the portico by the museum exit). *Open*: daily 8–8 (winter 9–1 and 3–5). Admission charge (moderate); joint ticket with Museo delle Sinopie.

Museo Nazionale di San Matteo
Pisa's main museum suffers from a gloomy atmosphere and poor displays. However, it contains notable paintings by Lippo Memmi, Simone Martini, Masaccio and others. Sculptures include works by Nicola and Giovanni Pisano, a superb bust by Donatello, and Andrea and Nino Pisano's famous *Madonna del Latte*. *Open*: daily 9–7 (Sunday 9–1). Closed Monday. Admission charge (moderate).

A famous experiment
During his sojourn at Pisa University, Galileo (see pages 106–7) dropped balls of different weight from the Leaning Tower to disprove Aristotle's theories on the acceleration of falling bodies.

The Duomo and Italy's most famous tower – built in 1173 and still leaning

A 'Paradise of Exiles'

■ **The art, architecture and landscapes of Florence and Tuscany have long provided a refuge for the world-weary poets, painters and writers of colder and more hellish climes. In the 19th century Shelley was to describe the region as a 'Paradise of Exiles'. His rapture, however, was not shared by all who wrote of their travels here.....■**

First thoughts

'I think it is the most beautiful city I have ever yet seen ... Domes and steeples rise on all sides ... On the other side there are the foldings of the Arno above: first the hills of olive and vine, then the chestnut woods, and then the blue and misty pine forests, which invest the aerial Apennines, that fade in the distance ... I have seldom seen a city so lovely at first sight as Florence.' Shelley (1792–1822), *Letter*

Top: Percy Bysshe Shelley (1792–1822) Below: Robert Browning (1812–89), poet and exile

Unfashionable Florence Early exiles passed Florence by. Cervantes and Chaucer, for example, shunned the city on their Italian journeys. Travellers of Protestant stamp, notably Goethe, ignored its Renaissance charms, preferring the relics of classical Rome. Montaigne, the first notable writer to record his impressions (1580), fails to mention even Raphael or Michelangelo. Thomas Gray and Hugh Walpole (1741) called Florence 'one of the dullest cities in Italy' – though for this pair (if Gray's journal is to be believed) sightseeing was hardly a priority. Describing their day, Gray wrote: 'We get up at twelve, breakfast till three, dine till four, sleep till six, drink cooling liqueurs till eight, go to the bridge [the Ponte Vecchio] till ten, sup till two, and so sleep till twelve again.'

The beginnings of tourism By the early 19th century, Florence was attracting more discerning visitors. The reasons they came are many – the obvious ones of art, history, health, beauty, scholarship, creative inspiration, and the more obscure ones of escape – from failure, from doomed relationships, from the strictures of the home country. The seductions of love and lust were undoubtedly a factor: hundreds were emboldened by the idea of a warm climate stimulating the passions to greater heights, a hypothesis summarised in a couplet from Byron's *Don Juan*: 'What men call gallantry, and gods adultery,/ Is much more common where the climate's sultry.'

Literary visitors At one time or another Tuscany played host, among others, to Milton, Trollope, George Eliot, Robert and Elizabeth Browning, Tennyson, Dostoevsky, John Ruskin, Stendhal, James Fenimore Cooper, Nathaniel Hawthorne, Mark Twain, Henry James, Aldous Huxley, E M Forster and D H Lawrence – not to mention the countless less famous exiles who set up residence in countryside villas (much

'Little Englander'
Tobias Smollett and
(below) Aldous
Huxley

as they do today). The region proved particularly alluring to the Romantics, tempting the likes of Shelley, who fled here to escape 'the shadows of his first marriage … the tumult of humankind, and the chilling fogs and rains of our own country.'

The down side Not everyone's Italian journeys were blessed with success or recorded with enthusiasm. Joseph Addison arrived at Calais and promptly fell in the harbour; Petrarch was injured by a horse; Walpole's dog was eaten by a wolf; Casanova was sexually assaulted by a policeman; and Tobias Smollett, surely the world's most miserable traveller, found dirt, disease and disillusion at every turn. Italian women, for example, he thought the most haughty, insolent, capricious and revengeful females on the face of the earth; accommodation was universally 'execrable'; he 'fared wretchedly at supper'; and services were offered with the most 'disagreeable importunity'.

For Aldous Huxley, the spectacle of Florence, 'that second-rate provincial town with its repulsive Gothic architecture and its acres of Christmas card primitives almost made me sick'. The good life also became too much for Dylan Thomas, who found the city 'a gruelling museum' and became 'sick … of drinking chianti in our marble shanty, sick of vini and contadini and bambini.' Laurie Lee bemoaned 'the streets laden with odours of meat and frying oil' … and abhorred the 'brick-faced British tourist' in the 'cheaper cafes … sweating and counting their crumpled money'. But then, as Goethe wisely observed, in an alien country 'every foreigner judges by the standards he brings with him'.

A gilded city
'Oh! How much beauty, when on a fair, clear morning, we look … on Florence. See where it lies before us in the sunlighted valley, bright with the winding Arno, and shut in by swelling hills: its domes, and towers, and palaces, rising from the rich country in a glittering heap and shining in the sun like gold.' Charles Dickens, *Pictures from Italy* (1840)

Fed up
'This is a pestilential place, smug little hills domed over with villas, and museums and churches that have been so much photographed and written about that one is fed up to the eyes with them long before one sets foot inside.' Violet Trefusis, *Letter* to Vita Sackville-West (1921)

A Madonna and Child *over the doorway of Andrea Pisano's octagonal Baptistery*

►► **Pistoia**   *IBCC6*

Pistoia is probably the least visited of Tuscany's first-division towns. Its Duomo, Battistero and Campanile, however, stand comparision with similar buildings in Pisa and Siena, and are complemented by the bonus of tremendous Romanesque pulpits in three of Pistoia's other churches. The city traditionally enjoyed a reputation for violence: Michelangelo called its citizens 'enemies of Heaven'; Machiavelli thought them 'brought up to slaughter and war'. In the 16th century pistols are said to have taken their name from the city's small *pistolese* daggers. Pistoia's ferocious reputation, however, failed to trouble Florence, to whom it remained subservient for most of its medieval history. Today its trade is in ornamental trees and shrubs, its nursery gardens being among the largest in Italy.

Piazza del Duomo►►, Pistoia's beautiful main square, is a revelation. The **Campanile**, once a Lombard watchtower, dazzles at its centre. The Gothic **Battistero** (1338–59) is also lovely to look at – the design was by Giovanni Pisano – but rather lacks interior interest. Other buildings include the Palazzo dei Vescovi, home to the **Museo della Cattedrale**, whose prize piece is Ghiberti's Reliquary of St James (1407). *Open*: guided tours only, Tuesday, Thursday and Friday 10, 11:30 and 3:30. Admission charge (inexpensive). The nearby Palazzo Comunale houses the **Museo Civico**, packed with six centuries' worth of mostly minor paintings. *Open*: daily 9–1 and 3–7 (Sunday 9–1 only). Admission charge (moderate).

A tiled porch and a lovely *Madonna and Child* by Andrea della Robbia usher you into the **Duomo►**, whose interior talking points include a font (entrance wall) by Benedetto da Maiano and the tomb (1337) of Cino da Pistoia, diplomat, teacher, poet and friend of Dante (right aisle). Overshadowing both, however, is the St James Altar (1287–1456), perhaps Italy's finest silver altarpiece (in the Cappella di San Jacopo, off the right aisle). Weighing almost a tonne, and decorated with 628 figures, its sculptors included Brunelleschi, who created the two *Prophets* on the work's left-hand side. Other highlights of the

Getting there
Trains from Florence on the Viareggio line take 35–45 minutes to reach Pistoia. Buses to and from Florence, Lucca and Pisa use the terminal at the railway station. If you are driving, note that the town centre is closed to traffic. Use the car parks off Via Pacinotti, north of the station.

Tourist information
Pistoia's central tourist office is at Piazza del Duomo 4 (tel: 0573/21 622). Information on the province of Pistoia is available from the Azienda Promozione Turistica Abetone, Pistoia, Montagne Pistoiesi. Their office is at Via Marconi 16 in San Marcello Pistoiese, a village towards Abetone.

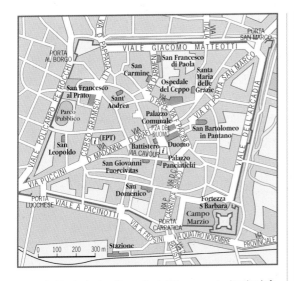

Ospedale del Ceppo

This working hospital takes its name from the hollowed-out tree trunk (*ceppo*) used by 13th-century Franciscan monks to collect alms (the name was later applied to many charitable foundations). The 15th-century façade, a copy of Brunelleschi's Ospedale degli Innocenti in Florence (see page 112), is famous for its *Seven Works of Mercy* – colourful terracottas by Giovanni della Robbia (1514–25). Contemporary figures including pilgrims, prisoners, the sick and the deceased are depicted with startling realism.

cathedral include the Cappella del Sacremento (to the left of the high altar), decorated with a bust of Donato de' Medici by Antonio Rossellini and a *Madonna and Saints* (often covered), started by Verrocchio and finished by Lorenzo di Credi.

See Pistoia's other lovely churches in the following order and you will be able to follow the chronological development of three pulpits whose carving marked a watershed in Italian sculpture. Each piece reveals the growing confidence of craftsmen whose revival of classical idioms was to pave the way for the Renaissance. The 12th-century church of **San Bartolomeo▶** has a pulpit by Guido da Como (1250). **San Giovanni Fuorcivitas▶▶** stood outside the city (*fuori città*) in its 8th-century incarnation. Inside is a pulpit (1270) by Guglielmo da Pisa, a pupil of Nicola Pisano, father of Giovanni (Giovanni carved the water stoup's *Four Cardinals*). Note also Luca della Robbia's terracotta *Visitation* on the left wall. **Sant'Andrea▶▶** contains the best of the pulpits, a work of 1301 by Giovanni Pisano superior even to the pulpit he began carving for Pisa's cathedral a year later.

Black and White

An accident in Pistoia allegedly caused the famous split of the Guelph ranks into Black and White factions. A child, the story goes, was sent to apologise for hurting his friend while playing with a sword. The friend's father chopped off his hand, saying 'Iron, not words, is the remedy for sword wounds.' The punishment divided Pistoia into rival camps – *Neri* and *Bianchi* (Black and White) – the ancestral names of the families concerned. The nicknames were soon taken up by rival factions among Florence's divided Guelphs.

Pistoia's vegetable market

Datini, the wealthy 14th-century Merchant of Prato

▶ **Prato** *IBCC5*

Prato is Tuscany's most prosperous but least obviously pretty city. However, its unappealing industrial outskirts (where some 75 per cent of Italy's textiles are produced) surround a tight historic core, a noted Renaissance church and one of Tuscany's most captivating fresco cycles.

Woollen mills first appeared in Prato in 1108, 56 years earlier than in Florence. Unable to control its political factions, the medieval city placed itself under the protection of Naples' Anjou rulers in 1313. Besieged in 1350 by the Florentines, who were concerned at Prato's commercial ascendancy, the city found itself sold out to Florence by the Queen of Naples a year later. Thereafter its fortunes followed those of its neighbour. Today, however, the stories are reversed, with Prato much the more commercially dynamic of the two former rivals.

Once through Prato's ugly suburbs, you find old Prato huddled within a hexagon of medieval walls and watched over by the **Castello dell'Imperatore**▶. The castle, built in the 13th century for Emperor Frederick II, served as a base for Imperial armies travelling between Germany and the emperor's dominions in Sicily and southern Italy. Now heavily restored, its walkways provide an excellent spot from which to enjoy an overview of the city. Concerts are held here in the summer. *Open*: daily 9–12 and 3–6 (Sunday 9–12 only). Closed Tuesday. Admission free.

To the north of the castle stands **Santa Maria delle Carceri**, an early Renaissance church begun in 1485 by Giuliano da Sangallo. With its piazza, it takes its name from the prison (*carceri*) that used to stand here. The church was built to honour a miraculous talking Madonna painted on one of the prison walls, the Madonna delle Carceri. The church betrays the influence of Brunelleschi and Alberti, its interior of the blandly harmonious type so familar in Florence. Decorative relief is provided by a fine enamelled frieze and tondi of the Evangelists (1490) by Andrea della Robbia.

Piazza del Duomo, Prato's broad main square, lies a few blocks north of the church and castle, flanked by Piazza del Comune and a garland of attractive medieval palaces. The **Duomo**▶▶, begun in 1211, is distinguished by the Pulpit of the Sacred Girdle, a lovely exterior pulpit designed by the artists Donatello and Michelozzo (1428–38) for ceremonial displays of the Virgin's girdle, Prato's most sacred holy relic (see panel opposite). The dancing putti (by Donatello) are copies, the originals now on display in the **Museo dell'Opera del Duomo, along with Maso di Bartolomeo's Reliquary of the Holy Girdle** (*open*: daily 9–12 and 3–6; Sunday 9–12 only; closed Tuesday; admission charge (moderate)). Above the main portal is a lovely terracotta lunette (1489) by Andrea della Robbia of the Madonna and Saints Stephen and Lawrence. The unusual, half-striped façade dates from 1385–1457.

Immediately on the left inside is the Cappella della Cintola (1385–90), built to house the sacred girdle. Its redoubtable bronze screen partly conceals an altar statuette of the Madonna and Child (a masterpiece by Giovanni Pisano) and a fresco cycle by Agnolo

Donatello and Michelozzo's Pulpit of the Sacred Girdle

The Sacred Girdle
According to tradition, the Virgin Mary tossed her girdle (*cintola*) to Thomas the Apostle at the moment of her Assumption as she hurtled heavenwards. He, in turn, bequeathed it to a priest, one of whose descendants married Michele Dogomari from Prato, who visited the Holy Land as a Crusader and remained there as a merchant. When the couple returned to Prato, the girdle accompanied them as part of the girl's dowry. It is displayed from Donatello's pulpit five times a year (on Easter Day, 1 May, 15 August, 8 September and Christmas Day).

Gaddi, *The Legend of the Holy Girdle* (1392–5). The nave's left-hand aisle contains a fine pulpit by Antonio Rossellino and Mino da Fiesole. The highlight of the interior, however, is Fra Filippo Lippi's superlative fresco cycle (1452–66) in the choir (behind the high altar), considered one of the great cycles of the early Renaissance. The left wall depicts scenes from the life of St Stephen, the right wall scenes from the life of John the Baptist. The dancing figure of Salome in the latter (*The Banquet of Herod*) is a portrait of Lucrezia Buti, the nun seduced by Lippi, who was himself a monk. Ironically, Lippi seduced her during a ceremony to honour the Virgin's girdle. She subsequently became the painter's mistress and mother of their son, Filippino Lippi, who was himself an accomplished artist.

The Fontana del Bacchino *in Prato*

The famous 'medieval Manhattan': San Gimignano's towers

Getting there
Take a train or SITA bus from Florence to Poggibonsi (80 minutes) and then a TRA-IN bus from the station forecourt to San Gimignano. The village is 55km from Florence by road. Parking is provided outside the walls on Viale Garibaldi.

Tourist information
San Gimignano's tourist office is at Piazza del Duomo 1 (tel: 0577/940 008). The village has just three central hotels but many private rooms for rent. For help in finding accommodation contact the Cooperativa Turistica, Via San Giovanni 125 (tel: 0577/940 809).

▶▶▶ San Gimignano *IBCC4*

San Gimignano may be among Tuscany's best-preserved medieval villages but it is far from being one of its least-discovered. During the summer, tour buses by the score roar in for their occupants to admire its famous towers so, to enjoy the ambience to the full, aim either to come out of season or to spend a night here. If time forces you to join the crowds, allow at least a morning to take in not only the towers and the little back streets, but also the glorious fresco cycles of the village's two main churches, the Collegiata and Sant'Agostino.

San Gimignano was inhabited by both the Etruscans and the Romans (though it is named after a 4th-century bishop of Modena). Its position on the Via Francigena, an important pilgrimage route between Rome and northern Europe, brought it to medieval prominence. The towers took root from about 1150, some 72 of them sprouting to create what is now, famously, dubbed a 'medieval Manhattan' (only 15 of the originals are still here). Built as status symbols – the higher the better – and as defensive outposts, the towers played a prominent part in the internecine feuds that ultimately proved to be the town's undoing. When nobles were not dousing one another in boiling pitch, or hurling rocks at their neighbours, they were kept busy fighting off the challenge of towns like Volterra and Poggibonsi. Weakened by such bickering, the town eventually put itself under Florence's protection (1348), a move that broke the nobles' power, rendering the towers obsolete – otherwise they might not have been allowed to survive. Thereafter, San Gimignano became a sleepy backwater (another factor in the towers' survival). Its only later claim to fame was a fictional appearance as 'Monteriano' in E M Forster's *Where Angels Fear to Tread*.

The present village is a pocket-sized place (less than 15 minutes' walk from one end to the other). Enter either by Porta San Matteo or by the fine southern gate, the Porta San Giovanni (1262). Then walk up Via San Matteo or Via San Giovanni to the interconnecting main squares – Piazza del Duomo and Piazza della Cisterna (named after its 13th-century well). Piazza del Duomo contains most of the action – the Collegiata and the Palazzo del Popolo, the latter home to the Museo Civico and Torre Grossa (the only tower you can climb). Be sure to brave the back streets, as well, wandering to the walls and the Rocca (castle) for fine views and quiet spots away from the crowds.

Collegiata►►► San Gimignano's cathedral in all but name (the village no longer has a bishop), the Collegiata was consecrated in 1148 and enlarged by Giuliano da Maiano between 1466 and 1468. Little in the plain Romanesque façade prepares you for the splendid interior, whose decorative scheme includes no less than four major fresco cycles. The first, on the right-hand (south) wall, is a 22-panel sequence of scenes from the New Testament (*c.*1381), long attributed to Barna da Siena, a follower of the great Sienese painter Simone Martini. Barna reputedly died in a fall from scaffolding whilst working on the cycle. Most critics, however, now credit the work to Lippo Memmi and assistants (1333–44).

A homely corner in San Gimignano

229

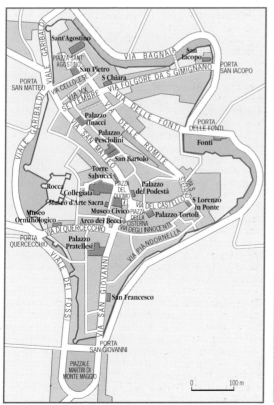

Biglietto Unico
A single ticket (*Biglietto Unico*) is available, covering admission to San Gimignano's Museo Civico, the Cappella di Santa Fina, the Museo d'Arte Sacra, and the small Museo Ornitologico.

Just watching life go by: a visitor enjoys the sunshine in this charming little town

Museo d'Arte Sacra
This small museum, entered to the left of the Collegiata, contains a collection of Etruscan finds, church silver, old wooden statues, valuable 13th-century Crucifixes and a *Madonna and Child* by Bartolo di Fredi. *Open*: daily 9:30–12:30 and 3–6 (winter 2:30–5:30). Closed Monday. Admission charge (moderate); *Biglietto Unico* available (see panel on page 229).

The Old Testament cycle on the left wall is less contentious, being signed and dated (1367) by Bartolo di Fredi. Its 26 episodes describe the stories of Genesis, Noah, Abraham, Joseph, Moses and Job. Biblical narrative aside, the paintings are remarkable for their human and incidental detail, full of ideas copied from Ambrogio Lorenzetti's influential frescos, *Good and Bad Government*, in Siena (see page 237).

The Collegiata's third cycle, on the rear wall, is Taddeo di Bartolo's *Last Judgement, Paradise and Hell* (*c.*1393) – perhaps the most entertaining of the three, if only for the wonderfully gruesome execution of its more lurid scenes. Close to the rear wall are two painted wooden statues of the Virgin Annunciate and the Angel Gabriel by Jacopo della Quercia (1421).

Off the south aisle, the Cappella di Santa Fina (1468), a Renaissance masterpiece by Giuliano da Maiano (1468), contains a ciborium and outstanding altar bas-reliefs (1472–7) by Giuliano's better-known brother, Benedetto da Maiano. Here, too, you will find the Collegiata's fourth fresco cycle, (*c.*1475), Domenico Ghirlandaio's depiction of episodes from the life of Santa Fina, one of San Gimignano's most revered saints (see panel opposite). *Open*: Cappella di Santa Fina daily 9:30–12:30 and 3–6 (winter; 2:30–5:30). Closed Monday. Admission charge (moderate); *Biglietto Unico* available (see panel, page 229).

Museo Civico►► Climb the Palazzo del Popolo's tower and then explore its civic museum and picture gallery. The palace's frescoed main hall, the Sala del Consiglio or Sala di Dante, is where Dante tried to persuade San Gimignano to join an alliance with Florence in 1300 (see pages 70–1). The room is dominated by Lippo Memmi's magnificent (but damaged) *Maestà* (1317), a not dissimilar work to Martini's superb fresco in Siena's Palazzo Pubblico. Upstairs are countless valuable paintings, including winsome pieces by Gozzoli, Pinturicchio, Filippino Lippi, Taddeo di Bartolo and others. San Gimignano's most endearing pictures, though, are the so-called *Wedding Scene* frescos by the more obscure Memmo di Filippuccio. Various interpretations have been placed on these 14th-century paintings, which are tucked away in one of the museum's smaller rooms. Some say they are a warning against the wiles of women, others that they are a harmless sequence of nuptial scenes. They show a wife riding on her husband's back, and a couple taking a shared bath before climbing into bed. *Open*: daily 9:30–12:30 and 3–6 (winter 2:30–5:30). Closed Monday. Admission charge (moderate); *Biglietto Unico* available (see panel on page 229).

Sant'Agostino▶▶ Barn-like, in the manner of most Augustinian churches, Sant'Agostino (1298) is known for the beautifully detailed frescos (1464–5) in the choir. The work of Benozzo Gozzoli, a painter born in San Gimignano, they depict scenes from the life of St Augustine. Elsewhere, the church has an altar (1495) by Benedetto da Maiano (in the Cappella di San Bartolo, to the right of the main door); frescos of the life of the Virgin (1374) by Bartolo di Fredi (south apse); a resounding *Coronation of the Virgin and Saints* (1483) by Piero Pollaiuolo (over the high altar); and *Four Bishops*, a marble relief by Tino da Camaino (part of the original tomb of San Bartolo, another of San Gimignano's patron saints). The third altar in the north aisle contains a redoubtable fresco of St Sebastian, commissioned from Benozzo Gozzoli in 1464 to celebrate the passing of a plague epidemic.

Santa Fina
Fina led a strange life. Born in San Gimignano in 1238, she desperately repented her sins after contracting a fatal illness at the age of 10 (her worst lapse, apparently, had been to accept an orange from a boy). She passed the next five years lying on a wooden board awaiting her death, which had been announced to her in a vision by St Gregory. In the meantime she kept busy by working miracles (some shown in Ghirlandaio's Collegiata frescos): she healed her nurse's paralysed hand; restored a choirboy's sight; and caused angels to ring the Collegiata's bells. At her death, violets blossomed from her board and wallflowers sprang from a tower in the village.

231

Pieve di Cellole
This beautiful 13th-century Romanesque church, one of the area's finest, lies 4km northwest of San Gimignano on the Certaldo road.

All part of the charm of San Gimignano: little frescoed nooks and crannies

■ **Monasteries have dotted Tuscany for over a thousand years, tucked away in the folds of forested slopes far from the debilitating cares of a decadent world. Three of the most beautiful lie close together in the tranquil countryside south of Siena......■**

232

St Galgano Guidotti
The abbey of San Galgano honours St Galgano Guidotti (1158–81), a monk whose old hermitage forms part of the circular chapel (1182–5) on Monte Siepi, the hill above the abbey. At the entrance to this chapel is a sword he thrust into a stone to symbolise his renunciation of his former knightly career (after his family and fellow knights had come to try and tempt him back to his old way of life). He was made a saint by Pope Urban III in 1185 as an example to other Christian knights. Around the chapel's walls are faint frescos (1344) by Ambrogio Lorenzetti showing scenes from Galgano's life.

Monte Oliveto Maggiore Tuscany's most-visited abbey was founded in 1313 by the Olivetans, or 'White Benedictines', a breakaway group who sought to return to the simple ideals of the earliest Benedictines. Today its buildings are mainly institutionalised affairs restored in the last century, but its setting is one of Tuscany's loveliest, secluded amid thick woodlands in the deep-cut hills south of Siena.

Most people come here to enjoy a fresco cycle that ranks with Tuscany's best. Located in the main cloister, the Chiostro Grande (1426–74), the cycle was started by Luca Signorelli, who painted nine panels (1497–8) depicting scenes from the life of St Benedict. Several years later (1505–8) the remaining 27 panels were completed by Il Sodoma, a remarkable painter who was invariably surrounded by a coterie of young boys and a menagerie of 'badgers, apes, dwarf asses, horses ... magpies, dwarf chickens, tortoises, Indian doves ...' The painter's own letters also spoke of three wives and 30 children.

Before you leave the abbey, be sure to go into the main church to see the beautiful inlaid woodwork of the choir (dating from 1503).

Open: daily 9:30–12:30 and 3–5:30. Admission free. The abbey is 9km east of Buonconvento on the SS451.

San Galgano Few places in Tuscany are as romantic as San Galgano. Roofless, its grassy nave looks to the heavens, its empty windows a playground for darting swifts. Vegetation curls across its ruined frescos, and the wind idles around its crumbling columns. Founded in the

Monte Oliveto Maggiore: details from the monastery – (top) interior and (right) exterior

Monasteries

13th century, and once Tuscany's largest Cistercian abbey (and one of the two largest in Italy), it was begun jointly by Italian monks and Cistercians from the Order's mother house at Citeaux (hence its amalgam of French and Italian architectural styles). Its abbots – who grew wealthy from the sale of wool – arbitrated in disputes between Tuscan cities, oversaw the building of Siena's Duomo, and held posts as *casalinghi* (accountants) on Siena's council.

By the end of the 14th century after years of inter-city strife, San Galgano's population of monks had dropped to a mere handful. Renewed settlement was thwarted by corruption, most notably the sale of its roof leading, a scam (worked by one of its abbots) that led to the nave's collapse in 1786. Thereafter the abbey mouldered and fell into disuse. Today some of the buildings have been restored and reoccupied by an Olivetan order of nuns.
Open: daily, dawn to dusk. Admission free. The abbey is 32km southwest of Siena off the SS73 Grosseto road.

Sant'Antimo Sant'Antimo's considerable appeal is both scenic and architectural. The first abbey here was reputedly founded by Charlemagne in 781, though most of the present Romanesque church – one of Italy's finest – dates from the beginning of the 12th century. The abbey declined during the 14th century, and was suppressed by Pope Pius II in 1462.

The exterior and interior sculpture is outstanding, particularly the nave capitals, a combination of French, Lombard and even Spanish influences. The sacristy (rarely open) forms part of the primitive Carolingian church, its entrance flanked by 9th-century pilasters. The small vaulted crypt dates from the same period. Above the nave runs a *matroneum* (women's gallery), an unusual feature once used to segregate the congregation. Equally unusual is the ambulatory, whose three radiating chapels (rare in Italian churches) were probably copied from French models.
Open: daily 9–12 and 2–7 (winter 10–12 and 2–4). Admission free. Sant'Antimo is 10km south of Montalcino.

Cypresses gird the abbey of Monte Oliveto Maggiore

233

Gregorian chant
Sant'Antimo is maintained by a small community of French Cistercian monks who sing a haunting Gregorian Mass every Sunday at 11am. Organ concerts are also held in the church during July and August.

SIENA

The gloriously intricate façade of Siena's cathedral

Getting there
Regular trains run to Siena from Florence (some involve changing at Empoli). Services run roughly every hour, and the journey time is 90 minutes. Once in Siena, cross the road from the station for buses to Piazza Matteotti, near the city centre (tickets are available from the station atrium). The centre of Siena is completely closed to traffic. Car parks are well signposted on the approaches to the city, but parking spaces can still be difficult to find.

Tourist information
Siena's tourist office is at Piazza del Campo 56 (tel: 0577/280 551). *Open*: daily 9–12:30 and 3:30–7. Closed Saturday afternoon and all day Sunday.

Hotel help
For assistance in booking a hotel, contact either the tourist office or Siena Hotels Promotion, Piazza San Domenico (tel: 0577/288 084).

▶▶▶   Siena   *IBCD3*

Italy's loveliest medieval city (the perfect foil to Florence), Siena is the one trip you should make in Tuscany if you make no other. A breathtaking piazza, the Campo, forms Siena's heart and is the setting for the Palio, Italy's most famous festival (see pages 240–1). The towering Palazzo Pubblico contains masterpieces of painting from the Sienese School, a genre further represented in the Pinacoteca Nazionale, one of Italy's leading provincial galleries. Siena's Duomo ranks among Europe's great Gothic buildings, and is filled with treasures ranging from Pinturicchio's vivid fresco cycle to sculptures by Pisano, Donatello and Michelangelo. The Museo dell'Opera del Duomo offers the most majestic of all Sienese paintings, Duccio's multi-panelled *Maestà,* not to mention a glorious aerial view of the city. Finally, Siena's streets harbour several churches, many shops and restaurants, and some of the region's loveliest medieval nooks and crannies.

Siena was reputedly founded by Senius, son of Remus, one of the two legendary founders of Rome – hence the many statues of the she-wolf, who suckled Romulus and Remus. A small Etruscan settlement was superseded by *Saena Julia,* a Roman colony founded by Augustus. By 1125 Siena was a free *comune* – though already sunk in the rivalry with Florence that was to dominate its

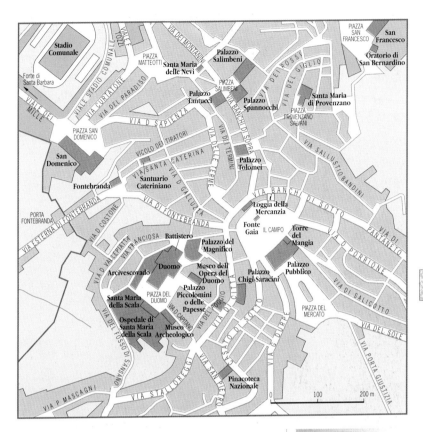

medieval history. The old enemy was defeated in 1260 at the Battle of Montaperti, the high point of a century during which its wealth made Siena one of Europe's major cities. Sienese bankers figured among the continent's wealthiest, and Sienese painters – men such as Duccio, Martini and the Lorenzettis – were at the cutting edge of Italian art. From 1287 to 1355 the city was ruled by the quasi-democratic Council of Nine, under whom the Duomo the Campo and the Palazzo Pubblico were completed.

The Black Death of 1348, during which three-quarters of Siena's population died, was a blow from which the city never fully recovered. Two charismatic saints emerged to dominate the ensuing period of spiritual uncertainty: St Catherine of Siena (1347–80) and St Bernardino (1380–1444). In the political sphere, Siena struggled against a succession of papal, imperial and autocratic rulers, owing allegiance to Charles V (from 1530) before suffering a devastating siege at the hands of Florence, and eventually succumbing to the military might of the Grand Duchy of Tuscany in 1559. After that, the city languished for centuries in a period of neglect. Today the outlook is rosier, the town a bustling provincial centre grown rich on banking and tourism.

The Campo►►► Siena sits on a Y-shaped ridge, ranged over three hills. At its heart, on the site of the Roman

Wine-tasting
Siena's Forte di Santa Barbara houses the Enoteca Italiana Permanente, a national wine library which claims to possess a bottle of every wine produced in Italy. Its bar offers wine by the glass or bottle. Views from here are superb, especially at sunset. *Open:* daily 3–midnight.

Nannini

Siena's favourite café is Nannini at Banchi di Sopra 22–4. The same family runs Nannini Gelateria on the corner of Banchi di Sopra and Piazza Matteotti.

Music

The Accademia Musicale Chigiana, Via di Città 89 (tel: 0577/46 152) organises classical concerts and recitals throughout the year. Some of the best take place during the Settimana Musicale Sienese (late August). Performances of opera and ballet are given in the Palazzo Pubblico's Teatro dei Rinnovati (tel: 0577/292 265).

The Duomo she-wolf, Siena's emblem – one of many to be seen in the city

forum, lies the Campo, a huge piazza. Its medieval rebuilding under the Council of Nine explains the nine sections of its fan-like brick pavement (also intended to symbolise the Madonna's cloak, sheltering Siena under its protective embrace). Cafés and restaurants on the perimeter of the Campo are expensive, but it is worth indulging in at least one pricey *cappuccino* to enjoy the square's endless street-life. The piazza's fountain, the Fonte Gaia, is a largely 19th-century copy of a 15th-century original.

Palazzo Pubblico►►► The Campo's southern flank is dominated by this great civic palace, built between 1297 and 1310 and still housing the city's municipal offices. From the courtyard an entrance to the left leads to the tower, the Torre del Mangia (102m high, with over 500 steps), allegedly named after its first bell-ringer, Giovanni di Balduccio, a renowned glutton and wastrel (whose nickname, *mangiaguadagni*, means 'eat the profits'). The views are outstanding. *Open*: daily 10–7 (winter and Sunday 9:30–1:30). Admission charge (moderate).

The ticket office on the right of the courtyard provides access to the **Museo Civico**, on the palace's upper floor (note the plan at the museum entrance). Quality is variable across the gallery's 18 rooms but the highlights represent some of the greatest of Tuscany's Sienese paintings. Ignore Rooms 1–7 initially (ceramics and 16th- to 18th-century paintings) and turn left into the Sala di Balia, frescoed by Spinello Aretino (1407) with scenes from the life of Pope Alexander III. Ahead lies the Anticamera del Concistoro, covered in frescos and *sinopie*, and beyond that the Sala del Concistoro, whose ceiling frescos (1529–35) by Beccafumi (see panel opposite) consist of a series of allegories on the virtues of Siena's medieval government (an artistic brief imposed on most of the Palazzo's painters over the centuries).

Doors off the Anticamera lead through the Vestibule and Anticappella respectively, the latter frescoed by Taddeo di Bartolo. To its left is the *Cappella* (Chapel), unmistakable behind an iron screen (1435–45) designed by Jacopo della Quercia, Siena's leading medieval sculptor. The frescos, *Scenes from the Life of the Virgin* (1407–8), are also by Taddeo di Bartolo. The altarpiece is by Il Sodoma. The large Sala del Mappmondo beyond contains two of the palace's highlights, Simone Martini's huge *Maestà* (1315–21) on the left wall, and his *Equestrian Portrait of Guidoriccio da Fogliano* (1328) on the right wall (though the attribution of this is disputed). Through to the right (in the Sala della Pace) are two more famous frescos, Ambrogio Lorenzetti's wonderfully detailed (though somewhat damaged) *Allegories of Good and Bad Government* (1338), once considered the most important cycle of secular paintings of the Middle Ages. *Open*: daily 9–7 (winter and Sunday 9:30–1:30). Closed Monday. Admission charge (moderate).

Duomo►►► A church has existed on the cathedral's current site since at least the 9th century. The present building dates from 1215–1376 – a period that also saw an aborted plan to extend the cathedral, a scheme whose half-finished results are still clearly visible to the right of the Duomo. Giovanni Pisano designed much of the fine lower façade (1285), though most of his original statuary now resides in the Museo dell'Opera del Duomo. The façade's upper half, a less harmonious undertaking, was added in the 14th century; the upper gable mosaics date from the 19th century.

The interior of the Duomo is even more dazzling than the façade. Its pavement (partly covered for protection) comprises 56 panels, designed between 1369 and 1547 by 40 of Siena's leading artists. Mid-way down the left aisle (fourth altar) is the Piccolomini altar, whose four lower-niche statues are early works by Michelangelo (1501–4). Immediately to its right is the entrance to the Libreria Piccolomini, beautifully frescoed by Pintoricchio

Frescoed vaulting and part of the font in the Battistero

Domenico Beccafumi
The outstanding Sienese painter of his time, Beccafumi (1484/6–1551) worked in Rome before returning to Siena to work in the Mannerist tradition of Bronzino and Andrea del Sarto. His best work is in Siena's Duomo and Palazzo Pubblico.

San Domenico
This huge red-brick 12th-century church is known for the only authentic portrait of St Catherine of Siena (located to the right of the entrance). Also worth seeing are the frescos by Sano di Pietro, Pietro Lorenzetti and Matteo di Giovanni, and Sodoma's *St Catherine in Mystical Ecstasy* (right nave). Catherine's house and sanctuary can be visited near by on Costa di San Antonio.

Church and oratory
The church of San Francesco's cavernous interior contains frescos by the brothers Pietro and Ambrogio Lorenzetti. To the right of the church is the Oratorio di San Bernardino, built on the spot where the Franciscan St Bernardino used to preach. Upstairs is a fine Mannerist fresco cycle by Sodoma and Beccafumi. *Open:* daily 10:30–1:30 and 3–5:30. Admission charge (inexpensive).

with scenes from the life of Aeneas Piccolomini, better known as Pope Pius II (see pages 216–17). The frescos (1502–9) were commissioned by his nephew, Pius III, who was pope for only 10 days. *Open:* daily 9–7 (winter 10–1 and 2:30–5). Admission charge (inexpensive).

Nicola Pisano's Gothic pulpit (1268), at the end of the left aisle, is the Duomo's masterpiece. To its left, in the corner chapel, seek out Tino da Camaino's tomb of Petroni (d.1313), copied throughout the 14th century, and, below it, the bronze pavement tomb (1426) of Bishop Pecci by Donatello. The hexagonal Cappella di San Giovanni Battista occupies a corner of the left transept, home to more frescos by Pintoricchio and a bronze statue of St John the Baptist (1457) by Donatello.

Outside the Duomo, be sure to see the **Battistero** (Baptistery) of 1317–82, reached down steps to the right and rear of the building. Inside, beneath the beautiful vaulting, stands a hexagonal font (1417–30) that is one of the most important sculptural works of the early Renaissance. Most of its bronze panels, depicting scenes from the life of John the Baptist, were cast by Donatello, Lorenzo Ghiberti and Jacopo della Quercia. Most of the frescos are by Vecchietta. *Open:* daily 9–1 and 3–6. Admission free.

Museo dell'Opera del Duomo►► Siena's excellent cathedral museum opens with the Galleria delle Statue (downstairs), whose central exhibit is an ochre-coloured tondo of the Madonna and Child by Donatello. Close by is a *Madonna and Child with Saints* by Jacopo della Quercia. The heavyweight wall statues – the work of Giovanni Pisano – were removed from the façade. A reverentially lit

Left: Siena's black-and-white striped Duomo and bell-tower stand out in contrast to the terracotta roofs of the city's medieval streets
Below: the Torre del Mangia overlooks the Campo

The perfect village
The village of Monteriggioni, a few kilometres north of Siena, is perhaps the most perfectly preserved fortified village in Italy. Its towers and fortifications are evocative from afar, and within its walls are a tiny huddle of streets, a superb new four-star hotel and a couple of good restaurants.

room on the first floor contains Duccio's magnificent *Maestà* (1308–11). Allow plenty of time to study both the main altarpiece and its many predella panels, all but three of which have been recovered after the painting was split up in the 18th century – Washington, London and New York have the missing pieces. Also here are Duccio's *Madonna and Child* and Pietro Lorenzetti's *Birth of the Virgin* (1342).

Further Sienese paintings grace the gallery's second floor, notably Beccafumi's *St Paul*, Simone Martini's *Blessed Augustine*, and the bizarre but influential *Madonna dagli Occhi Grossi* (Madonna of the Large Eyes), an anonymous work by the so-called 'Maestro di Tressa' (1220–30). Absolutely not to be missed is the superb view from the museum's external tower and balcony (signed *Ingresso al Panorama*). *Open*: daily 9–7:30 (winter 9–1:30). Admission charge (moderate).

Pinacoteca Nazionale▶▶▶ This extensive 36-room gallery at Via San Pietro 29 is a must if you enjoy the golden-hued and beautifully coloured paintings of the Sienese School. The one caveat is its preponderance of paintings depicting the Madonna and Child: over half the pictures commissioned in Siena between 1350 and 1550 were of the Virgin, and the *Maestà* – the Virgin Enthroned – was a Sienese invention. Paintings are arranged chronologically, and include works from all Siena's leading names – Duccio, Pietro Lorenzetti, Simone Martini, Ambrogio Lorenzetti, Sassetta, Giovanni di Paolo, Sano di Pietro, Beccafumi and many more. *Open*: daily 8:30–7 (Sunday 8–1; winter 8:30–1:30). Closed Monday. Admission charge (moderate).

■ **Siena's world-famous Palio is not staged just to entertain visitors. The twice-yearly horse race – Italy's most spectacular pageant – gives colourful expression to the fierce rivalries that have raged for 700 years among the town's 17 medieval districts, the *contrade*.....■**

240

Bound for glory: the start of another Palio

Seeing the Palio
Only the most determined visitor is likely to get a reasonable view of the Palio. Even if you arrive several hours before the race, the Campo will be hot, noisy and very crowded. Balcony places around the piazza are sold for high prices months beforehand. For advance booking you could try contacting Palio Viaggi, Piazza Gramsci 7 (tel: 0577/280 828). The only way to guarantee a cheap and comfortable view of the Palio is to watch the live broadcasts on national television. Alternatively, watch one of the practice runs that take place in the week before the big event.

A time-honoured tradition The Palio has taken place in some shape or form virtually every year since the 13th century. It takes its name from the *pallium*, an embroidered banner awarded to the winning *contrada*, and is held in honour of the Madonna. For this reason, the first race is run on the festival of the Visitation (2 July), the second (instigated in 1659) on 16 August, the day after the Feast of the Assumption. (Races are also occasionally run to honour a special event – see panel opposite.) The contest originally took place around the city streets, usually from an outer gateway to the Duomo. Regular races only began to be held in the Campo in 1656.

Siena's *contrade* Since the 13th century Siena has been divided into three administrative districts (*terzi*) – the *Terzo di Città*, the *Terzo di Camollia* and the *Terzo di San Martino* (corresponding roughly to the city's three hilly spurs). Each *terzo* is divided into smaller wards, or *contrade*, of which there were 42 in the 14th century, reduced to 23 in the 16th century. Today there are 17 *contrade*, each with its own church, social club, museum, fountain, flag and heraldic animal motif (from which the *contrade* take their names). Allegiance to the *contrada* is absolute: after a conventional baptism, for example, children are rebaptised in their *contrada* fountains. Each *contrada* is run by an assembly, elected democratically by all those born within that *contrada* and aged over 18. Special heralds attend weddings and funerals of *contrada* members, and signs of the *contrade* are visible everywhere as you walk around Siena. Each *contrada* holds an

annual parade, and the *alfiere*, the famous flag-throwers (not to mention the *tamborini*, the drummers), can often be seen practising in the streets.

Preparations for the Palio No more than 10 *contrade* take part in each Palio, so lots are drawn to make the selection. Horses and starting positions are also drawn by lot, though each *contrada* selects its own jockey, many of whom are drawn from the *butteri*, the traditional cowboys of Tuscany's Maremma region. Thereafter, anything goes. Horses are sometimes drugged, and jockeys bribed or ambushed. Alliances are forged and broken. Huge amounts of money change hands. Small wonder that jockeys are guarded day and night, allowed to communicate only through their bodyguards.

Rehearsals, processions and boundless pageantry fill the days before a race. A *contrada* banquet is held on the eve of battle. The following morning horses are taken to church to be blessed – 'go, little horse, and return a winner' are the priest's words (dung produced at this point is seen as an excellent omen). At around 5pm the pages, *tamborini* (drummers), equerries and *alfieri* (flag-throwers) of each *contrada* process to the Campo. In front of them march city officials and representatives from the old towns of the Sienese Republic.

The race At about 7pm the race is ready to roll. All but one of the horses are penned into a corner of the Campo (which has been covered in sand and lined with mattresses to lessen the dangers to horse and jockey). The lone rider charges when the group least expects it, and the race is under way. Jockeys beat their horses (and each other) with whips made from calf phalluses. Ninety seconds and three laps of the piazza later it is all over. Winning jockeys drink to their victory, while losers drown their sorrows. Celebrations go on for days, recriminations for decades.

Special events
Of the 600 Palios run since the 17th century, around 60 have been held to celebrate special events. For example, races took place in 1809 to mark Napoleon's victorious return to Paris; in 1849 to celebrate the opening of the Siena–Empoli railway; in 1945 to mark the end of World War II; in 1947 to record the sixth centennial of St Catherine's birth; and in 1969 to acknowledge the first lunar landing.

241

Non-events
It takes a lot to stop the Palio. Races were not held during the two world wars or during a cholera outbreak in 1885. In 1900 they were called off after the assassination of King Umberto I, and again in 1798 after a devastating earthquake (though this time only the July race was cancelled). During violent political rioting in 1919, Siena's left- and right-wing factions set aside their differences for the duration of the Palio.

Local rivalries start young in Siena: these tamborini, *members of one of the* contrade, *will practise all through the year*

Drive Siena to Montepulciano

A drive through the heart of the Tuscan countryside, visiting vineyards, ancient abbeys, Roman baths and several historic hill-towns (approximately 120km one way).

Leave Siena by the SS326 and after 5km take the SS438 for Asciano. This road passes through the *crete*, the so-called Sienese 'badlands' – a region of eroded clay hills covered in summer with sunflowers and rolling wheatfields. Modest **Asciano**► is a partially walled hill-town with two museums: the Museo d'Arte Sacra, home to a dozen or so important Sienese paintings, and the Museo Archeologico, filled with Etruscan finds from the surrounding area.

Continue south from Asciano, passing Monte Oliveto Maggiore►►►, Tuscany's most beautifully situated monastery (see page 232). From here follow the road southwest towards **Buonconvento**►, which boasts an excellent and little-known museum of medieval paintings, the Museo d'Arte Sacra at Via Soccini 17. *Open*: Tuesday and Thursday 10–12, Saturday 10–12 and 4–6, Sunday 9–1. Admission charge (inexpensive).

The drive south along the Ombrone Valley to **Montalcino**►► passes through delightful countryside. More verdant than the often eerie desolation of the *crete*, the landscape is rippled with the Brunello vineyards for

The hot springs that are now the focal point of the medieval piazza in Bagno Vignoni have been used since Roman times

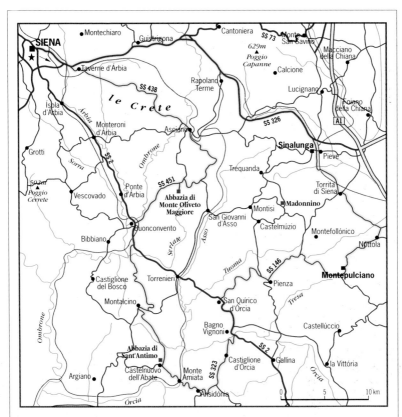

which the region is famous (see page 213). The village's *rocca* (castle), offering glorious views, has a lovely *enoteca* where you should stop to sample local wines. For non-alcoholic refreshment, visit the Fiaschetteria Italiana, an untouched turn-of-the-century café in the main square.

Some 10km south of Montalcino, set amid olive groves and ilex-covered hills, is the 12th-century abbey of Sant'Antimo, one of the region's most enchanting Romanesque buildings (see page 233). Continue southeast on minor roads before turning north beyond Ansidonia towards San Quirico. After the hilltop hamlet of Castiglione d'Orcia and the junction with the SS2 watch for the sign to **Bagno Vignoni▶▶**. The steaming sulphur pool in the village's main square is one of Tuscany's most memorable sights. The arcaded Renaissance *piscina* was built by the Medici, but the spa has been used since Roman times. More hot springs emerge near the Posta Marcucci hotel, where non-residents can bathe in the hotel spa.

Return to the main SS2 and drive north to **San Quirico▶**, which, despite its rather moribund appearance, merits a brief stop if you have time to explore its Collegiata, a pretty Romanesque church with outstanding carved portals, a good Renaissance choir and a 15th-century triptych of the Madonna and Saints by Sano di Pietro.

The final stretch of the tour follows the SS146 eastwards through **Pienza▶▶▶**, one of Tuscany's most interesting small towns (see pages 216–17). Hilltop **Montepulciano▶** is even more appealing (see pages 214–15). Both make convenient places to spend the night.

To return to Siena take the main road north from Montepulciano, to Nottola (7km) and then turn north to drive through Torrita to Sinalunga. Here pick up the main SS326 for Siena (42km).

Room for two more on one of Viareggio's well-groomed beaches

Getting there
Trains run to Viareggio directly from Florence roughly every hour. The journey time is about 90 minutes.

Tourist information
Viareggio's tourist office is at Viale Carducci 10, one block back from Viale Regina Margherita, the seafront promenade (tel: 0584/48 881 or 962 233). A summer-only kiosk operates at the station (Piazza Dante).

▶ **Viareggio** *IBCA5*

Viareggio, to all intents and purposes, is Florence-by-the-Sea. Almost any train bound here on a summer's morning is likely to be teeming with Italians heading for a day on the beach. The town marks the southernmost point of the **Versilia**, a mountain-backed riviera of beach resorts that stretches almost to the Ligurian border. As the Biarritz of this Tuscan riviera, Viareggio is the place to choose if you want an easily organised day by the sea from Florence. It is also the best of the resorts, rivalled only by **Forte dei Marmi**, an unaccountably chic little enclave beloved of writers, artists and would-be celebrities. This said, any of the Versilian resorts will do if all you want is an hour of sun and a dip in the sea. All are commercialised, and all are dominated by the so-called *stabilimenti*, private stretches of beach that charge for access and rent out towels, changing rooms and sun-loungers. This may sound a grim arrangement, but the sand is guaranteed to be clean and groomed (even if the water sometimes fails the odd safety standard). If you blanch at the thought of paying, the shore is also dotted with public beaches (*spiaggia libera*).

The beaches of Viareggio will be far from empty, and the *stabilimenti* rates are pretty steep, but the town has an elegant and relaxed atmosphere and the sand is excellent (over 100m wide and several kilometres long). The town is among Italy's oldest resorts, its long seafront promenade – fronting a grid-iron street plan – having been almost purpose-built in 1860. A fire in 1917 changed its appearance somewhat, the original boardwalk and wooden buildings giving way to palm-fringed boulevards and a medley of lovely Liberty-style buildings. The most notable of these is the Gran Caffè Margherita (near the marina), designed by Italian art nouveau iconoclasts Galileo Chini and Alfredo Belluomini.

Prices for most things in Viareggio are over the odds, particularly in the seafood restaurants – though these are some of Italy's best if you want to treat yourself. Even seafront pizzerias will land you with eye-opening bills. Picnic provisions can be bought from the market in Piazza Cavour, mid-way between the railway station and the seafront.

If you have time while in Viareggio be sure to head south and follow the famous Via dei Tigli – a 6km-long avenue of lime trees – to the lakeside village of **Torre del Lago Puccini►** (accessible by bus from Viareggio's Piazza d'Azeglio). Giacomo Puccini, born in nearby Lucca, spent the second half of his life here, composing all his best-known operas (with the exception of *Turandot*) on the edge of Lago Massaciuccoli (it was the lake, incidentally, that attracted Puccini, who came here to hunt, or – as he put it – to practise 'my second favourite instrument, my rifle').

The composer's house, the **Villa Puccini►**, is now a museum, set back from the lake and rather hidden behind trees and high iron railings. Its rooms contain numerous musical mementoes, including Puccini's favourite instrument, his piano. Nothing has been changed since the composer's death. The mausoleum of Puccini and his wife is placed, rather aptly, between the piano room and the gun room. *Open*: guided tours only, every 30 minutes, daily 10–12 and 4–7 (winter 10–12 and 3–5:30). Closed Monday. Admission charge (moderate).

The popular Festival Pucciniano takes place in venues around Torre del Lago Puccini during August. Concerts of the master's works are given in the village's open-air theatre. Details of the current year's programme can be obtained from the festival office, Piazzale Belvedere Puccini (tel: 0584/359 322).

Shelley's death
The English poet Shelley moved to Italy in 1818, aged 26, accompanied by his second wife Mary, author of *Frankenstein*. After four years in his 'Paradise of Exiles' (he coined the phrase), he drowned whilst sailing from Livorno to meet up with his fellow poet and exile, Byron. His corpse was washed up two weeks later at Gombo, just south of Viareggio. Byron and other friends cremated Shelley's body on the spot, 'pouring libations of wine, salt and frankincense on to the red-hot ashes'. Trelawney, one of the friends present, observed that 'the brains literally seethed, bubbled and boiled as in a cauldron … [but] what surprised us all was that the heart remained entire.' The said heart was returned to England, where it was laid to rest in Bournemouth. The poet's ashes were buried in Rome's Protestant Cemetery.

245

Art nouveau architecture is one of the pleasures of Viareggio

■ **Few ancient peoples were as enigmatic yet as culturally sophisticated as the Etruscans. Between 800BC and 400BC – when their civilisation was at its height – they controlled much of central Italy (Etruria) through a loose but prosperous confederation of cities.....■**

Top: Etruscan vase (c. 500BC), showing boxers fighting

Roman bullies?
'Because a fool kills a nightingale with a stone, is he therefore greater than the nightingale? Because the Roman took the life out of the Etruscan, was he therefore greater than the Etruscan?' D H Lawrence, *Etruscan Places* (1932).

246

Etruscan sites
Etruscan sites and museums in Tuscany can be found in Arezzo, Florence, Volterra, Chiusi and Grosseto. Some of the most interesting tombs that are regularly open to the public dot the countryside around Sovana in the south of the region.

Uncertain origins Where the Etruscans came from is one of history's great mysteries. They believed themselves to be Italy's indigenous people. Their alphabet has links with Chaldean Greek, suggesting roots in Asia Minor. Motifs in their funerary art suggest contact with Buddhism, whilst their tomb figures have a distinctly Asiatic cast. The Etruscan caste system and priestly oligarchy show parallels with the Brahmanism of 10th-century BC India. Scholarly evidence today suggests mixed roots – a blend of seafarers and indigenous tribes, with ethnic links to Asia Minor and trading ties with Greece. Trying to unravel the Etruscans' origins today, however, is rather like an archaeologist 3,000 years in the future trying to untangle the ethnic roots of the average 20th-century Englishman or American, where no single source can easily be isolated.

Etruscan cities The first Etruscan cities were probably established around the 8th century BC. Over the next 200 years the most powerful, known as 'lucomonies' (autonomous kingdoms), came together to form a loose 12-city federation, the Dodecapolis. Some of the cities – including Arezzo, Cortona, Chiusi and Volterra – are still important towns (as are Orvieto and Perugia in Umbria, and Cerveteri and Tarquinia in Lazio). Others, such as Vulci, Roselle and Vetulonia, are now little more than scattered ruins. Although most of the cities were concentrated in central Italy, Etruscan outposts spread as far south as Pompeii, and to Ravenna and Bologna in the north.

Etruscan fortunes took a turn for the worse in 474BC, a fateful year that saw the Etruscans defeated by the Greeks at the Battle of Cumae. After that, territory was

An Etruscan plate in the Museo Nazionale Etrusco in Chiusi, one of several museums in Tuscany packed with Etruscan artefacts excavated from tombs

The Etruscans

also lost to the Gauls and Samnites. Cities then fell in fairly rapid succession to the Romans. Veio was one of the first to go (in 396BC), Perugia one of the last (in 309BC). Some fought, others went quietly. Some, for a while, maintained a benign independence. All, however, were eventually assimilated, their people and customs absorbed by force or through intermarriage.

Tuscany is riddled with hundreds of Etruscan tombs. The half-hidden one pictured here is near Volterra

The Etruscan legacy Wander the streets of Volterra, it is said, and you encounter faces that might have come straight from the town's Etruscan tombs. Since so little else of Etruscan culture has survived, genetic continuity may appear at first glance to be one of the Etruscans' few historic bequests. History, however, has been side-tracked by the Romans, who deliberately set out to appropriate the culture of their predecessors and absorb it into their own. Etruscans, for example, were probably Rome's first settlers, and provided its first kings. Their alphabet passed into Latin, and thus into later European languages. The Romans also inherited many of the Etruscans' gods and divinations, and even their circuses, rituals and gladitorial games.

Much of the Etruscans' material culture has been lost because their cities were made mostly of wood. Almost all that remains are necropoli, the great 'cities of the dead' that surrounded every Etruscan settlement. Almost everything found (or known) about the Etruscans, there-fore, comes from tombs (the Etruscans, like the Egyptians, buried their dead equipped with everything they might need in the afterlife). This has given them an undeserved reputation for gloom and an obsession with death. In truth, they were lively and imaginative – 'effer-vescent as flowers', in the words of D H Lawrence – and possessed of highly developed social, cultural and political systems.

Life and death
'Death ... to the Etruscans was a pleasant continuance of living, with jewels and wine and flutes playing for the dance. It was neither an ecstasy of bliss, a heaven, nor a pur-gatory of torment. It was just a natural continuance of the fulness of life. Everything was in terms of life ... the things they did, in their early centuries, are as natural and easy as breathing.' D H Lawrence, *Etruscan Places* (1932)

VOLTERRA

Tourist information
Volterra's tourist office is
at Via G Turazza 2, off
Piazza dei Priori (tel:
0588/86 150).

Balze
Volterra's plateau is slowly
crumbling away. The best
place to see its famous
cliffs and chasms is
beyond Porta San
Francesco. On the way,
drop into the church of San
Francesco, known for its
fresco cycle of 1315, *The
Legend of the True Cross*
by Cenni di Francesco.
Most of its scenes are similar to Piero della
Francesca's famous cycle
in Arezzo (see pages
192–5).

Museo d'Arte Sacra
The tiny museum next to
the Duomo (entrance at Via
Roma 13) contains a col-
lection of sculptures, bas-
reliefs, bells, furnishings,
vestments, silverware and
illuminated manuscripts.
The best of the paintings
are Rosso Fiorentino's
Madonna of Villamagna
and Daniele da Volterra's
Madonna of Ulignano.
Open: daily 9–1. Closed
Monday. Admission charge
(inexpensive).

*Looking down on
Volterra's extensive
Roman remains*

►   **Volterra**   *IBCC3*

Commentators invariably describe lofty Volterra as grim
and forbidding – a city, in the words of D H Lawrence,
'that gets all the wind and sees all the world … a sort of
inland island, still curiously isolated and grim'. On the
wrong sort of day this atmosphere is all-pervasive.
Hunched behind medieval walls, the town is still inward-
looking; perched above a ring of brown-grey hills, it con-
tinues to be lord of all it surveys. At other times, Volterra
can be a delightful place, not only for its tremendous
views, but also for its superb Roman remains, numerous
parks and gardens, fine medieval buildings, and one of the
country's top Etruscan museums.

As Velathri, Volterra was one of the Etruscans' 12 cities,
its early prominence based on mining and an impregnable
position. In the 3rd century BC it became Roman
Volaterrae. A thousand years later it was briefly the capital
of the Lombard kings. Florence subdued the city in 1361,
then again in 1472, when Lorenzo de' Medici hired merce-
naries to defend Florentine claims to the town's alum
mines (alum was used as a fixative for dyes and was therefore vital for Florence's textile trade). A terrible siege and
sack ensued: the resulting slaughter was one of three
'crimes' Lorenzo confessed to Savonarola on his
deathbed. Volterra remained a Florentine vassal and part
of the Grand Duchy of Tuscany until unification in 1860.

The town's main square, **Piazza dei Priori►►**, is straight
out of the Middle Ages. Its **Palazzo dei Priori** (1208–57)
was Tuscany's first civic palace, and is still the town hall.
The Sala del Consiglio, on the first floor, boasts a large
fresco of the Annunciation by Orcagna (1383). Opposite
stands the **Palazzo Pretorio**, known for its Torre del
Porcellino (Piglet's Tower), named after the quaint (and
now much worn) carved boar to the right of the entrance.

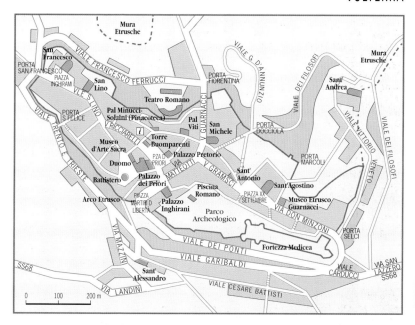

The 12th-century Pisan-style **Duomo►** has several noteworthy works of art. On the high altar stands a 1471 tabernacle by Mino da Fiesole. The pulpit to the left was assembled from 13th-century Pisan fragments in 1584. A chapel in the south transept contains a polychrome *Deposition* (1228), a redoubtable work in wood by an unknown Pisan sculptor. On the left (north) wall the second altar has a lovely *Annunciation* (1497) by Fra Bartolomeo. A separate room, off the north aisle, displays 15th-century terracotta figures depicting the Nativity and the Adoration of the Magi, the latter with a frescoed background by Benozzo Gozzoli.

Volterra's **Pinacoteca►** (art gallery) is housed in the Palazzo Minucci-Solaini at Via dei Sarti 1. Most of its works have been salvaged from churches around the town, including San Giusto al Bostro, a church swallowed up by the town's crumbling cliffs, the *balze* (see panel opposite). Highlights among the Sienese and Florentine paintings are works by Taddeo di Bartolo, Ghirlandaio and Luca Signorelli. The main treasure is Rosso Fiorentino's *Deposition* (1521), a masterpiece of Mannerist painting (in Room 12, on the first floor). *Open*: daily 9–1 and 3–6 (winter 9:30–1). Admission charge (inexpensive).

Given its worthy reputation, the old-fashioned layout of the **Museo Etrusco Guarnacci►►** may be a disappointment. The sheer surfeit of urns can seem overwhelming – there are over 600 of them ('an open book of life', in the words of D H Lawrence). Etruscan devotees, however, will find much to keep them happy. Particularly eye-catching is the *Ombra della Sera* (the 'Shadow of the Night'), an elongated 5th-century bronze figurine (used as a poker by the farmer who found it in 1879). The most famous work is Room 20's *Gli Sposi* (The Married Couple), a tomb cover which is reproduced on postcards all over the town. *Open*: daily 9–1 and 3–6:30 (winter 9–2). Admission charge (inexpensive).

Fortezza and park
Volterra's castle is two castles – the Vecchia (1343) and the Nuova (1475). The latter, also known as *Il Maschio* (The Male), after its battlemented tower, was built by Lorenzo de' Medici after the 1472 siege. It is linked to *La Femmina* (The Female) by a double rampart. Parts are currently used as a prison. The nearby Parco Archeologico is the best place in the town to enjoy a picnic or a siesta.

Teatro Romano
Volterra's Roman theatre is one of the best-preserved in Italy. Although it has been closed for some time, you can enjoy a view of it and the surrounding excavations north of Porta Fiorentina on Via Lungo le Mura del Mandorlo.

Itineraries

These suggested day-by-day itineraries should save you unnecessary legwork and valuable time spent in working out where to go when (to check opening times, see under individual entries in the A to Z sections and also pages 268–9).

One- or two-week itinerary

First week

Sunday Begin with the introductory walk on page 54, stopping at the tourist office, the Palazzo Vecchio and the Museo della Casa Fiorentina Antica. Fortify yourself with a restaurant lunch, then return to Piazza del Duomo to climb the Campanile and explore Piazza del Duomo.

Monday Start at the Museo di Firenze com'era, then visit Casa Buonarroti before buying a snack or a picnic lunch in the Mercato di Sant'Ambrogio (pages 114–15). Visit Santa Croce and its museum, then stroll to the Ponte Vecchio and enjoy an early evening walk (page 156) up to San Miniato al Monte. Take bus no 12 or 13 back.

Tuesday Take a train to Lucca or Pisa for the day.

Wednesday Devote the morning to the Uffizi. Spend the afternoon in Piazza del Duomo, seeing inside the Duomo and the Battistero and visiting the Museo dell'Opera del Duomo.

Thursday Start with a browse on and around the Ponte Vecchio, then walk to the Palazzo Pitti. Spend the rest of the morning looking at pictures there, then relax (perhaps with a picnic lunch) in the Giardino di Boboli. Walk to Santa Maria del Carmine to see the Brancacci chapel frescos, then visit Santo Spirito before finding a pleasant Oltrarno restaurant for dinner.

Friday Make an early start and take a long half-day over the walk in the north of the city (page 94), visiting as many of the churches and museums as you can. After a late lunch, rest your legs by taking the circular tour from Piazza San Marco on bus no 15 (see panel on page 186). If you still have the energy, get off the bus in Via de' Tornabuoni for some window-shopping.

Saturday Visit the Bargello and the Badia Fiorentina in the morning and pick up a pizza for lunch on the way to visit Santa Maria Novella and perhaps also Santa Trinita in the afternoon.

Second week

Sunday Spend the morning at the Museo Archeologico and the afternoon on a bus trip to one of the Medici villas (pages 170–1).

Monday and Tuesday Hire a car (see page 256) and visit San Gimignano and Siena, staying overnight and perhaps fitting in one of the drives on pages 198–9 or 242–3.

Wednesday Spend a leisurely day in Fiesole.

Thursday Visit the Museo della Fondazione Horne and the Museo Bardini, then in the afternoon either revisit the Uffizi or do some shopping.

Friday Take a train to either Arezzo or (for a longer day) Cortona for the day.

Saturday Spend a scientific last morning visiting the Museo Zoologico – La Specola and, back across the Ponte Vecchio, the Museo della Storia di Scienza. The afternoon is left free for shopping, revisiting places of special interest, packing – or just relaxing.

Weekend itinerary

Rather than trying in vain to 'do it all', combine a few of the main sights with time spent strolling, relaxing and enjoying the city's restaurants and shops. Introduce yourself to the city on Saturday morning with the walk on page 54, perhaps lingering a while in Piazza della Signoria and visiting the Museo della Casa Fiorentina Antica and Santa Maria Novella. Have lunch in a restaurant near the centre, then visit the Uffizi before crossing the Ponte Vecchio and walking up to San Miniato al Monte in the early evening (page 156).

Begin Sunday with a visit to the Bargello, then see one of the great churches: Santa Croce and its museum, or San Lorenzo and the Cappelle Medicee. After lunch, see Piazza del Duomo and climb Giotto's Campanile, marvelling at the view as you plan a more leisurely return visit to the city.

TRAVEL FACTS

Entry formalities

Citizens of the US and the British Commonwealth require passports, but visas are not necessary for visits to Italy that do not exceed three months. Visitors' Passports or Visitor Cards will suffice for citizens of European Union (EU) countries. Visas are usually required for longer stays and for nationals of other countries. It is a good idea to carry some form of identification (with a photograph) at all times in Italy.

By air

The small Peretola airport on the northwestern outskirts of Florence handles scheduled direct daily flights to and from London, Paris, Brussels, Dortmund, Frankfurt, Barcelona, Nice and Munich. Connections within Italy are available to and from Bari, Cagliari, Catania, Elba, Milan (Linate), Naples, Olbia, Palermo and Rome. For information on air travel, tel: 055/373 498. SITA buses connect Peretola and the city centre roughly every hour (journey time 15 minutes), arriving in Via Santa Caterina da Siena (behind the station). Tickets should be bought at the airport bar and punched on the bus.

Pisa's larger Galileo Galilei airport (tel: 050/500 707 or 216 073) handles more international flights, with numerous daily connections on national and charter airlines to most major cities in Italy and Europe. Hourly trains connect Pisa Aeroporto with Florence's main railway station (journey time 1 hour).

Bologna airport (1 hour by road or rail from Florence) also has scheduled flights from London, Paris and Frankfurt.

By train

Florence's main railway station, Santa Maria Novella, lies at the heart of central Italy's rail network. Direct international trains arrive here from Paris, Calais (summer only), Brussels, Amsterdam, Basel, Munich and other European cities. Fast main-line connections are also available from Rome (2 hours), Milan (3 hours), Pisa (1 hour), Bologna (1 hour), Verona (2 hours), Venice (3 hours), Genoa (2 hours) and Turin (4 hours). For train information, tel: 288 785 (9–5 only).

The station has left-luggage, exchange, restaurant and hotel-booking facilities. City buses leave from the concourse on its eastern

Pointing the way: road signs in Pisa

252

Fast and flashy, but unsuitable for Florence's traffic-clogged streets

side (to the left as you go out). Taxis depart from the front of the station. It is about 10 minutes' walk to the Duomo and Piazza della Signoria. A small tourist office is located at the southern end of the bus bays in Piazza della Stazione, to the east of the railway station.

A few trains (mostly night sleepers) use Florence's two minor stations, Rifredi (north of the city) and Campo di Marte (to the east).

By car
Florence sits on Italy's main A1 motorway, the Autostrada del Sole. To the north it links to Bologna (a busy, winding stretch of road with many tunnels); to the south it links to Arezzo and Rome. The closest exits to the city centre are Firenze–Certosa and Firenze–Signa. A fast motorway-standard road leaves the A1 south of the city at Firenze–Certosa to connect with Siena. The A11 motorway leaves the A1 at Firenze–Nord to connect with Prato, Pistoia, Lucca and the west-coast A12 motorway (for Genoa and La Spezia). The new Superstrada (not marked on many maps) runs parallel to the A11 to the south, linking Florence with Pisa, Livorno and the A12 motorway.

By bus
Tuscany is served by several long-haul bus companies (see under **Public Transport** on pages 258–9 for details).

Most have their terminals on or close to the main railway station in Florence. CLAP and Lazzi all arrive at Piazza della Stazione. COPIT uses Piazza Santa Maria Novella, just to the south. SITA is based in Via Santa Caterina da Siena, immediately off the western edge of Piazza della Stazione.

Customs For visitors aged 17 or over from EU countries, limits on duty- and tax-paid goods (i.e., bought in ordinary shops) are as follows:
• Tobacco: 800 cigarettes, 400 cigarillos, 1kg of tobacco or 200 cigars.
• Alcohol: 10 litres of spirits or 20 litres of fortified wine plus 90 litres of wine (not more than 60 per cent sparkling) plus 110 litres of beer.

For EU and non-EU visitors aged 17 or over, allowances for goods bought in duty-free shops (in airports or on board ships and planes) are:
• 200 cigarettes or 100 cigarillos or 50 cigar or 250g of tobacco
• 1 litre of spirits or 2 litres of table wine or 2 litres of fortified or sparkling wine
• An additional 2 litres of still table wine
• 60ml perfume, 250ml toilet water.

Travel insurance
It is highly recommended that you take out fully comprehensive travel insurance before travelling to Italy.

Climate

Despite its generally mild winters and warm summers, Florence has a surprisingly varied and extreme climate. Summers can be uncomfortably hot and oppressive, whilst winter temperatures often match those of northern European cities. Rainfall can be high until well after Easter, and tumultuous summer thunderstorms are fairly common (particularly in September). The best months for sightseeing are May, June and September. October and April are the third and fourth

Don't leave your umbrella at home: it has its uses, rain or shine, and the Tuscan climate can be unpredictable

wettest months respectively after January and November.

When to go

If possible avoid July and August, Florence's hottest and busiest months, and try instead to plan a visit for May, June, September or October. Hotels will be busy throughout the period May to September. If you are concentrating on Tuscany and its scenery, the countryside is at its best in May, when spring flowers are in full bloom. September's landscapes have a different beauty, burnt brown and gold by the summer sun.

National holidays

Shops, banks, offices and schools close on the following national holidays: 1 January (New Year's Day); 6 January (Epiphany); Good Friday; Easter Sunday; Easter Monday; 25 April (Liberation Day); 1 May (Labour Day); 15 August (Assumption); 1 November (All Saints' Day); 8 December (Immaculate Conception);

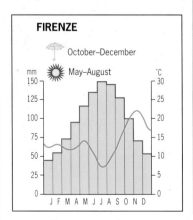

FIRENZE

October–December

May–August

mm / °C

150 / 30
125 / 25
100 / 20
75 / 15
50 / 10
25 / 5
0 / 0

J F M A M J J A S O N D

Christmas Day; 26 December (Santo Stefano). The feast of St John, Florence's patron saint, is celebrated on 24 June as a local holiday.

Accommodation is usually in short supply around the public holidays, and roads and railways will be especially busy.

Time differences

Italy is 1 hour ahead of GMT in winter, 2 hours ahead in summer. US Eastern Standard Time is 6 hours behind Italy: Sydney is 8 hours ahead in summer. Note that these time differences may vary by an hour for short periods in spring and autumn, since the seasonal time change takes place on different dates in different countries.

Money matters

The unit of Italian currency is the *lira* (plural *lire*), abbreviated to L. It is issued in the following denominations:
• **Notes** – L1,000; L2,000; L5,000; L10,000; L50,000; L100,000.
• **Coins** – L5 and L10 (both rare); L50; L100; L200; L500. The L200 telephone token (*gettone*) can be used as a coin.
Italy no longer has acute change problems, but presenting a L50,000 or a L100,000 note for a small purchase can still cause difficulties. All the zeros of Italy's currency can be confusing, so check change and all monetary transactions carefully.

Foreign exchange Many Florentine banks offer over-the-counter exchange (*cambio*) facilities (see page 264 for opening times). Increasing numbers have external automatic tellers that exchange all major foreign banknotes into lire. Exchange kiosks are also common. Those with the longest opening hours include the office in the railway station ticket hall and **Exact** (open daily from 8:30 until the evening; branches at Via dei Calzaiuoli 42r, Via Por Santa Maria 3r and Via Alamanni 9r). **American Express** is at Via Guicciardini 49r (tel: 288 751).

Credit cards Cash still reigns supreme in Italy, but the credit card (*carta di credito*) is gradually gaining acceptance. Most Florentine hotels and restaurants accept cards, though there may be more reluctance in smaller Tuscan towns. Credit cards are accepted at some petrol stations in cities, but are seldom accepted for petrol purchases elsewhere. The most commonly recognised cards are Mastercard, Visa, American Express and Diner's Club.

Exchange machines help reduce the queues of visitors in banks

255

Car rental

To rent a car you must be over 21 and hold a valid driver's licence. The big firms have offices at Pisa and Peretola airports. Enquire about fly-drive deals at travel agents before leaving home. All agencies are listed in the Yellow Pages (*Pagine Gialle*) under *Autonoleggio*. Be sure to read the small print, and to satisfy yourself that insurance cover is

A contented pillion passenger

Two wheels are quicker than four

adequate. Check all extra charges carefully (accident waiver, additional insurance) and note that VAT (IVA) will be added to the final bill.

The main car rental offices in Florence are as follows:

Avis Borgo Ognissanti 128r (tel: 213 629 or 239 8826)
Europcar Borgo Ognissanti 53r (tel: 236 0072/3)
Hertz Via Maso Finiguerra 33r (tel: 282 260 or 239 8205)
Italy by Car Borgo Ognissanti 134r (tel: 293 021 or 287 161).

Car breakdown

If your car breaks down, switch on the hazard warning lights and place a warning triangle 50m behind your car. Then call the Automobile Club d'Italia (ACI) emergency number (tel: 116) and give the operator your location and the car's make and registration. The car will be towed to the nearest ACI-affiliated garage. This service is free for foreign-registered cars. ACI have a special assistance number in Florence (tel: 24 861).

Driving tips

Whilst narrow and winding roads will probably be your only problem in rural Tuscany, note that Florence has a complicated one-way system and that much of the city centre is

completely closed to traffic for most or all of the day.

Documents Visitors bringing their own (foreign-registered) cars to Italy must be at least 18 years of age and carry the vehicle's registration and insurance documents and a full driving licence (*patente* in Italian). A green UK, red Eire or other European licence is acceptable if accompanied by a translation (available from ACI offices or the Italian State Tourist Office or motoring organisations in your country of origin). Translations are not required for the new (pink) EU driving licences.

Rules of the road Italian traffic rules are allied to the Geneva Convention and Italy uses European standard road signs (motorway signs are green, others blue). Driving is on the right and you should give way to traffic from the right unless there are

A picturesque but expensive way to see Florence

signs to the contrary. Tolls are payable on all but a handful of motorways (*autostrade*). The speed limit in urban areas is 50kph (31mph); outside urban areas it is 110kph (70mph) on dual carriageways, unless otherwise marked, and 90kph (56mph) on secondary roads. The limit on motorways is 130kph (81mph) for vehicles over 1100cc and 110kph (70mph) for vehicles under 1100cc. The wearing of front seat belts is compulsory. Police can impose heavy on-the-spot fines and take away your driving licence for many offences.

Accidents If you have an accident (*un incidente*) place a warning triangle 50m behind your car. Call either the ACI (tel: 116) or the emergency services (tel: 112 or 113). Do not admit liability or make statements

areas (such as central Florence), visitors may park outside hotels for unloading only (so hotels with private garages are at a premium). New peripheral car parks (*parcheggi*) are opening in Florence (notably at Piazza della Stazione). The most central long-term car park is at the Fortezza da Basso (linked to the centre by bus no 15). Other smaller car parks include Piazza Beccaria, Piazza Porta Romana, Piazza Libertà and Lungarno della Zecca Vecchia. Illegally parked cars may be towed away; call Parco Auto Requisite (tel: 355 321) to arrange recovery. Never leave valuables in parked cars.

Public Transport
Air Alitalia and its domestic affiliate ATI fly from Pisa to most national and international destinations (see **Arriving**, pages 252–3). Prices are high, however, and within Italy it is cheaper and often more convenient to travel by rail. Students and passengers aged between 12 and 25 qualify for 25 per cent reductions on certain Alitalia flights. There are also 30 per cent discounts on some night flights, plus 50 per cent savings for family groups (spouse and/or children travelling with you). For airport inquiries at Pisa Galileo Galilei, tel: 050/500 707. For Florence Peretola, tel: 055/373 498.

that might incriminate you later. Ask any witness(es) to remain. Make a statement to the police and exchange names, addresses, car details and insurance companies' names and addresses with any other driver(s) involved.

Petrol Petrol (*benzina*) in Italy is some of the most expensive in Europe. Diesel (*gasolio*) is cheaper. Petrol stations follow normal shop hours (closed 1–3:30pm and after 7pm) and many close all day Sunday and for the month of August (except on motorways). Do not rely on paying by credit card.

Parking Parking is extremely difficult in the centres of all Tuscan towns. Where street parking exists, it is seldom free except in areas with disc schemes, where you can park for a specified short period if you display your time of arrival. Town centres are often classified as limited traffic zones (ZTL or *zona di trafico limitato*), open only to public transport, residents' cars and taxis. In these

Bus (For information on buses within Florence, see page 186). About 10 bus companies serve Florence and Tuscany. For tickets and information on prices and timetables for long-haul buses (*autobus* or *pullman*), visit tourist offices or the individual offices below:
SITA Via Santa Caterina da Siena 15 (tel: 483 651)
Lazzi, Piazza della Stazione 4 (tel: 215 154)
CAP (Northern Tuscany) Largo Fratelli Alinari 9 (tel: 214 637)
CLAP (Northern Tuscany) Piazza della Stazione 15 (tel: 283 734)
COPIT (Northern Tuscany) Piazza Santa Maria Novella 22r (tel: 215 451)
CAT (Central and southern Tuscany) Piazza della Stazione 15 (tel: 283 734)

TRA-IN (Siena province) Piazza San Domenico, Siena (tel: 0577/221 221)

Train Florence is one of the hubs of the Italian rail network. It sits astride the main Rome–Milan line (connections to Bologna and Arezzo) and is the terminus for two lines to the west (one to Livorno via Pisa and Empoli, the other to Viareggio via Prato, Pistoia and Lucca). Direct lines run to Siena (sometimes with changes at Empoli) and Faenza in Emilia-Romagna (a lovely scenic ride). Italy's main west-coast route runs through Tuscany linking Orbetello in the south with Livorno, Pisa, Viareggio and Massa in the north (connections to Rome, Genoa and Turin).

• **Network** Except for a few private lines the Italian rail network – cheap, comprehensive and efficient – is run by the Ferrovie dello Stato (FS).

• **Trains** There are five basic train categories: *Pendolino* and *Inter /Euro City* stop only at major stations and require you to book in advance and-pay a supplement (*un supplemento*). *Espressi* and *diretti* make more stops, while *locali* halt at every station.

• **Tickets** (*biglietti*) These are available as single (*andata*) or return (*andata e ritorno*) in first (*prima*) or second class (*seconda classe*).

• **Fares** Fares are calculated on a kilometric basis and are among the cheapest in western Europe. Return tickets offer a 15 per cent discount on distances up to 250km.

• **Validity** Return tickets are valid for one day from the day of purchase for journeys up to 250km. They acquire an extra day of validity for each additional 200km up to a maximum of six days. If buying your ticket in advance (advisable at busy periods) be certain to specify your day of travel. To avoid a fine, be sure to validate your ticket by stamping it in the platform machine provided.

• **Reservations** Stations usually have separate ticket windows for reservations (*una prenotazione*) and sleepers (*una cucetta*).

• **Reductions** Discounts of 20 per cent are available for families with a *Carta Famiglia* (Family Card); for travellers between 12 and 26 with a *Carta Verde*; and for those over 60 with a *Carta d'Argento*. Cards can be purchased from main-line stations and are valid for a year.

• **Passes** The FS issue three main passes: the *Chilometrico*, valid for 3,000km of travel over a maximum of 20 journeys; the *Biglietto Turistico Libera Circolazione*, a first- or second-class travel-at-will card available for periods of 8, 15, 21 or 30 days; and a *Flexipass*, allowing unlimited travel: four days within a nine-day period, eight days within a 21-day period, or 12 days within any month).

• **Timetable** Be sure to buy the *Pozzorario*, a cheap bi-annual timetable widely available from bookshops and station kiosks.

Taxis Drivers are usually honest, but make sure the meter is switched on at the start of the journey. There is a standard minimum fare, and supplements apply to baggage, night services, and journeys to the airport. If you call a taxi, the meter starts when you make the phone call.

Santa Maria Novella station

Media

Florence's favourite newspaper (*giornale*) is *La Nazione*, a national broadsheet with its roots in Tuscany (much as *La Stampa* belongs to Turin, *La Repubblica* to Rome, and so on). It produces local editions with supplements for most Tuscan towns, plus full listings of daily events. The other most widely read quality papers are the progressive *La Repubblica* (which produces a lively Florentine edition) and the more conservative *Corriere della Sera*. Two exclusively sports-based papers are also popular, the *Gazzetta dello Sport* and the *Corriere dello Sport*. News magazines (*riviste*) also enjoy a large readership, notably *L'Espresso* and *Panorama*.

Foreign newspapers and magazines are readily available in Florence, usually from late afternoon on the day of issue (the railway station kiosks are the most reliable source). European editions of the *Financial Times* and the *International Herald Tribune* are also widely available.

Italian radio and television are both deregulated, and both offer a vast range of national and local stations. Standards are often low, with most Tuscan networks devoted mainly to advertising, pop music and old films. National stations are a little better, dividing equally between the three channels of the state RAI network and the stable of channels part-owned by Silvio Berlusconi (Canale 5, Rete 4 and Italia Uno).

Post offices

Florence's most central post office is at Via Pellicceria 8, tel: 216 122 (*open*: Monday to Friday 8:15–7 and Saturday 8:15–noon). There is another big post office at Via Pietrapiana 53–5; tel: 212 305 (same hours). Small town post offices (*posta* or *ufficio postale*) usually open Monday to Friday 8–2 and Saturday 8–12, longer in larger cities such as Florence and Siena (see above). All post offices close at noon on the last working day of the month.
• **Stamps** (*francobolli*) These can be bought either from post offices or from tobacconists (*tabacchi*) displaying a blue 'T' sign.
• **Post-boxes** These are small and red and marked *Poste* or *Lettere*.

An Italian post-box. Mail services can be very slow

Many of them have two slots – one for local mail (marked *Città*), the other for further afield (marked *Altre Destinazioni*).
• **International mail** Mail sent to and from Italy can take up to three weeks to arrive. You can speed matters by sending mail *espresso* (express) or *raccomandata* (registered).

Telephones in Italy are modern and easy to use

• **Poste restante** Letters can be sent *poste restante* to the main post office by addressing them *Fermo Posta*, followed by the name of the town. Counters 23 and 24 at Florence's Via Pellicceria office deal with *poste restante* mail. Take a passport when collecting mail and be prepared to pay a small fee (around L300 per item). Filing can be haphazard, so ask staff to check under your first and last names.

• **Telex, fax and telegrams** These can be sent from Florence's main post offices (the telegram office at Via Pellicceria is open until 10pm).

Telephones

Italy's state telephone company (SIP) provides public telephones in bars, on the streets and in special SIP offices. All are marked by red or yellow signs showing a telephone dial and receiver. In Florence, booths at the railway station are open 8am-8pm, while the main SIP office at Via Cavour 21r is open 24 hours.

Most phones accept L100, L200 and L500 coins, as well as a L200 token known as a *gettone*. The last are often given as change or can be bought from bars and *tabacchi*. The oldest phones (often in bars) usually only accept these tokens. Public phones are increasingly being modified to accept cards (*schede telefoniche*). Cards are available in L5,000, L10,000 and L15,000 denominations from *tabacchi*, SIP offices, automatic dispensers or shops displaying an SIP sticker. Remember to tear the corner off the card before using it.

Making a point: portable phones are Italy's latest status symbol

• **Timing of calls** Peak period on weekdays is 8:30am-1pm. The cheapest rate is 10pm-8am all week, while other times are classified as either standard (such as weekdays 1-6:30pm) or off peak (such as weekday evenings and Sundays). The cheap international rate covers all day Sunday, and 10pm-8am on other days for calls in Europe, 11pm-8am for the rest of the world.

• **Tones** The dialling tone on public phones is a sharp hum. A series of rapid pips means you are being connected, while long beeps indicate a ringing telephone at the other end. More rapid beeps mean 'engaged'.

• **International calls** Use a phone card or a *telefono a scatti* – a kiosk where you speak first and pay when your call is over; these are found in some bars, hotels, post offices and tourist offices and in most SIP offices. Dial 00 for an international line followed by the country code: 44 for the UK; 1 for the US; 61 for Australia and so on. (The code for Italy when calling from abroad is 39.)

• **Reversing the charges** To make a reverse-charge (collect) call, dial 15 (Europe) or 170 (Intercontinental) and ask to make *una chiamata con pagamento a destinazione*.

• **Area codes** The area code for Florence is 055 (omitted in this book on the assumption that you will be telephoning from Florence). Area codes are included for other towns.

Crime and the police

The sheer number of visitors to Florence makes them an obvious target for the unscrupulous. In this city as in others, all sorts of horror stories circulate of unwitting tourists fleeced by the criminal elite. Whilst crime certainly exists in Florence, few such tales have much basis in fact, and common sense and a few precautions should keep you safe.

Report any theft to your hotel and then to the police at the Questura, Via Zara 2 (tel: 49 771). They have a special department to deal with visitors' problems. They will also issue you with a special document (*una denuncia*) to forward with any insurance claims. Report loss of passport to the police and your nearest consulate or embassy.

- To contact the police in an emergency, telephone 112 or 113.
- Always carry cash in a belt or pouch – never in a pocket.
- Do not carry large amounts of cash. Use credit cards or travellers' cheques.
- Wear your camera and never put it down on café tables. Beware of strap-cutting thieves.
- Do not flaunt valuables. Better still, leave them at home.
- Leave jewellery in the hotel safe (not in rooms), especially items like chains and earrings which can easily be snatched.
- Hold bags across your front as the Florentines do – not hung over one shoulder where they can more easily be rifled or grabbed.
- Be careful of pickpockets on crowded buses, in street markets or anywhere where large groups of tourists congregate.
- After dark, avoid non-commercial parts of town, parks, and the area around the railway station.
- When driving always lock your car, and never leave luggage, cameras or valuables inside.

Consulates

- **Austria** Via dei Servi 9 (tel: 238 2014)
- **Belgium** Via dei Servi 28 (tel: 282 094)
- **Denmark** Via dei Servi 13 (tel: 211 007)
- **France** Piazza Ognissanti 2 (tel: 230 2556)
- **Netherlands** Via Cavour 81 (tel: 475 249)
- **Norway** Via G Capponi 26 (tel: 247 9321)
- **Spain** Via La Pira 21 (tel: 217 110)
- **Sweden** Via della Scala 4 (tel: 239 6865)
- **UK** Lungarno Corsini 2 (tel: 284 133)
- **USA** Lungarno Amerigo Vespucci 38 (tel: 239 8276)

The art of gentle persuasion. Italy has several different police forces

Travellers from Ireland, Australia, New Zealand and Canada should contact their embassy in Rome.

Emergency Telephone Numbers
Police (Carabinieri) 112
Emergency services (Police, Fire, Ambulance) 113
Fire (Vigili di Fuoco) 115
Car breakdowns 116
Questura (Florence Police Station) 49 771
Medical emergency(24-hour central number for all of Tuscany) **118**
24-hour tourist medical centre 475 411

Lost Property
Florence's lost property office is at Via Circondaria 19 (tel: 367 943). *Open*: daily (except Thursday and Sunday) 9–noon. Report losses of passports to the police and your consulate. Report general losses to the police at the Questura, Via Zara 2.

Health
The chief everyday health hazards are likely to be too much sun, air pollution (especially for asthma and allergy sufferers) and biting insects and snakes. Water is safe to drink unless marked *acqua non potabile*. Condoms (*profilattici*) are available over the counter from pharmacies and some supermarkets.

Be certain to take out health insurance before travelling (and keep all receipts for medicine and treatment). Free treatment is available to citizens of EU countries, but to be eligible you must bring the necessary documentation (Form E111) to Italy with you from your country of origin.

Pharmacies A chemist's shop (*farmacia*) is identified by a green cross. Pharmacies have the same opening hours as shops, but some take turns to stay open late and all night (the rota is displayed on pharmacy doors). Regular late-night outlets include the pharmacy at the railway station; Molteni, Via dei Calzaiuoli 7r; All'Insegna del Moro, Piazza San Giovanni 20r; and Paglicci, Via della Scala 61. Staff are well qualified to give advice on minor ailments, and can dispense many medicines over

Italian pharmacists can advise on minor medical problems and dispense a wide variety of medicines

the counter, including some normally only available on prescription in other countries. Remember to bring any prescriptions or doctor's notes that might be required to obtain medicine. Better still, bring with you from home enough medication to last the duration of your stay.

Doctors If you need a doctor (*un medico*) ask first at your hotel, telephone 118, or contact the Tourist Medical Service, Via Lorenzo il Magnifico 59 (tel: 475 411), which has multilingual doctors on 24-hour call. For first aid (often given free) or hospital treatment visit the Ospedale di Santa Maria Nuova, Piazza Santa Maria Nuova 1 (tel: 27 581).

Vaccinations Vaccinations are not necessary for entry into Italy unless you are travelling from a known infected area. Check current requirements if you are travelling from the Far East, Africa, South America or the Middle East.

Camping and self-catering

Most Tuscan campsites are on the coast. Most open seasonally (typically June to September) and are extremely busy during the peak months of July and August, when you must book ahead or arrive before 10am to have any hope of finding a place. Tourist offices have lists of sites and current prices. You might also invest in the widely available *Campeggi e Villaggi Turistici*, an exhaustive list of sites published by the Touring Club of Italy. Freelance camping is usually acceptable, but ask the landowner's permission first, and do not light fires.

Countless agencies rent villas or farmhouses in Tuscany. Most advertise in Sunday newspapers. Agencies and local tourist offices in Italy can also be helpful. Prices are considerably higher than for equivalent properties in France or Spain. Check matters such as whether you will be sharing your swimming pool (often you are) and whether the owner (or caretaker) lives on or near the property. It is essential to know exactly what is included in the rental price (water, electricity, maid service, cleaning and linen can all be extra). Water shortages can be a problem in summer.

Visitors with disabilities

Matters are improving but Florence, with its narrow, car-crowded streets and antiquated hotels and galleries, is still not the easiest of cities for visitors with disabilities. Lists of hotels from tourist offices usually indicate places suitable for the disabled. Italian state tourist offices abroad also provide lists of appropriate hotels and the addresses of Italian associations for travellers with disabilities in various towns and cities. Specific information is also provided in the British publication *Access in Florence*, available for a small fee from OUSA Office, Sherwood House, Sherwood Drive, Bletchley, Milton Keynes MK3 6AN (tel: 01908/71 131).

New public buildings in Italy must all be wheelchair-accessible, and museums generally are gradually improving their accessibility. A few Inter City trains, particularly on the Rome–Milan line, now have special wheelchair facilities. Staff at airports, stations and in galleries are usually helpful. Parts of central Florence usually closed to traffic are open to drivers with disabilities, and there are also special parking places. Restaurants present few problems, though it is advisable to call ahead to reserve a convenient table.

Opening times

Opening hours can be a thorny problem in Florence, where most of the 'sights' are churches, museums and galleries. Be sure to obtain a list of current opening times (*Orario di Apertura*) from one of the city's tourist offices.

• **Banks** Open weekdays 8:20–1:20. Some larger branches may also open 3–4pm.

• **Churches** No two Florentine churches seem to have the same opening times. Generally most open at 7 or 8am and close at noon or 12:30. They re-open between 3 and 4pm, closing finally between 6 and 7:30. Notable exceptions include the Duomo (open all day), Santa Croce (open all day in summer) and the Battistero (open afternoons Monday to Saturday, but Sunday morning).

• **Museums and galleries** Opening times are given under individual entries in the A to Z sections of this book and (for Florence only) on pages 268–9. Most large (usually state-run) galleries open 9–2 Tuesday to Sunday and close on Monday (a few close at 1pm). Notable exceptions are the Uffizi and the Museo dell'Opera del Duomo. Some other museums open in the morning and perhaps also in the afternoon (though Sunday is usually a half-day) and some of these museums close an hour or two earlier in the afternoon between about October and March. Closing days of smaller museums vary.

• **Parks** Public parks and gardens usually open from 9am to an hour before dusk, but both the Giardino dei Semplici and the Giardino di Boboli have more restricted opening hours.

• **Post offices** Open Monday to Friday 8–2, Saturday 8–12. Smaller post offices may not open on Saturday. Main post offices often stay

open for some services until 8pm. All post offices close at noon on the last working day of the month.
• **Restaurants** All restaurants have a statutory weekly closing day (*la chiusura settimanale*), often Monday. Many also close for one evening. Most close for part of August (sometimes July). See also page 175.
• **Shops and offices** These are normally open from 8:30 or 9am to 1pm, re-opening between 3 and 4pm, and closing at 7:30 or 8pm. Food shops close (for most of the year) on Wednesday afternoon. Most other shops are closed on Monday morning (except for the period from mid-June to mid-September when many stores close on Saturday afternoon). Many garages close on Sunday (except on motorways). Supermarkets and department stores usually open 9am–8pm (closed Sunday).

Places of worship
• **Church of England** St Mark's, Via Maggio 16 (tel: 294 764)
• **American Episcopal Church** St James's, Via Rucellai 9 (tel: 294 417)
• **Synagogue** Via L C Farini 4 (tel: 245 252/3)

Opening times of sights such as the Battistero can be unusual, so check first

Toilets
Public conveniences are rare in Florence, and are often grim. They are to be found at the railway station, in the basement of the Palazzo Vecchio and off the courtyard of the Palazzo Pitti. Otherwise you will probably have to use the facilities in bars and cafés. These are free, but are intended for the use of customers so you will be more welcome if you buy something first. Ask for *il gabinetto* or *il bagno*, and do not confuse *Signori* (Men) with *Signore* (Women). Some facilities may have an attendant and a small dish for gratuities – leave around L200.

Photography
Shops are always ready to serve Florence's countless visitors with films and photography paraphernalia. A film is *una pellicola*, slides are *diapositive*.

Tipping
A 10–15 per cent service charge (*servizio*) is usually included in

High fashion meets High Renaissance in one of Florence's luxury shops

restaurant bills, but waiters expect a small tip on top. For quick service in bars, do as the locals do and slap down a L100 or L200 coin with your till receipt when ordering. Theatre usherettes expect a small tip for showing you to your seats, and it is a good idea to give around L200 per visitor to custodians or sacristans who open up churches or museums out of hours. In taxis, round the fare up or tip 10 per cent.

Electricity
Current in Italy is 220 volts AC (50 cycles). Plugs are of the two-round-pin variety: a travel adaptor is useful. Some sockets have a third (central) earth socket, but still accommodate the standard two-pin plug. In older hotels and houses you may find two-pin plugs of different specifications. Here you will need to buy (or borrow) an Italian adaptor.

Etiquette
• **Churches** Do not wear shorts, mini skirts or skimpy tops in churches, and do not intrude while church

CONVERSION CHARTS

FROM	TO	MULTIPLY BY
Inches	Centimetres	2.54
Centimetres	Inches	0.3937
Feet	Metres	0.3048
Metres	Feet	3.2810
Yards	Metres	0.9144
Metres	Yards	1.0940
Miles	Kilometres	1.6090
Kilometres	Miles	0.6214
Acres	Hectares	0.4047
Hectares	Acres	2.4710
Gallons	Litres	4.5460
Litres	Gallons	0.2200
Ounces	Grams	28.35
Grams	Ounces	0.0353
Pounds	Grams	453.6
Grams	Pounds	0.0022
Pounds	Kilograms	0.4536
Kilograms	Pounds	2.205
Tons	Tonnes	1.0160
Tonnes	Tons	0.9842

MEN'S SUITS							
UK	36	38	40	42	44	46	48
Rest of Europe	46	48	50	52	54	56	58
US	36	38	40	42	44	46	48

DRESS SIZES						
UK	8	10	12	14	16	18
France	36	38	40	42	44	46
Italy	38	40	42	44	46	48
Rest of Europe	34	36	38	40	42	44
US	6	8	10	12	14	16

MEN'S SHIRTS						
UK	14	14.5	15	15.5	16	16.5	17
Rest of Europe	36	37	38	39/40	41	42	43
US	14	14.5	15	15.5	16	16.5	17

MEN'S SHOES						
UK	7	7.5	8.5	9.5	10.5	11
Rest of Europe	41	42	43	44	45	46
US	8	8.5	9.5	10.5	11.5	12

WOMEN'S SHOES						
UK	4.5	5	5.5	6	6.5	7
Rest of Europe	38	38	39	39	40	41
US	6	6.5	7	7.5	8	8.5

services are in progress. Many churches and galleries forbid the use of flash, or ban photography altogether.

• **Smoking** There are few non-smoking areas in restaurants or public places. Smoking is banned on buses.

• **Topless sunbathing** This is usually tolerated on more out-of-the-way beaches.

• **Bargaining** This is no longer appropriate in shops, though in markets (except food markets) and budget hotels you may be able to negotiate.

• **Hotels, restaurants and bars** Do try to speak Italian; it will be appreciated – however bad. Children are more than welcome in most hotels, bars and restaurants.

Women travellers

Women visiting Tuscany and Florence are likely to receive fewer uninvited approaches from 'Latin lovers' than in Rome or southern Italy. Such advances, while irritating, are unlikely to turn violent. The best remedy is to walk away. Resorting to put-downs or a well-chosen Italian swear word invariably makes matters worse. At night it is best to avoid areas such as the Cascine, the streets around the station and Santa Maria Novella. On trains, choose a compartment with other women.

Tourist offices

Visit a tourist office early in your stay to collect free information (such as maps, lists of events, museum opening hours and charges) which will be invaluable in planning your sightseeing. The most convenient tourist office in Florence is the one close to the Duomo and the Palazzo Medici-Riccardi at Via Cavour 1r (tel: 276 0381or 290 832). Details of other tourist offices in the city appear on page 186, and details of offices in other Tuscan towns appear on the relevant pages of the Tuscany A to Z section (pages 192–249). There is at least one tourist office open in Florence daily all year (see page 186 for exact times) . Elsewhere offices may close in the afternoon out of season. Offices in villages may have more limited opening times.

Italian State Tourist Offices abroad

Australia and New Zealand Orient Overseas Building, Suite 202, 32 Bridge Street, Sydney, NSW 2000 (tel: 02/247 7836)

Canada 1 Place Ville Marie, Montréal, Québec H3B 3M9 (tel: 514/866 7667)

Irish Republic 47 Merrion Street, Dublin 2 (tel: 01-666 397)

United Kingdom 1 Princes Street, London W1 8AY (tel: 0171-408 1254)

United States 630 5th Avenue, Suite 1565, Rockefeller Center, New York NY 10111 (tel: 212/245 4822)

A postcard home from the Ponte Vecchio

Opening times

As an aid to planning your time in Florence, this chart gives the opening hours for the city's most important galleries, museums and churches.

Page		Weekdays	Sunday	Closed
Galleries and museums				
52	Accademia	9–7 (winter 9–2)	9–2	Monday
56	Bargello	9–2	9–1	Monday
135	Biblioteca Laurenziana	9–1	—	Sunday
146	Cappella Brancacci	10–4:30	1–4:30	Tuesday
64	Cappelle Medicee	9–2	9–2	Monday
68	Casa Buonarroti	9:30–1:30	9:30–1:30	Tuesday
69	Casa di Dante	9–1	9–1	Tuesday
100	Cenacolo di S Apollonia	9–2	9–1	Monday
102	Chiostro dello Scalzo	9–1 Monday & Thursday	—	Friday to Sunday, Tuesday Wednesday
84	Forte di Belvedere	9–8 or dusk if earlier	9–8 or dusk if earlier	
87	Museo Archeologico	8:30–2	8:30–1	Monday
88	Museo Bardini	9–2	8–1	Wednesday
85	Museo Botanico	9:30–12:30 Monday, Wednesday, Friday	—	Tuesday, Thursday, Saturday, Sunday
90	Museo della Casa Fiorentina Antica	9–2	9–2	Monday
92	Museo di Firenze com'era	9–2	8–1	Thursday
121	Museo di Fotografo Alinari	10–7:30 (11.30 pm Friday and Saturday)	10–7:30	Wednesday
93	Museo della Fondazione Horne	9–1	—	Sunday
120	Museo Marino Marini	10–1, 4–7 (winter 3–6)	10–1, 4–7 (winter 3–6)	Tuesday
85	Museo di Mineralogia	9–1	—	Sunday
96	Museo dell'Opera del Duomo	9–7:30; (winter 9–6)	—	Sunday
143	Museo dell'Opera di Santa Croce	10–12:30, 2:30–6:30 (winter 3–5)	10–12:30, 2:30–6:30 (winter 3–5)	Wednesday
85	Museo di Paleontologia	9–1 Tuesday to Thursday, Saturday; 2–6 Monday	—	Sunday, Friday

Page		Weekdays	Sunday	Closed
100	Museo di San Marco	9–2	9–2	Monday
152	Museo di Santa Maria Novella	9–2	8–1	Friday
108	Museo Zoologico – La Specola	9–12 Tuesday & Saturday	—	Sunday, Monday, Wednesday to Friday
102	Museo Stibbert	9–1	9–1	Thursday
104	Museo di Storia della Scienza	9:30–1; (also 2–5 Monday, Wednesday, Friday)	—	Sunday
112	Ospedale degli Innocenti	8:30–2	8:30–1	Wednesday
113	Palazzo Medici-Riccardi	9–1, 3–6	9–1	Wednesday
116	Palazzo Pitti	9–2	9–2	Monday
122	Palazzo Vecchio	9–7	8–1	Saturday
160	Uffizi, Galleria degli	9–7	9–2	Monday

Churches

Page		Weekdays	Sunday	Closed
55	Badia Fiorentina	Under long-term restoration – check times locally		
60	Battistero	1:30–6	9–1	—
63	Campanile	8:30–6:50 (winter 9–4:30)	8:30–6:50 (winter 9–4:30)	—
	Cappella Brancacci	see under Museums and galleries opposite		
	Cappelle Medicee	see under Museums and galleries opposite		
76	Duomo	9:30–6	9:30–6	—
76	Crypt	10–5	—	Sunday
80	Dome	10–5	—	Sunday
110	Orsanmichele	9–12, 4–6	9–12, 4–6	
134	Sagrestia Vecchia (San Lorenzo)	10–11:45 (Monday, Wednesday, Friday, Saturday);4–5:45 (Tuesday, Thursday)	—	Sunday
132	San Lorenzo	7–12, 3:30–5:30	7–12, 3:30–5:30	—
136	San Miniato al Monte	8–12, 2–7 (winter 8–12, 2:30–6)	8–12, 2–7 (winter 8–12, 2:30–6)	—
138	Santa Croce	8–6:30 (winter 8–12:30, 3–6:30)	8–12:30 (not winter), 3–6:30	—
148	Santa Maria Novella	7–11:30, 3:30–6	7–11:30, 3:30–6	—
154	Santa Trinita	7–12, 4–7	7–12, 4–7	—
155	SS Annunziata	7:30–12:30, 4–7	7:30–12:30, 4–7	—
157	Santo Spirito	8–12, 4–6	8–12, 4–6	—

Glossary

These pages explain some of the artistic and architectural terms used in the book.

aedicule	decorative niche framed by columns
ambo	simple medieval pulpit, often with marble inlay
anfiteatro	amphitheatre
apse	semicircular recess behind church altar
architrave	a supporting beam above a column
atrium	inner entrance court of early house or church
baldacchino	a canopy on columns, usually over a church altar
battistero	baptistery
campanile	bell-tower
campo	square
camposanto	cemetery
cantoria	choir-loft
capital	top of a column
cappella	chapel
cartoon	full-size preliminary sketch for a fresco or painting
chancel	part of church containing altar
chiaroscuro	exaggerated light and shade effects in a painting
chiesa	church
chiostro	cloister
colombarium	part of a tomb, with wall niches for the dead
Comune	administrative department of an Italian town, city or village
confessio	crypt beneath a church's high altar
cornice	top of a classical façade
cortile	courtyard
Cosmati work	marble with inlay of coloured stones and glass
crypt	burial place of a church, usually under the altar
cupola	dome
diptych	two-panelled painting
duomo	cathedral
fresco	wall-painting on wet plaster (see pages 98–9)
graffito	incised decoration on a building or wall
intarsia	mosaic or inlay work in wood or stone
loggia	roofed gallery or outside balcony
lunette	semicircular space above door, window or vaulting

Italy's finest piazza: the Campo in Siena

Maestà	representation of the Madonna and Child in majesty
matroneum	women's gallery in early churches
narthex	vestibule of a church
nave	central space of a church
palazzo	palace, large house or apartment block
pendentives	four curved triangular elements on piers supporting a dome or cupola
peristyle	courtyard surrounded by colonnades
piano nobile	main floor of a palace
piazza	open space or square in a town or village
Pietà	image of the Madonna mourning the dead Christ
pietra serena	a light-coloured stone
pietre dure	semi-precious stones such as agate and amethyst
pinacoteca	picture gallery
porta	gate
portico	covered doorway
predella	small panel below the main part of an altarpiece
putto	cherubic child in painting or sculpture
sinopia	wall sketch for a fresco
stele	vertical headstone
stemma	coat of arms
teatro	theatre
terme	baths

The courtyard of the Palazzo Vecchio, with decoration by Vasari

tondo	round painting or relief
torre	tower
transept	transverse arms of a church
tribune	raised gallery in a church or the apse of a basilica
triptych	painting on three panels
trompe l'oeil	tricks using perspective to create the illusion of depth in a painting

Stemmi (the coats of arms of those who held public office) are found on many buildings

Italians respond well to foreigners who make an effort to speak their language (however badly). Many Italians speak at least some English, and most up-market hotels and restaurants have multilingual staff.

All Italian words are pronounced as written, with each vowel and consonant sounded. The letter c is hard, as in English 'cat', except when followed by i or e, when it becomes the soft *ch* of 'children'. The same applies to g when followed by i or e – soft in *giardino*, as in the English 'giant'; hard in *gatto*, as in 'gate'. Words ending in o are almost always masculine in gender (plural ending –i); those ending in a are feminine (plural –e).

Use the polite, third person (*lei*) to

Italians usually appreciate visitors' attempts to speak their language, so don't be afraid to try out a few phrases

speak to strangers: use the second person (*tu*) to friends or children.

Courtesies
good morning **buon giorno**
good afternoon/good evening **buona sera**
good night **buona notte**
hello/goodbye (informal) **ciao**
hello (answering the telephone) **pronto**
goodbye **arrivederci**
please **per favore**
thank you (very much) **grazie (mille)**
you're welcome **prego**
how are you? (polite/informal) **come sta/stai?**
I'm fine **sto bene**
I'm sorry **mi dispiace**
excuse me/I beg your pardon **mi scusi**
excuse me (in a crowd) **permesso**

Basic vocabulary
yes **sì**
no **no**
I do not understand **non ho capito**
left/right **sinistra/destra**
entrance **entrata**
exit **uscita**
open **aperto**
closed **chiuso**
good/bad **buono/cattivo**
big/small **grande/piccolo**
with/without **con/senza**
more/less **più/meno**
near/far **vicino/lontano**
hot/cold **caldo/freddo**
early/late **presto/ritardo**
here/there **qui/là**
now/later **adesso/più tardi**
today/tomorrow **oggi/domani**
yesterday **ieri**
how much is it **quant'è?**
when **quando**
do you have …? **avete …?**

Emergencies
help! **aiuto!**
Where is the nearest telephone? **Dov'è il telefono più vicino?**
There has been an accident. **C'è stato un incidente.**
Call the police. **Chiamate la polizia.**
Call a doctor/an ambulance. **Chiamate un medico/un'ambulanza.**
first aid **pronto soccorso**
Where is the nearest hospital? **Dov'è l'ospedale più vicino?**

HOTELS AND RESTAURANTS

The recommended hotels and restaurants in this section have been divided into three price categories:
- **budget** (£)
- **moderate** (££)
- **expensive** (£££)

Telephone numbers are given in the form you would use if phoning in Florence, so area codes are given only for places outside the city. If you telephone Florence from elsewhere, prefix the Florence numbers given here with the area code 055.

For Florence, a selection of cafés and bars is also given, on pages 279–80.

ACCOMMODATION

FLORENCE

Central covers the area immediately around Piazza del Duomo and Piazza della Signoria. The other districts are **West**, **East** and **North** (of Piazza del Duomo) and **Oltrarno** (south of the Arno).

Central

Bavaria (£) Borgo degli Albizzi 26 (tel: 234 0313). Reliable cheap option in a 16th-century palazzo, but becomes booked quickly.

Brunelleschi (£££) Piazza Santa Elisabetta 3 (tel: 562 068). Fine new four-star hotel incorporating beautifully converted medieval tower; in a quiet location behind Via dei Calzaiuoli.

Davanzati (£) Via Porta Rossa 15 (tel: 283 414). Friendly place close to the Museo della Casa Fiorentina Antica.

Della Signoria (£££) Via delle Terme 1 (tel: 214 530). Modern luxury hotel. Views of the Ponte Vecchio from upper floors. Nice breakfast terrace.

Helvetia e Bristol (£££) Via de' Pescioni 2 (tel: 287 814). Close to the Duomo, this luxury hotel dates from the 18th century, but was completely restored in 1989 with the aim of creat-ing the finest of all Florence's central hotels. Has largely succeeded, with its elegant and exclusive atmosphere, attention to period detail, evocative wood and marble bar, and a high quality in-house restaurant. Rooms are large and well-appointed, and most of the marble-tiled bathrooms have Jacuzzis. Very expensive.

Hermitage (££) Vicolo Marzio 1, Piazza del Pesce (tel: 287 216). Very well-known three-star hotel on the Arno overlooking the Ponte Vecchio; popular with British and American visitors. Fine terrace. Rooms on the street are double-glazed but rear rooms are quieter.

Maxim (£) Via de' Medici 4 (tel: 217 474). Immediately behind Via dei Calzaiuoli, a minute from the Duomo. Very friendly, multilingual owners. Many quiet if basic off-street rooms.

Pendini (££) Via degli Strozzi 2 (tel: 211 170). Busy but well-run and friendly 40-room three-star hotel near Piazza della Repubblica. Large and cosily furnished rooms.

Porta Rossa (££) Via Porta Rossa 19 (tel: 287 551). A wonderful old-fashioned hotel founded in the 14th century, with large if often spartan rooms and fine period decoration. Byron and Stendhal both stayed here.

Savoy (£££) Piazza della Repubblica 7 (tel: 283 313). Most central of the city's big luxury hotels: expensive, efficient but rather impersonal.

West

Aprile (££) Via della Scala 6 (tel: 216 237). Excellently converted former Medici home with many original features. Some rooms are modern, some medieval in flavour. There are some cheaper rooms but these are very small.

Bretagna (£–££) Lungarno Corsini 6 (tel: 289 618). Airy and recently upgraded rooms in charming *pensione* with excellent view over the Arno.

Cestelli Soggiorno (£) Borgo Santi Apostoli 25 (tel: 214 213). Tiny, family-run place in quiet medieval alley. Small, simple rooms, only one with private bath-room.

Excelsior (£££) Piazza Ognissanti 3 (tel: 264 201). The city's grandest hotel. Old-world, spacious and comfortable rooms, some of which overlook the river. The piazza, though, is not one of Florence's prettiest. Very expensive.

Grand Hotel (£££) Piazza Ognissanti 1 (tel: 288 781). Smaller but otherwise similar to the Excelsior opposite. Rooms are often more modern but with less character. Very expensive.

Kraft (£££) Via Solferino 2 (tel: 284 273). Quiet, comfortable rooms in choice of modern or traditional styles. Mannered rather than charming atmosphere. Fine upper terrace, moderate restaurant and small rooftop swimming pool with grand views.

La Mia Casa (£) Piazza Santa Maria Novella 23 (tel: 213 061). Popular and probably the best of the many budget options on this piazza.

Principe (£££) Lungarno Vespucci 34 (tel: 284 848). Small, elegantly old-world four-star. Many rooms have terraces overlooking the Arno. Small garden. Popular with US visitors.

Residenza (££) Via de' Tornabuoni 8 (tel: 284 917). Fine, no-frills old-world hotel on the top four floors of a 17th-century palazzo. Good value given the location, though street-front rooms can be noisy.

Tornabuoni Beacci (£££) Via de' Tornabuoni 3 (tel: 212 645). Hotel on the top three floors of a 14th-century palazzo. Rooms vary in quality – some are small and sparse. Dull dining room but excellent terrace for breakfast and drinks.

East

Balestri (££) Piazza Mentana 7 (tel: 214 743). Spacious and comfortable if short on style, this welcoming three-star hotel has been in the same family over four generations since 1888. It stands on a piazza just off the Arno between the Uffizi and Santa Croce.

Hotel J & J (£££) Via di Mezzo 20 (tel: 240 951). An intimate and quiet little hotel in a 16th-century monastery close to Santa Croce. Smart and tasteful rooms are all different, some with painted ceiings, others with terraces, small courtyard or views over the rooftops; attracts select clients from the world of fasion and design.

Liana (££) Via Alfieri 18 (tel: 245 303/4). Old villa hotel in the former British Embassy (1864–70). Fading and rather tastelessly decorated, but good value. Rooms face on to a peaceful garden.

Plaza Lucchesi (£££) Lungarno della Zecca Vecchia 38 (tel: 264 141). Smart four-star hotel on the Arno. Modern rooms with good bathrooms.

Regency (£££) Piazza Massimo D'Azeglio 3 (tel: 245 247). Intimate, exclusive club-like hotel with slick, rather vividly decorated rooms (though some are small for the price). The quiet piazza is 15 minutes' walk from the centre.

Rigatti (£–££) Lungarno Generale Diaz 2 (tel: 213 022). Charming and good-value hotel on the Arno between the Uffizi and Santa Croce, on the top two floors of the 15th-century Palazzo Alberti. The best rooms are superb, others can be small and simple. Good terrace, but rooms with river views are noisy.

Santa Croce (£) Via Bentaccordi 3 (tel: 217 000). Cheap, small and modern two-star hotel near Santa Croce.

North

Ariston (£) Via Fiesolana 42 (tel: 247 6980). Cheap choice east of Piazza della Santissima Annunziata.

Le Due Fontane (££) Piazza della Santissima Annunziata 14 (tel: 210 185). A comfortable and modern, if rather bland three-star hotel on one of Florence's best-known piazzas.

Loggiato dei Serviti (££–£££) Piazza della Santissima Annunziata 3 (tel: 289 592). A lovely, award-winning hotel in the vaulted interior of the Servites' 16th-century confraternity. The refined rooms are calm, cool and spacious. Advance booking is essential at busy times of the year.

Monna Lisa (£££) Borgo Pinti 27 (tel: 247 9751). Excellent public spaces belie the quality of the private rooms in this popular but now overpriced hotel, part of a 15th-century Renaissance palace. Some rooms are large and overlook a *cortile* (courtyard) and garden; others (notably the singles) are small and noisy and face on to the street.

Morandi alla Crocetta (££) Via Laura 50 (tel: 234 4747). Small, highly characterful and charming family-run three-star hotel in part of the old 16th-century Crocetta convent. Warm welcome and good value.

Rudy (£) Via San Gallo 51 (tel: 475 519). Quieter than some of the cheap hotels in this area (notably those on nearby Via Cavour). No private bathrooms in double rooms. 1am curfew.

Sampaoli (£) Via San Gallo 14 (tel: 284 834). Much the same as the Rudy, but without the curfew.

Splendor (£–££) Via San Gallo 30 (tel: 483 427). Reasonably priced, modest family-run hotel with bright, if unexceptional, rooms near San Marco and the Accademia.

Oltrarno

Annalena (££) Via Romana 34 (tel: 222 402). Long-established, famous and much sought-after *pensione*-style hotel – part of an old Medici *palazzo* – opposite the Boboli gardens. Beautiful public rooms. Most of the large bedrooms boast antiques and painted furniture; some have terraces and garden views.

Bandlni Sorelle (£–££) Piazza Santo Spirito 9 (tel: 215 308). This old-fashioned hotel's charm, value for money and location mean it is often fully booked months in advance.

Lungarno (££–£££) Borgo San Jacopo 14 (tel: 264 211). A modern hotel occupying a new building and the 13th-century Torre Marsili. Rooms are cosy and comfortable; 14 have river views; 13 are in the old tower.

Pitti Palace (££–£££) Via Barbadori 2 (tel: 239 8711). This modern and delightful little hotel, part of an up-market chain, is a favourite with American and British visitors. Lovely sitting room and terrace, but bedrooms are not the best at this price, and some can be noisy.

Silla (£–££) Via de'Renai 5 (tel: 234 2888). Fine old *palazzo* on the river, with a superb terrace looking over the Arno and a small park. Good value.

Villa Cora (£££) Viale Machiavelli 18 (tel: 229 8451). Although it is some way from the centre (free shuttle service), this hotel is among the Florentine elite. A fine villa in its own grounds, with stunning decor, attentive service and very high prices.

TUSCANY
Arezzo

Astoria (£) Via Guido Monaco 54 (tel: 0575 24 361). Central two-star hotel close to San Francesco.

HOTELS AND RESTAURANTS

Cortona

Cecco (£) Corso Italia 215–17 (tel: 0575/20 986). Extremely central if rather bland two-star hotel.
Continentale (££) Piazza Guido Monaco 7 (tel: 0575/320 251). Modern, comfortable and convenient three-star hotel.
Ostello Piero della Francesca (£) Via Borg'Unto 6 (tel:0575/354 546). Private hostel off Piazza Grande.
Ostello Villa Severi (£) Via Redi (tel: 0575/29 047). IYHF youth hostel in an old villa out of town (bus no 4 from the railway station).
San Luca (££) Piazza Garibaldi 1 (tel: 0575/630 587 or 630 504). Near a busy piazza on the southern edge of town; the hillside setting guarantees fine views from the reception areas, but rooms are simple and straightforward.

Chianti

Castello di Spaltenna (££–£££) Via Spaltenna, Gaiole in Chianti (tel: 0577/749 483). Very pretty converted monastery just outside Gaiole; popular restaurant.
Relais Fattoria Vignale (££–£££) Via Pianigiani, Radda in Chianti (tel: 0577/738 300). Highly elegant hotel with Michelin-starred restaurant. Located in a villa on a wine estate.
Salivolpi (££) Via Fiorentina, Castellina in Chianti (tel: 0577/740 484). Welcoming family-run hotel.
Tenuta di Ricavo (££–£££) 4km south of Castellina in Chianti on San Donato road (tel: 0577/740 221). Medieval hamlet transformed into a fine Swiss-run hotel.

Cortona

Athens (£) Via San Antonio (tel: 0575/603 008). One-star budget option.
Italia (£) Via Ghibellina 5 (tel: 0575/630 564). Reasonable two-star hotel on one of Cortona's nicer streets.

Ostello San Marco (£) Via Maffei 57 (tel: 0575/601 392). Central IYHF youth hostel.
Sabrina (£) Via Roma 37 (tel: 0575/630 397). Three-star facilities in tiny, central hotel.
San Michele (££) Via Guelfa 15 (tel: 0575/604 348). Fine four-star hotel and Cortona's top choice if price is not important.

Fiesole

Villa Bonelli (££) Via F Poeti 1 (tel: 055/59 513 or 598 941). One of Fiesole's more intimate and friendy hotels; 20 modestly but nicely furnished rooms, some with fine views of Florence.
Villa Sorriso (£–££) Via Gramsci 21 (tel: 055/59 027). Finding a cheap place to stay in Fiesole is a problem; this is the most reasonable of the places close to the centre.
Villa San Michele (£££) Via Doccia 4 (tel: 055/59 451). Under the same management as the famous Cipriani in Venice, this is one of Italy's most luxurious hotels. The villa, set in in its own extensive grounds and with a swimming pool, is said to have been designed by Michelangelo. While some of the 28 rooms are small and somewhat simple given their price, meals can be taken outdoors in a glorious loggia with stunning views over Florence.

Lucca

Diana (£) Via del Molinetto 11 (tel: 0583/492 202). First choice among the cheaper two-star hotels. Close to the Duomo.
Ilaria (£) Via del Fosso 18 (tel: 0583/47 558). A sort of glorified hostel nicely situated on one of the canals in the east of the city.
La Luna (££) Corte Compagni 12 (tel: 0583/493 634). Three-star hotel nicely located just west of Piazza Anfiteatro.
La Pace (£) Corte Portici 14 (tel: 0583/494 981). One

block north of San Michele in Foro.
Universo (££) Piazza del Giglio 1, near Piazza Napoleone (tel: 0583/493 678). An air of old-world, slightly faded elegance pervades Lucca's top central hotel. Standards (and views) vary from room to room.

Montepulciano

Duomo (£) Via San Donato 14 (tel: 0578/757 473). The best mid-range choice.
Il Borghetto (££) Via Borgo Buio 7 (tel: 0578/757 354). Montepulciano's top hotel; located off the Corso near Piazza Michelozzo.
Marzocco (£) Piazza Savonarola (tel: 0578/757 262). Another good mid-range choice situated just inside the town walls at the lower end of the Corso.

Monteriggioni

Hotel Monteriggioni (££–£££) Via Maggio 4 (tel: 0577/305 009). This brand new four star is one of the finest hotels in this part of Tuscany: beautifully appointed and located at the heart of one of Italy's most perfectly-preserved medieval villages: a good out-of-town alternative to staying in Siena.

Pienza

Dal Falco (£) Piazza Dante Alighieri 7 (tel: 0578/748 551). A restaurant with a few cheap rooms to rent.
Il Corsignano (£) Via della Madonnina 11 (tel: 0578/748 501). Pienza's best choice as a mid-range (three-star) hotel.
Il Chiostro di Pienza (££) Corso Rossellino 26 (tel: 0578/748 400). A conversion of the fomer San Francesco monastery, this beautiful hotel has modern rooms, good views and a lovely cloister. Patches of fresco remain in parts of the hotel.

Pisa

Amalfitana (£) Via Roma 44 (tel: 050/29 000). Pleasant and well-located two-star hotel just south of the Campo dei Miracoli.

Grand Hotel Duomo (££) Via Santa Maria 94 (tel: 050/561 894). Best of the town's modern and luxurious hotels if you wish to do Pisa in style. Roof garden, garage, and air-conditioning throughout.

Gronchi (£) Piazza Arcivescovado 1 (tel: 050/561 823). First choice among the cheaper hotels near the Campo.

Jolly Hotel dei Cavalieri (££) Piazza della Stazione 2 (tel: 050/43 290). Modern four-star hotel convenient for the station (and thus for the airport) but not for much else.

Pistoia

Firenze (£) Via Curtatone e Montanara 42 (tel: 0573/23 141). Pistoia's only two-star hotel; quiet and close to Piazza del Duomo.

Il Convento (££) Via San Quirico 33, Santomato (tel: 0573/452 651). Peaceful hotel 5km northeast of Pistoia near Ponte Nuovo. A converted 18th-century convent, with a swimming pool.

Patria (£) Via Crispi 6–8 (tel: 0573/25 187). Three-star hotel between the centre and the railway station, near San Giovanni Fuorcivitas.

Prato

Flora (£) Via Cairoli 31 (tel: 0574/20 021). Modern, middling three-star hotel near Santa Maria dei Carceri.

President (££) Via Simintendi 20 (tel: 0574/30 251). Prato's only four-star hotel, and – like most of the city's accommodation – aimed at business people.

San Marco (£) Piazza San Marco 48 (tel: 0574/21 321). Convenient three-star hotel located between the railway station and Castello.

Stella d'Italia (£) Piazza del Duomo 8 (tel: 0574/27 910). Perfect position for a formerly grand but now faded, central, two-star hotel.

San Gimignano

Bel Soggiorno (££) Via San Giovanni 91 (tel: 0577/940 375). There is little to choose between this and the nearby Leon Bianco – though you may have to take full pension here during high season.

La Cisterna (££) Piazza della Cisterna 24 (tel: 0577/940 328). The oldest and perhaps the nicest hotel in San Gimignano.

Leon Bianco (££) Piazza della Cisterna 8 (tel: 0577/941 294). Another fine old hotel on the main square.

Le Vecchie Mura (£) Via Piandornella 15 (tel: 0577/940 270). One of the best budget choices after the convent and youth hostel; friendy management and rooms – some with views – above a restaurant in the southeast corner of the village.

Villa San Paolo (££–£££) (tel: 0577/955 100)One of several country villas dotted around the countryside close to San Gimignano; located on the road for Certaldo, 4km north of the village. Beautiful hillside setting, with ample terraces, tennis court and swimming pool.

Ostello della Gioventù (£) Via delle Fonti 1 (tel: 0577/941 991). IYHF youth hostel in the northern part of the village.

Siena

Atena (££) Via P Mascagni 55 (tel: 0577/286 313). Modern three-star hotel just outside the city walls to the south. Most rooms have good views.

Duomo (££) Via Stalloreggi 34 (tel: 0577/289 088). Ideally placed and perfectly comfortable three-star hotel south of the Duomo.

Il Palio (£) Piazza del Sale 19 (tel: 0577/281 131). Large two-star (so a better chance of vacancies).

Locanda Garibaldi (£) Via Giovanni Dupre 18 (tel: 0577/284 404). Modest but excellent and budget-friendly choice just off the Campo.

Palazzo Ravizza (££–£££) Pian dei Mantellini 34 (tel: 280 462). Quiet and very nice three-star hotel at the southern end of Via Stalloreggi, but usually insists on full-board.

Piccolo Hotel Etruria (££) Via delle Donzelle 1–3 (tel: 0577/288 088). Good central two-star hotel just off Via di Città.

Volterra

Etruria (£) Via Matteotti 32 (tel: 0588/87 377). On the main street. Probably the best overall choice, with good value for money.

Nazionale (££) Via dei Marchesi 11 (tel: 0588/86 284). D H Lawrence stayed here while researching *Etruscan Places*. Modernised since then, but rooms are small.

San Lino (££–£££) Via San Lino 26 (tel: 0588/85 250). Volterra's best hotel; four-star.

Villa Nencini (££) Borgo Santo Stefano 55 (tel: 0588/86 386). Pleasant hotel with pool and garden, just outside the city walls.

RESTAURANTS

FLORENCE

Most of the restaurants listed are within 10 minutes' walk of Piazza del Duomo. The areas covered are **North**, **West** and **East** (of Piazza del Duomo and Via dei Calzaiuoli) and **Oltrarno** (south of the Arno).

North

Almanacco (*Centro Vegetariano Fiorentino*) (£) Via delle Ruote 30r (tel: 475 030). This unsigned spot is one of the city's few vegetarian restaurants. You pay a 'membership fee' (L10,000) but can then return as often as you like. The food is cheap, the menu changes every day and the atmosphere is relaxed and convivial. Closed Monday and weekend lunchtimes.

Antellesi (£) Via Faenza 9r (tel: 216 990). Cheap, charming and inviting place close to the Cappelle Medicee. Simple wooden tables and easy-going atmosphere. Traditional dishes such as *bistecca* and *ribollita* together with interesting one-offs. Arrive early to be sure of a table. Closed Sunday.

Cafaggi (££) Via Guelfa 35r (tel: 294 989). A classic two-roomed *trattoria* that has been in the Cafaggi family for 60 years. Many ingredients, such as wine and olive oil, come from the family's Chianti estate. Fish dishes are good. To keep costs down choose from three set-price menus: *turistico*, *leggero* (light) and *vegetariano* (vegetarian). Closed Sunday evening, Monday lunchtime and August.

La Taverna del Bronzino (££–£££) Via delle Ruote 25r (tel: 495 220). Orientated towards expense accounts: top-notch cooking, rarefied but unstuffy atmosphere. Closed Sunday.

Le Fonticine (££) Via Nazionale 79r (tel: 282 106). A noted Florentine institution whose owners (from Emilia-Romagna) give added refinement to classic local dishes such as *cervello fritto* (fried brains) and *pappardelle di cinghiale* (pasta and wild boar). Excellent home-made pastas. Closed Sunday, Monday and August.

Mario (£) Via Rosina 2r (tel: 218 550). No pudding or coffee, just basic Tuscan fare served to a bustling mix of students and market traders. Arrive early. Open for lunch only. Closed Sunday.

Palle d'Oro (£) Via Sant'Antonino 43r (tel: 288 383). Simple and spartan, but cheap and well-cooked basic dishes attract large lunchtime crowds. Booths and tables at the rear; good take-away section at the front. Closed Sunday and August.

Sabatini (£££) Via Panzani 9a (tel: 282 802). Formerly one of Florence's top restaurants. Still super-smart, but now only occasionally superlative, though the Italian-International cuisine is always reliable. Excellent service and cellar, but very expensive. Closed Monday.

San Zanobi (££) Via San Zanobi 33r (tel: 475 286). Light, inventive and superbly presented cooking; measured and very civilised dining room. Closed Monday.

West

Al Lume di Candela (££–£££) Via delle Terme 23r (tel: 294 566). 'By Candlelight' has a reputation for romantic dining *à deux*, but the smoochy setting and cooking are international rather than Florentine in flavour. Closed lunchtime and Sunday.

Belle Donne (£) Via delle Belle Donne 16r (tel: 238 2609). Tiny and wonderfully decorated place (festoons of flowers and mountains of fruit and vegetables). Shared wooden tables with paper tablecloths; daily menus on a blackboard and accomplished Tuscan cooking. Closed weekends and August.

Cantinetta Antinori (££) Palazzo Antinori, Piazza Antinori 3r (tel: 292 234). Definitely a place for a treat – but be sure to dress up. Owned by one of Tuscany's oldest and most famous wine families (wine, cheese and oils come from the family estates), the restaurant's exquisite panelled salons form part of a 15th-century *palazzo* and are always filled with immaculately groomed Florentines. Closed weekends and August.

Cocco Lezzone (£££) Via Parioncino 26r (tel: 287 178). A famous, rather chic restaurant whose white-tiled dining room dates from the building's past use as a dairy. High prices and top-class Tuscan cooking, but tables are communal and you are expected to move on quickly to make way for new customers. Closed Sunday, Tuesday evening and August

Il Contadino (£) Via Palazzuolo 71r (tel: 238 2673). A students' and backpackers' haven: no concessions to decorative niceties, but some of the cheapest food in the city. Closed Sunday.

Il Latini (£) Via Palchetti 6r (tel: 210 916). An always full Florentine institution, but not to all tastes: communal tables, a rowdy atmosphere and cheap Tuscan classics – though its immense popularity has brought an increase in prices and a slight fall in standards. Closed Monday, Tuesday lunchtime and August.

East

Acquacotta (£) Via dei Pilastri 51r (tel: 242 907). Cheap, three-roomed eating place with reliable Tuscan dishes. Named after a traditional Florentine vegetable soup (literally 'cooked water'). Closed Tuesday evening, Wednesday and August.

Alle Murate (£–££) Via Ghibellina 52r (tel: 240 618). One of the city's rising stars, a few doors down from the Casa Buonarroti. An excellent choice for innovative and very good cooking, as well as for its noted cellar. Surprisingly reasonable prices (at present), with several good set-price menus. Open evenings only. Closed Monday and August.

Buca dell'Orafo (£) Volta dei Girolami 28r (tel: 213 619). Fair prices and a simple, friendly *trattoria* feel ensure this place is always packed with Florentines and foreigners alike. Closed Sunday, Monday and August.

Cantina Barbagianni (££) Via Sant'Egidio 12 (tel: 248 0508). A cellar bar restaurant with interesting Tuscan food and courteous service. Try the *assaggio di primi* to sample a variety of different starters. Closed Saturday and Sunday (Sunday and Monday lunch in winter).

Cibrèo (££) Via dei Macci 118r (tel: 234 1100). Extremely well-known place (off the Sant'Ambrogio market) whose relaxed and attractive restaurant – renowned as a touchstone of Tuscan cooking – has spawned a similarly well-executed café, delicatessen and cheaper *bistro* in the same area (entered from Piazza Ghiberti 35r). Closed Sunday and Monday.

Da Ganino (£–££) Piazza dei Cimatori 4r (tel: 214 125). Good places close to the Duomo and Via dei Calzaiuoli are hard to find. This place makes an alternative to nearby Paoli (see below). Small, old-fashioned interior, safe cooking, and a few tables on the tiny piazza outside for outdoor eating (note also the reasonable Birreria Centrale next door, also with outside tables). Closed Sunday.

Da Pennello (£) Via Dante Alighieri 4r (tel: 294 848). Cheap and cheerful spot now so well known it is often hard to find a table. Book ahead to enjoy the famous *antipasti* and the summer terrace. Closed Sunday evening and Monday.

Enoteca Pinchiorri (£££) Via Ghibellina 87 (tel: 242 777). Often described as Italy's best restaurant and wine cellar (reputedly 80,000 bottles of Italian and French vintages). Lovely 15th-century setting and award-winning cooking, though the ceremony and the seriousness may not be to all tastes. Closed Sunday, and Monday lunchtime.

Il Tirabusciò (£) Via de' Benci 34r (tel: 247 6225). Very fairly priced (with

special cheap set menu at lunch), with a welcoming atmosphere and thorough-going local cuisine. Closed Thursday.

La Baraonda (££) Via Ghibellina 67r (tel: 234 1171). Currently one of the city's most popular restaurants. Closed Sunday.

Paoli (£–££) Via dei Tavolini 12r (tel: 216 215). The food here is nothing special, but the vaulted and frescoed medieval dining room is one of the city's most atmospheric. Just off Via dei Calzaiuoli; book or arrive early. Closed Tuesday.

Oltrarno

Borgo Antico (££) Piazza Santo Spirito 6r (tel: 210 437). A pleasant restaurant with outside tables in one of Florence's most charming squares. Book in summer. Closed Monday.

Camillo (££–£££) Borgo San Jacopo 57r (tel: 212 427). Lively, family-run place of long-standing appeal to foreign (especially US) visitors. Higher prices than the food merits, and over-long menu, but the cooking is consistently good. Closed Wednesday and Thursday.

Da Omero (£) Via Pian dei Giullari 11r (tel: 220 053). A long way to come (south of the Forte di Belvedere), but worth it in summer for outdoor eating with a lovely view across the city. Closed Tuesday.

Il Barone di Porta Romana (£–££) Via Romana 123 (tel: 220 585). Elegant but relaxed ambience, sensible prices and a large garden for summer *al fresco* eating make this a favourite with Florentines. Closed Sunday.

Osteria del Cinghiale Bianco (£–££) Borgo San Jacopo 43r (tel: 215 706). Another place popular with visitors, partly for the robust food, partly for the setting – a 14th-century tower near the Ponte Vecchio. Closed Tuesday and Wednesday.

Ruggero (£) Via Senese 89, beyond Porta Romana (tel:

220 542). Tiny, traditional *trattoria* with reliable and occasionally exceptional food. Closed Tuesday and Wednesday.

CAFÉS AND BARS

FLORENCE

Alpina Via degli Strozzi 12r. Sicilian *cassata* is a speciality among the ice-creams here.

Caffè Cibrèo Via del Verrocchio 5r. Cosy and beautiful wood-panelled café with a handful of tables. Top-notch *cornetti* and pastries.

Caffè du Monde Via San Niccolò 103r. Open from 10pm until dawn. Frequented by the famous and the not-so-famous.

Caffelatte Via degli Alfani 39r. A former dairy that still sells milk, butter and cheese, but is also excellent for tea, coffee, lunch, breakfast or brunch.

Caruso Caffè Via Lambertesca 16r. Central Latin American-style late-night spot. Good cocktails.

Donnini Piazza della Repubblica 15. The most modest of this piazza's 'Big Four' cafés (see pages 22–3). Excellent hot sandwiches.

Festival del Gelato Via del Corso 75r. More than 100 flavours of ice-cream.

Frilli Via San Niccolò 57. Long-established and among the city's best ice-cream parlours.

Giacosa Via de' Tornabuoni 83r. Favoured meeting place of the slightly smarter set. Famed as the birthplace of the *negroni* cocktail.

Gilli Piazza della Repubblica 39r. Florence's oldest café – the grandest and most tempting of the four on this piazza. Lovely *belle-epoque* interior; renowned cocktails and *marrons glacés*.

Giubbe Rosse Piazza della Repubblica 13–14r. Once a retreat for literary and artistic types, now popular with aging Florentines who come for the piano music and the banter of the red-waistcoated waiters.

Il Granduca Via dei Calzaiuoli 57r. The best central *gelateria*.

Il Rifrullo Via San Niccolò. Popular with young, well-groomed Florentines. Open until late. Nice garden open in the summer.

Il Triangolo delle Bermude Via Nazionale 61r. Handy for the station. 'New wave' ice-cream in madly exotic flavours.

La Dolce Vita Piazza del Carmine 5r. Chic post-modernist bar on one of Oltrarno's biggest squares. Quiet by day but packed with bright young things late at night, especially when live bands are performing (Thursdays from 11pm).

La Loggia Piazzale Michelangelo 1. Big and busy and away from the centre, but famous for one of the classic views over the city.

Mago Merlino Via dei Pilastri 31r. Vaguely alternative place known for its books, games, tarot-card and palm readers, and Indian, Chinese and Turkish music. Open until late.

Manaresi Via de' Lamberti 16r. Considered by many to pour the best cup of coffee in the city. A large selection of roast and ground coffee can be bought here too.

Paszkowski Piazza della Repubblica 6r. Grand café with piano music and the occasional chamber orchestra playing light melodies to elderly Florentines lingering over their drinks.

Perchè No? Via dei Tavolini 19r (just off Via dei Calzaiuoli). Centrally situated ice-cream parlour, excellent for *semi-freddi* and countless types of cone.

Procacci Via de' Tornabuoni 64r. No tea or coffee here, only cold drinks and wine, but the draw is the famous truffle

sandwiches (ask for *un panino tartufato*).

Rex Caffè Via Fiesolana 23r. American-style bar favoured as a rendezvous before and after a night on the tiles.

Rivoire Piazza della Signoria 5r. Not as exclusive as in times past, and now mainly frequented by foreigners, this is still the city's best-known café. Expensive, but worth it at least once for its outdoor tables and the views on to Piazza della Signoria.

Uffizi Galleria degli Uffizi. The Uffizi gallery's café offers grand views over the Piazza della Signoria.

Vivoli Via Isola delle Stinche 7r (off Via Ghibellina between the Bargello and Santa Croce). Florence's most famous ice-cream parlour – many consider Vivoli's the best ice-cream in Italy (or the world!).

RESTAURANTS

TUSCANY
Arezzo
Buca di San Francesco (£) Via San Francesco 1 (tel: 0575/23 271). Average food in a popular medieval setting, but convenient for San Francesco and Piero della Francesca's frescos. Closed Monday evening and Tuesday.

Cecco (£) Corso Italia 215 (tel: 0575/20 986). Old-fashioned, long-established family restaurant with peasant dishes, including famed *ravioli*, from Arezzo's past. Closed Monday.

Chianti
Badia a Coltibuono (£) Badia a Coltibuono, near Gaiole in Chianti (tel: 0577/749 424). Famous restaurant in the grounds of an 11th-century convent that uses ingredients (such as oils and wines) from its adjoining estate. Tours and cookery courses are available. Closed Monday.

Castello di Spaltenna (££) Via Spaltenna, Gaiole in Chianti (tel: 0577/749 483). Lovely, flower-filled medieval restaurant in a hotel on the outskirts of Gaiole. Refined cooking with occasional surprises. Closed Monday and Tuesday lunch.

Pietrafitta (££) Pietrafitta 10, Località Pietrafitta (tel: 0577/741 123). Recently opened, neatly appointed place run by American-Australian proprietors. Cooking mixes Italian and international to fine effect. Good wine list with plenty of New World choices. Closed November to Easter.

Taverna del Bindolo (£) Via Trento e Trieste 4, Castellina in Chianti (tel: 0577/741 163). Large, newly restructured but still pleasantly rustic restaurant. Porcini mushrooms and truffles feature among the classic Tuscan dishes. Closed Tuesday.

Trattoria il Gabbiano (£) Via Chiantigiana 4, Ponte a Gabbiano (north of Greve on the SS222 Florence – Siena road; tel: 055/821 127). Rustic Tuscan food and surroundings. Waiters reel off the day's specialities at the table, but menus are available if you ask. Very good value. Closed Friday.

Vignale (££) Via XX Settembre 2; Radda in Chianti (tel: 0577/738 094). Cooking with plenty of skilful light touches, but the prices, the rather uncomfortable setting and the service may not be to all tastes. Closed Thursday and from November to March.

Cortona
Grotta di San Francesco (£) Piazzetta Baldelli 3 (just off Piazza della Repubblica; tel: 0575/630 271). Good, basic and relaxed *trattoria*.

La Loggetta (£) Piazza Pescheria 3 (tel: 0575/630 575). Right at the heart of Cortona, this lovely medieval restaurant looks down on to Piazza della

Repubblica from its evocative loggia. Cool, calm interior and assured traditional cooking. Closed Monday.
Tonino (££) Piazza Garibaldi 1 (tel: 0575/603 100). A serious place with serious prices, a long menu and a good cellar. Closed Tuesday.

Lucca
Buca di Sant' Antonio (£) Via della Cervia 3 (tel: 0583/55 881). Standards are not as high as they were in Lucca's most famous restaurant, but this is still a reliable choice for local specialities at reasonable prices. Closed Monday and Sunday evening.
Giulio in Pelleria (£) Via delle Conce 47 (tel: 0583/55 948). Bright, lively and extremely busy neighbourhood restaurant, so be sure to book ahead. Closed Sunday and Monday.
Solferino (££–£££) Via delle Gavine 50, San Marcario in Piano (tel: 0583/59 118). Located off the SS439 in a hamlet 5km west of Lucca off the N439 road, the Solferino has been one of the most famous and respected Tuscan restaurants for several generations. Food and wines are excellent. Closed Wednesday and Thursday lunch.

Montepulciano
Cantuccio (£) Via delle Cantine 1 (tel: 0578/757 870). A good alternative to the Diva.
Diva (£) Via di Gracciano nel Corso (tel: 0578/716 951). The best place to eat in a town which is not over-blessed with top-class restaurants. Located in the lower part of town just inside the walls. Closed Tuesday.
Il Marzocco (££) Piazza Savonarola 18 (tel: 0578/757 262). Reliable and basic family-run hotel restaurant. Closed Wednesday.

Pienza
Il Prato (£) Viale Santa Caterina 1–3 First-ranked among Pienza's handful of restaurants. Plenty of well-prepared regional specialities. Closed Wednesday.
Latte di Luna Via San Carlo 2 (tel: 0578/748 606). Amiable and easy-going *trattoria* with small outside terrace for *al fresco* eating.

Pisa
Ai Ristori dei Vecchi Macelli (££) Via Volturno 49 (tel: 050/20 424). Pleasant atmosphere and light Tuscan cooking with the odd twist. Fish, game and seafood specialities, and great puddings. Closed Wednesday and Sunday lunch.
Sergio (£££) Lungarno Pacinotti 1 (tel: 050/580 580). Smart, expense-account-orientated restaurant with fine, if elaborate cooking and appropriately grand wines, service and setting. Closed Sunday and Monday lunch.

Pistoia
Leon Rosso (£) Via Panchiatichi 4 (tel: 0573/29 230). Adequate restaurant in a city not known for its culinary sophistication. Closed Sunday.

Prato
Osvaldo Baroncelli (££) Via Fra Bartolomeo 13 (tel: 0574/23 810). Forty years under one owner seem to have ensured high standards in this restaurant on the edge of the medieval centre. Closed Sunday.
Il Pirana (£££) Via Valentini 110 (tel: 0574/25 746). A modern interior and a semi-industrial suburban setting barely detract from one of the most highly regarded fish restaurants in the region. Closed Sunday and lunchtime on Saturday.

San Gimignano
Da Graziano (££) Via G Matteotti 39a (tel: 0577/940 101). Excellent food and wine at reasonable prices in a small hotel just outside the city walls. In summer you can eat outside on a pretty terrace. Closed Monday.
Le Terrazze (£) Albergo La Cisterna, Piazza della Cisterna 24 (tel: 0577/940 328). A terrace with fine views and a medieval dining room complement good regional cooking in this village-centre hotel restaurant. Closed Tuesday and Wednesday.

Siena
Ai Marsili (£) Via del Castoro (tel: 0577/47 154). Occasionally erratic cooking, but a central location (just south of the Duomo), reasonable prices and an attractive old dining room make this place the equal of Le Logge, its Sienese rival. Closed Monday.
La Torre (££) Via Salicotto 7–9 (tel: 0577/287 548). This once unknown old-fashioned *trattoria* just off the Campo has now been discovered. The atmosphere remains, the food is good, but prices have crept up. Arrive early to secure one of the handful of tables. Closed Thursday.
Il Campo (££) Piazza del Campo 50 (tel: 0577/280 725). This is the best of the expensive, tourist-orientated eating places on the Campo. Closed Tuesday.
Osteria Le Logge (££) Via del Porrione 33 (tel: 0577/48 013). Siena's prettiest restaurant, but now expensive and often fully booked, so make early reservations. Closed Sunday.

Viareggio
Romano (£££) Via Mazzini 120 (tel: 0584/31 382). Perhaps Tuscany's best fish restaurant. Closed Monday.

Volterra
Etruria (£) Piazza dei Priori 8 (tel: 0588/86 604). Volterra's best *trattoria* is conveniently situated on the main square. Good for game specialities in season. Closed Thursday.

Index

a

accidents 257–8
accommodation 274–7
  Arezzo 275–6
  camping 264
  Chianti 276
  Cortona 276
  Fiesole 276
  Florence 172–3, 274–5
  last-minute bookings 172
  Lucca 276
  Montepulciano 276
  Monteriggioni 276
  Pienza 276
  Pisa 276–7
  Pistoia 277
  Prato 277
  prices 173
  reservations 172
  San Gimignano 277
  Siena 277
  villa accommodation 264
  Volterra 277
Addison, Joseph 223
Agostino di Duccio 53, 161, 168, 239
airports and air services 252, 258
Alberese 197
Alberti, Leon Battista 120, 148, 168, 170
Albinia 196
Alfieri, Vittorio 142
Allori, Cristofano 119
Alpi Apuane 191, 196
Ammannati, Bartolommeo 57, 127, 169
Andrea da Firenze 153
Andrea del Castagno 58, 79, 100, 155, 168
Andrea del Sarto 102, 118, 155, 169, 171, 220
Angelico, Fra 83, 100, 101, 102, 168, 202, 203
antiques fairs and markets 193, 209
antiques shops 179
Arezzo 190, 192–5
  accommodation 275–6
  antique fair 193
  Casa di Vasari 192
  Duomo 192
  festivals 17, 195
  Fortezza Medicea 195
  getting there 193
  Giostro del Saracino 195
  Museo Archeologico 193
  Palazzetto della Fraternità dei Laici 192
  Passegio del Prato 195
  Piazza Grande 192
  Pieve di Santa Maria 192
  restaurants 280
  San Domenico 192
  San Francesco 192–5
  tourist information 192
Arno 130–1

Arnolfo di Cambio 77, 122, 138, 158
art
  artists' materials 181
  cartoons 99
  fresco 98–9
  glossary of terms 270–1
  Mannerism 169
  pre-Renaissance art 158–9
  Renaissance art 167–9
  tondo (round panel) technique 119
artists and architects
Agostino di Duccio 53, 161, 168, 239
Alberti, Leon Battista 120, 148, 168, 170
Allori, Cristofano 119
Ammannati, Bartolommeo 57, 127, 169
Andrea da Firenze 153
Andrea del Castagno 58, 79, 100, 155, 168
Andrea del Sarto 102, 118, 155, 169, 171, 220
Angelico, Fra 83, 100, 101, 102, 168, 202, 203
Arnolfo di Cambio 77, 122, 138, 158
Baccio di Montelupo 110
Baldovinetti, Alesso 137
Bandinelli, Baccio 57, 59, 127, 169
Barna da Siena 229
Bartolini, Lorenzo 141
Bartolo di Fredi 230, 231
Bartolomeo della Gatta 202, 203
Bartolomeo, Fra 100, 101, 119, 206, 208–9, 249
Beccafumi, Domenico 93, 236, 237, 238, 239
Bellini, Giovanni 164
Benedetto da Maiano 59, 141, 151, 230, 231
Bicci di Lorenzo 79, 193, 203
Bonanno 219
Botticelli, Sandro 58, 109, 162–3, 168
Bronzino, Agnolo 169, 206
Brunelleschi, Filippo 76, 80–1, 96, 112, 132, 134, 144, 157, 167, 224
Canova, Antonio 117, 141, 142
Caravaggio 119, 165
Cassioli, Giuseppe 141
Cavalcanti, Andrea 79
Cavallini, Pietro 159
Cellini, Benvenuto 57, 86, 169
Cenni di Francesco 248
Cimabue 158, 159, 161, 192

Civitali, Matteo 206, 207, 208
Credi, Lorenzo di 214–15, 225
Crivelli, Carlo 103
Daddi, Bernardo 97, 111
Daniele da Volterra 248
Desiderio da Settignano 59, 133, 142
Domenico Veneziano 161
Donatello 58–9, 97, 133, 134, 142, 149, 167, 238
Dürer, Albrecht 164
Dyck, Anthony van 118
Fedi, Pio 86
Gaddi, Agnolo 79, 141, 226–7
Gaddi, Gaddo 79
Gaddi, Taddeo 141, 143
Gentile da Fabriano 162
Gerini, Lorenzo 202
Ghiberti, Lorenzo 61, 62, 80, 167, 224
Ghirlandaio, Domenico 109, 151, 152, 154, 168, 206, 230, 249
Giambologna 57, 58, 86, 112, 127, 169
Giotto di Bondone 63, 93, 142–3, 158, 159, 161
Giovanni da Milano 141
Giovanni del Biondo 97, 141
Giovanni di Paolo 169, 215, 216
Giuliano da Maiano 230
Goes, Hugo van der 163
Gozzoli, Benozzo 113, 168, 231, 249
Guercino, Il 209
Guglielmo da Pisa 225
Guido da Como 220, 225
Leonardo da Vinci 58, 163, 168
Lippi, Filippino 93, 119, 145, 147, 150, 151, 157, 227
Lippi, Fra Filippo 119, 162, 168, 227
Lorenzetti, Ambrogio 161, 232, 237
Lorenzetti, Pietro 103, 192, 203
Manetti 137
Mantegna, Andrea 164
Marini, Marino 120
Martini, Simone 93, 161, 237
Masaccio 145, 146, 147, 149, 150, 167
Maso di Bianco 141
Masolino da Panicale 145, 146, 147
Matteo di Giovanni 216
Memmi, Lippo 161, 229, 230
Memmo di Filippuccio 231

Michelangelo 12, 52, 53, 56–7, 64, 65, 66–7, 68, 80, 123, 135, 137, 143, 164, 168–9, 237
Michelino, Domenico di 78
Michelozzo di Bartolommeo 83, 100, 113, 123, 137, 155, 167, 214
Mino da Fiesole 55, 227
Monaco, Lorenzo 52, 100, 162
Nanni di Banco 110
Nardo di Cione 149, 152
Neri di Bicci 90, 154
Orcagna, Andrea 86, 110, 111, 152, 157
Parmigianino 164
Perugino, Pietro 92, 118, 169
Piero della Francesca 162, 169, 192, 193, 194
Piero di Cosimo 83
Pietro da Cortona 117, 201
Pintoricchio 237–8
Pisano, Andrea 61, 63, 97
Pisano, Giovanni 158–9, 220, 221, 225, 226, 237
Pisano, Nicola 158, 206, 220–1, 238
Pisano, Nino 149
Pollaiuolo, Antonio 89, 97, 162, 168
Pollaiuolo, Piero 162
Pontormo, Jacopo 144, 163, 164, 169, 171
Pozzo, Andrea del 215
Quercia, Jacopo della 169, 206, 208, 237, 238
Raphael 118, 119, 164, 169
Rembrandt 165
Ricci, Stefano 141
Robbia, Andrea della 208, 224, 226
Robbia, Giovanni della 225
Robbia, Luca della 78, 97, 167, 225
Rosa, Salvator 117
Rossellino, Antonio 140, 141, 225, 227
Rossellino, Bernardo 140, 141, 216, 217
Rosso Fiorentino 118, 133, 164, 169, 248, 249
Rosso, Vincenzo 127
Rubens, Peter Paul 118, 165
Salviati, Francesco 74, 75
Sangallo, Antonio da 214
Sangallo, Giuliano da 157
Sano di Pietro 243
Sansovino, Andrea 93
Sansovino, Jacopo 93
Santi di Tito 149

Sassetta 169
Signorelli, Luca 169, 202, 203, 232, 249
Signorini, Telemaco 92
Sodoma, Il 232, 237, 238
Spinello Aretino 137, 141, 192, 236
Tacca, Pietro 112, 114
Taddeo di Bartolo 215, 230, 237, 249
Talenti, Francesco 63, 77, 110
Tino da Camaino 79, 88, 220, 231, 238
Tintoretto 118, 206
Titian 118, 164
Tribolo, Niccolò 170
Uccello, Paolo 78, 152–3, 162, 167
Vasari, Giorgio 123, 129, 148, 192
Vecchietta 216, 238
Verrocchio, Andrea del 157, 168
Asciano 242
  Museo Archeologico 242
  Museo d'Arte Sacra 242
Aspertini, Amico 208

B

Baccio di Montelupo 110
Badia a Coltibuono 198
Bagno Vignoni 243
Baldovinetti, Alesso 137
ballet and modern dance 184
balze 248
Bandinelli, Baccio 57, 59, 127, 169
bankers, medieval 32–3
banks 264
Bardini, Stefano 88
Barga 16, 196
Barna da Siena 229
Baroncelli, Bernardo 75
Bartolini, Lorenzo 141
Bartolo di Fredi 230, 231
Bartolomeo della Gatta 202, 203
Bartolomeo, Fra 100, 101, 119, 206, 208–9, 249
Battistero 60–2
Beccafumi, Domenico 93, 236, 237, 238, 239
bella figura 14
Bellini, Giovanni 164
Benedetto da Maiano 59, 141, 151, 230, 231
Bennett, Arnold 116
Bicci di Lorenzo 79, 193, 203
birdwatching 196
Boccaccio 55, 71, 150, 151, 159
Bolgheri 196
Bonanno 219
Boniface VIII 70, 71
bookshops 178, 180
Botticelli, Sandro 58, 109, 162–3, 168
Bronzino, Agnolo 169, 206

Browning, Elizabeth Barrett 73
Brunelleschi, Filippo 76, 80–1, 96, 112, 132, 134, 144, 157, 167, 224
Bruni, Leonardo 140, 142
Buonconvento 242
  Museo d'Arte Sacra 242
Buontalenti 84 84
bus services 253, 258–9
Byron, Lord George 64, 164, 245

C

cafés and bars 22–3, 176, 185, 279–80
Camaldoli 196
camping 264
Canova, Antonio 117, 141, 142
Cappello, Bianca 171
car rental 256
Caravaggio 119, 165
Carrara 196
Carretto, Ilaria 206
Casanova 223
Casentino 191, 196
Cassioli, Giuseppe 141
Castellina in Chianti 199
Castello di Brolio 198
Castelnuovo di Garfagnana 196–7
Catiline 28–9
Cavalcanti, Andrea 79
Cavallini, Pietro 159
Cellini, Benvenuto 57, 86, 169
Cenni di Francesco 248
Charlemagne 36, 233
Chianti 191, 198–9, 276, 280
Chimera 87
Chiusi 246
churches and chapels (Florence)
  Badia Fiorentina 55, 72
  Baptistery 60–2, 72
  Cappella Bardi 141, 142–3
  Cappella Baroncelli 141, 142
  Cappella Brancacci 145, 146–7
  Cappella Capponi 144
  Cappella del Cardinale del Portogallo 136, 137
  Cappella Castellani 141, 142
  Cappella del Crocifisso 137
  Cappella di Filippo Strozzi 150–1
  Cappella dei Pazzi 143
  Cappella Peruzzi 141, 142–3
  Cappella dei Principi 64–5
  Cappella Rucellai 120
  Cappella Sassetti 154
  Cappella Strozzi 149, 152
  Cappelle Medicee 64–5
  Cappellone degli Spagnoli 153
  Medici Chapels 64–5

Ognissanti 98, 109
Orsanmichele 110–11
San Lorenzo 94, 132–5
San Marco 100
San Martino del Vescoco 69
San Miniato al Monte 136–7
Santa Croce 98, 138–43
Santa Felicita 144
Santa Margherita de' Cerchi 69
Santa Maria del Carmine 98, 145
Santa Maria del Fiore (Duomo) 76–81
Santa Maria Maddalena 59
Santa Maria Maddalena dei Pazzi 92
Santa Maria Novella 98, 148–53
Santa Reparata 76–7
Santa Trinita 98, 154
Santissima Annunziata 94, 98, 155
Santo Spirito 157
Cimabue 158, 159, 161, 192
cinema 184
Civitali, Matteo 206, 207, 208
Clark, Kenneth 111
classical music 183
Clement VII 42–3
climate 254
clubs and discos 185
Compagnia dei Bianchi 154
conversion charts 266
Corfino 197
Cortona 190, 200–5
  accommodation 276
  antiques fair 200
  getting there 200
  Giardini Pubblici 202
  market 200
  Museo dell'Accademia Etrusca 202–3
  Museo Diocesano 203
  restaurants 280–1
  San Domenico 202
  San Francesco 201
  San Nicolò 202
  Santa Maria del Calcinaio 203
  tourist information 201
crafts 18–19, 115
Credi, Lorenzo di 214–15, 225
credit cards 255
crete 191, 242
crime 25–6, 187, 262
Crivelli, Carlo 103
Crucifix (Cimabue) 131, 143
currency 255
customs regulations 253

D

Daddi, Bernardo 97, 111
Daniele da Volterra 248
Dante 12, 55, 69, 70–1, 72, 78, 140, 158
Decameron 150, 151

Desiderio da Settignano 59, 133, 142
Dickens, Charles 129, 223
disabled visitors 264
Domenico di Michelino 79
Domenico Veneziano 161
Donatello 58–9, 97, 133, 134, 142, 149, 167, 238
driving
  accidents 257–8
  car breakdown 256
  car rental 256
  documents 257
  driving tips 256–7
  parking 258
  petrol 258
  regulations 257
  to Florence and Tuscany 253
Dumas, Alexandre 73
Dürer, Albrecht 164
Dyck, Anthony van 118

E

Easter celebrations 75
electricity 266
Eliot, George 63, 116
emergency telephone numbers 263
entry formalities 252
etiquette 266–7
Etruscans 28, 246–7

F

fabrics 179
Facaros, Dana 116
fashion and style 14–15, 178
Feast of the Annunciation 101
Fedi, Pio 86
Ferragamo, Salvatore 15
festivals 16–17, 183, 215, 240–1
  Arezzo 16, 17
  Barga 16
  Bravio delle Botti 17, 215
  Cantiere Internazionale 16, 215
  Estate Fiesolana 16, 82, 183
  Festa del Grillo 17
  Festa degli Omaggi 17
  Festa del Rificolone 17
  Festa di San Giovanni 17
  Fiesole 16, 183
  Florence 16, 17, 183
  food and wine 16–17
  Gioco del Ponte 17
  Giostra del Saracino 17, 195
  Giostro dell'Orso 17
  Lucca 16, 17
  Luminara 17
  Luminara & Regatta di San Ranieri 17
  Maggio Musicale 16, 183
  Montepulciano 16, 17, 215
  music 16, 183

INDEX

Palio 17, 240–1
Pisa 17
Prato 17
San Paolino 17
Santa Croce 17
Scoppio del Carro 17
Settembre Lucchese 209
Settimana Musicale 16
Siena 16, 17
Torre del Lago 16
Fiesole 28, 82–3
Badia Fiesolana 83
Cappella Salutati 83
Duomo 83
festivals 16, 82, 183
Museo Archeologico 83
Museo Bandini 83
San Domenico 83
San Francesco 83
Sant'Alessandro 83
Teatro Romano 83
Villa Medici 83
walk 83
Firenze Nuova 24–5
Florence 10–187
Accademia del Cimento 104
Accademia della Crusca 170
Accademia, Galleria dell' 52–3
accommodation 172–3, 274–5
airport 252
Antica Farmacia di San Marco 180
Badia Fiorentina 55, 72
Baptistery 60–2, 72
Bargello, Museo Nazionale del 56–9
Biblioteca Laurenziana 135
cafés and bars 22–3, 176, 185, 279–80
Campanile di Giotto 63
Capitano del Popolo 57
Cappella Bardi 141, 142–3
Cappella Baroncelli 141, 142
Cappella Brancacci 145, 146–7
Cappella Capponi 144
Cappella del Cardinale del Portogallo 136, 137
Cappella Castellani 141, 142
Cappella del Crocifisso 137
Cappella di Filippo Strozzi 150–1
Cappella dei Pazzi 143
Cappella Peruzzi 141, 142–3
Cappella dei Principi 64–5
Cappella Rucellai 120
Cappella Sassetti 154
Cappella Strozzi 149, 152
Cappelle Medicee 64–5
Cappellone degli Spagnoli 153
Casa Buonarroti 68
Casa di Dante 69
Cascine, Le 73, 114

Cathedral Works Museum 96–7
Cere Anatomiche 108–9
Chiostrino dei Voti 155
Chiostro degli Aranci 55
Chiostro dei Morti 155
Chiostro di Sant'Antonino 100
Chiostro dello Scalzo 102
Chiostro Verde 152
climate and when to go 254
consulates 262–3
Corridoio Vasariano 129
Cosimo I (Giambologna) 127
crafts 18–19, 115, 181
crime and personal safety 25–6, 187, 262
David (Michelangelo) 52–3
Duomo 76–81
emergencies 262–3
essential sights 51
Farmacia di Santa Maria Novella 180
fashion and style 14–15
festivals 16, 17, 183
floods 19, 26, 47, 130–1
Florentines 12–13
food and drink 20–1, 174–7
Forte di Belvedere 84, 156
Galleria d'Arte Moderna 123
Galleria del Costume 120
Galleria Palatina 117–19
Giardino di Boboli 84–5
Giardino del Cavaliere 85
Giardino dei Semplici 85
history 28–47
itineraries 250
Judith and Holofernes (Allori) 119
La Vittoria (Michelangelo) 123
The Last Supper (Ghirlandaio) 109
Loggia dei Lanzi 86
Loggia del Pesce 115
Loggia dei Rucellai 121
lost property 263
markets 114–15
Marzocco 127
Medici Chapels 64–5
Mercato Centrale 114
Mercato Nuovo 115
Mercato delle Piante 115
Misericordia 77
Museo Archeologico 87
Museo degli Argenti 119–20
Museo Bardini 88–9
Museo Botanico 85
Museo della Casa Fiorentina Antica 90–1
Museo di Firenze com'era 92
Museo della

Fondazione Horne 93
Museo Marino Marini 120
Museo di Mineralogia 85
Museo Nazionale di Antropologia ed Etnologia 95
Museo dell'Opera del Duomo 96–7
Museo dell'Opera di Santa Croce 143
Museo di Paleontologia 85
Museo delle Porcellane 117
Museo di San Marco 94, 98, 100–2
Museo di Santa Maria Novella 152–3
Museo Stibbert 102–3
Museo di Storia della Fotografia Fratelli Alinari 121
Museo di Storia della Scienza 104–5
Museo Zoologico – La Specola 108–9
Museum of Florence as it Was 92
Museum of the History of Science 104–5
Museum of the Old Florentine House 90–1
National Museum of Anthropology and Ethnology 95
Neptune Fountain 127
Nicchia di Dante 69
nightlife 182–43
Ognissanti 98, 109
opening times 50, 264–5
Opificio delle Pietre Dure 19
orientation 50–1
Orsanmichele 110–11
Ospedale degli Innocenti 94, 112
Ospizio dei Pellegrini 100
Palatine Gallery 117–19
Palazzo dell'Arte della Lana 110
Palazzo dei Castellani 104
Palazzo Corsi-Alberti 93
Palazzo Davanzati 90–1
Palazzo Medici-Riccardi 94, 98, 113
Palazzo Nonfinito 95
Palazzo Pazzi-Quaratesi 58
Palazzo Pitti 116–20
Palazzo Rucellai 120–1
Palazzo Salviati 69
Palazzo Strozzi 121
Palazzo Vecchio 122–3, 126
Palio dei Cocchi 149
parking 258
Pianta della Catena 92
Piazza dei Ciompi 114–15
Piazza del Duomo 50, 54
Piazza della Repubblica 54
Piazza Santa Maria Novella 148, 149

Piazza Santissima Annunziata 112
Piazza Santo Spirito 115
Piazza della Signoria 26, 51, 54, 126–7
Pietà (Michelangelo) 96
places of worship 265
planning your visit 11
Podestà 56, 57
police 262
pollution 26
Ponte alla Carraia 109
Ponte Vecchio 128–9
population 24
Porcellino (Tacca) 114
practical details 186–7
Primavera (Botticelli) 162
Priori 122
public transport 186
railway station 252–3
restaurants 21, 174, 277–9
Sagrestia Nuova 78
Sagrestia Vecchia 134–5
San Lorenzo 94, 132–5
San Lorenzo (market) 114
San Marco 100
San Martino del Vescoco 69
San Miniato al Monte 136–7
Sant' Ambrogio 114
Sant' Apollonia 94, 98, 100
Santa Croce 98, 138–43
Santa Felicita 144
Santa Margherita de' Cerchi 69
Santa Maria del Carmine 98, 145
Santa Maria del Fiore (Duomo) 76–81
Santa Maria Maddalena 59
Santa Maria Maddalena dei Pazzi 92
Santa Maria Novella 98, 148–53
Santa Reparata 76–7
Santa Trinita 98, 154
Santissima Annunziata 94, 98, 155
Santo Spirito 157
Sasso di Dante 72
shopping 178–81
Silver Museum 119–20
Studiolo di Francesco I 123
toilets 265
tourism 24
tourist offices 267
tourist pass 187
Trinità (Masaccio) 150
Uffizi, Galleria degli 160–5
Venus de' Medici 164
Via del Corso 72
Via della Porcellana 54
views 51
Villa Medicea di Careggi 170
Villa Medicea di Castello 170
Villa Medicea della Petraia 170–1

Florence (continued)
  Villa Medicea di Poggio
    a Caiano 171
  walks 54, 72, 94, 156
  Zoological Museum
    108–9
food and drink
  beer 177
  cafés and bars 22–3
  cheeses 210
  coffee 176
  drinking water 177
  eating out 174–5
  festivals 16–17
  Florentine specialities
    21
  medieval food 20
  olive oil 208
  shopping for 180–1
  soft drinks 177
  tea 176
  Tuscan specialities
    210–11
  vegetarian food 175
  wines and liqueurs
    176–7, 212–13
foreign exchange 255
Forte dei Marmi 244
Franchi, Jacopo 79

G

Gaddi, Agnolo 79, 141,
  226–7
Gaddi, Gaddo 79
Gaddi, Taddeo 141, 143
Gaiole 198
Galileo Galilei 104,
  106–7, 221
Garfagnana Valley 191
gay clubs 185
Gentile da Fabriano 162
Gerini, Lorenzo 202
Ghiberti, Lorenzo 61, 62,
  80, 167, 224
Ghirlandaio, Domenico
  109, 151, 152, 154,
  168, 206, 230, 249
Giambologna 57, 58, 86,
  112, 127, 169
Giotto di Bondone 63,
  93, 142–3, 158, 159,
  161
Giovanni da Milano 141
Giovanni del Biondo 97,
  141
Giovanni di Paolo 169,
  215, 216
Giuliano da Maiano 230
Goes, Hugo van der
  163
Goethe 222, 223
Gombo 245
Gozzoli, Benozzo 113,
  168, 231, 249
Gray, Thomas 222
Grotta di Buontalenti
  84
Gualberto, Giovanni
  154
Gucci 14
Guelph-Ghibelline con-
  flicts 36–7
Guercino, Il 209
Guglielmo da Pisa 225
Guido da Como 220,
  225

H

Hannibal 202
Hare, Augustus 57

health 263
health insurance 263
medical treatment
  263
pharmacies 263
vaccinations 263
history of Florence and
  Tuscany 28–47
  Austrian and French
    rule 45
  banking 32–3
  barbarian invaders 31
  Etruscans 28, 246–7
  Guelph-Ghibelline
    conflicts 36–7
  Margraves 31
  Medici family 33, 38–9,
    42–4, 61
  Medici popes 42–3
  medieval prosperity
    32–3
  merchant guilds 34–5
  modern times 46–7
  myth and legend 28–9
  naming of Florence 29
  Roman domination
    30–1
  Savonarola 40–1, 100,
    102, 123
  self-determination 46
  world wars 46–7
Horne, Herbert Percy
  93
Howells, W D 77
Huxley, Aldous 223

I

Inquisition 107, 139

J

James, Henry 204, 208
jewellery shops 179–80
John XXIII 61

L

Lago di Burano 196
language 272
Lassels, Richard 80
latrines 91
Lawrence, D H 246,
  247
Lawrence, Frieda 127
Lee, Laurie 191, 223
Leonardo da Vinci 58,
  163, 168
Levigliano 196
Lippi, Filippino 93, 119,
  145, 147, 150, 151,
  157, 227
Lippi, Fra Filippo 119,
  162, 168, 227
Longfellow, Henry
  Wadsworth 63, 108
Lorenzetti, Ambrogio
  161, 232, 237
Lorenzetti, Pietro 103,
  192, 203
Lucca 190, 204–9
  accommodation 276
  Caffè di Simo 207
  Casa di Puccini 207
  city walls 209
  Duomo di San Martino
    205–6
  festivals 16, 17, 209
  getting there 204
  market 208

Museo Nazionale
  Guinigi 208–9
Piazza del Anfiteatro
  208
restaurants 281
San Cristoforo 207
San Frediano 207–8
San Michele in Foro
  206–7
Santa Maria
  Fortisportam 209
Torre Guinigi 209
tourist information 204
Volto Santo 206
Lusitania, Jacopo di
  136

M

Machiavelli, Niccolò
  124–5
Manetti 137
Mantegna, Andrea 164
marbled paper 181
Maremma 191, 197
Margrave Ugo 55
Margraves 31
Marina di Alberese 197
Marini, Marino 120
markets
  Cortona 200
  craft market 115
  Florence 114–15
  Lucca 208
  Mercato Centrale 114
  Mercato Nuovo 115
  Mercato delle Piante
    115
  Piazza dei Ciompi
    114–15
  San Lorenzo 114
  Sant'Ambrogio 114
Marlia 209
Marsuppini, Carlo 140,
  142
Martini, Simone 93, 161,
  237
Masaccio 145, 146, 147,
  149, 150, 167
Maso di Banco 141
Masolino da Panicale
  145, 146–7
Massa 196
Matteo di Giovanni 216
McCarthy, Mary 58–9,
  66
media 260
medical treatment 263
Medici, Cosimo de'
  38–9, 100, 102, 134
Medici family 33, 38–9,
  42–4, 61
Medici, Giuliano de'
  74–5
Medici, Lorenzo de' (the
  Magnificent) 39,
  74–5, 120, 248
Memmi, Lippo 161, 229,
  230
Memmo di Filippuccio
  231
merchant guilds 34–5
Michelangelo 12, 52, 53,
  56–7, 64, 65, 66–7,
  68, 80, 123, 135,
  137, 143, 164,
  168–9, 237
Michelino, Domenico di
  78
Michelozzo di
  Bartolommeo 83,
  100, 113, 123, 137,
  155, 167, 214

Milton, John 196
Mino da Fiesole 55,
  227
Monaco, Lorenzo 52,
  100, 162
monasteries
  Monte Oliveto
    Maggiore 232, 242
  San Galgano 232–3
  Sant'Antimo 233, 243
money 255
  banks 264
  credit cards 255
  currency 255
  foreign exchange 255
Montaigne 170, 222
Montalcino 191, 242–3
Monte Oliveto Maggiore
  232, 242
Montefeltro, Federico da
  162
Montepulciano 190,
  214–15, 243
  accommodation 276
  Corso 214
  Duomo 215
  festivals 16, 17, 215
  getting there 214
  Museo Civico 215
  Palazzo Cantucci 215
  Palazzo Comunale
    215
  Piazza Grande 215
  restaurants 281
  San Biagio 214
  San Francesco 215
  Sant' Agostino
    214–15
  Santa Lucia 215
  tourist information
    214
  Vino Nobile 213
Monterchi 194
Monteriggioni 191, 199,
  239
Monti dell'Uccellina 197
Mugello 191, 196
museums and galleries
  (Florence)
  Accademia, Galleria
    dell' 52–3
  Bargello, Museo
    Nazionale del 56–9
  Cathedral Works
    Museum 96–7
  Cere Anatomiche
    108–9
  Galleria d'Arte
    Moderna 120
  Galleria del Costume
    120
  Galleria Palatina
    117–19
  Museo Archeologico
    87
  Museo degli Argenti
    119–20
  Museo Bardini 88–9
  Museo Botanico 85
  Museo della Casa
    Fiorentina Antica
    90–1
  Museo di Firenze
    com'era 92
  Museo della
    Fondazione Horne
    93
  Museo Marino Marini
    120
  Museo di Mineralogia
    85
  Museo Nazionale di
    Antropologia ed
    Etnologia 95

Museo dell'Opera del Duomo 96–7
Museo dell'Opera di Santa Croce 143
Museo di Paleontologia 85
Museo delle Porcellane 117
Museo di San Marco 94, 98, 100–2
Museo di Santa Maria Novella 152–3
Museo Stibbert 102–3
Museo di Storia della Fotografia Fratelli Alinari 121
Museo di Storia della Scienza 104–5
Museo Zoologico – La Specola 108–9
Museum of Florence as it Was 92
Museum of the History of Science 104–5
Museum of the Old Florentine House 90–1
National Museum of Anthropology and Ethnology 95
Palatine Gallery 117–19
Uffizi, Galleria degli 160–5
Zoological Museum 108–9
music festivals 16, 183

Nanni di Banco 110
Napoleon 204
Nardo di Cione 149, 152
national holidays 254–5
Neri di Bicci 90, 154
newspapers and magazines 260
Nightingale, Florence 143
nightlife 182–5
  cabaret 183
  cinema 184
  classical music 183–4
  clubs and discos 185
  concert halls 182
  gay clubs 185
  late-night bars 185
  listings 182
  music festivals 16–17, 183
  opera 183, 184
  rock, pop and jazz 184–5
  theatre 183
  ticket agencies 183

Oltrarno 51
opera 183, 184
Orcagna, Andrea 86, 110, 111, 152, 157
Orecchiella 191, 196–7

Parco Naturale della Maremma 191, 196, 197
parking 258
parks and gardens
  Cascine, Le 73, 114
  Giardino di Boboli 84–5
  Giardino del Cavaliere 85
  Giardino dei Semplici 85
  regional parks 196, 197
Parmigianino 164
passeggiata 23
passports and visas 252
Pazzi Conspiracy 74–5
Pazzi, Jacopo de' 58, 74
Perugino, Pietro 92, 118, 169
Petrarch 223
petrol 258
pharmacies 263
photography 265
Pienza 191, 216–17, 243
  accommodation 276
  Duomo 216
  getting there 216
  Museo della Cattedrale 216
  Palazzo Piccolomini 217
  Pieve di Corsignano 216
  restaurants 281
  tourist information 216
Piero della Francesca 162, 169, 192, 193, 194
Piero di Cosimo 83
Pierozzo, Antonino 100
Pietro da Cortona 117, 201
Pintoricchio 237–8
Pisa 190, 218–21
  accommodation 276–7
  airport 252
  Battistero 220–1
  Campo dei Miracoli 218
  Camposanto 221
  Duomo 219–20
  festivals 17
  getting there 218
  Leaning Tower 218–19
  Museo Nazionale di San Matteo 221
  Museo dell'Opera del Duomo 221
  Museo delle Sinopie 221
  Palazzo dell'Orologio 220
  restaurants 281
  Santa Maria della Spina 220
  tourist information 218
Pisano, Andrea 61, 63, 97
Pisano, Giovanni 158–9, 220, 221, 225, 226, 237
Pisano, Nicola 158, 206, 220–1, 238
Pisano, Nino 149
Pistoia 190, 224–5
  accommodation 277
  Battistero 224
  Black and White factions 225
  Campanile 224
  Duomo 224–5

festivals 17
getting there 224
Museo Civico 224
Museo della Cattedrale 224
Ospedale del Ceppo 225
Piazza del Duomo 224
  restaurants 281
San Bartolomeo 225
San Giovanni Fuorcivitas 225
Sant'Andrea 225
tourist information 224
Pitti, Luca 116
Pius II 216, 238
plagues 150
Poggio a Caiano 171
police 262
Pollaiuolo, Antonio 89, 97, 162, 168
Pollaiuolo, Piero 162
Pontormo, Jacopo 144, 163, 164, 169, 171
porcelain 180
postal services 260–1
Pozzo, Andrea del 215
Prato 190, 226–7
  accommodation 277
  Castello dell'Imperatore 226
  Duomo 226–7
  festivals 17
  getting there 226
  Museo dell'Opera del Duomo 226
  restaurants 281
  Sacred Girdle 226, 227
  Santa Maria delle Carceri 226
  tourist information 226
Pratomagno 191, 196
public transport 258–9
  bus services 258–9
  domestic air travel 258
  rail passes 259
  rail services 259
  taxis 259
  travel discounts 258, 259
Pucci, Emilio 14–15
Puccini, Giacomo 207, 245

Quercia, Jacopo della 169, 206, 208, 237, 238

Radda in Chianti 198–9
radio and television 260
rail services 252–3, 259
Raphael 118, 119, 164, 169
regional parks 196, 197
relics 96
Rembrandt 165
Renaissance 166–9
restaurants 164, 175, 277–81
  Arezzo 280
  Chianti 280
  Cortona 280–1

Florence 21, 174, 277–9
holidays and closing 175
Lucca 281
Montepulciano 281
Pienza 281
Pisa 281
Pistoia 281
Prato 281
San Gimignano 281
Siena 281
smoking in 174
types of 174
vegetarian 175
Viareggio 281
Volterra 281
Riario, Girolamo 74
Ricci, Stefano 141
Robbia, Andrea della 208, 224, 226
Robbia, Giovanni della 225
Robbia, Luca della 78, 97, 167, 225
rock, pop and jazz 184–5
Rogers, Samuel 65
Rosa, Salvator 117
Rossellino, Antonio 140, 141, 225, 227
Rossellino, Bernardo 140, 141, 216, 217
Rosso Fiorentino 118, 133, 164, 169, 248, 249
Rosso, Vincenzo 127
Rubens, Peter Paul 118, 165
Ruskin, John 64, 77, 151, 206, 221

Salviati, Francesco 74, 75
San Galgano 232–3
San Gimignano 191, 228–31
  accommodation 277
  Collegiata 229–30
  getting there 228
  Museo d'Arte Sacra 230
  Museo Civico 230–1
  Pieve di Cellole 231
  restaurants 281
  Sant'Agostino 231
  tourist information 228
San Pellegrino in Alpe 197
San Quirico 243
Sangallo, Antonio da 214
Sangallo, Giuliano da 157
Sano di Pietro 243
Sansepolcro 194
Sansovino, Andrea 93
Sansovino, Jacopo 93
Sant'Antimo 233, 243
Santi di Tito 149
Sassetta 169
Savonarola, Girolamo 40–1, 100, 102, 123
self-catering 264
Servites 155
Sesto Fiorentino 180
Shelley, Percy Bysshe 73, 160, 222, 223, 245

shopping 178–81
  antiques 179
  art and antiquarian
    bookshops 180
  artists' materials 181
  clothes 178
  English-language books
    178
  fabrics 179
  food and drink 180–1
  herbs and flowers
    180
  jewellery 179–80
  leather goods 178–9
  marbled paper 181
  markets 114–15
  opening times 178
  perfumes and toiletries
    180
  porcelain 180
  shipping arrangements
    178
  terracotta pots 179
  tourist guides and
    maps 178
Siena 190, 234–41
  accommodation 277
  Battistero 238
  Campo 235–6
  contrade 240–1
  Duomo 234, 237–8
  Enoteca Italiana
    Permanente 235
  festivals 16, 17
  getting there 234
  Museo Civico 236–7
  Museo dell'Opera del
    Duomo 238–9
  music 236
  Oratorio di San
    Bernardino 238
  Palazzo Pubblico 234,
    236–7
  Palio 17, 240–1
  Pinacoteca Nazionale
    234, 239
  restaurants 281
  San Domenico 237
  San Francesco 238
  Torre del Mangia
    236

tourist information 234
Signorelli, Luca 169,
    202, 203, 232,
    249
Signorini, Telemaco 92
Sixtus IV 74, 75
Sloane, Sir Francis 170
smoking 267
Smollett, Tobias 164,
    223
Sodoma, Il 232, 237, 238
Sovana 246
spa 243
Spinello Aretino 137,
    141, 192, 236
St Catherine of Siena
    237
St Cosmos and St
    Damian 134
St Fina 231
St Francis 138, 139
St Galgano Guidotti
    232
St Lawrence 134
St Minias 136
St Zenobius 61
St Zita 208
stamps 260
Stazzema 196
Stendhal 142
Stibbert, Frederick 103
Story, William Wetmore
    64

T

Tacca, Pietro 112, 114
Taddeo di Bartolo 215,
    230, 237, 249
Talamone 197
Talenti, Francesco 63,
    77, 110
taxis 259
telephones 261
terracotta pots 179
Testi, Fulvio 213
textiles industry 32
theatre 183
Thomas, Dylan 223
time 255

Tino da Camaino 79, 88,
    220, 231, 238
Tintoretto 118, 206
tipping 265–6
Titian 118, 164
toilets 265
topless sunbathing 267
Torre del Lago Puccini
    16, 245
tourist offices 267
travel discounts 258, 259
travel insurance 253
Trefusis, Violet 223
Tribolo, Niccolò 170
Trollope, Anthony 118,
    130
Tuoro sul Trasimeno 202
Tuscany 188–249
  essential sights 190
  festivals 16–17
  food and wine 210–13
  history 45, 246–7
  landscape 191, 196–7
  literary exiles 222–3
  monasteries 232–3
  scenic drives 191,
    198–9, 242–3
  Tuscan towns 190
  villages 191
Twain, Mark 77, 130,
    164

U

Uccello, Paolo 78,
    152–3, 162, 167
Urban VIII 107
useful words and
    phrases 272

V

vaccinations 263
Vallombrosa 196
Vasari, Giorgio 123, 129,
    148, 192
Vecchietta 216, 238
Verrocchio, Andrea del
    157, 168

Versilia 244
Vespucci, Amerigo 109
Vespucci, Simonetta
    109
Via dei Tigli 245
Viareggio 244–5, 281
villa accommodation
    264
Villa Medicea di Careggi
    170
Villa Medicea di Castello
    170
Villa Medicea della
    Petraia 170–1
Villa Medicea di Poggio a
    Caiano 171
Villa Puccini 245
Volpaia 199
Volpi, Elia 90
Volterra 190, 247, 248–9
  accommodation 277
  balze 248
  Duomo 249
  Fortezza 249
  getting there 248
  Museo d'Arte Sacra
    248
  Museo Etrusco
    Guarnacci 249
  Palazzo dei Priori 248
  Palazzo Pretorio 248
  Piazza dei Priori 248
  Pinacoteca 249
  restaurants 281
  San Francesco 248
  Teatro Romano 249
  tourist information 248
  votive offerings 155

W

Walpole, Hugh 222, 223
when to go 254
Wilde, Oscar 87
wines and spirits 176–7,
    212–13
women travellers 267
Worldwide Fund for
    Nature (WWF)
    reserves 196

PICTURE CREDITS AND CONTRIBUTORS

Picture credits

The Automobile Association wishes to thank the following photographers and libraries for their assistance in the preparation of this book:

J ALLAN CASH PHOTOLIBRARY spine Fountain of Neptune. THE BRIDGEMAN ART LIBRARY, LONDON 28a black figure vase, Bucchero ware, Etruscan, 6th century BC, Museo Archaeologico, Chiusi/K & B News Foto, Florence; 39 *Adoration of the Magi* by Sandro Botticelli (1444/5–1510) Galleria degli Uffizi, Florence; 40b *Portrait of Savonarola* by Fra Bartolommeo (*c* 1472–*c* 1517) Museo di San Marco dell'Angelico, Florence; 88 *Adoration of the Christ Child with the Young St John the Baptist* by Pseudo Pier Francesco Fiorentino (fl.1475–1500) Museo Bardini, Florence; 101 *The Annunciation* by Fra Angelico, (*c* 1387–1455) Museo di San Marco dell'Angelico, Florence; 116 *The Parting of Venus from Adonis*, 1707–8 (fresco) by Sebastiano Ricci (1658–1734) Palazzo Pitti, Florence; 118 *Portrait of an Unknown Man* (detail) by Titian (Tiziano Vecellio) (*c* 1485–1576) Palazzo Pitti, Florence; 124b *Portrait of Machiavelli* by Santi di Tito (1536–1603) Palazzo Vecchio, Florence; 145 *Adam and Eve Banished from Paradise* by Tommaso Masaccio (1401–28) Brancacci Chapel, Santa Maria del Carmine, Florence; 146–7 *St Peter Visited in Jail by St Paul*, *c* 1480 by Filippino Lippi (*c* 1457/8–1504) Brancacci Chapel, Santa Maria del Carmine, Florence; 161 *The Madonna di Ognissanti*, *c* 1310 (post-restoration) by Ambrogio Bondone Giotto (*c* 1266–1337) Galleria degli Uffizi, Florence; 246a Etruscan vase showing boxers fighting *c* 500BC, British Museum, London. MARY EVANS PICTURE LIBRARY 45b Napoleon I; 74 Pope Sixtus IV; 222a Shelley; 222b Robert Browning. KIT HOARE 45a Tuscan landscape. HULTON DEUTSCH COLLECTION LTD 47 floods, books needing rebinding; 130a floods 1966–7; 130b floods; 131 flood damage. TIM JEPSON 57 courtyard, Bargello; 108 Museo Zoological. THE MANSELL COLLECTION LTD 36a Frederick Barbarossa's Court; 36b Frederick Barbarossa; 41 Savonarola; 42b Pope Giovanni de Medici; 68 Giuliano de Medici; 75a Giuliano; 75b Lorenzo; 104 instrument, Galileo; 106a Galileo; 106b Galileo; 223a Tobias Smollett; 223b Huxley. ROYAL GEOGRAPHICAL SOCIETY 43 map. SPECTRUM COLOUR LIBRARY 67 *Madonna and Child* by Michelangelo. DAVID WALSH 102–3 Fra Angelica; 149 *Trinità* by Masaccino. ZEFA PICTURE LIBRARY (UK) LTD 17 Siena, Palio race; 28b figure (Etruscan); 52 interior of Accademia Gallery; 53 *David* by Michelangelo; 240b Siena, Palio race; 241 drummers.

The remaining photographs are held in the Automobile Association's own photo library (AA PHOTO LIBRARY) and were taken by Clive Sawyer, with the exception of the following pages: 16b, 20–1, 20, 24–5, 37, 38a, 48–9, 70a, 77, 80b, 92, 111, 154, 166–7, 182b, 187, 194, 238a, 241, 252, 256a, 258–9, 260a, 263, 271a (Jerry Edmanson); 210b, 211 (Eric Meacher); the cover and pages 4a, 4b, 12b, 19, 26, 30–1, 31b, 56, 66, 80a, 81, 82, 84–5, 148, 151, 152b, 156, 168, 183, 190a, 191, 196–7, 196b, 198, 203, 210a, 212a, 212b, 225, 227a, 228, 229, 230, 231, 232a, 232b, 233, 234, 242, 245, 246b, 248, 251, 262, 267 (Ken Paterson); 73 (James Robertson-Taylor); 7, 151, 162, 175a, 253, 255 (Barrie Smith); 18–9, 181 (Wyn Voysey).

Contributors

Series adviser: Christopher Catling **Joint series editor**: Susi Bailey
Copy Editor: Julia Brittain **Designer**: Jo Tapper
Verifier: Kerry Fisher **Indexer**: Marie Lorimer